Exploring
North Carolina's
Natural Areas

Exploring North Carolina's Natural Areas

Parks, Nature Preserves, and Hiking Trails

EDITED BY DIRK FRANKENBERG

The University of North Carolina Press

Chapel Hill and London

Designed by April Leidig-Higgins
Set in Minion by Keystone Typesetting, Inc.
Maps by Eric Ringler, Polaris Cartography
Manufactured in the United States of America

The paper in this book meets the guidelines for
permanence and durability of the Committee on
Production Guidelines for Book Longevity of the
Council on Library Resources.

Library of Congress Cataloging-in-Publication Data
Exploring North Carolina's natural areas: parks,
nature preserves, and hiking trails / edited by Dirk
Frankenberg
p. cm. Includes bibliographical references (p.   )
ISBN 0-8078-2547-6 (cloth: alk. paper) —
ISBN 0-8078-4851-4 (pbk.: alk. paper)
1. Natural areas—North Carolina—Guidebooks.
2. Natural history—North Carolina—Guidebooks.
3. Ecotourism—North Carolina. 4. North Carolina—
Guidebooks. I. Frankenberg, Dirk.
QH76.5.N8 E86 2000   508.756—dc21 99-055917

04 03 02 01 00   5 4 3 2 1

This book is dedicated to the citizens of the state of North Carolina, the good people who, through public and private efforts, have preserved for future generations natural areas like those that first led our state to be called "the goodliest land under the cope of Heaven."

Contents

The Piedmont

The Mountains

Preface

This book owes its origins to the tagline of a previous book of mine, which characterized it as "an ecotourist's guide to the North Carolina coast." That phrase led Anne Taylor, director of the Office of Environmental Education of the North Carolina Department of Environment and Natural Resources, to corner me at a meeting and ask, "What can you and others like you do to help people better understand and appreciate North Carolina's natural heritage?" This led to a meeting of authors of books about the state's natural history to discuss her question in the summer of 1997. That meeting hatched the idea of a book that would present driving tours of some of the state's most attractive and interesting natural areas, identify learning experiences in each tour, and make the tours and experiences accessible to a wide general audience, from schoolchildren to adults.

The authors and other consulting naturalists worked together to develop a "must include" list of natural areas for the book. The areas included here were suggested by several naturalists, but many other suggested areas could not be included. As a result, we know that there are more great natural places in North Carolina than those described in this book. We see the present book as a first step in a continuing process of describing the state's natural areas for the public, and we hope a series of similar publications will follow from this one. The authors also agreed to allow their work to be used as the basis for "virtual fieldtrips," made available to schools over the Internet. We hope these virtual trips—now included in the multimedia area of the Learn NC website (http://www.learnnc.org)—will help meet the goal of making the book's content accessible to schoolchildren.

As you will see from the table of contents, the book is organized into five sections. The introduction is an overview of the state's geology, climate, and plant and animal life. This section is designed to introduce readers to the environmental processes that form and sustain the natural heritage of our state. The other four sections of the book describe tours of natural areas in the Coast, Coastal Plain, Piedmont, and Mountain Regions of the state. Each tour can be accomplished in less than a day, but each can be expanded to several days if visitors choose to explore all stops along the route. Each tour has a map of the recommended route and identifies the things to be seen and learned along the way. Photographs are included of sites along most of the tour routes.

Many avenues for further reading and study are opened up by the broad range of topics touched upon in this book. The introduction describes geological phenomena from plate tectonics to sedimentation, climate from global change to microclimate, and biota from plant community ecology to species adaptation. The tours cover an even wider range of topics than the overview. Most are primarily ecological in approach, but some are geological and some mix biology, ecology, history, and culture. All tours identify natural areas where visitors can make firsthand observations from hiking trails, bicycle paths, and bodies of water. Thus it is not likely that any suggested readings list could cover all possible areas of reader interest, but the titles listed in the "Suggestions for Further Reading" section at the end of the book include those that authors of this book have found useful. They are listed in categories that reflect topics covered in the introduction and tours, that is, biota, climate, ecology, geology, and natural areas. All focus on North Carolina, although some describe phenomena of surrounding regions as well. Most entries contain a brief description of the book's coverage.

This book exists because more than fifty North Carolina naturalists volunteered their time to make it happen. Thirty-two of this number volunteered to write one or more of the tours that make up the bulk of the book. But these authors were not the only naturalists who helped. Many others spent time and freely offered suggestions, advice, and assistance. The book could not have been written without the participation of naturalists across the state. I must thank all of them at the outset. Participants in this project came from state agencies, universities, conservation organizations, and private companies. Volunteers from North Carolina's Department of Environment and Natural Resources ranged from Secretary Wayne McDevitt through assistant secretaries, program directors, and staff at all levels. I must make special mention of the roles of Anne Taylor; Linda Pearsall, head of the Natural Heritage Program; and Betsy Bennett, director of the State Museum of Natural Sciences. All three of these energetic and capable people helped whenever and however help was needed. The book owes much to their efforts. Naturalists from conservation groups and private companies also helped; several contributed tour descriptions, but others assisted in less visible ways. Professor Robert Peet of the University of North Carolina at Chapel Hill helped identify places to include and people to write about them, as did Chuck Roe, director of the Conservation Trust for North Carolina and former head of the state's Natural Heritage Program. Jane Preyer and Doug Rader of the Environmental Defense Fund and many others also talked with me as the project moved along. All of these helped in important ways. Suffice it to say that North Carolina's naturalists are exceedingly enthusiastic, conscientious, and supportive people. Everyone whom I contacted did whatever he or she could to make this book possible.

The book's subject matter owes much to the citizens of North Carolina and to their elected representatives in the General Assembly. The people have supported preservation of natural areas, and the General Assembly, acting through direct appropriations or through citizen boards of the North Carolina Natural Heritage Trust, the Clean Water Management Trust Fund, and the state's Division of Parks and Recreation, have made such preservation possible.

The book's completion owes much to the staffs of the University of North Carolina's Marine Science Program and the University of North Carolina Press. The Marine Science Program agreed to let me spend my time on this project that covered somewhat more than marine sciences and also allowed Jim Gray to process, and reprocess, the words that make up the text. Jim did this time-consuming task willingly and well, albeit with a modest level of good-natured griping. The staff of the University of North Carolina Press took our drafts and turned them into the book you have before you. David Perry, the editor-in-chief, provided encouragement throughout and negotiated the rather unusual contract through which royalties from book sales will go to support environmental education programs in the state's Department of Environment and Natural Resources. His colleagues Dave VanHook and Pam Upton kept up with the myriad details that must be attended to in any undertaking of this sort. Finally, I and all the authors owe a debt of gratitude to Laura Cotterman, our copyeditor, whose interest and expertise in natural history greatly improved all parts of the manuscript.

Exploring
North Carolina's
Natural Areas

Introduction

DIRK FRANKENBERG

The tours in this book will guide you to some of North Carolina's most interesting and beautiful natural areas. These areas are some of our best examples of a landscape once controlled exclusively by natural processes. Unfortunately, we do not have perfect knowledge of what that original landscape was like because human use of the landscape began well before anyone described it. The use and manipulation of the landscape by humans have increased in both scope and intensity during the last four hundred years. The areas described in our tours are less modified than their surroundings—some because their topography or location made them too expensive to develop, others because they have been left alone for many years since their last use in agriculture or forestry, and some because they were preserved early in our history for the enjoyment of future generations. These areas give us the best idea we can get of North Carolina's environmental heritage. This book is written to introduce more people to that heritage by directing them to the best-preserved, publicly accessible examples of North Carolina's natural landscape. This overview describes the major forces that created and sustain that landscape.

North Carolina's natural landscape resulted from long and continuing interactions between its land, its climate, and its living things (biota). The land itself was formed in two episodes of mountain building, each followed by long periods in which the mountains were reduced by rock weathering and erosion. The climate changed, cooling as North America moved north from its equatorial origin and cyclically with global changes of temperature and rainfall. The biota began adding its contributions to the landscape as soon as plants colonized the land about 440 million years ago. Both plants and animals have influenced land, climate, and landscape development ever since. Plants growing on weathered rock stabilize the surface, decrease erosion rates, add organic matter, and retain water, all of which make the once barren surface more conducive to further colonization by living things. Plants and animals also influence the climate by increasing the rate at which water moves from soil to air and by providing organic matter to absorb and release heat and water, thereby reducing daily and seasonal ranges of temperature and humidity. Interactions between land, climate, and biota have also played major roles in landscape development. Both the forces and their interactions are important to North Carolina's natural heritage—a heritage of greater richness and biological diversity than that of almost any other state.

The Land

The area we now call North Carolina has existed as part of the earth's geology almost half as long as the earth has had a solid crust. The oldest rocks in North Carolina are metamorphically modified sediments that form the core of the Blue Ridge Mountains. The sediments that formed this rock were eroded from the earliest continental material in North America about 2.6 to 1.8 billion years ago. The sediments, much modified by recurring periods of heat and pressure, now form part of the Elk Park Massif, a feature that will be seen on the Roan Mountain driving tour.

The first rocks formed within what is now North Carolina resulted from a collision between continents about 1.8 to 1 billion years ago. This collision formed the Grenville Mountains and changed sediments from the earlier continent into sandstone, then into true metamorphic rocks called gneisses. The Grenville Mountain–building events thrust these and other rocks up out of the seafloor into mountains tens of thousands of feet tall. At their bases, some mountains in the Grenville chain were flooded by molten granite forced upward from earlier continental rock underlying the seafloor. These "intrusions" rarely reached the surface of the crust; most formed subsurface layers, called "dikes" when they are vertically oriented and "sills" when horizontal. Some of these layers have now been exposed by erosion and form the granite outcrops of the Piedmont and the granite peaks of Stone Mountain, Looking Glass Rock, and others seen on our tours in the mountains. Thus rocks formed during the Grenville period are the basement rocks of today's Appalachians—exposed in some places but covered in most with layers of other materials added later in our story.

The Grenville Mountains, spectacular in their prime, did not last. Rock weathering and erosion ate away at them, undeterred by plant cover, soil formation, or protective organic matter. (Plants did not invade the land for another 400 million years.) In addition, forces in the earth's crust that formed the Grenvilles reversed, pulling apart the recently formed continent to create new seaways among its fragments. Thus the rocks of the Grenvilles were weathering and fracturing at the same time. In 150 million years (a short period in geologic time), the Grenvilles were nothing more than a core of metaphoric rocks near sea level, and layers of sediments on the floor of newly opened oceans. But ocean floors often reverse the gravitational rule—"what goes down must come up." That is what happened to the eroded roots of the Grenvilles—they came up during geologic uplifts as the seaways closed and new mountains, the Appalachians, were formed.

A lot of interesting geological events took place during the 500-million-year period during which the Grenville continent split and came back together, but this is not the place to describe those events in detail. Fred Beyer has done that well in his book, *North Carolina: The Years before Man—A Geologic History* (see "Suggestions for Further Reading"). Suffice it to say that the pulling apart of the Grenville continent began about 800 million years ago and lasted 300 million years. The forces that spread apart continental fragments (called terranes by geologists) created new oceans with their associated seafloors and sediments. The largest of these oceans was the proto-Atlantic, the predecessor of our Atlantic, but several smaller coastal oceans and seaways formed at the same time.

The spreading stage reversed again after 300 million years. The newly formed oceans, seas, and seaways began to shrink as continents and continental fragments were pushed toward one another. These movements were destined to form modern North Carolina. Unsurprisingly, this moving together of continental material did not occur without some major disruptions. The heavy, basaltic rocks of the seafloors fractured and sank beneath the lighter continental rocks as the seaways were obliterated. Massive stresses built up where rock masses slid past one another—forces that spawned both earthquakes and volcanoes like those that now occur in California and Washington, where similar processes (transform faulting and subduction, respectively) are going on today. In ancient North Carolina volcanoes spewed ash and lava for hundreds of millions of years. We now have 10,000-foot-deep layers of this ash along our border with Virginia, for example. Other materials from these volcanoes landed in the shrinking seas to form layers that became the Carolina Slate Belt and other northeast-to-southwest-trending rock formations in the Piedmont. Volcanic ash and calcium carbonate deposited in these seas formed the slate and marble that is mined throughout the region today. The rocks of these old seafloors can be seen in quarries located along our tours of the Uwharrie Mountains of the central Piedmont.

The most dramatic events of the post-Grenville period, however, were those associated with origins of the Appalachian Mountains. These, like the Grenvilles before them, formed when major continents collided. North American and Euro-African plates of the earth's crust collided over a period of over 500 million years, obliterating the proto-Atlantic as well as what remained of the marginal seas between continental fragments. Rocks and sediments involved in these collisions were changed by heat and pressure (metamorphosed) into new and more permanent minerals. The later stages of the crustal collisions thrust surface rocks northwestward over 100 miles and forced vast slabs of rock up and over their northwestern neighbors to form both today's Appalachian Mountains and the ridge and valley topography further west. The original Appalachians were as tall as the Grenvilles, and like the Grenvilles they began to erode immediately after they formed. The overthrust origins of the Appalachians established the erosion pattern that followed because the eastern slope of the new mountains was steeper than the western slope. As a result, swift-running streams stripped more material off the eastern slope, steepening it to the slope we see today and isolating the mountains of the western Piedmont, several of which you will see during the tours of Pilot Mountain, Hanging Rock, and Crowders Mountain.

Erosion was not the only process to effect changes on the newly formed landmass of North Carolina. This land, built during millions of years of continental collision, fractured when crustal forces reversed to form the modern Atlantic Ocean. These fractures broke the continent and allowed large blocks to settle deeper into the crust, forming depressions. These depressions are now called Triassic basins after the period (208–245 million years ago) during which they formed. Features such as the Dan and Deep River Triassic basins occupy much of the central Piedmont today. They trend from northeast to southwest and they, as well as the solidified remnants of molten rock that oozed upward in vertical dikes along their flanks, have a continuing impact on Piedmont topography and soil types. Harry LeGrand's tour of the central Piedmont takes you through the Durham Triassic basin and to the "Butner Gumbo" soils formed from dark, magnesium-rich (and therefore basic) mafic dike rocks deep in the crust. As you will discover on this tour, the basic (that is, relatively high pH) soils derived from these mafic rocks support different plants than are found on the typically acidic Piedmont soils around them.

The most obvious effect of the continental splitting, however, was the development of a seaward slope on the eastern side of the mountains down which weathered products of Appalachian erosion began to move. At present, all but 5,000 feet of the original mountains' mass has found its way east. Some of that material formed sediments of the Coastal Plain, including those of the Sandhills (observable on two of our tours). However, more of the eroded material went into the ocean to form our continental shelf and slope. These sedimentary structures now reach thicknesses of over 10,000 feet off North Carolina. Thus North Carolina grew eastward with materials eroded from the mountains. This fact is important to keep in mind when visiting either end of our state. In the west, you should be thinking about negative space—that is, the volume of the landscape not filled with mountains. As you view the mountains on our tours, bear in mind that those rocks were once deep within the earth's crust, much of which has been eroded away to form the negative space of the valleys. Similarly, as you visit the mountains of the western Piedmont on our tours (Kings, Crowders, Pilot, etc.), bear in mind that all the land surface was once at the level of these peaks and that most of it has been eroded away. When you visit the western edge of the Coastal Plain along Interstate 95, recall that this was once the seacoast, and that the eroded remnants of the post-Grenville continental fragments are hundreds of feet under your feet. When visiting the seacoast, don't think that the landscape is flat and topographically dull; think of the thousands of feet of mountain and Piedmont rock fragments that lie between the soles of your feet and the continental rocks that first fractured to open the Atlantic.

The erosion that stripped away the Appalachian surface did not occur without continental reaction. As the weight of overlying rock was removed, deeper layers moved upward much as water in a spring continues to bubble upward as earlier volumes flow away. The slowly rising surface of the land continued to erode, keeping the surface of the Piedmont always above sea level and creating hills and valleys in areas of more and less erosion-resistant rocks. The gently rolling hills of our Piedmont are the record of this rising and eroding surface, which is called by geologists a "peneplain," that is, "almost a plain." The gradual rise and erosion of the Piedmont created soils that are largely formed in place. That is, the soils of the Piedmont result from weathering of the underlying rocks, so soil maps are similar to rock maps. The plants that live in these soils also have the same distribution as the rocks: soils and plants have evolved together over the last 200 million years.

If erosion caused the slow uplift of land in the west, the growing layers of eroded material weighed down and depressed underlying rocks in the east. This subsidence created a flat, level surface that was alternately flooded and exposed as sea level rose and fell. Much of the sediment brought to the coast was dissolved or worn away to nothingness, leaving only the most resistant materials (quartz sand) behind. Thus the sands of the Coastal Plain are the survivors of the vast post-Appalachian erosion. These sands have been, and continue to be, shifted about by currents of wind and water, a fact that will be obvious if you take our tours of the coastal zone. In addition, the sea's retreat has left distinct surfaces of successively older seafloors on the Coastal Plain. These surfaces, and the ancient shorelines that mark their seaward margins, account for much of the Coastal Plain's modest topography. The old shorelines—called "the seven steps to the sea" by geologists control drainage patterns, river courses, soil types, flooding regimes, and human settlement patterns. You will see the sandy ridges that characterize these old shorelines as you drive across the Coastal Plain on our tour routes (Weldon to the Great Dismal Swamp or through Croatan National Forest, for example).

The Climate

Climate and weather have influenced North Carolina's natural landscapes for as long as there have been landscapes to influence. Climate is treated second in this overview because it is partly controlled by land, and its influence on present landscapes extends back thousands rather than the millions of years it took for the landforms to develop. Climate and weather are related, but not identical. The difference was put succinctly by Mark Twain, who said, "Climate is what you expect, weather is what you get." Scientists try to improve on that homily by defining climate as "the prevailing atmospheric phenomena and conditions of temperature, rainfall, wind, etc. in a region" and weather as "the condition of the atmosphere at a given place and time." For our purposes both climate and weather are important because both influence the types and distribution of natural landscapes. Climate conditions, both past and present, have significant effects. Our landscapes are biologically diverse, in part because our present climate is diverse and continues to change from conditions in the recent past.

North Carolina has a broad range of climate conditions due to its three distinct regions: the Appalachians, the Piedmont, and the Coastal Plain. This topographical variety, along with the presence of the Gulf Stream off the coast, gives North Carolina the greatest climate variability of any state east of the Mississippi River. Statewide variability occurs in both rainfall and temperature. The Piedmont section of the state is warmer in the summer and drier year round than either the mountains or the Coastal Plain. This temperature pattern results from the inherent coolness of higher elevations in the mountains and the proximity of the eastern part of the state to the waters of our coastal ocean and sounds. The Piedmont is subject to neither condition and is warmer as a result. The wetter climates of the mountains and coast are linked to the same causes. The higher elevations of the mountains force surface air to rise and cool, causing much of its water vapor to condense into liquid and fall as rain. In the Coastal Plain, proximity to large water masses provides a ready source of evaporated water to air masses that move over land, warm, and rise to produce rainfall by the same process. In the Piedmont, neither of these rainfall sources occurs, and we are stuck with the ubiquitous "widely scattered thunderstorms" as a source of rainfall.

Past climate conditions also have easily observable effects on North Carolina's natural landscapes. During the ice ages that reached their maxima about 18,000 years ago, North Carolina escaped glaciation but was cold enough that tundra plants flourished in our mountains, cold prairie grasslands grew in the Piedmont, and conifer forests of spruce, fir, and white pine prevailed in the Coastal Plain. The Coastal Plain was also wider than it is today because the combination of a cold ocean and frozen water stored in northern glaciers lowered the sea level more than 300 feet. In fact our coast was located where the outer edge of the continental shelf is today. As the climate warmed and glaciers retreated, North Carolina landscapes changed. By 13,000 years ago the conifer forests had invaded the Piedmont and temperate hardwood forests occupied the south Coastal Plain. By 10,000 years ago the present forest type distributions were pretty much in place, but, as you will see when you tour our state, "relict" forests and species still occupy unusual places where the microclimate is cooler or wetter than surrounding areas. We have Piedmont plants in the Coastal Plain, mountain plants in the Piedmont, and Canadian plants in the mountains. Such occurrences are pointed out in our tours of all three regions.

Despite all the diversity and temporal variability of our climate, it is still possible to summarize by saying that it is characterized by warm summers and mild winters with 40 to 60 inches of rainfall spread relatively evenly across the year. This equitable situation derives from the combined effects of three major factors: our latitude—in the global wind belt known as the "band of prevailing westerlies" but far enough north to be affected by both the airflow known as the jet stream and the seasonally migrating "polar front"; our location with respect to oceans and the rest of the continent—close enough to both the Atlantic and the Gulf of Mexico to get moisture from them, but southeast of continental areas from which dry, and often cool, air reaches us; and our topography—mountainous in the west, leaving parts of the state in a "rain shadow," with flat or rolling Piedmont and Coastal Plain areas providing little topographic control over wind fields or movement of weather fronts and rainfall patterns.

The influence of weather on North Carolina landscapes is sometimes as observable as the influence of climate, as when hurricanes, floods, or tornadoes knock down trees to create decades-long openings in our forest canopies. But weather influence can also be more subtle, as when cold air flows down a valley floor to create "frost hollows" in depressions, leaving "thermal belts" of warmer air along the valley walls—a process that leads apple producers in our mountains to locate their orchards on the side slopes rather than on the valley floors or the ridge crests.

Generalizations about the weather of North Carolina are not impossible. Peter J. Robinson, professor of geography at the University of North Carolina at Chapel Hill and coordinator of the state climate program, has categorized the state's weather as falling into four major types:

1. Cold, dry, and relatively cloudless when the polar front is south of the state and continental or polar air covers us—frequent in winter but infrequent in summer.
2. Warm, moist, and relatively humid with clouds when the polar front is north of the state and maritime tropical air covers us—causing rainfall around thunderstorms in summer and prolonged drizzle in winter.
3. Rapidly changing conditions between types 1 and 2 when the polar front passes through the state—more common in winter than in summer.
4. Rapidly changing weather with clouds and rain when low pressure systems pass through the state—common in both summer and winter.

Robinson's thoroughness compels him to include hurricanes and other extreme events like tornadoes and ice storms as additional weather types, although, fortunately for us all, these are infrequent.

Thus, North Carolina's weather is dominated by alternating periods of tropical and polar/continental air masses separated by periods of rapidly changing conditions marked by precipitation events. North Carolina weather is changeable—perhaps not as variable as New England weather (about which Mark Twain said, "If you don't like it, wait a few minutes"), but changeable nonetheless. The complexities of North Carolina weather and climate make predictions and summaries difficult. Both public and private organizations provide weather predictions daily. Analyses of regional climate variations are provided by the state climate program. This office integrates findings on interactions among land, air, and sea to provide information on regional and local climate variations through data services, personal visits, fax, and telephone, as well as through the Internet (http://www.nc-climate.ncsu.edu). The office also maintains and operates a network of agrometeorological stations across North Carolina. This network, consisting of eighteen stations spread across the state, a telecommunications center, and systems to perform analysis and storage of data, is dedicated to providing precision agrometeorological and climatological data to North Carolina citizens and institutions. Efforts are currently under way to expand the AgNet and combine other observation stations in North Carolina to form a comprehensive climate-environment observations network (NC ECO NET) that will have a continuous weather-monitoring site in each North Carolina county.

The Biota: Plants and Animals of Natural Landscapes

To most people, the most interesting aspects of natural landscapes are the plants and animals that live in them. Plants are the most visible features of terrestrial landscapes. In terrestrial settings, animals are harder to see because they are small (insects), hidden (amphibians and small mammals), or cautious and fast moving (larger mammals and birds). In aquatic settings, animals sometimes dominate landscapes—as in oyster reefs—but this is rare. In most cases, plants dominate the landscape visually and provide physical structure to the environment in which animals live. In all cases, plant photosynthesis provides the organic energy that sustains the animals' food chain. For these reasons, most descriptions of natural landscapes focus on the type and distribution of plants and give only secondary attention to the animals that live among them. That approach is followed in this book as well.

The type and abundance of plants that characterize a natural landscape are controlled by both biological and nonbiological factors. Plant distribution is directly related to substrate (rocks and soils), setting (elevation, topography, slope, etc.), and climate (temperature, moisture, wind, salt spray, etc.). The major biological processes that control plant distribution are adaptation and succession.

These processes underlie the unique ability of living organisms to invade unoc-cupied habitats and change both themselves and the habitat to establish a func-tional ecological system. The importance of these two processes justifies defining them here: adaptation is the modification by which an organism or species be-comes better fitted to its environment; succession is a sequence of ecological changes whereby one group of plants and animals successively gives way to an-other until a recurring assemblage of organisms naturally associated with each other and their physical environment is established. Such recurring assemblages of organisms are known as "natural communities" by ecologists.

In North Carolina, adaptation has produced organisms well fitted to natural environments of many types. North Carolina environments range in elevation from sea level to the highest point east of the Mississippi; from hot, dry pockets of soil on granite outcrops to cool, tidally inundated swamp forests of the lower Coastal Plain; from mountain coves packed with winter snow to porous-soiled subtropical barrier islands near the Gulf Stream. This range of environments is filled with well-adapted species. The driving tours in this book will take you through environments where much of this adaptive diversity can be observed firsthand.

The ecological process of natural succession characterizes most North Carolina landscapes because most areas have been disturbed by humans. North Carolina's first major industry was forestry, and its second was agriculture. As a result, almost all accessible land has been cleared by logging, farming, or both. Exceptions in-clude the wettest of wetlands, the steepest of slopes, and a few areas of nondevelop-ment. Somewhat surprisingly, the largest areas of undisturbed natural commu-nities are the marshlands along our coasts and Coastal Plain rivers. These habitats have deep, soft soils that made them unsuitable for development until large earth-moving machines became available. Regulations now protect these marshes from dredge-and-fill projects; so, for better or worse, if you want to see a landscape that looks much like it did when humans first looked upon it, go visit a salt marsh. Our tours of downeast Carteret County, the White Oak River, the Cape Fear Estuary, and Brunswick County wetlands will take you to all the salt marshes you might want to see.

The process of natural succession dominates the Piedmont section of the state, where almost all the land has been logged and farmed. A detailed description of the process and the plants that characterize each successive stage can be found in Michael A. Godfrey's *Field Guide to the Piedmont: The Natural Habitats of Amer-ica's Most Lived-in Region, from New York City to Montgomery, Alabama* (see "Suggestions for Further Reading," under "Ecology"). In brief, seventy-five years of ecological study have shown that bare Piedmont soils (abandoned fields being the classic example) are occupied successively by grasses, plants of the aster family,

broomsedge and goldenrod, pines, and finally hardwoods. The particular species and duration of each successional stage differ in habitats of different moisture levels, but grass and aster stages last only a year or two, the broomsedge/
goldenrod stage lasts two or more years before being overgrown by pines, and
pines last fifty to one hundred years before being replaced by a community dominated by hardwoods.

Natural succession also dominates much of the landscape in mountain and
Coastal Plain sections of the state. Land once used for farming and forestry is now
being converted to other purposes. Abandoned land goes through many of the
same general stages as occur in the Piedmont, but species and time frames differ
sufficiently to make a full description beyond the scope of this overview. Suffice it
to say that natural communities are dynamic systems that change continuously.
During succession these changes often occur in similar sequences in areas of
similar exposure, moisture, elevation, and soils. These changes decrease, but do
not stop, when a recurring natural assemblage of species is established. Disturbance of these assemblages by fires, windstorms, floods, or other extreme events
initiates further successional changes, creating a mosaic pattern of stages within
areas occupied by the same recurring assemblage.

Recent studies of plant communities have led ecologists to revise their views of
the permanence and uniformity of such assemblages. Extensive evidence of the
mosaic nature of such systems is not consistent with an earlier theory that a stable
"climax community" would form and remain relatively unchanged at the end of
the successional sequence. Evidence from field studies of such sequences have
revealed that succession does not always proceed in the order first described.
Michael Godfrey admits that his own field observations show the generally accepted successional sequence "to be violated as often as followed" but states his
belief that it still remains "a good first approximation" of what happens when
natural plants reestablish themselves on abandoned land. There are also ecologists
who challenge the long-cherished notion that nature is organized into distinct
communities at all. These scientists interpret plant distributions in natural landscapes as representing only the interplay between physiological adaptations of
individual species and gradients of physical factors in the environment. In this
view, the "recurring assemblages" of plants usually defined as communities are
nothing more than the common occurrence of species with similar adaptations
occupying sites with similar soils and microclimates. This disagreement among
experts is unlikely to be resolved anytime soon, but readers should be aware of it as
they make their own observations of plant distributions in the natural areas described in this book.

The most complete descriptions of plant distributions in North Carolina is
based on the concept that plants occur in communities, that is, "distinct and

recurring assemblages of plants, animals and fungi naturally associated with each other and their physical environment." This treatment is found in an important book, *Classification of the Natural Communities of North Carolina*, by Michael P. Schafale and Alan S. Weakley. The authors modestly call their work "approximations," and the latest (1990) version is the third in an evolving sequence. It and earlier versions can be obtained from the North Carolina Natural Heritage Program (see "Suggestions for Further Reading").

Schafale and Weakley recognize the variation in plant assemblages by identifying both subtypes and variants of the "natural communities" they describe, and they are well aware of the flux in their field. Nevertheless, they describe North Carolina's natural communities as occurring in one of four systems: terrestrial, palustrine (relating to marshes and wetlands), estuarine (relating to the mixed salt and fresh waters where rivers enter the sea), and marine. Each community can include tens to hundreds of species, and there are of course many community subtypes, but Schafale and Weakley's work provides ample support for the proposition that North Carolina harbors a great level of natural diversity.

If one thinks back of the information in this chapter, the underlying causes of North Carolina's diversity are not difficult to discern. We have a broad range of rock types, elevations, and topography. We have isolated outcrops of rock that have intruded into our landscape from deep in the earth, as well as those whose resistance to weathering have allowed them to survive millions of years of erosion (e.g., the isolated monadnocks of Pilot Mountain, Hanging Rock, Chimney Rock, and Kings Mountain). The erosion that was not resisted has given us a wide variety of soils. The rolling hills remaining after erosion have thin, porous soil at their crests, thicker, more water-retentive soils on their flanks, and deep rich soils along the rivers that separate them from one another. The eroded particles not retained in the hills and rivers have been carried seaward to produce the thick wedge of sediment that makes up our Coastal Plain. We have a barrier island coastline with some islands far offshore (the Outer Banks) and others barely separated from the mainland (our southern coast). We have the Gulf Stream bringing warm water and a subtropical climate to our southern coast, and cool waters originating from the Labrador Current come to us from the north. These waters carry different species—a difference that increases the diversity of our marine life. We have rivers draining from quite different sources, some rising in the mountains, others in the Piedmont, and still others in the Coastal Plain. Each is isolated from its neighbors and thereby has provided speciation opportunities for aquatic organisms of different river systems. Where these rivers meet the sea they form mouths of different sizes as well as the second-largest estuarine coastal lagoon system in the nation (Pamlico Sound). The climate over this landscape is generally favorable to living things but has enough variation, seasonality, and extreme events to encourage continuing adaptation among the organisms exposed to it. All in all, North Carolina's diverse natural biota is a living reflection of the diverse geological and climatological landscapes of the state. Much of this landscape has been modified by humans in ways that reduce its natural diversity. As a result, the biota has also been diminished, but, as I believe you will see from the driving tours that follow, an impressively large number of unmodified and natural areas have been preserved in our state by public and private action.

The Coast

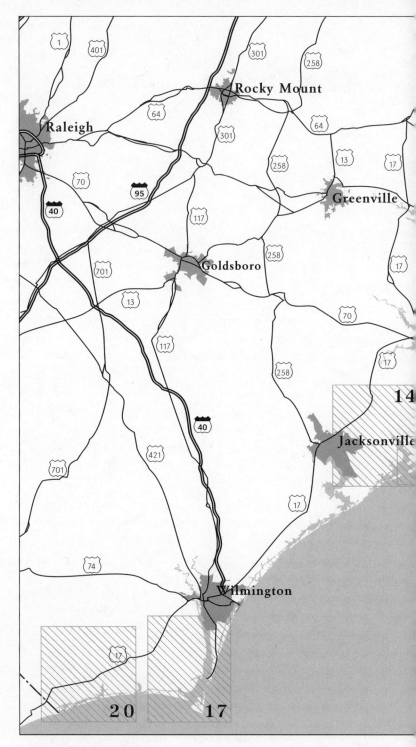

FIGURE 1. Coastal tour routes
Numbers in boxes indicate figure numbers for individual tour route maps.

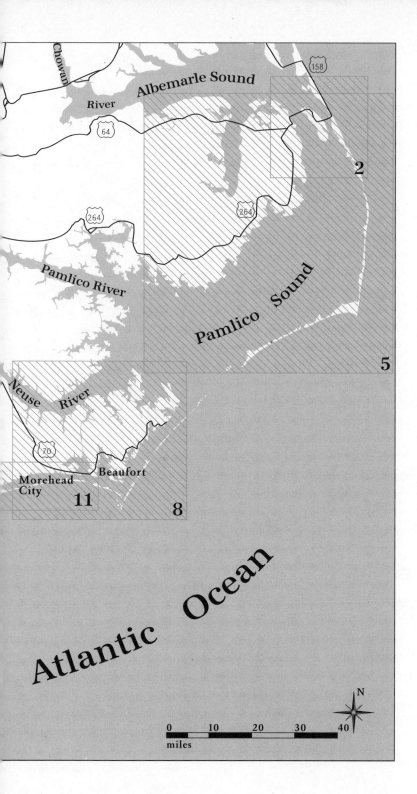

Old and New on the Outer Banks

Maritime Forests, Inlets, and Development

DIRK FRANKENBERG

This tour takes you to old and new maritime forests, tidal inlets, and areas of human development. The tour begins at the oldest maritime forest on the Outer Banks (Nags Head Woods) and ends 25 miles later at Pea Island National Wildlife Refuge. Along the way you will see the state's largest sand dune at Jockey's Ridge State Park, a National Natural Landmark at Nags Head Woods Ecological Preserve, and an array of coastal habitats in a national seashore (Cape Hatteras) and a national wildlife refuge (Pea Island). You will also see how human use of Outer Banks real estate has changed over the last 160 years. The tour passes by houses built as long ago as the 1830s and as recently as yesterday.

If you take this tour you will learn that the only constant in barrier island habitats is constant change. You will observe change in sand dunes when wind-blown sand moves across the dune surfaces. You will see that change in tidal inlets is as constant as it is in dunes. The tour will take you to where Oregon Inlet formed in 1846 as well as to its present location almost 2 miles to the southeast. You will also learn how changes in dunes and inlets are caused by currents of wind and water. These currents are fully sufficient to move dunes over buildings, shift inlets away from lighthouses built to mark their location, and move ship channels out from under the bridges that were built over them. Finally, you will learn the vital role that rooted plants play in holding sand in place against these currents of wind and water. The tour will take you past vegetated habitats ranging from a mature maritime forest in Nags Head Woods, to a planted stand of slash pine, to young forests just beginning to replace shrub thickets. I hope you will take time to walk into these areas on a windy day so you can feel firsthand how the plants block the wind and reduce sand movement. Such walks will convince you that if it weren't for plants, all of the Outer Banks would be as unstable as the flanks of Jockey's Ridge.

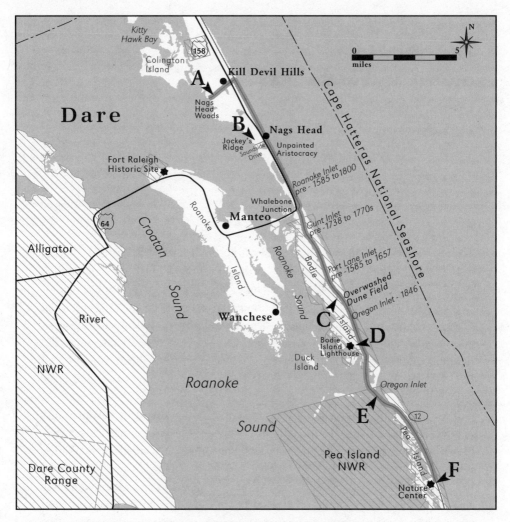

FIGURE 2. Outer Banks tour route—Nags Head Woods to Pea Island

A. Nags Head Woods Ecological Preserve and Run Hill

This tour begins at The Nature Conservancy Interpretive Center in Nags Head Woods. This center is reached from US 158 by West Ocean Acres Road at milepost 9.5 (look for the saltwater taffy store and the "timeless" McDonald's at the intersection). West Ocean Acres Road passes through a typical sequence of plant communities ranging from shrub thickets near US 158, through juvenile then mature pine forest for about 0.75 miles, then rises steeply up and over the crest of an old sand dune and plunges into Nags Head Woods, one of the oldest, most diverse, and most beautiful maritime forests on the East Coast. The Nature Conservancy Center is on the left about 1.5 miles west from the highway (near where power lines cross the dirt road that West Ocean Acres Road becomes after it crosses the dune ridge).

The biota of Nags Head Woods is exceptionally diverse for a barrier island maritime forest. Eleven species of oak, ten ferns, three pines, two magnolias, two cedars, two willows, five milkweeds, four goldenrods, and three cattails are found among the more than 300 species of plants identified to date. Over 100 species of birds, 65 species of land vertebrates (amphibians, reptiles, mammals), and 6 species of freshwater fish also live here. This extraordinary diversity is made possible by the unusual protection from salt spray afforded by tall dune ridges that surround the forest on three sides. You crossed one of these ancient dunes on West Ocean Acres Road on your way into the forest; others are visible from the public road through it. Water-filled low areas between these dunes add aquatic and edge habitats to that of the forest itself. This forest would be interesting in any setting, but on a barrier island it is a "must visit" site.

Nags Head Woods is so unusual that both the state government and The Nature Conservancy (a privately funded organization) have spent money to preserve a large fraction of it in the natural state. The National Park Service listed it as a National Natural Landmark in 1974 and the North Carolina chapter of The Nature Conservancy made it one of its first protection projects in 1977. The Nature Conservancy has now acquired 420 acres of the forest itself, owns another 390 acres jointly with the town of Nags Head, and leases yet another 300 acres from the town. The forest boasts miles of well-marked nature trails, guided field trips during the summer, and children's nature camps in July. Visiting hours vary with the season, so visitors are asked to call for information on programs and trail access at the time of their visit (252-441-2525). Access via the public dirt road beyond The Nature Conservancy Interpretive Center is available at any time, and the preserve is worth seeing even if you can't arrange to visit the center or the nature trails that radiate from it.

The trails from The Nature Conservancy Interpretive Center are a real treat. If you can, you should arrange your tour to reach the center when it is open. The staff will provide you with trail guides and give you advice about which trails are of the right length and rigor for your interest and abilities. All trails pass through relatively open forest of oaks, gums, maples, and hollies and near permanent and seasonal wetlands. My personal favorite passes back over the dune ridge toward the ocean, goes under the power line, and circles through a full range of maritime and swamp forests before returning.

If your tour cannot be arranged to dovetail with the Interpretive Center's hours, an always-open substitute is available from the Nags Head Town Park on West

Barnes Street at milepost 11 of US 158. The park is on the left before you get to the Medical Center, and the trailhead is at the southwest corner of the parking area. This half-mile trail may be initially misleading because it begins on an uphill stretch across a sparsely vegetated, seaward-facing dune ridge; but soon thereafter it traverses thickets and enters a magnificent maritime forest that extends all the way to the west side of the banks. This trail is worth hiking because it passes through most of the vegetation types found on the Outer Banks—dune grasslands, shrub thickets, and maritime forests—with all the diversity for which Nags Head Woods are famous.

To continue the primary tour, turn left after leaving The Nature Conservancy Interpretive Center. A few hundred yards will take you to a T-junction near the Nags Head Sanitation Service facility; turn right on Boundary Road. Boundary Road passes through well-preserved stands of maritime forest and goes past a series of freshwater ponds. The road may have deep puddles after rains, but it eventually rises up along an old dune ridge, then exits Nature Conservancy property and becomes West Martin Street. Note the houses built within the maritime forest. These are sited as the original settlers of the Outer Banks sited theirs, that is, they are nestled among well-established forests and separated from the destructive power of the sea by ancient dune ridges.

Continue along West Martin Street for a short distance, then go left on Ninth Avenue and left again on West Air Strip Road to the foot of Run Hill dunefield. Park your car along the road and climb Run Hill near its southern border with Nags Head Woods. As you climb the northeast face of the dune, note its steepness and loose sand—evidence of recent sand deposition by winds from the southwest. As you reach the crest, note that the southwest face of the dune is equally steep and loose. You have just examined physical evidence that records the two prevailing wind directions on the Outer Banks. The depositing dune face that you climbed to reach the crest was formed by southwest winds. The dune face that is moving over Nags Head Woods was formed by northeast winds. Note also the sand-trapping ability of dune vegetation at Run Hill's crest: sea oats and American beachgrass crown the tops of the dune hummocks, and trailing sand ridges are visible behind them. These hummocks record the direction of the strongest prevailing winds—in this case, from the northeast.

The most dramatic views from the crest of Run Hill are to the south into Nags Head Woods and to the southwest across forest, thicket, freshwater marsh, salt marsh, and Roanoke Sound (Figure 3).

Both of these views explain why Nags Head Woods is well protected from salt spray. Run Hill itself forces salt-laden winds to rise above the forest canopy—a situation most obviously revealed along the southwestern edge of the dune field. Roanoke Island protects the woods from large, spray-producing waves in Albe-

FIGURE 3. View from Run Hill. Note Nags Head Woods to left of dune and Roanoke Sound in distance. (Photo by D. Frankenberg)

marle and Pamlico Sounds. Jockey's Ridge (the giant dune just west of US 158 at milepost 13) protects the woods on the south, and the tall dune ridge you crossed on the way to and from The Nature Conservancy Interpretive Center protects the woods on the east. Together, these barriers provide a protective box that isolates the woods from salt spray and allows development of the diverse forest you have just seen. Another interesting view from Run Hill is north to the Wright Brothers Memorial at the crest of the next large dune. This dune is uniformly covered with a lawn, a result created by importing topsoil and nonnative grasses to the area in the 1920s. These exotic imports stabilized the dune, making it completely different from the unstable dunes from which the Wrights actually flew. To appreciate the difference, you may want to visit the memorial; it has a replica of the original plane, interesting exhibits and presentations on early flight, and photographs showing the desertlike unvegetated dune the Wright brothers knew.

B. Jockey's Ridge State Park and Soundside Drive

This driving tour continues south on US 158 (reached by returning to West Martin Street; turn left to get to the highway, then right to head south). As you drive south, note modern house and business sites on exposed mid-island "flats" and on the artificial oceanfront dunes. Unsurprisingly, these sites are susceptible to being flooded by stormy seas and covered over by migrating dunes (a fate known on the Outer Banks as "being sanded"). Drive south on US 158 to the main entrance to Jockey's Ridge State Park. If you want to learn more about the natural history of the largest sand dune on the East Coast, enter the park and visit the natural history museum/interpretive center in the park's office building. If you are content to limit yourself to observation of, and hiking over, the dune, continue past the park entrance and the dune itself to milepost 13 and turn right onto West Soundside Drive. Look northwest from the US 158/Soundside Drive intersection to see the top of a sanded minigolf facility sticking up out of the dune. This cupola stands as mute testimony that "sanding" really can happen to Outer Banks buildings. Further down West Soundside Drive are other places where Jockey's Ridge has covered both land and property.

The main body of Jockey's Ridge is north of West Soundside Drive, but the dune and its actively depositing southwest face are best seen from a point about 0.25 miles west of US 158. Here, the road is wide enough for parking and the dune is close enough to climb. If you do climb the dune, you will be able to see the peak of Jockey's Ridge to the north with its hang-gliding students and sandboarders, but you will be far enough away to enjoy the natural dunescape and ponder the size of the main dune.

Geologists attribute the large dunes of the northern Outer Banks to the alternating windfield of the Banks. As is clear from West Soundside Drive, the dominant winds here are from the northeast, but the dunes wouldn't be as high as they are if southwest winds didn't also help them grow. The alternating flows of air combine to concentrate sand at the dune crest, thereby making it taller.

At the west end of Soundside Drive you will find a parking lot and the Roanoke Sound beach access. After you have seen as much as you like of this site, follow Soundside Drive back across the Banks to the coastal road known as Virginia Dare Trail. Note the "flats" between the coastal road (Virginia Dare Trail) and US 158— relatively flat areas once covered with trees that were cleared for farming in the eighteenth century. These areas are now sites for residential and commercial development. A few patches of shrub thicket dominated by wax myrtle (southern bayberry), groundsel (cotton bush), dune elder, and yaupon holly have returned on vacant lots, but not to an extent useful for nature study.

East Soundside Drive intersects with Virginia Dare Trail (NC 12) among what some historians call the Unpainted Aristocracy—the oldest summer cottages on the Outer Banks. Some of these houses have sections that were built in the 1830s. All those built before the Civil War have been moved to the ocean side of the island, because none were built there before the 1880s. The first cottage on the oceanfront was built by W. G. Pool, a doctor from Elizabeth City. Nags Head was already a leading seashore resort—had been since the mid-1850s—but the earliest visitors followed the lead of previous inhabitants and built their cottages and hotels as far back from the ocean as possible. Pool began a new trend by building his own house on the shore, and he encouraged others to do so by giving 130-foot-wide building lots to his friends' wives. About forty of the cottages built in this period remain today and together have been designated a historic preservation district. Most are now set on pilings to allows waves and sand to pass beneath them.

Turn right on Virginia Dare Trail, observing both the old houses and the new construction with wave-blocking foundations. History, as well as common sense, tells us that the early construction practice is far less susceptible to storm damage than the modern style. It is hard not to wonder how and where houses would be built on the Outer Banks were it not for publicly financed (and therefore relatively cheap) flood and storm damage insurance underwritten by the federal government.

c. Cape Hatteras National Seashore, Old and New Inlets, and Pea Island Nature Preserve

The driving tour enters Cape Hatteras National Seashore just past the place where NC 12 intersects with US 64/264 at an area known as Whalebone Junction. You reach this junction by continuing south on Virginia Dare Trail until it becomes a divided highway (i.e., US 64 and 264), then turning left at a stoplight where NC 12 heads south toward Cape Hatteras and Ocracoke.

A booth offering information about Cape Hatteras National Seashore is located on NC 12 immediately south of Whalebone Junction. Brochures and on-site personnel provide information on road conditions (NC 12 is sometimes closed by flooding or wind-blown sand) and answer questions. Just beyond the information booth, on the west side of the road, are large freshwater marshes and ponds. These formed atop the floodtide delta deposits of three old inlets—Roanoke, Port Lane, and Gunt (see map). Thickets sometimes interfere with the view, but the old inlet sediments combine to make Bodie Island over a mile wide at this point. Roanoke Inlet is the most famous of the three because most historians believe it provided access to Sir Walter Raleigh's first colony during the late 1500s. It was open before 1585 and closed about 1800. Gunt Inlet, 2 miles farther south, was smaller and shorter-lived. It opened in the 1730s and closed in the 1790s. Port Lane Inlet existed from before 1585 until the 1650s and was located somewhere south of Gunt Inlet. The tidal flats inshore of these three inlets provide low, water-saturated land that makes ideal waterfowl habitat. Hunters have long used these lands for recreation and continue to do so even though they are now part of Cape Hatteras National Seashore. The area provides habitat for thousands of geese (Canadian and snow), tundra swans, ducks, herons, egrets, ibises, pelicans, coots, gallinules, shearwaters, gulls, terns, and others too numerous to mention. Bird-watching platforms are established at several points along the road, as are hunting blinds that can be reserved in hunting season through the enforcement section of the National Park Service (Route 1, Box 675, Manteo, NC 27954; 252-473-2111). A good bird identification book such as Roger Tory Peterson's *A Field Guide to the Birds*, along with rubber boots, binoculars, and insect repellent, are recommended accessories for those who utilize these platforms and blinds.

D. Coquina Beach, Bodie Island Lighthouse, and Bodie Island Dike Nature Trail

Five and three-tenths miles south of Whalebone Junction there is a crossroads. The road on the ocean side leads to the beach, where one can see an excellent example of recent dune changes and the remains of a four-masted wooden schooner that wrecked here in 1921. The sound side road leads to Bodie Island Lighthouse, built in 1874 on what was then the northern shore of Oregon Inlet. The interesting Bodie Island Dike Nature Trail takes off from near the lighthouse. Both sides of the road are worth exploring.

The road to the beach ends in a new parking lot built to replace one that was destroyed when ocean waves and currents washed over the dunes in the Halloween storm of 1991. Trails from the new lot lead to the shipwreck, on the landward side of the artificial dune, and dramatic evidence of the 1991 dune overwash. This major overwash event sanded the earlier bathhouse and destroyed the seaward-most section of what was once a loop road to the U.S. Coast Guard Station visible in the distance. Pieces of the road decorate the new, higher land surface produced by overwashed sand. The source of that sand is readily apparent when you look at the flat beach and note the absence of the artificial seawardmost dune. That dune was destroyed by the overwash event, and its sand was pushed over the road and bathhouse and into the thicket beyond (Figure 4). Further evidence of this sand movement can be seen as you walk toward the old Coast Guard Station. What was once a continuous line of artificial dunes is now represented by two or three hummocky dunes with eroded faces on all sides other than the one facing inland. Still farther north, you will find the loop road blocked to a depth of more than 20 feet by sand.

The beach access facilities at Coquina Beach have been relocated in keeping with National Park Service policy, which states that "natural shoreline processes (erosion, deposition, dune formation, inlet formation, and shoreline migration) that are not influenced by human actions will be allowed to continue without abatement except where control measures are required by law. . . . Managers will plan to

FIGURE 4. Previous bathhouse covered by sand in 1991. (Photo by D. Frankenberg)

phase out, relocate, or provide alternative facilities for park developments located in hazardous areas that cannot reasonably be protected." Dune overwash damage is now repaired only in areas where North Carolina has a legal right to protect transportation infrastructure (NC 12 and the Herbert Bonner Bridge over Oregon Inlet) or where the Park Service is obligated to protect significant cultural resources (Cape Hatteras Lighthouse).

The road to Bodie Island Lighthouse and the Bodie Island Dike Nature Trail lies directly across NC 12 from the road to Coquina Beach. The road is flanked by nonnative slash pines planted in the early twentieth century and natural thickets growing in the protection provided by these trees. A few small live oaks are just getting started. This is about as new a maritime forest as can be found on the Outer Banks. Mid-nineteenth-century maps of the area show it dominated by sand flats, grasslands, and marshes. Compare this forest with Nags Head Woods to get a sense of old and new forests and the level of protection from wind and salt spray that they each provide.

The Bodie Island Lighthouse was built in 1874 to mark Oregon Inlet, now the only navigable access from sound to ocean between Cape Hatteras and Chesapeake Bay. This inlet opened in 1846 and was named Oregon after the first ship to pass through it. The lighthouse is not open to visitors, but the parking area provides access to the Bodie Island Dike Nature Trail, an easy and highly informative trail reached by the marl road at the southwest corner of the lighthouse loop road. About 0.25 miles down this road is the entrance to the nature trail. There are informative brochures in a self-serve dispenser near the trail entrance. In case the supply is exhausted, know that the trail is more than 6 miles long and can be hot and buggy in summer. It is a loop trail, but you may wish to consider turning back before completing its full length. The trail features freshwater marshes (station 2), a stand of loblolly pines planted by the National Park Service in 1962 as part of an erosion control effort (station 3), a natural shrub thicket (station 4), a diked area where freshwater habitats occur east of a plank-faced earthen dam (stations 5–6), and saltwater habitats to the west (stations 5–8). Ultimately the trail returns through dunes to the lighthouse. It provides excellent bird-watching opportunities and seems little used during the nonsummer months. Interesting views from the trail are made more scenic by the lighthouse to the north and the bridge over Oregon Inlet to the south. Such views provide food for thought. All the land between the lighthouse and Oregon Inlet was build by sand deposited in the inlet since 1874. The only constant in barrier island habitats is constant change.

E. Oregon Inlet

There are four major features that should be observed at Oregon Inlet: (1) the southward extension of Bodie Island into the inlet, (2) the extensive and complex flood-tide delta west of the bridge, (3) evidence of an ebb-tide delta represented by an arc of breakers extending from one side of the inlet to the other just offshore of the beach, and (4) the swift tidal currents that sweep through the inlet to create all of the preceding features. Unfortunately, all features are rarely observable at the same time, but all can be seen from the Herbert Bonner Bridge.

The features of Oregon Inlet are, of course, only specific examples of general features found in all barrier island inlets. Oregon Inlet is more dynamic than most because more sand (500,000 to 1,000,000 cubic yards per year) is moving past it. As a result, the inlet has shifted almost 2 miles since 1849 (about 250 feet per year). The entrance to the inlet has moved landward over 1,800 feet during the same period. Oregon Inlet continues to move. Bodie Island is extending into the inlet from the north, covering a distance of about a mile since the bridge was built in 1960. This extension has forced the channel south, where it is now trying to erode the north end of Pea Island. The attempt was succeeding until the U.S. Army Corps of Engineers constructed a rock seawall to trap sand there. This "sand-retaining structure" has been built as an apparent substitute for a controversial pair of mile-long rock jetties planned by the corps as a way of "stabilizing" the inlet. You can park at the foot of the bridge on Pea Island to see for yourself how the sand-retaining structure is working and ponder the advisability of building jetties in an environment as changeable as that of Oregon Inlet.

F. Pea Island Wildlife Refuge

Pea Island is a U.S. Fish and Wildlife Service wildlife refuge that extends from Oregon Inlet to the town of Rodanthe. Hunting is prohibited, and those interested in natural areas are free to explore almost everywhere except in bird-nesting areas and stands of threatened or endangered plants. Much of the northern half of the refuge is managed to enhance its use by migratory waterfowl and other birds. About 4 miles south of Oregon Inlet is a nature center with trails that follow dikes separating freshwater ponds built for waterfowl. The trail is worth visiting, both for bird watching and for viewing the surrounding habitat. The trail follows the dike for about half a mile, and there are field-glass-equipped platforms every few hundred feet. A good bird identification guide and your own binoculars will greatly enhance appreciation of the waterfowl. Many experienced birders say this site is the best available on the Outer Banks. You will see sandpipers, plovers, immature gulls and terns, herons, swans, and snow geese depending on the season. Fall is probably the most interesting time for watching migrating birds that stop over on their way down the Atlantic Flyway.

The nature trail extends for a 2-mile circuit around a large pond, but a walk to and from the two-story observation platform at the end of the dike will expose you to most of the species present. Greater privacy for longer, uninterrupted viewing can be obtained with greater distance from the trailhead, so let your commitment to birding be your guide. It is useful to get as far as the turn in the trail (about one-half mile) because it is only from there that visitors can see the extensive salt marsh on the sound side of Pea Island. The marsh here shows characteristic zonation patterns with thicket plants along the base of the dike, followed by freshwater marsh plants (cattails, common reed) in the middle distance and salt marsh species (black needlerush, smooth cordgrass) near the creeks and sound. As in most ecological transitions, the change is not uniform with distance. Marsh plants are extremely sensitive to immersion cycles, so small differences in the height of the marsh surface or distance from a tidal creek alters zonation dramatically. This phenomenon is well illustrated in the marsh beyond the pools. The zonation here is decidedly patchy with thicket-covered high spots (hummocks) among all types of marsh vegetation.

Outer Banks from Ocracoke to Pea Island
Merging of Sand and Sea

STANLEY R. RIGGS

This 55-mile tour passes through a large portion of the Cape Hatteras National Seashore (CHNS), which encompasses over 30,000 acres extending from Ocracoke Inlet north to southern Nags Head. The CHNS consists of four islands and three inlets and includes three lighthouses, numerous historic lifesaving and lighthouse keepers stations, vast areas of empty ocean beaches, estuarine marshes, shorelines, dunefields, and maritime forests. Within but not part of the CHNS are numerous historic fishing villages such as Ocracoke, Buxton, Avon (Kinnakeet), and Rodanthe. Our trip will end in the Pea Island National Wildlife Refuge (PINWR), a 6,000-acre managed wildlife refuge that is home to hundreds of bird species and offers miles of trails for wildlife and barrier island observation (also included in the preceding tour description).

The Outer Banks of North Carolina are home to one of the most famous coastal environments in the world, and on this tour through the heart of the Banks you will learn about the characteristics of a barrier island coastline. The present-day barrier island system is perched on top of, and is largely controlled by, the underlying geologic framework. You will visit numerous places where this framework results in significant barrier island responses and differential shoreline erosion. You will also experience a diverse range of habitats, observe modern coastal processes in action, and see numerous examples of the major conflict between a not-so-fragile, dynamic, high-energy, storm-dominated system and a very fragile human infrastructure of highways, bridges, and buildings.

A. Ocracoke Village

This tour is best begun in Ocracoke because to do so almost requires that you take the ferry trip across Pamlico Sound—one of the world's greatest estuarine lagoons. This ferry ride not only is awesome, but it sets the proper scene for your trip up the thin and dynamic ribbon of sand that is the North Carolina Outer Banks. To get to Ocracoke you take an approximately 2½-hour car ferry ride across Pamlico Sound from either Cedar Island, in eastern Carteret County, or Swan Quarter, in south-

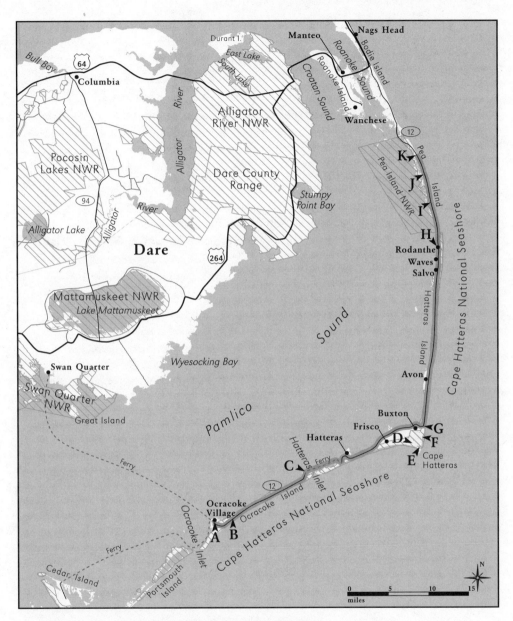

FIGURE 5. Outer Banks tour route—Ocracoke to Pea Island

ern Hyde County, for $10 per vehicle. Several ferries a day travel in both directions and from both destinations; however, it is recommended that you make reservations in advance by calling 1-800-BY-FERRY. The trip can also be taken in reverse order by driving south on NC 12 from Nags Head. If you have taken my advice and chosen to start at Ocracoke, park in the CHNS Visitors Center parking lot and take an extended and leisurely walking or bike tour of the town (bikes can be rented from numerous locations along Silver Lake Road). The places that should be visited include the following: the CHNS Visitors Center, Ocracoke Preservation Museum, Silver Lake (locally known as The Creek), the Ocracoke lighthouse, old cemeteries, and the many historic houses tucked safely among the dunes and live oaks of an old maritime forest. Guided island walks and public talks are available at certain times of the year—ask at the visitors center and museum.

Private ferries are available from Ocracoke to the Cape Lookout National Seashore (CLNS) and the historic village of Portsmouth, a former trade center established in 1753 to manage the shipping through Ocracoke Inlet. The CLNS consists of 55 miles of uninhabited barrier islands including Core Banks, Drum Inlet, Cape Lookout, Barden Inlet, and Shackleford Banks.

The village of Ocracoke dates back to the early 1700s when ship pilots and pirates (including the well-known Blackbeard, or Edward Teach) settled here because of the extensive shipping industry through Ocracoke Inlet. Today there are more than 100 historic houses and buildings within the Ocracoke Historic District that date from the 1880s to the 1930s. In addition, the 65-foot-tall Ocracoke lighthouse and associated dwelling date back to 1823, making it the oldest operating lighthouse in North Carolina. Be sure to walk down some of the narrow, rutted, sandy lanes such as East Howard Street with its old houses, cemeteries, and sprawling live oaks. This walk provides the wonderful feeling of "the way it used to be" in Ocracoke Village, where the permanent population ranges up to 600. The recent boom in tourism has brought massive changes to the village, including summer populations of about 5,000 and hundreds of thousands of visitors each year. As you leave Ocracoke Village pay special attention to its physical location. Situated on a land mass that is significantly landward of the barrier island, it is actually separated from the main part of the barrier island by a large salt marsh. The road crosses the marsh and gently curves onto the back side of the Ocracoke barrier island. The marsh between the two islands was far more extensive in the past. Construction of the artificial barrier dune ridge prevented the normal process of barrier island overwash from taking place and allowed for the growth of shrubs and transition vegetation now seen here.

B. Ocracoke Barrier Island and Barrier Dune Ridges

Take NC 12 from Ocracoke Village to the first CHNS parking area and walkway north of the airport. Walk on the boardwalk toward the beach and stop midway. First, notice the location of the village. Now notice the linear barrier dune ridges that parallel the shoreline and are crossed by the walkway.

In the 1930s a major change took place on the Outer Banks that has significantly impacted the barrier islands and led to the ongoing development boom there. Construction of barrier dune ridges changed the entire equilibrium and dynamics of these barrier islands. Barrier dune ridges essentially eliminate the overwash process, greatly modify the type and abundance of vegetation across the island, and alter the effects of the back-barrier estuarine processes. However, the greatest impact of all can be traced to increased economic growth in response to the false sense of security that these barrier dune ridge structures produce. The dune ridges epitomize the constant conflict between the natural processes of this dynamic, mobile, high-energy system and the fragile human infrastructure built upon it.

In the 1930s the Civilian Conservation Corps work program built dune ridges down the entire length of the Outer Banks from the Virginia line to Ocracoke Inlet. This social welfare program resulted in one of the great capitalistic success stories of this century. Massive sand fences were built out of shrubbery brought over from the mainland swamps. The fencing successfully trapped sand and built a continuous dune ridge along this entire coastal expanse. The ridge was up to 20 feet high and often consisted of multiple rows of dunes, as can be seen at this stop. The resulting barricade was like a fortress against the angry ocean waves and led to an increased sense of security that allowed the rapid sale of oceanfront property to summer visitors who did not understand winter coastal storms, overwash, and the dynamic nature of coastal environments.

As you drive along the barrier system, notice the extensive artificial dune ridge system. Almost all of these barrier dune ridges have been rebuilt many times since the 1930s in a never-ending attempt to protect the buildings and roads that shelter the dune ridges. For example, 1.9 miles of NC 12 on the north end of Ocracoke were relocated in 1988, and 1.4 miles of the dune ridge were rebuilt. This was redone in 1996, but erosion of the dune ridge continues, with over 3.3 miles of the road vulnerable once again. Keep your eyes open and you will see dune ridges in every stage of destruction by natural processes and every stage of reconstruction by humans. Today's winter storms guarantee the future of a major coastal industry associated with poststorm bulldozer beach scrapping, nylon sand bag construction and emplacement, sand fencing, fence building, beach grass planting, and demolition of buildings that fall to breaches in the all-too-penetrable wall of the dunes.

The beach in this area is a southeast-facing shoreline compared to the east-facing beaches that you will see north of Cape Hatteras. Winter storms from the northeast produce offshore winds, which result in lower wave energy on the beaches. In addition, this beach is in close proximity to Ocracoke Inlet, resulting in an increased abundance of sand at this locality. Consequently, this is the widest beach, with the most gentle slope, that you will see on this tour. Compare the width and slope of this beach to steeper and narrower beaches in the middle of

Ocracoke Island and at Cape Hatteras (Figure 6), where there is both a deficiency of sand and more wave energy on the beach.

c. Hatteras Inlet

Follow NC 12 to the North Carolina Department of Transportation ferry dock for Hatteras Inlet. This free ferry runs approximately every hour during the winter and every half hour during the rest of the year; in forty minutes it delivers you and your car to Hatteras Island.

Hatteras Inlet is one of only three major inlets that drain the entire Albemarle-Pamlico estuarine system to the west (Figure 5). Hatteras Inlet lies along the southeast-facing portion of the Outer Banks situated between Cape Hatteras and Cape Lookout. The vast estuarine area to the west is the shallow, low-salinity waters of Pamlico Sound. Hatteras Inlet has been open at least since the mid-1800s. Inlets are extremely important holes in an otherwise continuous sand dam. Inlets allow for the two-way exchange of fresh water from the land and salt water from the oceans. This results in the estuaries' acting as great mixing basins composed of mixed-salinity water or brackish water that ultimately will be discharged through the inlet.

As you ride the ferry across Hatteras Inlet, notice the following inlet features: (1) a small, well-developed ebb-tide delta on the ocean side (the zone where the ocean waves are breaking); (2) a vast region of shallow sandy flats on the estuarine side that constitutes the flood-tide delta; (3) extensive spoil piles resulting from regular dredging used to "control" active channel migration; (4) a long sand spit on the northeast side of the inlet, displaying an increasing degree of vegetation growth away from the inlet; and (5) a set of piles remaining from the erosion of the former U.S. Coast Guard station located on the southwest side of the inlet. The latter two points demonstrate that the inlet has been actively migrating toward the southwest through time. Use your binoculars to check for the interesting migratory birds and animals on the spoil piles within the inlet.

d. Buxton Woods

In Buxton, turn south off of NC 12 toward the Cape Hatteras lighthouse. At a four-way stop sign before the lighthouse, turn right or southwest for a short distance past the relocated lighthouse to a parking area for the Buxton Woods Nature Trail. The interpretive trail represents the first of what will be many efforts by the state to make educational use of the acres of maritime forest in Buxton Woods that have been purchased to preserve this important and unusual feature of the Outer Banks.

Between the town of Frisco and where you are parked, you have been driving through the maritime forest known as Buxton Woods—one of the largest remaining maritime forests on the Outer Banks. You may have noticed that the road crossed many east-west-oriented beach ridges and between-ridge swales. The swales or "sedges" contain extensive freshwater ponds and marshes with abundant wildlife. This short nature trail follows the dunes that top one ancient beach ridge and descends to the edge of a freshwater sedge. The forest here is dominated by live oaks and cedars with hollies and other small hardwoods in the understory. The flooded swale to the north of the trail is dominated by freshwater grasses and sedges of many kinds.

Due to the great width of Buxton Woods and the height of the many sand ridges, there is an abundant freshwater resource here that is not duplicated in most other portions of the Outer Banks—another reason why it is worth preserving the woods for future generations.

E. Cape Point

Continue driving south to the Cape Point parking area just beyond a campground. It is worth making the less-than-a-mile walk to Cape Point, one of the most popular surf fishing spots on the U.S. Atlantic Coast. The point is a high-energy, mobile system that responds dramatically to changing energy regimes as it flip-flops east and west, depending upon seasonal and annual storm patterns. Extending over 10 miles seaward from Cape Point are the infamous Diamond Shoals. Each of North Carolina's capes has a similar set of very shallow, cross-shelf sand shoals, which create the navigational conditions that have caused coastal Carolina to be labeled the "graveyard of the Atlantic."

Diamond Shoals separates two major ocean currents and biological regimes. To the north is water once associated with the Labrador Current and containing coldwater fauna and flora, while to the south is the tropical Gulf Stream and its associated warmwater fauna and flora. These two currents control the water conditions, species of fish, types of shells on the beach, and storm patterns for the Outer Banks. Their interaction over the Diamond Shoals results in an awesome display of the dynamics between waves, currents, winds, and the sand shoals. Often waves from either side of the shoals meet head on, throwing spray high in the air.

To the west of Cape Point is one of the very few growing beaches on the Outer Banks. Only local and relatively small segments of the North Carolina shoreline are presently characterized by beach accretion (the opposite of beach erosion). These accretionary areas generally occur on the flanks of cape structures and headlands and represent temporary episodes of coastline building toward the sea (a process termed prograding) rather than the more characteristic and longer episodes of erosion during which beaches recede landward. During episodes of progradation, these shorefaces are relatively stable and are characterized by beach ridge accretion and dune ridge development.

F. Cape Hatteras Lighthouse

Backtrack from Cape Point to the Cape Hatteras lighthouse parking lot.

The base of the first Cape Hatteras lighthouse, which was more than 3,000 feet from the shoreline when it was built in 1820, finally fell into the sea during a storm in March 1980. The present lighthouse was built in 1872 between 1,600 and 2,500 feet from the shoreline. Thus, the shoreline north of Cape Point has been receding at an average rate of between 12 and 20 feet per year (annual rates range from 6 to 35 feet per year) since the lighthouse was constructed. In contrast, the shoreline west of Cape Point has been accreting and has migrated seaward at about the same rate. This is how the vast sequence of beach ridges that make up Buxton Woods was formed (Figure 5).

The Cape Hatteras lighthouse (Figure 6) is the tallest lighthouse in the United States. If you are here during the summer season and are physically fit, you should climb the lighthouse for an awesome view of the Outer Banks. From there you can observe the following coastal features:

1. To the south are Cape Point and Diamond Shoals. On a clear day you can see the 120-foot-high Diamond Shoals light tower about 11 miles offshore from the lighthouse. This tower not only marks the outer end of the shoals, but it sits approximately on the outer edge of the continental shelf, where the cold Labrador Current runs into and deflects the warm Gulf Stream Current northeast into the North Atlantic.

2. To the northeast are three groins built in 1969 to protect the U.S. Naval facility (now belonging to the U.S. Coast Guard) and the lighthouse. Notice how the groin field has effectively held the sand and temporarily prevented shoreline recession. Also notice the severely eroded updrift (north) and downdrift (south) shorelines, which have continued to recede, leaving the groined area behind as a major headland. The southernmost groin was repeatedly breached, allowing waves to reach the base of the lighthouse.

3. To the north are the Buxton overwash area, the "going-to-sea" motels, and NC 12 following construction of the groin field in 1969. The road, motels, dune ridge, and beach, in the area of the Buxton Inlet, have been rebuilt many times since the groins were built. Notice the very narrow character of the Buxton overwash zone, which has contained numerous historic inlets. The abundant

FIGURE 6. Cape Hatteras Lighthouse in original location. (Photo by S. Riggs)

salt marsh islands immediately west of the Buxton overwash area formed on the shallow flood-tide deltas after the historic inlets closed. West of the barrier is the vast Pamlico Sound estuary (Figure 5). Strong northwest winds associated with offshore hurricanes moving north along the coast can cause major storm tides to pile up in the crook, causing severe flooding and damage from Pamlico Sound.

4. To the west is the very wide, east-west-oriented Hatteras Island (Figure 5). This island consists of multiple sets of beach ridges and swale structures that support Buxton Woods. The sand ridges support the maritime forest, while the swales between them contain marshes and freshwater ponds. The ponds are part of the groundwater system of the Buxton Woods, which is the largest freshwater resource on the Outer Banks. In recent years this water has supplied the rapid growth and development in the towns of Hatteras, Frisco, Buxton, and Avon. However, a shortage of water has become so severe on the Outer Banks that many villages have now built desalinization plants to supply their fresh water.

Since 1966 the CHNS has been involved in an ongoing battle to "save the lighthouse." This effort has included building the three groins and rebuilding them on several occasions, carrying out several major beach nourishment projects, setting numerous layers of rock revetments, deploying many layers of nylon sandbags, planting artificial seaweed, and even tearing up and dumping the asphalt from the adjacent parking lot. There were also engineering studies to design structures that would allow the lighthouse either to stand as an island within the encroaching ocean or to be picked up and moved inland on reinforced railroad tracks. In 1999 the lighthouse was successfully moved 2,900 feet to its new location 1,600 feet inland from its original position. Future generations will now enjoy the symbolic and historic Cape Hatteras lighthouse. Retreat from an eroding shoreline and rising sea level is a critical management response for the maintenance of both barrier islands and the structures built upon them.

G. Buxton Overwash

Backtrack once again to NC 12 and turn right (east); continue east and then north to the first CHNS parking area beyond the last buildings in Buxton and on the west side of NC 12.

This stop—Buxton overwash—is a classic example of a "going-to-sea" highway (and, perhaps, going-to-sea motels, visible at the north edge of Buxton). Along this portion of the Outer Banks, an ongoing and very costly battle is being waged between human development and ocean dynamics. The Buxton overwash zone occurs in the big bend area where the orientation of the Outer Banks changes to form Cape Hatteras (Figure 5). Due to the geometry and great size of Pamlico Sound, storm tides commonly cause the estuarine water to pile up in the bend, resulting in severe flooding, erosion, overtopping, and even the formation of new inlets. To the west are numerous sand shoals and salt-marsh islands that represent flood-tide deltas of previous inlets. The last major inlet through the barrier island at this location formed during the Ash Wednesday Storm of 1962; it was subsequently filled in by the U.S. Army Corps of Engineers. Inlets will form through this area again in response to future storms.

Walk from the parking lot west to the Pamlico Sound shoreline along one of the numerous footpaths. Look north along the barrier island and imagine that the high dune ridge isn't there. Notice that the barrier is very narrow and consists of a gently sloping surface that gradually declines from the top of the ocean beach down to the estuarine shoreline. This is the profile of a classic overwash barrier island. However, superimposed on top of this natural barrier island profile today is an abnormally high, bulldozed barrier dune ridge that has been rebuilt many times in desperate efforts to "hold the ocean" and protect the highway and motels. Notice the coarse gravelly sand that forms the sediment all the way across the island to the Pamlico Sound shoreline. This sand was derived from the beach every time the barrier dune ridge was blown out by storms and the overwash processes resumed.

While on the estuarine side of the barrier, notice that the vegetation is strongly zoned across the island, grading downslope from a few species of grasses on the dunes, to a shrub thicket with many plant species in the middle of the island, to a few species of salt-marsh grasses along the estuarine shoreline. The brackish-water salt-marsh plants are predominantly *Juncus* (black needlerush, a dark-colored rush with sharp points) and *Spartina* (green-colored smooth cordgrass). When the marsh grasses die, they accumulate through time to form a bed of peat, which is actively being eroded to form a small undercut scarp along the estuarine shoreline. Look carefully around these clumps of grass and associated peat to see how many different kinds of shellfish and snails you can find living in this important wetland habitat.

Walk across the barrier dune ridge to observe the east-facing ocean beach, which is very steep and narrow. This is a high-energy beach system, compared to the beaches south of Cape Hatteras. Because of the higher energy levels, this beach is composed of very coarse sands and gravels, often contains major beach cusps or indentations, and is characterized by steeply sloping surfaces on the front side of the barrier dune ridge. If you happen to be here on a very high tide or when a strong storm has built up a storm surge, you probably will observe the rapid erosion of the bulldozed barrier dune ridge, which is severely out of equilibrium with the wave dynamics. A major storm will eliminate this dune ridge totally, and the barrier island will again become an overwash zone, producing fans of sediment that bury the highway and build the barrier island westward into Pamlico Sound. This is how the barriers maintain themselves through time in response to rising sea level. The artificial barrier dune ridges temporarily stop this process, while shoreline recession continues. The result is often oversteepened beaches such as those in this area.

H. Cape Rodanthe and Wimble Shoals

Drive north on NC 12 through Salvo and Waves to Rodanthe. Turn east at the sign for the Rodanthe fishing pier, park in the lot, and walk to the beach.

At this location, geologic formations created during the Pleistocene era (1.6 million to 10,000 years ago) control the geometry of the Outer Banks. The Oregon Inlet to Cape Hatteras segment of the Outer Banks (Figure 5) is perched on an old land surface that extends seaward off mainland Dare and Hyde Counties and forms a submarine headland. This old land mass defines the geometry of the Outer Banks and hence creates the major change in barrier island orientation. The submarine headland forms a shallow shoal structure on the inner shelf called Wimble Shoals, which extends northward from the Rodanthe pier. Wave refraction around Wimble Shoals produces one of the best surfing spots on the Atlantic Coast, as well as a minor cape structure. Notice that to the north and south of the pier the shoreline is rapidly eroding, causing it to recede and form the minor coastal feature I call Cape Rodanthe. New housing developments within the highly eroding segments of shoreline to the north and south have lost many houses to the sea over the past decade.

I. New Inlet and Pea Island National Wildlife Refuge

Return to NC 12, turn north, and drive out of Rodanthe and into the PINWR for about 5 miles until you see a parking area on the west side of the road and the remnants of a wooden bridge over the water.

The PINWR extends from Rodanthe to Oregon Inlet and encompasses about 6,000 acres of Hatteras barrier island, with its fresh and brackish water ponds, plus about 25,700 acres of shallow Pamlico Sound waters. This refuge is managed to support specific wildlife species—food crops are planted, vegetation is controlled with prescribed burning and mechanical cutting, and water level and salinity in the impoundments are managed to encourage maximum food production. The refuge, situated on the Atlantic Flyway, was established in 1938 to provide habitat for migratory waterfowl. With over 265 species of birds that occur regularly and 50 species that are occasional visitors, the PINWR is considered to be a birder's paradise.

This is the site of a series of small inlets, repeatedly named New Inlet, that have opened and closed frequently over the centuries. These inlets were relatively small and, hence, little used because the larger, longer-lived Roanoke, Gunt, and Oregon Inlets to the north provided the primary discharge through the barrier islands. New Inlet closed completely in 1922, and there was an unsuccessful attempt to open the inlet artificially in 1925. In 1933 New Inlet reopened during a hurricane and remained open until 1945. Remnants of the wooden bridge built across New Inlet during the last period it was open stand today as a monument to the dynamic nature of inlets and impermanence of human structures. One cannot help but wonder about the destiny of the great Oregon Inlet bridge.

J. Pea Island Going-to-the-Sea Highway

This next segment is a "driving stop" since there is no place to actually get off the highway along this stretch of road.

Turn north onto NC 12 and notice that the road curves west onto a new black asphalt surface completed in 1997. This road replaces the "going-to-the-sea" highway that is visible veering off to the east, and which is now covered with a new barrier dune ridge (Figure 7). Driving along this section of road, you can get a feel for the major cost of building and maintaining a barrier dune ridge along the entire length of the CHNS. The dune ridges were built under the mistaken impres-

FIGURE 7. NC 12 being protected by artificial dune. (Photo by S. Riggs)

sion that the natural island system needed protection. Miles of sandbags along the old road represent another monument to attempts to preserve a fixed highway on a moving barrier island.

A widespread desire to preserve NC 12 has led the state of North Carolina to adopt an official "hold the line" policy with respect to the processes of coastal erosion. While development has exploded on the Outer Banks, this road has been quietly rebuilt and relocated for decades at incredible costs, for the purpose of providing services to the people who arrived via the highway. Now there is an expectation that the road will always be there, and it is supported by the infallible justification that the road provides hurricane evacuation routes for the people who followed decades of unlimited growth and development. A recent study for the North Carolina Department of Transportation concluded that the 20 miles of NC 12 between Kitty Hawk and Ocracoke are vulnerable or will be in the near future. Preservation efforts are short-term fixes for large-scale problems that have been developing for decades and are now at crisis levels; little fixes will not work anymore. In many places, the barrier is already too narrow, which means the state must begin to implement a set of realistic alternatives such as estuarine causeways, expanded use of ferries, or maintaining vulnerable portions of highway as gravel-based temporary segments that allow movement of traffic and occasional overwash with less-costly rehabilitation. Do we really need to maintain a paved road system that allows the public to speed through this beautiful coastal system at 70 miles per hour? We must begin to manage this high-energy, physically dynamic system by acknowledging, understanding, and working with its natural processes.

K. Pea Island Visitors Center and Hiking Trails

Turn north on NC 12 and continue for several miles to the PINWR Visitors Center on the west side of the highway.

Wildlife interpretive exhibits are located in the PINWR Visitors Center. Hike to the beach to get another view of the "going-to-the-sea" highway and associated efforts to save it with sets of nylon sandbags and a brand new barrier dune ridge. Notice all stages of scarping and destruction of the older barrier dune ridges. The North Pond wildlife trail provides prime wildlife viewing from miles of dikes that extend to, and continue along, the edge of Pamlico Sound. Observation platforms with spotting scopes are scattered along the trail, as described in the preceding tour.

Downeast Lowlands

Being Swallowed by the Sea

STANLEY R. RIGGS
AND DIRK FRANKENBERG

This 48-mile tour takes you through various habitats along the "downeast" Carteret peninsula that form uplands between the Neuse River and the Back Sound–Core Sound estuarine systems (Figure 8). You will see that the edges of the peninsula are being flooded by rising sea level. This flooding is converting low topography into the vast wetlands that characterize this portion of our coast. You will see coastal habitats ranging from cliffs to creeks and observe the processes that form them and the complex North Carolina coastal systems of which they are a part. In addition, you will see the dramatic effects of human activities upon these natural systems, as well as the consequences of the natural processes upon the economy of the region.

This tour will enable you to learn how the Neuse River and its tributaries are being drowned by rising seas, and how the land along and between drainages has evolved into wetland habitats. You will learn that this process of land being swallowed by the sea has been going on for over ten thousand years as the earth's climate and oceans warm and the continental glaciers continue to melt.

A. Pine Cliff Recreation Area in Croatan National Forest

Pine Cliff is part of Croatan National Forest, which consists of 157,000 acres encompassing many unique estuarine and wetland habitats. Pine Cliff is the trailhead for the 21-mile-long Neusiok hiking trail, which runs from the low-brackish water of the Neuse River estuary south to Oyster Point on the saltier water of the Newport River estuary. The trail traverses diverse habitats ranging from sandy beaches, salt marshes, blackwater creeks, and cypress swamps, to upland hardwood and pine forests, and scattered upland pocosins (the latter is a Tuscarora Indian word meaning "swamp-on-a-hill"). Pine Cliff is reached from US 70 in Havelock by following NC 101 east for about 5 miles, then NC 306 north for another 4 miles.

The Neuse River has two major parts. Upstream is the freshwater riverine

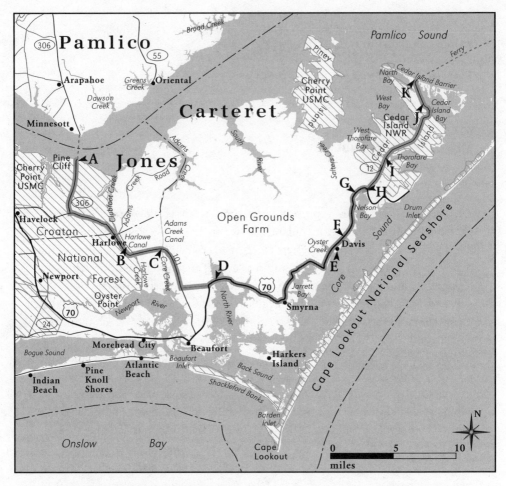

FIGURE 8. Downeast lowlands tour route

component, a low-gradient river that drains the red-clay soils of the North Carolina Piedmont. The river flows downhill to the Coastal Plain and southeast across the Coastal Plain to New Bern. Just west of New Bern the bottom of the river valley drops below sea level and becomes flooded by the sea. This is the beginning of the Neuse River estuary, a great mixing basin that is separated from the ocean by the sand dam of the Outer Banks barrier islands. The Neuse River estuary widens and deepens in the seaward direction as the fresh river water (less than 1 part per thousand, or ppt, salinity) mixes with salty ocean water (35 ppt salinity) to produce tea-colored, low-brackish estuarine water (1 to 10 ppt salinity). The fresh water–salt water mix is ultimately discharged into the ocean through four "inlets" that also act as outlets.

The Neuse River estuary at Pine Cliff generally has low-brackish (1–10 ppt salinity) to medium-brackish (10–20 ppt salinity) water. Pine Cliff is situated significantly closer to the freshwater input at the head of the estuary than to the saltwater input at Ocracoke Inlet (Figure 8). The salinity at Pine Cliff is highly variable and is primarily dependent upon recent storms and the stage of the river (flood or drought). On the beach are the robust shells of Rangia clams and the delicate shells of Macoma clams that live offshore; both can live in waters with low- to medium-brackish salinities.

The beach at Pine Cliff consists of a severely eroding, high-sediment bank shoreline composed totally of sand from a Pleistocene barrier island. We know it is old because of the well-developed soil horizon visible in the middle of the sediment bank. The shoreline is rapidly receding, as evidenced by the large number of pine trunks on the beach. Also visible sticking up out of the water are the central tap roots of former pine trees. At the base of the eroding bank lies a narrow sandy beach that extends offshore for over 100 yards as a series of broad, shallow sandy shoals. It is the erosion of the sediment bank that supplies all of the sand for this beach and the offshore shoals. If this shoreline, or any others like it along the estuaries, were to be bulkheaded to stop the erosion, there would soon be no more beach.

If you are here on a nice calm day, you will notice that the small waves are nowhere near the sediment bank—the shoreline is not eroding under these conditions. When the wind blows hard, however, wind tides pile the waters up to higher levels and intensify the wave energy at the beach. A strong "nor'easter" will blow water into the estuary, creating a high storm tide on this beach; the water will rise to the base of the high-sediment bank and waves will erode it. This is when bank erosion is at its maximum and when new sand is produced for the beach.

B. Harlowe Canal

Return to NC 101, turn left (east), and go through North Harlowe to Harlowe. Turn left (east) on Adams Creek Road, cross the Harlowe Canal bridge, and go about 100 yards, then turn right (south) on Ball Farm Road; follow it until you cross a second Harlowe Canal bridge and return to NC 101. Turn left (south) on NC 101 and in about 1 mile you will cross the Harlowe Canal for the third time.

Harlowe Canal is a navigational ditch dug across the interstream divide between Clubfoot Creek, a north-flowing tributary of the Neuse River, and Harlowe Creek, a south-flowing tributary of the Newport River. The canal was dug in the nineteenth century along the route of a Native American portage or canoe drag. This is a wonderful area for wildlife observation; canoes and kayaks can be launched under any of the bridges.

As you cross each bridge notice the distribution of vegetation types. From the first (north) bridge look north and see the upstream marshes of Clubfoot Creek. The first and second bridges are on the interstream divide, where the canal is cut into low-sediment banks that rise several feet above water level. The water here is fresh and has the color of black coffee; the banks are dominated by upland forest vegetation. The third (south) bridge crosses the upper estuary of Harlowe Creek, where you will notice a broad salt marsh composed of mixed *Juncus* (dark-colored needlerush) and *Spartina* (bright-green-colored smooth cordgrass). Here the creek is beginning to flood and the water is becoming slightly salty (low-brackish), as indicated by the presence of salt-marsh grasses. Notice the effects of rising sea level, which causes the water table to rise in the uplands adjacent to the marsh and results in some die-off of fringing vegetation, including the loblolly pines.

c. Adams Creek Canal

Continue to drive east on NC 101 for about 3 miles, cross over the high-rise bridge, turn left (north), and drive west back to Adams Creek Canal at the end of the road.

Adams Creek Canal is much larger than the Harlowe Canal because it is part of the Intracoastal Waterway that extends along the Atlantic and Gulf Coasts from Maine to Texas. The Intracoastal Waterway carries small boat traffic with less than a 14-foot draft through predominantly inland and protected waters. This regularly maintained canal was dug across the high interstream divide separating Adams Creek, a north-flowing tributary of the Neuse River, from Core Creek, a south-flowing tributary of Newport River. Notice that the sediment banks drop into deep water with no fringing marsh.

Clearly posted next to the boat ramp is the first of many similar signs that you will see at all stops along this tour. The North Carolina Marine Fisheries sign states, "Closed Area—Unlawful to Take Oysters, Clams, or Mussels." Wherever our coastal waters are too polluted for harvesting healthy shellfish, you will see these signs posted. If you look up and down the waterway you will see what is causing the pollution here: houses, many with septic tanks that discharge waste and nutrients into the groundwater and thence into surrounding coastal waters. Other types of pollutants also get into the canal from boat engines and leaky bilges, marinas, and parking lots.

D. North River Estuary

Drive east and south on NC 101 for 2 miles, then turn left (east) onto Laurel Road for 2.3 miles, turn right (south) on Merrimon Road for 2.5 miles, turn left (east) onto US 70 and drive about 0.8 miles to a pull-off area on the right side (south) and just before the North River estuary bridge.

Marshes fringing the North River estuary are composed primarily of brown *Juncus* rush with scattered patches edged with the bright green of *Spartina* grass. *Juncus* has a very wide tolerance for fluctuations in salinity and therefore is the dominant marsh plant in irregularly flooded marshes and in areas with highly variable salinities. The dominance of *Juncus* in this marsh suggests that the site is irregularly flooded and that salinities vary from fresh during rains and periods of freshwater runoff to saline when evaporation increases the saltiness of the water standing in the marsh. Notice that the *Spartina* grows primarily in the regularly flooded low marsh where salinity is less variable because of the regular input of salt water along either the outer marsh edge or along small tidal creeks that penetrate the marsh. Whenever *Juncus* occurs directly on the marsh shoreline, there is usually an erosional scarp where marsh recession is the dominant process. If the marsh shoreline is stable or accreting, *Spartina* grass forms a bright green fringe (Figure 9). Briefly walk into the marsh and see how many other kinds of plants you can find. Pay particular attention to where each plant type occurs relative to small-scale changes in topography and drainage within the marsh.

The North River is a south-flowing tributary to Back Sound estuary, and both have been drowned by rising sea level. You are parked in the middle of this wide estuary on a road dam that has cut off the northern segment from the southern segment, except for a small opening under the bridge. This road dam has a significant impact upon the dynamics of this estuarine system by restricting water exchange and, thus, decreasing tidal amplitude and salinity upstream.

Notice that there is more *Juncus* in the marsh north of the bridge than there is to the south. This reflects the lower tidal amplitude and lower salinity waters, which result from the road dam between the two marsh segments. The marsh is significantly wider along the road itself because it has grown out into the shallow waters created by the road fill. During low tide you can see extensive sand shoals that make for good clam habitat. Many of the shoals have become covered with shells and now are dominated by oyster reefs. Be advised, however, that "No Shellfishing" signs are posted nearby.

As a freshwater river and its associated floodplain descend below sea level, three major segments form along the resulting drowned-river estuary—upper, middle, and lower estuarine segments. You are now in the middle estuary, a wide body of water fringed by salt marsh. To the north the North River narrows down to form the upper estuary—a narrow creek through broad estuarine salt marshes. We drove over this segment of an estuary at Harlowe Creek. Far to the south is the lower North River estuary, where the fringing marsh has been completely eroded away and the estuarine shoreline is an eroding sediment bank. We saw this part of an estuary on the Neuse River at Pine Cliff.

The fringing marsh in the middle estuary is eroding on the seaward side and expanding on the landward side. Along the estuarine marsh shoreline, wave energy

FIGURE 9. Marsh along Salter Creek. Note plant zonation—*Spartina*, *Juncus*, pines. (Photo by D. Frankenberg)

undercuts the soft black sediment composed of organic debris from the salt-marsh plants. Most marsh shorelines within the Pamlico-Albemarle system of North Carolina are eroding on the seaward side at rates ranging from a few to tens of feet per year. The resulting organic detritus either enters the marine food chain, or it ends up forming the organic-rich sediments that settle out in the central basin of the estuaries. On the landward side, the marsh grasses grade into a transition zone of shrubbery and stunted trees and finally into upland forest vegetation. With rising sea level, the marsh expands up the slope and replaces the upland vegetation. The evidence for this process is the large number of tree skeletons that you will see in the transition zone and the adjacent marsh throughout this tour (see Figure 9). Construction of bulkheads and other forms of human interference with this long-term process preserves the trees but results in a net loss of salt marsh.

E. Davis

Continue east on US 70 through the towns of Bette, Otway, Smyrna, and Williston to Davis. At the stop sign in Davis turn right (southwest) and go two blocks to the brown sign for the ferry to Cape Lookout National Seashore; turn left and go one block to the waterfront.

From the Davis waterfront you can look out over Core Sound to Core Banks on the far shore. Core Sound's waters are medium- to high-brackish (10–30 ppt salinity). The higher salinities are due to the proximity of two inlets through the barrier islands (Barden Inlet to the south and Drum Inlet to the north). Because Core Sound is a large water body, storm tides can be high and wave energy can be strong, resulting in severely eroding shorelines. Notice the rock rip-rap and bulkheads along the sediment bank shorelines in Davis. Tourism is an increasingly important business for many coastal villages; Davis is one of several places where you can catch a private ferry to Cape Lookout National Seashore—a 55-mile piece of the Outer Banks. The uninhabited barrier islands that make up the national seashore (Core Banks, Cape Lookout, and Shackleford Banks) form a natural sand dam that separates the estuarine waters of Back, Core, and Pamlico Sounds from the salt waters of the Atlantic Ocean.

F. Oyster Creek, King Point Marsh, and Brett Bay

Return to us 70, turn right (northeast) on the highway, and drive about 1.8 miles to the Oyster Creek bridge. Cross the bridge and turn right onto the old bridge road base in front of the crab house.

For the next mile or so, the highway runs through a fringing marsh on the west side of Brett Bay, a drowned river estuary that has already lost its eastern side to sea level rise and shoreline erosion. Look carefully in the distance off Piney Point and you can see a few final remnants of marsh barely rising above the water; this is all that remains of the opposite shoreline. Results of this drowning process are small open embayments. This is the origin of most irregularities along the thousands of miles of North Carolina estuarine shoreline.

Notice the elevation of the road dam through the marsh and how it has severely changed the dynamics on the two sides of the highway. The marsh on the northwest side is dominated totally by *Juncus*, while the southeast side is a mixed *Spartina* and *Juncus* marsh. This suggests the presence of fresh to low-brackish water on the northwest and low- to medium-brackish water on the southeast. Also notice the excellent example of transition vegetation between the marsh and upland forest; a large number of tree skeletons reflect the shifting habitats as the marsh migrates slowly landward in response to rising sea level.

G. Entrance to Open Grounds Farm

Continue to drive north on us 70 for about 5 miles from Oyster Creek, then turn left (west) onto a private road with a large metal gate containing the initials "O G" and a small brick house on the south side.

This is the private entrance to Open Grounds Farm, a major agribusiness corporation. Please do not trespass; stop here just long enough to notice the vast open area to the west. You have been driving around this megafarm since you left the Intracoastal Waterway at the North River. Since then you have passed many roads coming out of the farm; however, all of them have steel gates with a dense perimeter forest so you cannot see what is back there or how they do business.

This megacorporation farm bought the heart of the so-called Carteret Pocosin in the 1970s and began clearing, ditching, and draining. The farmed land extends from ditch bank to ditch bank and is treated with fertilizers, pesticides, insecticides, trace-elements, and animal waste. These chemicals are not designed to leave the fields, yet some flow into shallow groundwater or adhere to sediment grains and thereby flow into the estuaries. During heavy rainfalls and storms, soils and chemicals wash into ditches, which flow into adjacent estuarine waters. That the cumulative impact of this massive operation has adversely affected the surrounding estuarine waters is indicated by the presence of "No Shellfishing" signs along every estuarine creek draining this farm.

H. Salter Creek and North Bay

Continue north on US 70 and cross the new high-rise bridge over Salter Creek and North Bay; at the base of the bridge turn left (north) onto a gravel road and drive to the boat launching ramp.

You are parked in the transition zone between the middle estuarine segment of Nelson Bay (south) and the upper estuarine segment about 100 yards to the north. Northward, Nelson Bay closes down to form Salter Creek, which consists of a narrow creek and wide marsh. Southward the estuary widens as shoreline erosion narrows the marsh until it disappears entirely in the lower estuarine segment where the shoreline is dominated by eroding sediment banks.

As you drive back to US 70 notice the large number of drainage ditches dug within the marsh. Each ditch can be recognized by a straight line of small pines, cedars, and shrubbery that grow on the spoil dredged from the ditch. For decades it was standard practice to drain the marshes to rid the coastal region of mosquitoes, which were considered to be health hazards. However, thousands of miles of ditching did not eliminate mosquitoes or other biting insects. Only recently have we learned that each species of mosquito and insect has different breeding habits and habitats. Consequently, the process of ditching and draining may have reduced one species but benefited many others. It disrupted the natural drainage system of the marsh, which in turn affected the marsh vegetation and the breeding patterns of countless marine species. This procedure was finally eliminated in North Carolina in the 1980s.

1. Cedar Island *Juncus* Marsh

Return to US 70, turn left (northeast) onto NC 12, drive about 3 miles to the base of the new high-rise bridge over Thorofare Canal, and turn left (west) onto the old bridge road.

You are in the middle of the Cedar Island National Wildlife Refuge, a 14,480-acre wilderness at the northeast end of the Carteret peninsula. The refuge contains about 11,000 acres of salt marsh dominated by *Juncus*, with local areas of *Spartina* (Figure 10). The remaining acreage is woodland composed of longleaf, loblolly, and pond pines; live oak; wax myrtle; gallberry; red bay; and yaupon. Over 270 species of birds have been observed in the wildlife refuge, along with deer, black bears, raccoons, otters, minks, squirrels, and rabbits. An incredible population of hardy mosquitoes and deer flies make the refuge their home. Refuge managers periodically utilize prescribed burning to manage the woods and marshes.

The new high-rise bridge crosses Thorofare Canal, a navigational ditch connecting Thorofare and West Thorofare Bays (see Figure 8). The canal was dug across the interstream divide, which consists of a vast *Juncus* marsh. The low, sloping surface of the Carteret peninsula systematically decreases in elevation to the northeast, and at this location it is essentially just below sea level. All upland forest and transitional zone vegetation on the interstream divide has been drowned by rising sea level as the marsh has migrated across and buried the former forest. If you dug a hole here through several feet of marsh peat, there would be many stumps and logs on the former forest floor below the peat.

The salt marsh surface grows vertically through the accumulation of organic matter in the form of peat, potentially keeping up with rising sea level. However, around the marsh perimeter rising sea level has deepened the adjacent waters, allowing for increased wave energy, increased rates of shoreline erosion, and horizontal recession or shrinking of the marsh. As sea level continues to rise over the next century (it is presently rising at the rate of about 1 foot per 100 years), erosion will completely eliminate the Cedar Island marsh, producing an open bay. This future Thorofare Sound will extend from Core Sound on the southeast to West Bay of Pamlico Sound on the northwest, totally isolating Cedar Island. All sounds in North Carolina, including Core, Pamlico, Croatan, and Roanoke Sounds, originated in this manner.

Several factors are critical in determining the characteristics of the awesome Cedar Island marsh. The marsh is located at the east end of the large Neuse River estuary, which consists of low- to medium-brackish water. Core Sound on the east side of the marsh receives salt water via two small inlets through Core Banks; consequently, both tides and salinities are minimal. The marsh is situated at the

FIGURE 10. Cedar Island Marsh along Thorofare Bay. (Photo by D. Frankenberg)

south end of Pamlico Sound, a vast shallow estuarine water body subject to strong winds and high wind tides that flood and drain the marsh on an irregular basis. Strong northeast and southwest storms cause storm tides and high wave energy. Thus, the Cedar Island Marsh is an irregularly flooded, brackish-water marsh dominated by *Juncus* that is being severely eroded along the shoreline. Its future at the bottom of the new Thorofare Sound is not far off.

Brackish marshes like the Cedar Island marsh are among the most productive habitats in the world. Wind- and storm-tide flooding carry nutrients into the marsh and sweep dead plant material into the estuaries and adjacent ocean-shelf waters. This organic detritus forms the basis of many food chains for marine organisms. Brackish marshes are essential for maintaining many different populations of estuarine and marine fish and shellfish; they are also valuable as terrestrial wildlife habitat.

J. Cedar Island Village

Return to NC 12, turn left (north), and drive northeast across the marsh and the transition zone into the upland woods. Bear left (northwest) at the next road junction and drive slowly along the winding road through the village of Cedar Island for 4 miles to the North Carolina Wildlife Resources Access parking area at the end of the road and on the east side of the Cedar Island Ferry terminal.

This portion of the tour is a drive through the Cedar Island fishing village (there is no good place to park). Notice that the long, linear village is built upon a higher beach ridge that is a continuation of the Lola Road beach ridge. Seaward of the village are the very shallow and protected waters of Cedar Island Bay, with the Cedar Island barrier visible in the distance. The last 0.5 miles, after you have left the village and are approaching the ferry terminal, crosses a marsh that forms the interstream divide between Cedar Island and the Cedar Island barrier and separates North Bay estuary from Cedar Island Bay (see Figure 8). As you approach the businesses before the ferry terminal, you are climbing onto the Cedar Island barrier. All the shallow and protected water bodies around Cedar Island are excellent for exploring by canoe or kayak.

к. Cedar Island Barrier and Pamlico Sound

Park in the North Carolina Wildlife Resources Access parking area located due east of the Department of Transportation's Cedar Island Ferry terminal; turn right (east) just before the ticket booth and car lanes for the ferry, and follow the signs to the water.

The ferry harbor has been built out into Pamlico Sound. The size of the rock walls gives an idea of the magnitude of winter northeast-storm tides and wave energy experienced at the south end of Pamlico Sound. During these storms weather reports warn of "flooding at the southern end of Pamlico Sound." Strong southwest winds during the summer cause abnormally low water levels in the Cedar Island area as the waters of Pamlico Sound are pushed northward with flooding around Roanoke Island. Sloshing of Pamlico Sound water levels produces very irregular (in both time and size) wind tides or storm tides. Since adjacent inlets through the barrier islands consist of small channels through the sand dam, only minor amounts of ocean (salt) water penetrate into Pamlico Sound, minimizing the effects of ocean tides.

The fossiliferous limestone used in construction of the ferry harbor and parking lot are large blocks of the Castle Hayne Formation of Eocene age (about 40 million years old). The fossils in this limestone are predominantly ancient clams that lived on a prehistoric subtropical continental shelf off the coast of North Carolina. Because the original shells have been leached away, the imprints left behind result in tremendous porosity and permeability, which is essential for a good groundwater aquifer. Consequently, the Castle Hayne Limestone is one of the best aquifers in the United States and is considered a critical source of groundwater for many coastal communities and businesses. It is also a source of aggregate and crushed rock used by the construction industry for roads, bridges, railroads, and so on. Look carefully at these rocks from an ancient ocean to see how many different kinds of fossil organisms are recognizable.

We are standing at the end of the Carteret peninsula where the land surface slopes below sea level to form a headland that continues below Pamlico Sound, having been swallowed by the rising sea level. The Cedar Island barrier formed on the end of Carteret peninsula because the slope of the land is low, a large supply of sand is available from shoreline erosion, and high levels of wave energy are available to build the barrier beach. The Cedar Island barrier and associated back-barrier estuaries, including North Bay, Cedar Island Bay, and Back Bay (Figure 8), form a small-scale barrier island system analogous to the larger-scale Outer Banks produced by the higher-energy Atlantic Ocean. This is a great place to explore the intricacies of a miniature coastal system by canoe or kayak.

The barrier beach is composed of very pure, white, fine-grained quartz sand. The few shells that are found on the beach are from organisms living on the offshore sand flats and include the razor clam, the oyster, and a small and delicate clam called *Mulinea*. You will also find fragments of the abundant blue crab. The portion of beach between low water and the storm beach is often dominated by very small worms that live below the sand surface in pinhole-sized burrows. Another type of worm produces small sand mounds around its burrows. Many shorebirds that you see wading on these sand flats and beaches are feeding on these worms.

If the water level is low when you are on the beach, look for green-colored sand. In the wet zone just above the shoreline, you will notice a green coloration that grades from very light where the sand is almost dry to very dense green where the sand is still wet. This is microalgae growing in the water around each sand grain. Notice that the algae can only grow if the sand is wet and if it is not moving; no green-colored sands occur in the surf zone or where waves are breaking because the algae gets crushed by moving sand grains. However, if the sand stays wet and has not been disturbed for many days, the algae can grow so thick that it actually forms a mat and binds sand grains together. On a hot day notice that the green sands will start to "blister" and bubble up with small gas bubbles being released into the water. This is oxygen, a byproduct of photosynthesis by the algal plants. On hot sunny afternoons when the water becomes extremely warm, these shallow pools become almost a soup. Storms break up the mats and distribute the algae in the water column, where it becomes food for many estuarine and marine organisms.

Notice the extensive shallow sand shoals that extend a considerable distance offshore. Wade across these shoals and observe how waves break as they ride up onto each shoal, and how waves erode, transport, and deposit sand to modify a beach or form an extensive field of ripple marks. Formation or destruction of each of these features is work that requires energy; it is the energy in waves and currents that do the work of erosion, transport, and deposition of sand. You will notice that every time the energy level changes, the processes of deposition and erosion change as the beach constantly readjusts itself to the fluctuating energy input.

Landward of the active beach is a small vegetated dune. On the west side of the ferry harbor the dunes are better developed and are steepened toward the Pamlico Sound side. The base of this erosional scarp is the zone reached by winter storm tides. Notice that the barrier east of the ferry harbor has a low and thin cover of dune grass, whereas the grass is thick and lush to the west. This difference demonstrates the impact of grazing animals upon the dunes. A large horse herd grazes to the east of the harbor, as indicated by the scattered piles of horse manure on the east barrier beach; there are no horses on the west barrier beach.

Bogue Banks

Natural Habitats on a Developed Shoreline

DIRK FRANKENBERG

This 20-mile tour takes you along Bogue Banks—one of the most developed barrier islands on the North Carolina coast. As you will see, public and private agencies have worked together to protect a wide spectrum of natural habitats in parks and natural areas nestled among residential developments. These habitats include excellent examples of dune, dune grassland, shrub thicket, evergreen maritime forest, salt marsh, and swamp forest. The tour takes you to habitats in a state park, a state natural area and aquarium, and a nature trail established and managed by the North Carolina Coastal Federation. Between these pockets of preserved nature you will view the result of fifty years of residential development—cottages built in the forties, motels of the fifties, country club communities from the seventies, multistory motels and conference centers of the eighties, and gated communities of million-dollar homes of the nineties. The preservation of natural areas on a residentially developed and developing barrier island is increasingly rare, but the fact that several of the Bogue Banks preserves were recently established suggests that other islands could still achieve some of Bogue's mix of residences and green space.

The major lesson to be learned from this tour is how attractive the presence of nature preserves among residential development can be. The unusual mix of developed and natural areas gives this tour a wide range of other learning opportunities as well. You can focus on nature and learn about the environmental processes that form and shape our southern barrier islands. You can focus on development and learn how humans have used and built upon the shore at different times. But I recommend that you do both: observe how nature dominated or controlled human use of the barrier island early on, yet today humans dominate and control nature. This approach will help you understand why recurring and predictable extreme events such as hurricanes and northeasters continue to be termed "natural disasters" when they strike developed shorelines. This term is applied whenever human development that has survived nonextreme events fails

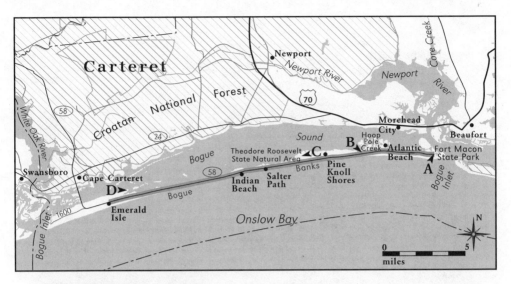

FIGURE 11. Bogue Banks tour route

catastrophically under conditions that are extreme but well within the historic range of conditions that occur on coastal barrier islands.

A. Fort Macon State Park and Nature Trail

This tour begins at Fort Macon State Park at the eastern end of Bogue Banks and NC 58. Fort Macon was built in the 1820s and 1830s to guard Beaufort Inlet. Although it was captured by Union troops during the Civil War, the fort faced its greatest risk of destruction not from warfare but from the migration of Beaufort Inlet. This threat was eliminated when a rock jetty was built to protect the fort after the inlet moved more than 1.5 miles toward it between 1948 and 1995. Inlet migration of this magnitude is quite common on barrier islands, although in this case it was probably increased by repeated dredging of the Beaufort Inlet navigation channel. But even before the channel was deepened during World War II, the inlet had migrated more than a mile from its 1866 position.

A good place to start your tour is on the ramparts of Fort Macon overlooking the inlet. Not only will you get a feel for nineteenth-century warfare, but you can contemplate the dredging required to maintain a 42-foot-deep, 600-foot-wide channel through this historically shallow inlet. From your vantage point on the ramparts, you can observe the 0.5-mile-wide modern inlet and compare it mentally to the 2-mile-wide inlet that was here when the fort was built. Most of the land you see across the inlet did not exist prior to 1866.

FIGURE 12. Well-vegetated, stable dunes in Fort Macon State Park. (Photo by D. Frankenberg)

There are several other sites worth visiting within the park. One is the Elliot-Cones Nature Trail near the fort. This trail follows a well-signed route through a shrub thicket community—a natural community that is nearly impenetrable without a maintained access trail. The trail leads into a young maritime forest of red cedars and live oaks. Older maritime forest can be visited on the left side of the road leading to the beach parking lot near the park entrance. Here the gnarled trunks of the live oaks give mute testimony to the difficulty faced when land plants try to grow upward into the salt spray from the hostile environment of the nearby sea.

Once you are inside the beach parking lot, the dunes and sea beach are accessible by foot. Be aware that the dunes here are more "natural" than the beach. Dune plants can cover a variable percentage of the soil; relatively complete cover leads to the hummocky dunefields seen in Figure 12. Sand dredged from the nearby inlet has been added to the beach here many times—a procedure that preserves the position of the beach, but makes it unnatural and unable to sustain normal populations of animals like ghost and mole crabs.

From the beach and dune you will get another view of human development that may be inconsistent with extreme events. The condominiums that stretch away to the west were all built at the state-required setback from the beach. This requirement is based on the average erosion rate. Unfortunately, average erosion rates mean little under the high water and waves of a hurricane. Bogue Banks has not felt a full-force hurricane for over fifty years. The condos observable from the beach are behind dunes that have been preserved to provide sand should beach erosion occur. Other developments you will see between here and the next tour stop did not take that wise precaution.

B. Hoop Pole Creek Nature Trail

About 4 miles west of the entrance to Fort Macon State Park on NC 58 you will find a new nature trail established by the North Carolina Coastal Federation. The trailhead is opposite Hardees on the east side of the Atlantic Beach Shopping Center, and a box containing informative trail guides is provided at the trail entrance. This trail meanders through a 30-acre tract purchased with funds from the North Carolina Clean Water Management Trust Fund—an innovative program established by the North Carolina General Assembly in 1996 to preserve un-developed lands that help sustain good water quality. The trail passes through land of both natural and historic importance. Soon after entering the trail you will pass Hoop Pole Creek, where Union soldiers landed to attack Fort Macon in April 1862. Beyond the creek the trail becomes a paved road through excellent examples of maritime forest and to areas that provide views of shrub thickets, salt marshes, tidal flats, shellfish beds, and open waters with sea grass beds. The land that supports these habitats was formed on the flood-tide delta of an old inlet. Early charts of this coast show that a series of inlets opened and closed at and near the eastern end of Bogue Banks. Sand carried through these inlets on flooding tides was deposited on the sound side of the inlet to form what scientists call a flood-tide delta. You did not see such a delta at Beaufort Inlet because it was dredged away to make the navigation channel, but all the low-lying land on the inshore side of Bogue Banks between here and Fort Macon was built naturally from sediments of the early deltas. An exceptional view of these lands is available from the high bridge to Morehead City, from which you can observe several examples of development on filled salt marshes—a practice that is no longer permitted, thanks to the North Carolina Coastal Area Management Act.

c. Theodore Roosevelt State Natural Area and Nature Trails, North Carolina Aquarium at Pine Knoll Shores

The next stop on this driving tour is about 4 miles west of Hoop Pole Creek on NC 58. This stop is a triple-header for nature lovers: an interpretive center set in the middle of a natural area containing two nature trails. I suggest visiting the aquarium first as its interpretive exhibits will help you understand what you saw at Fort Macon and Hoop Pole Creek, as well as what you will see on the nature trails and on the remainder of the tour. The aquarium also exhibits aquatic organisms, provides presentations by knowledgeable staff who can answer your questions, and houses a store that offers books for further study.

The best part of this site for nature-oriented visitors, however, is the two nature trails. These are both worth hiking as they provide access to different wetlands across the transition from fresh water to salt water. The freshwater trail, known as the Alice Hoffman Trail, is reached from within the aquarium building. Less than a mile long, this easy trail is self-guiding; plastic laminated trail guides are available at the end of the boardwalk/viewing platform behind the aquarium. Spend some time on these viewing platforms: they overlook Bogue Sound, salt marsh, and maritime forest and are equipped with binoculars so visitors can observe birds and other wildlife of these habitats.

The Alice Hoffman Trail beyond the platforms, a "must see" part of this stop, passes through most types of freshwater habitats found in the 265-acre Theodore Roosevelt State Natural Area. The topography of this area consists of a series of sandy ridges separated by low-lying wetlands. Such ridge-and-swale topography almost always forms along coasts where sediments are reworked by waves, tides, and wind to build new lines of dunes. The process of dunes migrating back from the sea under the influence of onshore winds is well and easily understood; but many people are surprised to learn that new dunes can also form seaward of older ones if the sand supply is large. Dune ridges formed by both processes occur in the Roosevelt Natural Area and elsewhere along western Bogue Banks.

The Alice Hoffman Nature Trail begins on an old dune ridge beside a swale that is now inhabited by salt marsh. The trail, named for the woman whose children donated this land to the state, follows the ridge east through a diverse maritime forest dominated by loblolly pines, laurel oaks, and live oaks and provides views of salt marshes and Bogue Sound (Figure 13). Maritime swamp forests with maples, sweet gums, and ash occur in swales south of the ridge and are observable both at a distance and from bridges. One of these bridges even floats so as to avoid disruption of the forest floor. Swamp forests are unusual on barrier islands. This one lacks some of the typical species, but Carolina ash, water oak, ironwood, and swamp dogwood are found. The swamp forest floor is covered with ferns during warm months.

The second nature trail, the Theodore Roosevelt Trail, is reached from the south side of the parking area across from the aquarium entry ramp. Although it is over a mile long, this trail offers easy walking along and between two ridges beside a swale that supports a freshwater swamp near the trailhead and communities across the transition to salt marsh as it proceeds west to Bogue Sound. This trail honors Theodore Roosevelt's dedication to conservation. His eldest son married Alice Hoffman's niece and was heir to the family's Bogue Banks property. The trail

FIGURE 13. Salt marsh and pond along Alice Hoffman Nature Trail in Roosevelt Natural Area. (Photo by D. Frankenberg)

begins in a maritime forest of live oak, cedar, and loblolly pine with an understory of dogwood and American holly, then moves back and forth between the two ridges as it progresses west toward Bogue Sound. Periodic views of the swale to the south provide glimpses of the sequence of communities from freshwater maritime swamp forest to brackish salt shrub, brackish marsh, and salt marsh. Brackish salt shrub has a marshlike layer under cedars, wax myrtles, and sea ox-eye. Brackish salt marsh is dominated by black needlerush, although along this trail it contains dead cedars as well. Salt marsh is dominated by smooth cordgrass and spike grass. The forest on the ridges becomes progressively less diverse as pines drop out, leaving mostly live oaks and cedars in the overstory with hollies underneath. The hollies here support a rich growth of reddish lichen, which gives their trunks a distinctly mottled appearance.

D. Western Half of Bogue Banks

Development along the western half of Bogue Banks covers a wide spectrum of styles and ages. If this spectrum interests you, you may want to drive through Pine Knoll Shores on your way back to NC 58. Pine Knoll Shores was an early community development that preserved much of the original vegetation—mostly large loblolly pines and live oaks—and most of the land surface topography. An exception to the latter is an extensive canal system that brings salt water into the center of the island. These canals may provide a conduit for sea water if the dunes along NC 58 are ever overwashed during a hurricane. West of Pine Knoll shores are good, bad, and historic examples of barrier island development. Good examples have structures hidden within the maritime forest canopy, thereby preventing fragmentation of these forests with new openings. Bad examples include buildings constructed on the seawardmost dune, unnecessary holes in the forest canopy, excessive crowding of mobile homes in "parks," and filled inlets serving as amusement parks. Some of the bad examples trace their origins to times when shorefront property was not highly valued. The town of Salter Path was established by people who built summer "camps" on unclaimed property during the early twentieth century. If no one cared enough about the property to pay taxes on it, it seems reasonable that inexpensive housing would be built upon it. Emerald Isle, the last town you will pass, has done quite well with recent development practices. Some scientists worry that roads leading straight back from the sea may encourage new inlets to form during hurricane flooding, but the pervasive ridge-and-swale topography of western Bogue Banks keeps several areas of high land available to block cross-island water movement.

Two places you might want to visit while in Emerald Isle are Archer Point, off Lee Street, and Bogue Inlet at the west end of SR 1600. Neither of these two places has much (if any) public parking, but the interesting things can be seen in a quick stop. Lee Street is the westernmost street that crosses the salt marsh separating Archer Point, a high and densely forested beach ridge, from the main part of Bogue Banks. Look for it about 3.5 miles after entering Emerald Isle from Indian Beach. Archer Point appears to be at least 3,400 years old, presumably having formed when sea level rise first began to slow down after the last period of glaciation. If this is true, the bulk of Bogue Banks was formed later than, and seaward of, this old ridge. If you visit, you will see that the Archer Point landform extends east as a series of ridged islands in Bogue Sound (Long to Wood Islands), so it must be a part of the early antecedent topography of Bogue Banks. Bogue Inlet is interesting because it has been dredged less than Beaufort Inlet and therefore includes tidal deltas. To reach the inlet turn west on SR 1600 at the westernmost island stoplight on NC 58. Continue to the southwest corner of the island where you will see a beach access ramp surrounded by "No Parking" signs. Slip furtively to the crest of the ramp to see the beach, Bogue Inlet, and its flood-tide delta inshore and breaker-outlined ebb-tide delta offshore. This inlet moved dramatically westward during Hurricane Bonnie in 1998. The inlet channel used to be hundreds of yards offshore, but the high tides and currents of Bonnie caused it to move west to its present location just off the beach. Local homeowners were not amused by this relocation of the inlet. If you look straight across the inlet you will see Bear Island, the main attraction of Hammocks Beach State Park. The White Oak River tour in this book tells you how to get to the island and what you can see while there. But now, rush back to your car and get away before the police come in response to one of the parking violation calls they seem to receive regularly.

White Oak River from Source to Sea

Natural Communities on a Blackwater River

DIRK FRANKENBERG

This 30-mile tour takes you the full length of a relatively undeveloped blackwater river, and if you take it you will see most of the natural communities that flank such rivers. These include five distinct types of wetlands, a range of aquatic systems from creek to river and tidal estuary, as well as old ocean shorelines left behind by falling sea level, fossilized remains of shells from ancient seas, and the full spectrum of coastal landforms and natural communities. You will also see examples of how natural landforms and communities have been modified for forestry, farming, and housing development. By and large, however, you will visit natural areas, including those preserved in two state game lands (Hofmann State Forest and Croatan), as well as in a national forest (Croatan) and a state park (Hammocks Beach).

The major environmental lesson to be learned from this tour is how waterfront plant communities change along the estuarine transition from salt to fresh water. You will also learn about coastal landforms and the forests they sustain. You will see pine savannas on the old shorelines, pond pine and pocosin wetlands on old seafloors, and swamp forests, freshwater marshes, and salt marshes on the riverine floodplains. You will see a full range of coastal water bodies ranging from freshwater creeks and rivers to an estuary and, finally, the ocean. If you visit Bear Island in Hammocks Beach State Park, you will see the mouth of the White Oak River at Bogue Inlet and the natural communities of one of North Carolina's least developed coastal barrier islands. It will take a full day to complete the tour, mainly because of the ferry trip to Bear Island. Without the trip to Bear Island it will take only half a day, and you will be left with an understanding of blackwater rivers, estuaries, and the natural communities they sustain.

You will learn the most about the sequence of natural communities along waters of changing salt content if you follow this tour from one end to the other, but it makes absolutely no difference if you start at the river's source in Hofmann State

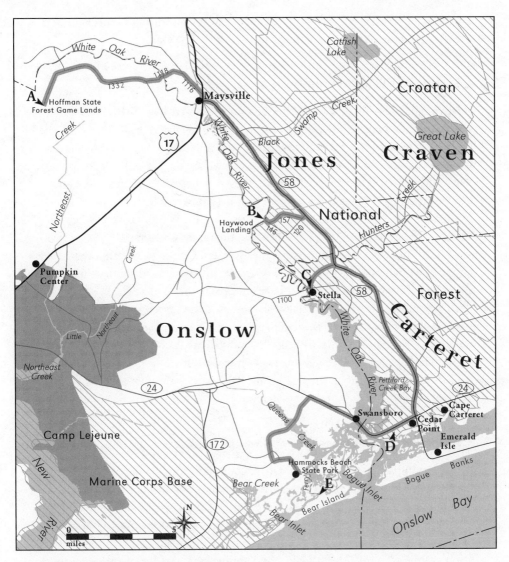

FIGURE 14. White Oak River tour route

Forest or at the river's mouth at the west end of Bear Island. I have arranged the tour description to follow the river from source to sea because I think this order best illustrates important points about the detrimental effect of salt water on higher plants, but you may arrange your tour in whatever way suits your time and interests. I have included the full spectrum of habitats and river sections on the tour; but if time is short, I urge you to focus on three of the five places mentioned—Haywood Landing, Cedar Point (both in Croatan National Forest), and

Bear Island in Hammocks Beach State Park. These are all "five star" environmental sites that should not be missed on any tour of the White Oak.

A. Source of the White Oak: Upstream of Maysville

Upstream of Maysville, the freshwater sections of the White Oak River are easy to visit by car or bicycle but challenging by boat. Downstream of Maysville, the reverse is true. Upstream the river is narrow and shallow but is crossed by bridges. If you decide to drive upstream, a full tour can be had on a 15-mile road trip from Maysville. You will see more than just the river because wetlands and forests border the roads. To take this upstream tour depart Maysville to the northeast on NC Bike Trail 3 (Fourth Street, SR 1116). Turn left on Gibson Bridge Road after about 1.2 miles (SR 1118). Cross the river and turn right on White Oak River Road (SR 1332). This road more or less parallels the river through wetland, field, and forest. Pocosin and pond pine wetlands occupy low-lying land south of the road. These habitats have been drained for agriculture in several places.

To return to Maysville turn right on Emmett Lane (SR 1333, Forest Road [FR] 3004); follow it about 1.1 miles, cross the river, and take a right onto SR 1116. If you want to see Hofmann State Forest and the White Oak Pocosin source of the river, you will have to brave dirt roads west of White Oak Road on the southside of the river or west on SR 1116 on the north side. These are both quite passable in two-wheel-drive vehicles except after heavy rains.

B. Freshwater Reaches of the River to Haywood Landing

Before leaving Maysville, you should drive south on US 17 just far enough to cross the White Oak as it flows through a private campground. The river is still small here but is navigable all the way to the coast by canoe or kayak. Looking downstream from US 17 you will see where the river widens and deepens and is bordered by swamp forest dominated by cypress, gum, willow oak, and red maple. This forest will be seen up close at Haywood Landing, the next major stop. You must return to Maysville and head south on NC 58 to get there.

Haywood Landing is a "must see" site for environmental tourists. It is reached from NC 58, most easily from the aptly named Loopy Road (FR 157), but also by Haywood Landing Road, which is reached via Point Road. Loopy Road is 7.2 miles south of the NC 58/US 17 intersection in Maysville; it is marked with "Haywood Landing" signs and passes through managed loblolly pine forest to its junction with Haywood Landing Road. Haywood Landing Road is built close to the edge of a sandy ridge that drops down to a bottomland hardwood forest to the north. Bottomland hardwood forests differ from swamp forests in frequency of flooding and in the existence of a well-developed understory. Bottomland hardwood forests in North Carolina are usually dominated by willow oak, red maple, and sometimes white cedar. The understory of these forests consists of shrubs such as swamp magnolia and swamp bay, as in this forest north of Haywood Landing Road. Other typical shrub and vine species in this forest include ironwood and buckeye, greenbrier and poison ivy. If you stop about 125 yards east of Haywood Landing, you will see a path leading down to the bottomland. Look to your right as you descend the path and examine the holes in the bank. At the back of these holes is fossil shell material about 20 to 30 million years old (late Oligocene to early Miocene). Two other holes to the right and left of the path also expose these fossils. Another exposure of the fossiliferous layer is on the east bank of the river near the boat ramp (reached by a path at the west edge of the picnic area). The fossils do not seem very dramatic—they are mostly small clam shells with a few snails. Close examination of this material has shown that these shells represent a relatively diverse assemblage including six species of bivalves and four species of snail. By fossil standards, these are also very good specimens—termed the "best preserved fossil molluscs for their age along the Atlantic Coast of North America" by J. G. Carter and his colleagues who authored *Fossil Collecting in North Carolina* in 1988 (Bulletin 89 of the North Carolina Geological Survey).

Haywood Landing itself is west of the bottomland fossil site. There is a cement ramp for launching boats, a picnic area with chemical toilets, a trail along the river, and excellent views of swamp forest habitat. Haywood Landing is on the tidal freshwater section of the river. If you visit at any time other than dead high tide, you will see a high tide line above the water. The maximum range here is about 1 foot, so high tides regularly flood the forest floor, eliminating plants that cannot tolerate complete immersion. Most of the shrub and vine components of the nearby hardwood bottomland forest cannot tolerate immersion, nor do oaks, ash, and sycamore. Red maple and willow oak occur in both swamp forests and hardwood bottoms. Tidal freshwater marshes are also visible at Haywood Landing; these are dominated by cattails and sawgrass, but also include numerous wildflowers that bloom in spring and summer. The swamp forest here is dominated by bald cypress, tupelo, and black gum.

Upland Forests and Wetlands between Haywood Landing and Stella

There are several types of forest that occur on the uplands away from the banks of the White Oak River. The largest acreage of forest is managed for production of timber from loblolly pines. These are the forests you will pass through as you drive along NC 58 between Haywood Landing and Stella, and most of these forests are in

Croatan National Forest—the largest single tract of forest in the White Oak area. Almost all of the loblolly pine forests grow on land that was modified from the original pond pine and pocosin habitat by extensive systems of drainage ditches. The canals to which these ditches connect can be seen all along the freshwater sections of the river. This drainage systems lowers the groundwater table in the ditched areas, allowing loblolly pines to grow in habitat previously too moist for them. Runoff from these modified areas reaches the river much more rapidly than would normally be the case. Oystermen and clammers claim that shellfish catches have gone down as the drained area has expanded, but there is no scientifically established relationship between the two.

If you want to see the undrained forest types of the White Oak watershed, you will need to get fairly far off the beaten track. These areas occur along the road to Great Lake and along hiking trails in Croatan Forest's Pond Pine and Pocosin Wildernesses (Figure 14). Detailed descriptions of these roads, trails, and natural communities are found in my 1997 book, *The Nature of North Carolina's Southern Coast* (see "Suggestions for Further Reading") and are covered in the Croatan National Forest tour later in this book.

c. Fresh Water–Estuarine Transition: Stella and the Middle Reaches

The freshwater reaches of the White Oak grade into the salt-tinged waters of its estuary somewhere between Haywood Landing and Stella. Exactly where depends on recent rainfall history. Stella, however, is a place where salt water occurs frequently enough to eliminate freshwater marshes and sustain salt marshes. This transition can be seen easily from the bridge at Stella, the "metropolis" reached from NC 58 by turning west on Kuhns Road and continuing west on Stella Road (Figure 14). There is parking on both sides of the bridge. Looking north of the bridge you will see cattails and sawgrass at the water's edge fronting extensive black needlerush marshes. Cattails and sawgrass grow in fresh water; black needlerush tolerates salt. Salt builds up in poorly drained marsh soils when sea water evaporates from its surface—hence the observed distributions of marsh plants. Looking to the south from Stella bridge, you will see only salt marshes (mostly black needlerush but sometimes with smooth cordgrass at the water's edge). Salt marshes will be seen repeatedly between Stella and the sea, bordering the river almost continuously along the middle reaches of the White Oak. Often these marshes occur between the water and the base of the 30-foot sandy ridges that characterize this area's ancient shoreline. The mid-reaches of the river itself are wide and shallow, in keeping with its origin as a river floodplain recently flooded by rising sea level. If

FIGURE 15. Salt marsh and forest in the mid-reaches of the White Oak. (Photo by D. Frankenberg)

the White Oak were a bigger river and/or had a higher sediment load, its mid-reaches would be filled with salt marshes; but the middle section remains as open water because sea level is rising faster than sediment moves downstream to fill it. The bottom of this section of river grades from mud and silt at Stella to sand-sized particles close to Swansboro.

D. Salt Marsh and Sound Views at Cedar Point Recreation Area

Salt marshes are the habitat to visit in the mid-reaches of the White Oak, and there are many great places to observe them. One of the best is the Cedar Point Recreation Area and its Tidelands Trail (Figure 15). The habitats viewable from this trail make this site one of the five-star features of this tour.

The Cedar Point Recreation Area is west of NC 58 off VFW Road, which is 0.6 miles north of the intersection of NC 24 and NC 58 in Cape Carteret (Figure 14). The Tidelands Trail leads north from the picnic area parking lot and offers great salt marsh views. Following along the marsh, the trail passes by all the expected salt-marsh plants (sea ox-eye, spike grass, black needlerush, and smooth cordgrass), but you may also find "high marsh" species scattered through a scrubby maritime forest at the edge of the marsh. This distribution of salt-marsh plants under trees

FIGURE 16. Mouth of the White Oak at Bear Island. (Photo by D. Frankenberg)

of the maritime forest is unusual. It may represent a transition that is under way from forest to marsh as increasingly frequent flooding with salt water kills back the forest and expands the extent of the salt marsh.

E. Mouth of the White Oak: Bear Island and Hammocks Beach State Park

This tour, like meals for children, has saved the best for last. Bear Island in Hammocks Beach State Park, an unspoiled, fascinating place, is your "dessert." The island offers excellent examples of salt marsh, dunefield, and maritime thicket communities, as well as one of the most reliably safe beaches along our coast. Most visitors concentrate on the beach, but there is much to discover on a walk through the dunes and thickets. Bear Island is only about 3.5 miles long, so one can walk down the beach and back through the dunes in an hour or two. Few visitors seem to leave the beach, but the dunescapes of Bear Island are truly stunning.

The island is reached by ferry. The mainland ferry dock is at the park headquarters, accessible from NC 24 via Hammocks Beach Road (SR 1511) about 2 miles west of Swansboro (Figure 14). The ferry runs daily between Memorial Day and Labor Day and on weekends in May, September, and October. At other times, the island can be reached by small boats that can, with permission, be launched from the park headquarters. There is also water taxi service from Swansboro; the best way to obtain a list of water taxis is by calling the park at 910-326-4881.

The highest land on Bear Island is on the north shore (the shore where the ferry lands). In some places this shoreline supports a maritime forest, whereas in others the dunes extend almost to the back-barrier salt marsh. The dunefield on Bear Island, the most extensive one in southern North Carolina, is large, active, and moves inexorably into and over maritime forests, thickets, and grasslands.

Grasslands and thickets develop in interdune areas, especially where seaward dunes offer some protection from ocean-derived salt spray. Note that sea oats dominate the most exposed locations, while salt meadow cordgrass, bluestem, broom sedge, and shrub thickets are found in less exposed habitats (Figure 16).

The dunefield on Bear Island not only is as extensive and diverse as any along the southern North Carolina coast, but it also offers up many interesting artifacts. In the open dunes you will find areas where whole clam and scallop shells are abundant. Park personnel call these areas "seagull microwaves." Gulls collect the living shells on the beach, carry them into the dunes, and wait until they open in the hot sun.

The beach at Bear Island is a classic example of the dissipative type—that is, a beach that dissipates the energy of breaking waves over a broad, relatively flat surf zone. The diagnostic feature of such beaches is that they have at least three waves breaking in the surf zone at any one time. I have never seen surf at Bear Island without three simultaneous breakers, and I have been there when eight to ten waves were breaking simultaneously.

The eastern end of Bear Island can be reached by boat or by walking along the beach. The trip is worth the effort because you can see Bogue Inlet's tidal deltas (Figure 16) and evidence of sediment driven through the dunes by Hurricane Fran in 1996. The maritime forest on Bear Island is painful to visit; its pines were decimated by Hurricane Fran and a subsequent pine bark beetle infestation.

Lower Cape Fear River by Car and Ferry

DIRK FRANKENBERG

This tour will take you along the banks of, and across, the biggest river in eastern North Carolina. It is no surprise that the Cape Fear dominates the landforms and natural habitats near its mouth. You will travel down the west bank to see how the river interacts with the mainland to create creek drainages, swamp forests, and marshes. You will spend thirty minutes on the river during a ferry ride from Southport to Fort Fisher, then explore the ways the river interacts with seacoast barrier islands. These interactions are largely natural, but you will see places where they have been changed by humans through the blocking of inlets, building of forts, and dredging of channels. You will also see how these modifications and nature's hurricanes have affected the native natural communities. There will also be unmodified natural communities to view along the estuary and in grasslands, on dunes, and on beaches.

The major lesson to be learned from this tour is that big rivers have big impacts on everything that borders them. This is not surprising, but the way it plays out in specific settings is interesting, unexpected, and educational. On the land side west of the river, for instance, you will see dead trees along tidal marshes and will learn that rising sea level is increasing the saltiness of water flooding the marshes. You will also learn that the uplands near the Cape Fear support the state's greatest number of natural communities and of plant and animal species that are federally classified as threatened or endangered. These uplands have ponds, and the rivers and creeks that drain them support a range of environmental conditions that make this area a center of natural diversity along the entire East Coast. On the sea side east of the river you will learn that a successful coastal engineering project blocked New Inlet from flowing into the Cape Fear River, thereby limiting the river's flow to a single mouth rather than two. You will also learn how the beach erosion that threatened historic Fort Fisher has been controlled by the placement of rocks on the shoreface, and of the resultant beach erosion downstream. You will gain an appreciation for the effects of hurricanes on a wide range of natural habitats and communities as you drive through private and public lands to visit two state historic sites (Brunswick Town and Fort Fisher), an estuarine research

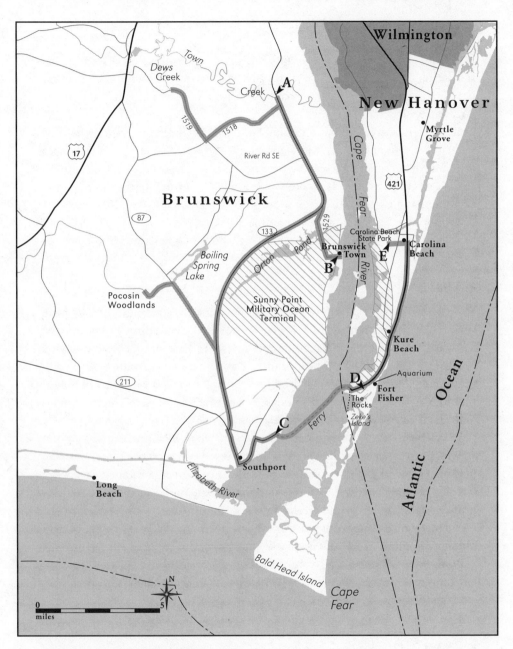

FIGURE 17. Lower Cape Fear River tour route

reserve (Zeke's Island), a state aquarium at Fort Fisher, and a state park at Carolina Beach.

As with most tours, this one can be made in either direction. I recommend starting on the west side of the river because that leaves hiking and beach areas for later, but there is no particular educational reason for conducting the tour in one direction or the other.

To reach this tour's initiation point from Wilmington, leave the city heading west on the combined US 17/74/76 and NC 133 and watch carefully for the NC 133 exit immediately after crossing the Brunswick River. The exit is a diamond interchange, so get off as soon as you can and turn left at the foot of the ramp to head south. NC 133 crosses Town Creek about 5 miles from US 17/74/76. Keep your eye peeled for views of salt and freshwater marshes east and west of NC 133. Many of these may be familiar as they are often seen in movies filmed near Wilmington.

A. Town Creek

Town Creek is interesting for several reasons. First, it is a typical coastal plain stream that rises in wetlands a few miles inland and passes through bottomland hardwood forest, swamp forest, freshwater marsh, and salt marsh before emptying into the Cape Fear estuary. It flows under NC 133 just as its waters are beginning to get salty and freshwater tidal marsh merges with salt marsh. If you look carefully at the salt marshes east of NC 133, you will see many examples of pines and hardwoods that have died as a result of saltwater exposure increasing as sea level rises.

Town Creek is also interesting for the ease with which its source can be found. If you are interested in such things, drive south on NC 133 and take a side trip on the first road to the right (SR 1518, Bucks Road), then right again on SR 1519 to its crossing of Dews Creek. This forested wetland is the type that initiates drainage into Coastal Plain rivers and creeks. In transit to this forest you will have passed over a sandy ridge supporting a dry forest dominated by scrub oak. The ridge is an old shoreline, and its dry soils contrast with the waterlogged ones of nearby fresh- and saltwater wetlands. This contrast can give you an idea of the spectrum of environments that support such a wide diversity of plants and animals as exist along the western shore of the Cape Fear River.

B. Brunswick Town Site and Salt Marshes

The tour continues south on NC 133 about 4.5 miles to another side trip through Orton Plantation to Brunswick Town on SR 1529 (Orton Plantation Road). The round trip is only about 5 miles long and is worthwhile for its spectacular views of Orton Pond (Figure 18), which is home to alligators and water turkeys (*Anhinga*),

FIGURE 18. Freshwater pond west of Cape Fear River. (Photo by D. Frankenberg)

as well as wetland and upland forests. The Brunswick Town site provides panoramic views of the Cape Fear River and its extensive salt marshes, as well as a chance to tour the earthworks of a Civil War–era fort and the site of one of North Carolina's earliest settlements. The small museum on the site is well worth visiting.

Continue south on NC 133 for another side trip up NC 87 to the Boiling Spring Lakes area and nearby longleaf pine savanna, pocosin, and pond pine woodland habitats (Figure 17). The lakes here are artificial, but extensive grassy wetlands like those that occur naturally are found along their edges. To reach this spectrum of wetlands, go west off NC 87 on North Shore Road just north of the lake. Although dirt, the road is well maintained and easily passable in two-wheel-drive vehicles. About 0.1 mile down this road there is a road to a dam on the left. This area provides a good place from which to view the wetlands both within and beside the lakes. Driving farther along North Shore Road will lead you through pocosins, pond pine woodlands, and longleaf pine savannas. The same communities and transitional types are also found along highways NC 133, NC 87, and NC 211.

c. Southport and Its Ferry Terminal

The tour continues south on NC 87/133 to Southport and its Cape Fear ferry terminal. Southport is a charming town and well worth a visit of its own. Naturalists will be pleased with the town's successful effort to save live oaks and other trees remaining from the maritime forest that once occupied the site of the town. Birders will be delighted with the opportunity to view wading birds (herons, egrets, and ibis) that nest in the summer on Battery Island off Southport's waterfront.

The real reason, however, to visit Southport is to catch the ferry northeast of downtown (Figure 17) and to observe some rare woodland communities that occur near the ferry terminal. The state-run ferry service up and across the Lower Cape Fear estuary departs about every 50 minutes from 8 A.M. to 6 P.M. from late March to mid-November, and half as frequently from November 15 through March. The vehicle fare is $3, and pedestrian fare is fifty cents. There is no better way to observe the Cape Fear estuary than from the river itself. In addition, the time you spend waiting to load can be put to good advantage by observing two rare forest types on private land near the ferry terminal. Deep ravines in a sandy terrace create ideal habitat for these two forest types. Swamp forest with pocosin plant understory predominates on the ravine floor, and a rare coastal fringe evergreen forest occupies the slopes. The slope forest is relatively open, with loblolly pine, laurel oak, live oak, and water oak making up the canopy and holly, yaupon, and red bay in the understory. The ridges between the ravines support a different pine and oak community in which longleaf pine dominates the canopy over relatively dense stands of turkey oak and laurel oak. You may or may not be pleased to learn that American alligators are seen frequently in these ravines.

The ferry will take you to the landing at Fort Fisher, on the east side of the Cape Fear. The Fort Fisher area offers several opportunities for nature study, as it provides easy access to "The Rocks" and Zeke's Island Estuarine Research Reserve. The Rocks are a 3-mile-long breakwater built in 1891 to keep the Cape Fear to a single mouth. It now offers waders a unique opportunity to see algae and animals that live attached to rocky substrate. Oysters, mussels, sea anemones, starfish, and sea urchins can all be found along with hundreds of other smaller and less conspicuous forms. This feature is also much used by sport fisherman and by birds that eat the fish that prey on the animals on the rocks. The rocks are flooded at high tide and slippery with algae at all times, so plan your walk to avoid being stranded and place your feet carefully to avoid falling.

D. Zeke's Island Estuarine Research Reserve

The Rocks can also be used to reach Zeke's Island, where extensive salt marsh and maritime shrub habitats can be observed. These and other habitats in Zeke's Island Reserve are, however, more easily reached from a nature trail at the North Carolina Aquarium at Fort Fisher. This trail takes you to sites greatly impacted by the winds and floodwaters of Hurricane Fran in 1996. Fran flooded this site with over 7 feet of sea water, much of which gradually drained into the soils of low-lying areas. The long period of inundation combined with the toxic effects of the salt killed the vegetation almost completely. The nature trail used to begin in a cedar and pine maritime forest. This forest has been completely destroyed, but higher ground further down the trail looks essentially the same as it did before the hurricane hit. The grasslands and salt marshes that stretch away for miles to the southeast also look just as they did before the hurricane. About 0.75 miles from the parking lot a side trail leads to a World War II–era bunker in which Robert Edward Harrell—known as the Fort Fisher Hermit—lived from 1955 until his death in 1972. Beyond the bunker the research reserve encompasses 1,165 acres of unspoiled marsh, shrub, dune, and oceanfront beach. Thus this may be the place you plan to combine a nature walk with a beach trip. The beach can be reached from the nature trail, but you must wade through a salt pond behind the dune line. You can avoid this muddy experience by returning to the aquarium and walking to the beach along a raised trail. There is also a sandy road along the back of the dune line, but it is only suitable for off-road vehicles. When you visit the aquarium be sure to see the hurricane flooding display on the tower outside the entrance. It dramatically points out how deep the storm surge flood from Fran and other historically damaging hurricanes has been. The tower is over 20 feet high to include Hurricane Camille's 23-foot surge. No one who sees and understands this tower's message will wonder why residents are urged to evacuate beach communities when major hurricanes threaten.

The aquarium's hurricane flood tower should be kept in mind as you drive down the exit road and see the tall (and to my eye, incredibly ugly) sand barricade bulldozed to protect the bathhouse parking lot and US 421 south of Fort Fisher State Park. This sand pile was made necessary by beach retreat on the south side of a beach-hardening project designed to protect Fort Fisher's seaward ramparts from shorefront erosion. The rationale for the project was cultural, not environmental, so I will leave any conclusions about the wisdom of this solution to history; but if you want to see what happens to beaches downstream of erosion control structures, park at the bathhouse and walk out on the beach to the north. There you will see the stone erosion control structure with the beach about 200 to 500 feet back from its prestructure location. Publicly owned beach and dune have been eroded away, perhaps in a justifiable trade for protected ramparts, but only time will tell the full environmental cost of the deal. Fort Fisher is well worth visiting if you are interested in mid-nineteenth-century coastal warfare or underwater archaeology: displays on both subjects are excellent. The environmental part of this tour finishes up at Carolina Beach State Park, reached by driving north on US 421 to Down Road just south of Snows Cut.

FIGURE 19. Salt marsh and maritime forest along the Cape Fear. (Photo by D. Frankenberg)

E. Carolina Beach State Park

Carolina Beach State Park is one of the jewels of the North Carolina State Park System. It occupies 1,173 acres on the northwest corner of the island and was created in 1929 when the Intracoastal Waterway was dredged through this peninsula. The park provides areas for camping and picnicking, as well as a marina with slips and a launching ramp. The main attraction for those interested in nature, however, is the more than 5 miles of trails laid out through forest and lowland plant communities. One of these trails—referred to as "Nature Trail" on signs and as the "Fly Trap Trail" in park literature—is the only one I know that explicitly identifies areas where you can find the often-poached Venus flytrap and other insectivorous plants. A stop at the park office to obtain trail maps is a good idea because existing roads and walkways are easily confused with official trails. The descriptive brochure for the Fly Trap Trail even provides drawings of sixteen plants typical of the three major forest types in the park and discusses animals—including the endangered red-cockaded woodpecker—that are found in the park's forests.

Carolina Beach State Park contains representative areas of at least nine different plant communities. Three of these—longleaf pine savanna, pond pine woodland, and pocosin—are seen from the Fly Trap Trail. An additional six communities are found along the 2.25-mile Sugarloaf Trail, which is reached from the southeast corner of the marina parking area. The Sugarloaf Trail gets its name from a 50-foot-high relict sand dune whose unvegetated top rising above the forest canopy has been used as a landmark for ships in the Cape Fear River since 1738. The trail reaches Sugarloaf along the banks of the Cape Fear River after passing through a short section of estuarine fringe loblolly pine forest. The bank of the river is occupied by salt marsh plants, with salt meadow cordgrass located between the upland and the taller, smooth cordgrass at the water's edge (Figure 19). The trail continues to Sugarloaf itself, then swings back through sand ridges supporting a forest community with an open canopy of longleaf pine and a distinctive understory of turkey oak sometimes interspersed with yucca. This community is called "xeric sandhill scrub" by plant ecologists, although park literature refer to it as "the dry sand ridge community." The trail continues past three more interesting habitats located in low-lying depressions within the sand ridge area. These areas support freshwater wetland communities that range from seasonally flooded grasslands to a permanent lily pond.

Carolina Beach State Park has a remarkably diverse flora. A 1990 study by David Sieren and Karen Warr of the University of North Carolina at Wilmington reported over 240 species present, including 30 that are described as "rare" by the state's Natural Heritage Program. This diversity and presence of rare species is partially a function of the diverse soil types, topography, and hydrology of the park lands. Four distinct soil types are distributed in a complex mosaic over topography that ranges from high dune ridges, through organic-rich muds in pocosins, to limesink depression ponds and grasslands. The ridge, swale, and depression topography produces complex freshwater drainage patterns of creeks, seeps, swamps, and ponds. The Cape Fear River provides brackish tidal water that floods the west and north sides of the park property.

Brunswick County

Savanna to the Sea

DIRK FRANKENBERG

This tour leads you across Brunswick County—one of North Carolina's richest counties from an environmental and ecological standpoint. A 1995 inventory of its natural areas and rare species showed that it has the highest level of species richness of any similarly sized area in the United States and pointed out that it supports a greater diversity of natural communities (thirty-six) and more endangered or threatened species (fifteen) than any other county in North Carolina. A spectrum of this biological richness can be seen on this 36-mile tour from the pine savannas and pocosins of Green Swamp to the unspoiled beaches and dunes of Bird Island. This route leads you past forests, swamps, and marshes, along a blackwater river, to an undeveloped barrier island. The topography along the route is almost as interesting as the biota: wetlands and sand ridges alternate across the landscape. You will pass by land that is almost all in private hands, but you can stop in places where public access is allowed, namely, at The Nature Conservancy's Green Swamp Preserve off NC 211, at several spots along the Shallotte River, and at Bird Island, which is partially owned by the U.S. Army Corps of Engineers (Figure 20).

Three major points that can be learned from this tour: the role of changing sea level in shaping coastal land forms; the habitat characteristics of wetland forests, swamps, and blackwater rivers; and the ever-changing nature of barrier islands as they respond to the energy of the ocean by migrating, as inlets fill, sand spits elongate, and beaches flatten and erode.

These learning opportunities are interconnected by the fact that sea level change plays a central role in establishing topography, river courses, and shoreline dynamics on sedimentary coastlines. The crucial information to remember is that sea level falls when the climate cools and rises when it warms. The world's climate cooled and sea level fell to 300 feet below current levels 20,000 years ago. Brunswick County changed from being a warm seacoast like it is today to a cold and stormy inland sand plain. As sea level fell, rivers extended seaward and eroded deep channels into the ever-widening coastal plain, and coastal barrier islands like today's were stranded and resembled the sandy ridges you will see on this tour.

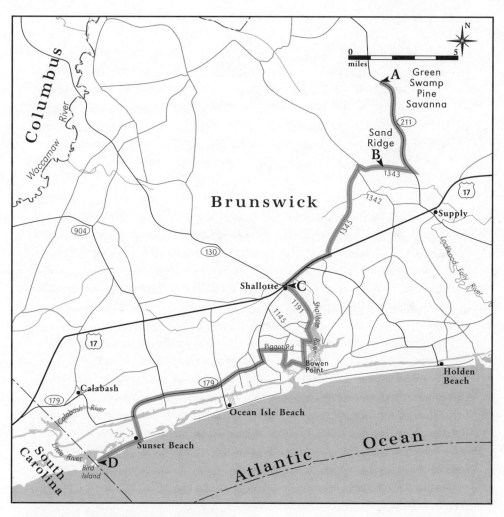

FIGURE 20. Brunswick County tour route

Sea level has risen continuously since the climate was at its coldest about 17,000 years ago, and its current level is only about 20 feet lower than it was about 120,000 years ago.

The topography that formed as sea level fell and rose is observable today. The Green Swamp occupies a large but shallow bowl, sometimes interpreted as the floor of an ancient lake. Sandy ridges scattered across the Coastal Plain may represent old lakeshores and riverbank levees, while long linear ridges oriented parallel to the seacoast are probably old shorelines from eras of higher sea level. This topographic context and scenario are helpful to keep in mind as you follow the tour route to the sea that is described below.

A. Green Swamp

This tour begins at The Nature Conservancy's Green Swamp Preserve off NC 211. The Nature Conservancy tract is located on the east side of the highway about 18.5 miles south of Bolton (a town on US 74/76), and about 7 miles north of Supply (a town on US 17). There is a small parking lot located just south of a flooded borrow pit and north of a loblolly pine plantation. Many trees near the parking area are marked by bands of white paint. Before entering the woodland, you may wish to use insect repellent and tuck your pant legs into your socks (both ticks and chiggers can be abundant here).

To reach the longleaf pine savanna where David Attenborough filmed Venus flytraps for his Public Broadcasting System TV documentary, *The Private Life of Plants*, take the grassy road/trail along the edge of the borrow pit, follow it southeast when it turns, and continue to the edge of a pocosin-filled pond pine woodland. Look closely ahead of you on the left for a small opening that leads to a rudimentary boardwalk made of two-by-fours that carries you over seasonally flooded soils (note the sphagnum moss in the lowest areas) to the longleaf pine savanna about 30 yards to the east (Figure 21).

This longleaf pine savanna is as natural and biologically complete as any in the state—hence its appearance on TV. It is a great place to explore on your own. Keep your eye peeled in summer for carnivorous pitcher plants, sundews, and Venus flytrap among the wiregrass, running blueberries, and huckleberries that characterize the ground cover under the pines. The carnivorous plants trap and extract nutrients from unwary insects to supplement the minimal supplies available in the soils, which are rich in organic matter but poor in nutrients. As you tour the longleaf pine savanna, keep in mind that this forest type once occupied an estimated 55 million acres between Virginia and Texas, of which only about 1 percent remains as you see it here. Former longleaf pine areas now support loblolly pine plantations or southern mixed hardwood forest—loblollies where the forest is managed for timber production, mixed hardwoods anywhere that fire is suppressed. Longleaf pines require periodic fires. Once these were touched off naturally by lightening, but both Native and modern Americans set fires to maintain savannas for hunting and forest products. The Nature Conservancy periodically burns this forest to maintain it, as you can see from the charred bark both here and in the loblolly stand you passed through to get here. If this were not done, hardwoods would come to dominate the understory and eventually shade out the pine seedlings and create a mixed hardwood forest to replace the savanna. The unremarkable-appearing wiregrass at your feet is mostly responsible for the fires. It grows from underground roots, and its dry shoots support the fast-spreading

FIGURE 21. Longleaf pine savanna in Green Swamp Preserve. (Photo by D. Frankenberg)

but relatively cool fires that clear the forest floor of hardwood seedlings, thereby maintaining the savanna vegetation.

Return to your car by reversing the route you took here. Even if you took anti-bug measures before entering the preserve, you may want to examine yourself for fellow travelers before proceeding. The sooner you rid yourself of any unwanted companions, the less scratching you will do later.

B. Old Shorelines

The tour continues south on NC 211 toward Supply—turn left when leaving the Nature Conservancy parking area. Keep your eye on the land to the left (east) of the road, as there are good examples of both pond pine woodland with pocosin plant understory and an open longleaf pine savanna within 0.75 miles of the parking area. About 2 miles further south you will cross the first of many sandy ridges. About 3 miles south on NC 211 brings you to Little Macedonia Road (SR 1343); turn right onto another sandy ridge. Follow SR 1343 to a T-intersection; turn left on Makatoka Road (SR 1342), then bear right immediately onto Royal Oak Road (SR 1345), which will take you to US 17. All along the state roads you will find rolling hills, often of fine white sand, suggesting their origin as sand dunes on old shorelines.

C. Shallotte: Shallotte River and Estuary

At the intersection of Royal Oak Road and US 17, turn west briefly, then left again onto US 17 Business into Shallotte. As you pass through downtown Shallotte watch for the Camp United Methodist Church on the banks of the Shallotte River. Park in the church parking lot or across the street so you can walk over the river on the bridge. Upstream you will see a typical marsh of low-salinity brackish water (i.e., one-sixth to one-eighth the salt content of ocean water). The dominant plant here is black needlerush, although some areas of giant cordgrass form a lighter green and taller fringe along part of the waterline. On the downstream side of the bridge you can see the transition from low to middle salinity (about half as salty as sea water). The high banks of the river support red cedar trees, the marsh still has lots of black needlerush, but an increasing area is occupied by smooth cordgrass—a shorter but more salt-tolerant relative of the giant cordgrass seen upstream. If you look closely on the east bank of the river, you will see an orange sign indicating the official "salt line" that separates management regimes for inland fisheries from those for marine fisheries. This sign shows that the state sees the Shallotte River bridge as the upstream limit of ocean water, although you will recognize that high tides and onshore winds may move salt water farther upstream, and periods of heavy rain and runoff will move the boundary further downstream.

The tour continues down the west bank of the Shallotte River estuary by traveling south on a sequence of roads close to the water. These roads begin at the first left on the west side of the bridge; this road may not be signed, but note that the next left is Copas Road (SR 1191). Copas Road extends along a high sandy bluff that defines the western edge of the Shallotte River floodplain—here occupied largely by irregularly flooded salt marsh dominated by black needlerush with a river-bordering fringe of smooth cordgrass, in other words, a typical mid-salinity marsh much like that seen downstream from the US 17 Business bridge in Shallotte. Regretfully, Copas Road provides only glimpses of these typical estuarine marshes, but almost all side roads to the east lead to panoramic views from the edge of the bluff. Roads in a development called The Rock lead to particularly good vistas of the upper Shallotte estuary. A good case can be made that salt marsh vistas like this one greeted the first Europeans that visited these shores. Not much development can take place in salt marshes, so they remain in their natural state.

The tour continues across a series of sandy ridges and low-lying swales that probably formed as the falling sea level stranded barrier islands of shorelines at higher sea levels than those of the present. Most of the interridge swales have been reinvaded by today's rising sea level, so you will cross creeks bordered by salt marsh at several points. You will also have to drive around some of the larger creeks. This is what you do when you continue straight onto Middle Dam Road (SR 1146), then turn left onto Village Point Road (SR 1145), which leads back to the bluff along the river. The river floodplain gets wider and wider as you approach the mouth, and, unsurprisingly, the marshes along it are increasingly dominated by the salt-tolerant smooth cordgrass. You can follow the bluff to its terminus at the Intracoastal Waterway by following Piggott Road past views from Lloyd's Oyster House and from Holden Seafood to Hughes Dock 77 Marina, located on the southeast corner of Bowen Point. Unfortunately you cannot see Shallotte Inlet from here because the view is blocked by an earthen dam built by the Army Corps of Engineers to contain dredged spoil from their periodic deepening of the Intracoastal Waterway. There is, however, a very good view of the sand flats and high-salinity salt marsh that stretch across the lower Shallotte estuary to its eastern bluff roughly 0.75 miles away.

D. Development, Development, and Bird Island

The tour continues from Bowen Point to Bird Island through roughly 9 miles of coastal development. There are gated communities with marinas and golf courses,

FIGURE 22. Mad Inlet and Bird Island. (Photo by D. Frankenberg)

condos, beach cottages, motels, single family homes, an airfield, and service businesses ranging from landscapers to medical care. This is rapidly becoming the norm along our southern coast, but a visit to Bird Island will restore your faith in nature conservation. So persevere and use the next few miles as a chance to eat, shop, or find a place to spend the night.

The easiest way to get to Bird Island's access point is to take Village Point Road back to Piggott Road and head west to NC 179; turn left and follow the signs for 7 miles to Sunset Beach. Sunset Beach is reached by a unique one-lane drawbridge over the Intracoastal Waterway and a causeway across well-developed high-salinity salt marsh. This marsh is much like that seen at a distance from Hughes Dock 77 Marina. You can park along the causeway for a closer look if you wish to. Upon reaching Sunset Beach turn right on any road and follow it to one of the last few roads on the west end of the island. Parking is not easy on Main Street (the coastal road), but is possible on the side roads; each of these roads has beach access on the shore side of Main Street, so walk on with confidence to the wide sand beach that stretches west to Bird Island.

The beach walk to Bird Island is made interesting by the beach itself—a flat strand with a broad surf zone of many breakers. This is a classic example of a dissipating shoreface where wave energy is dissipated gradually in the surf zone. The opposite extreme is a reflective beach where much of the wave energy is reflected back out to sea by a steep shoreface and narrow surf zone. Another interesting spot on the west end of Sunset Beach is the extensive sand spit that now links it to Bird Island (Figure 22). Prior to the two hurricanes of 1996, this dune-covered spit led to Mad Inlet—an inlet for a 200-foot-wide creek that connected the ocean to the Intracoastal Waterway (as shown on page 215 of *The Nature of North Carolina's Southern Coast*—see "Suggestions for Further Reading"). This inlet was closed when hurricane winds and waves moved sand westward to fill the creek almost completely. You will see that Mad Inlet is now only a trickle across the beach, and navigation to the waterway is no longer possible. The elongated sand spit west of Sunset Beach is also used as a nesting area for shorebirds and sea turtles. If you visit in summer, you will probably see turtle nests marked and fenced off as part of a turtle conservation program.

Elongating sand spits present on obvious disadvantage to those who seek what lies beyond them: the walk gets longer along with the spit. It is now over a 1.5-mile walk from the west end of Sunset Beach to what's left of Mad Inlet and Bird Island. The good news is that the crowds decline with distance along the beach. Bird Island itself is always uncrowded and often all but deserted. For those who enjoy nature without crowds, the long walk is the only price you pay.

Bird Island has a beach as extensive as Sunset's, large sand dunes, and extensive areas of salt marsh and maritime shrub thicket. The southern end of the island (beach and dunefield) are controlled by the U.S. Army Corps of Engineers and are therefore publicly accessible. The north end of the island is currently privately owned by a family in Greensboro who plan to keep it in its natural state. Negotiations to purchase the island have been under way for many years, and efforts to raise funds for its preservation have now begun. Bird Island has long been used by the public for bird watching, picnicking, and other low-disturbance activities. I will leave your use of this area to your own discretion, but emphasize that at the time of this writing the north end of Bird Island was still privately owned.

The Coastal Plain

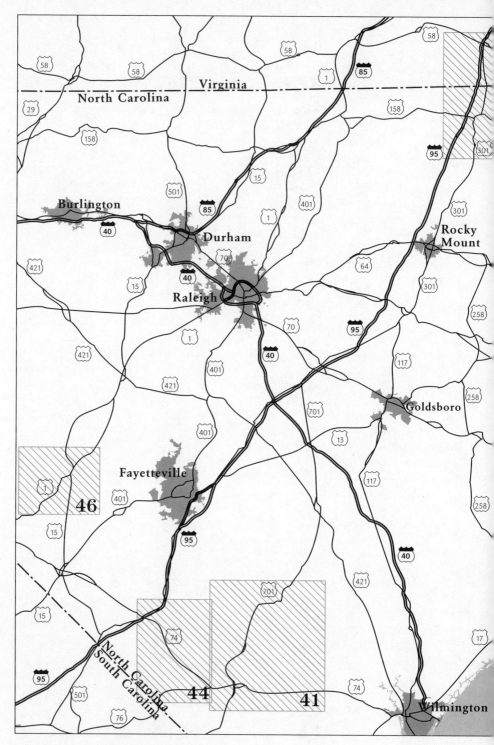

FIGURE 23. Coastal Plain tour routes
Numbers in boxes indicate figure numbers for individual tour route maps.

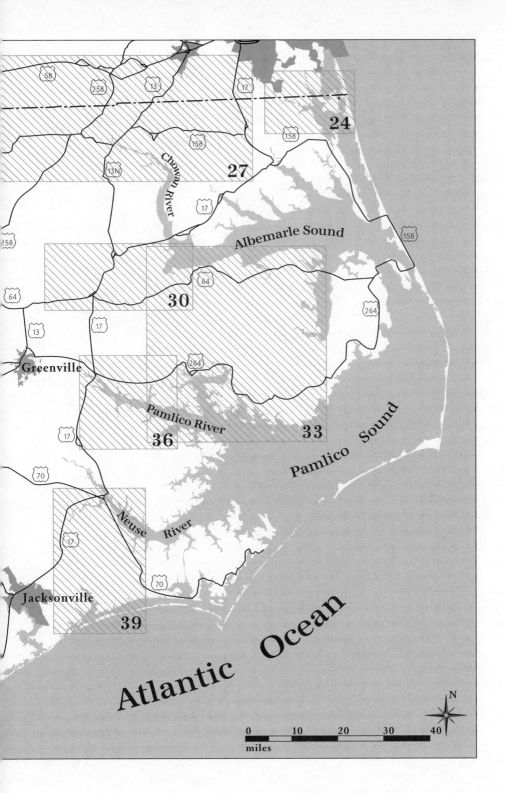

58

258

13

17

24

158

158

27

Chowan River

13N

17

17

258

Albemarle Sound

158

64

64

30

264

13

17

Greenville

264

36

Pamlico River

33

Pamlico   Sound

17

70

Neuse   River

70

17

36

Jacksonville

39

Atlantic   Ocean

N

0   10   20   30   40
miles

Currituck Sound's Mackay Island

YATES M. BARBER

This tour will take you to Mackay Island, a National Wildlife Refuge in the upper reaches of Currituck Sound that is accessible by land and by ferry. On a low-lying peninsula that separates Currituck Sound and Back Bay, Virginia, Mackay Island consists of extensive fresh to brackish marshes that are managed to support wildlife. There are forested ridges within the marshes that also provide extensive and varied habitat for wildlife.

The refuge is a unit of the U.S. Fish and Wildlife Service Refuge System, whose mission is to "administer a national network of lands and waters for the conservation, management and, where appropriate, restoration of the fish, wildlife, and plant resources and their habitats within the United States for the benefit of present and future generations." Mackay Island Refuge (Figure 24) meets this mission by conserving and managing not only terrestrial animals and birds, but by serving also as a vital nursery area for the young of numerous species of marine fishes including croaker, spot, mullet, blue crab, flounder, menhaden, and others that spawn in the ocean, but whose larvae and juveniles migrate into estuarine areas to complete their early life stages.

The major lesson to be learned from this tour is that nature is resilient and can restore itself when human "improvements" have unexpected impacts. Upper Currituck Sound is a case study of unanticipated outcomes of coastal "improvement" projects. Mackay Island Refuge was founded as a partial response to the unanticipated loss of waterfowl following dredging of the Intracoastal Waterway and the intrusion of both salt water and pollution following removal of a lock at Great Bridge, Virginia. The gradual restoration of the upper Currituck is an ongoing story of the successful reversal of habitat-damaging "improvements." Full appreciation of this story requires an understanding of the upper Currituck's history.

Environmental History of Upper Currituck Sound

In the eighteenth century Currituck Sound was a saltwater sound connected to the Atlantic Ocean by an inlet through the Outer Banks at the point where the

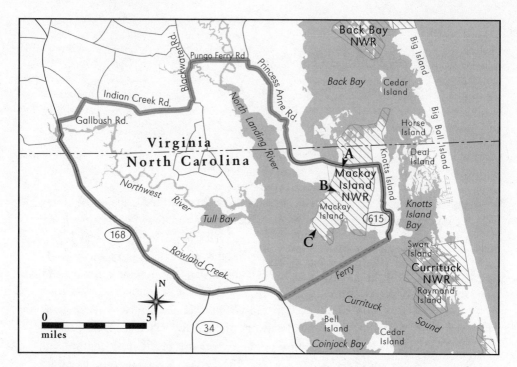

FIGURE 24. Mackay Island tour route

state line between Virginia and North Carolina now crosses. Scattered deposits of oyster shells in the sound bottom testify to a previously high salt content of these waters, as do an abundance of historical records and the "relict" stands of black needlerush (a salt-tolerant species), which are scattered through the local fresh-water marshes.

Currituck Inlet closed in the 1820s, following construction of the Dismal Swamp Canal, which was initiated in 1793. Closure of the inlet was an unanticipated outcome of the diversion of the headwaters of the Northwest River by the canal. The new canal reduced the discharge through Currituck Inlet below that was needed to keep the inlet open. This was the first "improvement" to have an unanticipated outcome in Currituck Sound, and it was a big one. Nearly 200 square miles of brackish salt water and salt marsh were converted to freshwater lagoon and marsh. In 1897 this change was declared "one of the most important geological changes in the coastal United States of recent times."

As the water in the sound became fresh, vast beds of submerged aquatic vegetation (SAV) developed, bringing huge numbers of waterfowl. Ultimately it brought wealthy hunters and their hunting clubs and spawned the economy of market hunting among the less wealthy. The excesses of market hunting nationwide led to its being banned in 1916, but not before major damage had been done to the bird populations of the Atlantic Flyway.

A second "improvement" to the upper Currituck had the unanticipated outcome of destroying much of the SAV that supported the waterfowl. In the 1917–30 interval when the Army Corps of Engineers enlarged the Albemarle-Chesapeake section of the Intracoastal Waterway, millions of cubic yards of dredge spoil were pumped into the upper end of Currituck Sound; this caused serious turbidity problems that essentially shaded out the SAV. In addition, a navigation lock was removed at Great Bridge, allowing pollution and salt water from Norfolk Harbor to enter Currituck Sound. Restoration of a lock at Great Bridge in 1932 initiated the recovery of the SAV, which was in good condition by the 1950s.

Unfortunately, a new threat to SAV in upper Currituck Sound appeared in the mid 1960s. Eurasian water milfoil (a noxious exotic plant) appeared near Knotts Island, and by 1970 virtually the entire sound (100,000 acres) plus the 24,000 acres of Back Bay in Virginia were blanketed with milfoil rather than with the wildlife-sustaining SAV. The milfoil outbreak combined with changes wrought by other "improvements" to decimate the black bass fishery. That fishery had boomed briefly in the 1970s, but declined drastically as the sound became turbid and salty. By 1988 virtually all the SAV had disappeared and the popular large-mouth black bass population was close to extinction. The problem was caused by high and variable salt content of the sound brought on by five years of drought, Virginia's pumping of ocean water into Back Bay, intrusion of salt water through Virginia Beach Canal No. 2 during northeast storms, and withdrawals of water from the Northwest River for domestic use. All of these except the drought were additional unanticipated outcomes of human attempts to "improve" the water supply quality and land drainage of the burgeoning Southside Virginia area.

By 1998 Currituck's water had freshened and some SAV had returned to both Currituck and Back Bay. These changes resulted from heavy rainfall, a cessation of the pumping of salt water into Back Bay, and a decline in the number of severe northeast storms. However, a year or so of drought or a recurrence of several severe northeast storms could cause the SAV to decline again, bringing with it the decline of the recently improved freshwater fishing.

The 8,646-acre Mackay Island National Wildlife Refuge (NWR) is situated in the extreme northeastern corner of North Carolina (7,772 acres) and in the extreme southeastern corner of Virginia (874 acres). If you are traveling from Virginia, go to Princess Anne Road (VA 615) in Virginia Beach and continue south to the North Carolina state line. Follow NC 615 about one mile. The entrance to the refuge office/visitor contact station is on your right.

If you are traveling from any point in North Carolina, go to the village of Currituck on NC 168 and take the Currituck Sound Ferry to Knotts Island. The ferry is free and has capacity for 18 cars (motor homes and travel trailers are allowed). It departs the Currituck Courthouse landing at 6 A.M., 9 A.M., 11 A.M., 1 P.M., 3:30 P.M. and 5:30 P.M., seven days a week. (Should you be unable to board the ferry, a land route is described at the end of the tour description). To ensure a spot on the ferry, arrive about twenty to thirty minutes before departure time.

From the Knotts Island Ferry landing, travel north on NC 615 for about 8.1 miles. The entrance to the refuge office/visitor contact station will be on the left side of the road. This contact station is normally open from 8 A.M. to 4 P.M., Monday through Friday. By all means, stop at the visitor station and secure the excellent brochure, map, and bird list and the latest information on refuge activities.

Even though you will be crossing Currituck Sound at its northern end, the forty-five-minute ferry ride of about 5 nautical miles will provide you an opportunity to grasp the vast size and unique nature of Currituck Sound—a body of water about 100,000 acres in size, 34 miles long, with an average depth of only 5 feet. Back Bay in Virginia is actually the northern tip of Currituck Sound and thus adds 24,000 acres, with an average depth of 4 feet, to the above figures.

Situated as it is at the north end of Currituck Sound, Mackay Island Refuge is strategically positioned along the Atlantic Flyway, making it an important wintering area for thousands of ducks, geese, and swans during the fall and winter. It was established primarily as a wintering ground for greater snow geese and other migratory waterfowl, but many other wildlife species occur here as well. They include wading birds, shorebirds, songbirds, mammals (such as raccoon, fox, white-tailed deer, muskrat, nutria, and otter), and reptiles and amphibians. Fresh- and brackish-water fishes of several species occur in the refuge's impoundments (ponds), canals, and bays. About 74 percent of the refuge consists of slightly brackish marsh habitat dominated by cattail, black needlerush, and giant cordgrass.

The history of Mackay Island is almost as interesting as that of the sound in which it sits. The island was owned by several prominent people prior to its acquisition by the U.S. Fish and Wildlife Service in 1960. A hunting club was located there in the early 1900s; one of its members was the famous North Carolina novelist, Thomas Dixon. In 1918 Joseph P. Knapp, a wealthy publisher, insurance magnate, and philanthropist, purchased the property. Knapp later enlarged his holdings by purchasing many additional small tracts, especially in the marsh areas.

Knapp was a generous philanthropist. He provided gifts to the Currituck County school system and was an early wildlife conservationist. He was the founder of the More Game Birds in America organization, which eventually became Ducks Unlimited, Inc., a world renowned private waterfowl conservation organization. In the 1930s Knapp produced as many as 35,000 ducks per year at his Mackay Island property for release into the wild. These efforts were an attempt to help restore the national population of waterfowl, which had plummeted during the market hunting and dust bowl eras. Knapp also invited scientists to study Currituck Sound's environmental problems in the 1920s, when the construction of the Intracoastal Waterway brought destruction to the waterfowl habitat.

Modern Mackay Island

On your visit to the Mackay Island National Wildlife Refuge, you will see how Joseph Knapp's legacy has been sustained through the practice of modifying habitats for wildlife. The most obvious of these modifications are the impoundments constructed in marshes. These systems give the wildlife managers effective control over water levels. Such control is necessary because Currituck Sound/Back Bay has a unique wind-driven system of tides rather than the astronomical tidal systems found in most coastal estuaries. Strong northerly winds blow the water out of Currituck Sound, often dropping its level by 2 feet or more. Conversely, strong southerly winds blow water into Currituck Sound, resulting in tides of 1 to 2 feet above the normal sound level. These wind tides can persist for a few hours or several days or weeks. Of course, strong northerlies occur more often in winter, and the southerlies occur more often in summer. These wind tides provide an important "flushing" of the sound, ridding it of excess nutrients and pollutants and moving a vast quantity of detrital materials into Albemarle and Pamlico Sounds. This plant debris is an important food source to the ecosystem in these lower sounds.

Impoundments permit control of water levels to favor the growth of food or cover plants for waterfowl, other nesting birds, muskrats, and so on. Flooding of food-producing areas is often used to make the food available to wintering waterfowl.

You will see wood duck nesting boxes at several sites on the refuge. The natural hollows in trees that "woodies" prefer for nesting are in short supply because there are few old hardwood trees in the area. The timber was cut prior to 1915 and again in the late 1950s just before the U.S. Fish and Wildlife Service acquired the property. Nest boxes are a practical and effective way to increase nesting opportunities for wood ducks. You will also see nesting platforms that have been placed to facilitate nesting by ospreys.

An important aspect of marsh management at the refuge is the use of fire. Each year refuge staff burn about 1,500 acres of marsh habitat. This reduces the buildup of marsh peat and prevents invasion by woody shrubs and trees. It also opens the marsh, permitting greater access for snow geese, other waterfowl, and other wildlife to feed in the area. Snow geese are noted for their habit of foraging on plant roots in these open marsh areas (Figure 25).

The Mackay Island staff have recorded 182 species of birds on the refuge. These

FIGURE 25. Snow geese feeding at Mackay Island. (Photo courtesy of U.S. Fish and
Wildlife Service)

birds are not all at the refuge all the time; but with the great variety of habitats, you
should be able to see a significant variety in one day. Be sure to bring your
binoculars and a bird book. Bring your camera also; telephoto lenses will give the
best results.

Where to See Wildlife

The best locations from which to see wildlife are along the Marsh Causeway (NC
615), Mackay Island Road, and Refuge Trails A, B, and C. Trail A is a 0.3-mile loop
off the Marsh Causeway and is open year round. Trail B, the Mackay Island Trail, is
a 3.8-mile loop around the East Pool. Trail C, the Live Oak Point Trail, is a 6.5-mile
loop around all three refuge impoundments. Trails B and C trailheads are on the
Mackay Island Road at the second gate (Dike Gate). These trails are open only
from March 15 through October 15. Activities permitted on the trails are wildlife
viewing, photography, hiking, and bicycling (mountain bikes recommended).

All portions of the refuge are open to wildlife-dependent recreation from March
15 through October 15. However, major portions of the refuge are seasonally closed
to all public use from October 16 through March 14 to provide wildlife rest areas.
Special "Open Road Days" are held throughout the year when visitors may drive
the dike and trail system around the impoundment to view wildlife.

Year-round public use, as indicated, is permitted in the following portions of the
refuge: (1) Corey's Ditch and the canal on the north side of the Marsh Causeway

FIGURE 26. Bank fishing at Mackay Island. (Photo courtesy of U.S. Fish and Wildlife Service)

(the section of NC 615 that crosses the Great Marsh) are open to fishing and crab-bing, and (2) Mackay Island Road from its junction with NC 615 to the Dike Gate.

Sport fishing is allowed in all canals, bays, and ponds from March 15 through October 15. The Marsh Causeway (NC 615) and the bridge at Corey's Ditch are open all year to fishing and crabbing from the bridge and the north side road shoulder. Mackay Island Road (to the Dike Gate) is open all year to bank fishing (Figure 26). Commercial fishing, trot lines, eel and crab pots, bait traps, and nets are pro-hibited. On the refuge, a North Carolina fishing license is required to fish in North Carolina waters and a Virginia fishing license is required to fish in Virginia waters. The refuge impoundments (East Pool, Middle Pool, and West Pool) are open to bank fishing only from March 15 through October 15 each year.

All refuge waters, ponds, and bays are closed to boating from October 16 through March 14. A launching ramp for small boats is located on the Mackay Island Road for use at other times. For summer visits, bring your canoe or kayak and you can double your wildlife viewing fun.

Public deer hunts (by permit only) are conducted during the fall (September–December). Additional hunting information may be obtained by calling the refuge office in early to mid-August.

Alternate Route to Mackay Island NWR

In the event you miss the ferry at Currituck, an alternate route is available. Drive north on NC 168 to the Virginia state line (12 miles). Proceed north on VA 168

(Battlefield Boulevard) for 2 miles to Gallbush Road on the right. Turn right (east) on Gallbush Road, and proceed 1.7 miles to its junction with Indian Creek Road. Turn right (east) on Indian Creek Road, and proceed 3.2 miles to the intersection with Blackwater Road. Turn left (north) on Blackwater Road, and go 1.8 miles to Pungo Ferry Road. Turn right (east) on Pungo Ferry Road, and go 2.8 miles to the intersection with Princess Anne Road (VA 615). Turn right (south) on Princess Anne Road, and you are now on the approach to Mackay Island NWR, as described above for Virginia. Go 6 miles to the North Carolina state line, plus 1 mile to the refuge office on your right.

Should you need, or choose, to travel this alternate route, your time will not be wasted because you will be able to observe the explosive urban growth that is now overrunning Currituck County, North Carolina, and the southeastern section of Virginia, as well as the Currituck Sound tributaries that drain these developments. You may ponder the unanticipated outcomes of this phase of development. You will see two wetland mitigation projects being developed (as of 1998) in connection with the widening of NC 168. These are located about 3.5 miles north of Currituck and just south of Sligo; one is on the west side of NC 168 and the other on the east side slightly further north.

After you enter Virginia on NC/VA 168 you will cross the Northwest River, one of Currituck Sound's major tributaries. On Blackwater Road you will cross Blackwater Creek, a tributary of the North Landing River. On Pungo Ferry Road you will cross the North Landing River (and the Albemarle-Chesapeake section of the Intracoastal Waterway), another of Currituck Sound's main tributaries.

The Pungo Ferry has been replaced with a high-rise bridge over the North Landing River, which gives you an excellent, though brief, view of the oxbows created in constructing the Intracoastal Waterway. The extensive wetlands you see at this crossing are now largely dedicated to conservation uses. On the alternate route you will also pass the entrance to Northwest River Park on Indian Creek Road. This large swampland park is operated by the City of Chesapeake and is one of a few access points on the Northwest River.

You can return to Currituck village by way of the ferry after your refuge visit. Or conversely, if you use the ferry to reach Knotts Island, you can follow the alternate land route in reverse to return to Currituck.

For additional information about the refuge, write or call Mackay Island National Wildlife Refuge, P.O. Box 39, Knotts Island, NC 27950-0039; 252-429-3100.

The author gratefully acknowledges the assistance of the personnel of the Mackay Island National Wildlife Refuge in preparing this chapter and for permission to use the map and to reproduce here excerpted text from the refuge brochure.

Wetlands, Swamps, and Forests

Merchants Millpond to the Great Dismal Swamp

HENRY C. HAMMOND
AND PENNY LEARY-SMITH

This 75-mile tour takes you from the Piedmont's seaward edge in Weldon to one of the most famous swamps in the United States—the Great Dismal. Along the way you will see the Coastal Plain of eastern North Carolina, where water, soil, and plants form habitats of primeval beauty. You will pass through towns that preserve the architectural heritage of the river-dependent culture of early European settlers of the Coastal Plain and the current uses that humans make of these drainage-challenged soils.

The major lesson you can learn from this tour is how water and soil control landforms and the natural habitats they sustain. Seemingly minor differences in elevation and soil type have major effects on vegetation. You will see how water plays a central role in wetlands, how it interacts with plants and soils to take on colors that are distinctive of its environmental origins, and how Coastal Plain residents have managed this water over the last 230 years of history in this region. Finally, you will learn the difference between the Piedmont and Coastal Plain sections of our state because when you turn east off of Interstate 95 onto US 158 you truly and figuratively have entered the Coastal Plain and are headed toward the ocean. This tour passes through six Coastal Plain counties—Halifax, Northampton, Hertford, Gates, Pasquotank, and Camden—plus a small sojourn into the Commonwealth of Virginia. It can be done in one long day, although some of the stops may inspire you to take a more leisurely pace or to come back later for something you missed.

A. Weldon Landing: Border between the Piedmont and the Coastal Plain

The "fall line" between the Piedmont and the Coastal Plain is visible from the North Carolina Wildlife Access boat ramp on the Roanoke River at Weldon. Look

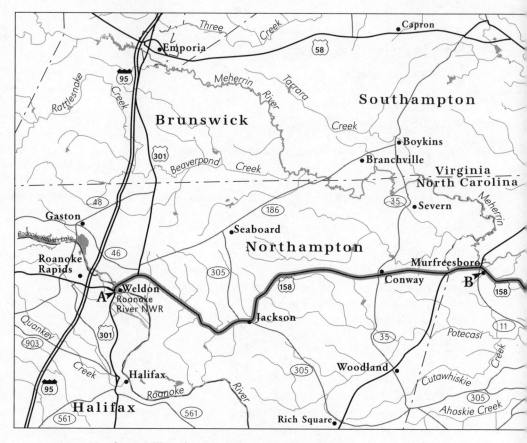

FIGURE 27. Merchants Millpond to Great Dismal Swamp tour route

upstream and you will see a highway bridge, a railroad bridge, and parts of another old bridge, as well as many rocks and rapids in the river. Look downstream and you will see a broad flat river, few rocks, steep banks, and large hardwood trees overhanging the water. The river is generally clear, except for a red tint picked up from the red clay of upstream landscapes. This is the area of the river where rockfish come to spawn in the spring. Here and at Halifax are the last places the Roanoke can be crossed during low water without a boat or a bridge. We know that trails used by Native Americans came to this point on both sides of the river, and that our ancestors used these trails as a basis for the roads and railroads of today. By the year 1830, Weldon was the terminus for four railroad lines, one canal, and one of the few interstate roads. You had to go through Weldon to go anywhere.

Back on US 158 cross the Roanoke and head into Northampton County. The land here is sandy and ever so slightly rolling. It has been cleared and tilled repeatedly, for these are some of the oldest farms in America. Note how much the

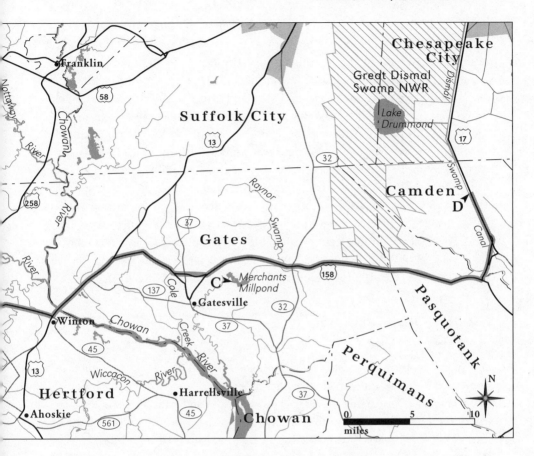

farms vary in size, age, and condition. The soils also vary greatly—ranging in color from black to tan to chalk white. Next you will pass through Jackson, with its wonderful old Greek Revival courthouse, and on to Conway and Murfreesboro.

B. Murfreesboro

If you choose to stop in Murfreesboro, take NC 158 Business into the downtown. This town has more colonial homes and buildings than most others in eastern North Carolina. Wander around—you won't get lost; look for the house with the gingerbread trim. When you are ready to move on, turn left on US 258 and go north to the rest area. During this short drive you will have crossed over the west leg of the Meherrin River. You actually may not have noticed it, for it is 50 feet below the level of the road. Decades ago, the Meherrin was used to move farm commodities to market. Along the banks of this river you can find fossils. One of the unusual plants that grows on these steep banks is mountain laurel. In the spring when this is in bloom you might think that you are hundreds of miles west, as this is a remnant of the flora, now mostly restricted to the mountains, left behind in this cool valley as the climate warmed after the last period of glaciation.

Drive back to us 158 and east through Mapleton to just outside of Winton. There us 158 joins with us 13 to cross over the Chowan River into Gates County. The Chowan at this point is wide and deep and carries a heavy load of silt from the farms and forestry clearings upstream. Several miles northeast of the Chowan, us 158 turns off to the right toward Roduco. Farther along, on the edges of fields, you will begin to see a mix of swampland trees, vines, and shrubs. All of these species are adapted to wet soil. As you near the third stop, the species composition of the forest changes to include more of those trees that grow in standing water. You should begin seeing brown signs pointing the way and picture signs, with binoculars, saying, "Wildlife Viewing Area." Turn right on sr 1400 and about a mile down you will come to the canoe access area of Merchants Millpond State Park.

c. Merchants Millpond State Park

This is truly a forest in a lake (Figure 28). The lake is artificial, in that there is a dam and spillway, but it has existed for more than 175 years and therefore supports unusually mature swamp forests. In earlier times there was a mill, but this is not so important now. Notice that the large cypress, tupelo, and gum trees and the lake together create a beautiful parklike sanctuary. For this part of the tour you must leave your car and travel by canoe across the lake and back up the streams that feed it. Fortunately, travel by canoe forces you to focus your attention on nature. The blend of physical and mental effort, along with the sounds of nature, makes this trip almost spiritual.

The geology of this area is very stable and the sediment on the lake bottom both seals the lake and provides important substrate for plants and animals. These same sediments are also responsible for the color and acidity of the water. The lake bottom is where turtles and over a dozen species of frogs burrow and rest for the winter. Many fish also depend on lake sediments for food and protection. The dominant trees growing out of the lake are bald cypress and tupelo gum—some of these trees are 500 to 1,000 years old.

The bald cypress is a special tree and is the essence of Merchants Millpond's uniqueness. Cypress trees can stand in water all the time, except that the seeds must be dry for part of the first year. Thus, the presence of cypress in the middle of the lake indicates that at some time in the past the lake dried up enough for cypress seeds to sprout and start growing. If you could peel the bark off of a cypress tree (please don't try), you would see that it grows in a slow-ascending spiral; one

FIGURE 28. Merchants Millpond—a forest in a lake. (Photo courtesy of Merchants Millpond State Park)

reason that these trees live so long is that they twist when they bend. Spanish moss hangs from most of the trees in this forest, and the sunlight that filters through this gray lace seems to soften every view. The cypress "knees" and flared trunks form islands for lots of other smaller plants to grow above the water. The variety of ferns and wildflowers is outstanding. The colors in the spring and fall are spectacular, as is the variety of types of plants, ranging from the tiny duckweed, water fern, and liverworts that float on the surface of the water (sometimes blanketing huge portions of the lake) to the largest tupelo gum that three men together can't reach around. The stumps of these giants support swamp rose, royal ferns, and red maples above the water. The fragrances and smells of this place are almost as diverse as the plants.

Animals abound at Merchants Millpond. From insects (we highly recommend that you use insect repellent and examine yourself for ticks after a visit) to the elusive bobcat—Merchants Millpond has it all. The fishing is varied, and we wonder if you will catch that 15-pound bass that got away last time we were there. Sunfish, bream, warmouth, bowfin, long-nosed gar, and the occasional pickerel are to be found. Reptiles and amphibians—toads, frogs, turtles, and snakes—provide excitement with their antics and calls. There are always great blue herons and wood ducks lurking about in the pond (Figure 29). At dusk owls, chuck-will's-widows, and whippoorwills will serenade you to sleep if you decide to camp over. Every

FIGURE 29. Great blue heron in the millpond. (Photo courtesy of Merchants Millpond State Park)

season on the pond is different. If you visit in winter you will learn that the bald cypress trees lose their needles—the only North Carolina conifer that does.

The park is open year-round and offers rental canoes, fishing, and camping for both families and groups. Information on the availability of these facilities can be obtained from the park office in Gatesville. The telephone number is 252-357-1191.

D. Dismal Swamp Canal

After you leave Merchants Millpond get back on US 158 and drive east. In about 7 miles you will pass through the crossroads town of Sunbury. About 15 miles farther on you will see signs directing you to US 17 North (this is just outside Morgans Corner). You will have noticed by now that the farm fields are bigger—some seem to stretch all the way to the horizon like a giant quilt of different rectangles. Crops grown in these counties vary from peanuts to sunflowers to aromatic sage (recognizable as huge purple flower beds). After traveling on US 17 for several miles you will see a large bridge rising high out of the farm fields. As you start up over the bridge you will probably notice that it seems to span only a narrow grove of trees. But you may be able to discern a reflection from something watery in that grove. This is the Dismal Swamp Canal. A large sailboat with a very tall mast may be passing just beneath you. Some distance on, you will come to the Dismal Swamp Canal Welcome Center on the left side of the highway.

Stop here: this is a very interesting place. Boats on the waterway stop at a 150-foot dock, and you can park and enjoy a picnic if you brought one. From the dock you will be able to see a very straight canal stretching out in both directions. The color of the water is similar to that of Merchants Millpond, but this seems clearer. The water level in the canal is approximately 8 feet above sea level. At this point you will probably start wondering how oceangoing boats got this high up. Where did the water come from to lift them?

The boats got here through a set of locks. You can visit the lock near South Mills to see how a heavy boat can be lifted that 8 feet. A simple explanation is that the boat enters into a three-sided box. The gate then closes behind it and water is pumped into the box, raising the water level to the level of the waterway. The reverse happens at the other end of the canal to lower the boat back down to the Elizabeth River for transit to the Chesapeake Bay.

So where does the water come from that is in the canal? The water comes from Lake Drummond, which is in Virginia. Lake Drummond and the Great Dismal Swamp form a pocosin (a lake on a hill). The lake is some 20 feet above sea level. A feeder ditch was dug from the lake to the canal to keep it filled. This was done over 100 years ago. Numerous stories and legends have been born out of the fascinating history of the Dismal Swamp and its canal.

Did George Washington once own part of the Great Dismal Swamp? Did slaves from the South escape along the canal? Did young couples elope out of Virginia along the canal to get married in North Carolina? Did the inspiration for "Show Boat" actually come from a floating theater that once traveled the canal? Was the tea-colored water of Lake Drummond and the canal so good that it was sold as the shipboard water of choice for passage back to the old world? The answer to all these questions is yes. You must come back sometime to hear the stories.

What kind of boats did they have back then? There were some steam boats but most cargo was loaded on a barge and then towed with a long rope by oxen or mules walking along a road or tow path on the banks of the canal. A single horse can tow a very large barge as compared with pulling a wagon or cart along a rough muddy road.

If you have a canoe with you, it is great fun to paddle along this canal and listen to the wind through the trees that have been left along the banks of the canal for shade and erosion protection. Along the feeder ditch and other secondary canals to the west you may see or hear all kinds of wildlife including black bears and bobcats. The west side of the canal is protected as a natural area in the form of the Great Dismal Swamp National Wildlife Refuge: 250 square miles. Some old logging roads and canals are the only access from this side into this wet and wonderful wilderness, but the road access into the wildlife refuge is from the Virginia side.

Lower Roanoke River Floodplain

Swamps and Wetlands

IDA PHILLIPS LYNCH
AND J. MERRILL LYNCH

This 45-mile tour will take you to one of the wildest areas in the state, the lower Roanoke River floodplain—a 3- to 5-mile-wide water-dominated wilderness that is essentially roadless yet accessible by several road crossings and boat landings. This area is one of the five major brownwater ecosystems in the Southeast, and it contains the largest least-disturbed, intact bottomland hardwood forest ecosystem remaining in the mid-Atlantic region.

You will see forests, landforms, wildlife, and birds, although what you will see of the last two depends on the time of year you visit. Forests range all the way from bottomland forest types and large backswamps to vast tracts of bald cypress and water tupelo swamp forests. Landforms in the floodplain include natural levees, swamp sloughs (river meander depressions), low and high ridges separated by swales, and ancient river channels. Two hundred and fourteen bird species, including eighty-eight breeding species (forty-four of these being Neotropical migrants) give the Roanoke floodplain the highest diversity of birds in the North Carolina Coastal Plain. These species include a large resident wood duck population, wintering waterfowl such as mallards and black ducks, and a number of land birds, including the federally listed endangered bald eagle. The Roanoke's rich swamp forests and bottomlands boast some of the state's greatest numbers of white-tailed deer and wild turkey, as well as thriving populations of black bear, river otter, and bobcat.

Birds typical of rich floodplain forests are common here during the breeding season, including Louisiana waterthrush, American redstart, Kentucky warbler, red-eyed and yellow-throated vireos, great-crested and Acadian flycatchers, and six species of woodpeckers. Some of the larger birds that are easily observed on the Roanoke are the barred owl, red-shouldered hawk, and great blue heron. More uncommon species that are found in the floodplain include Swainson's and cerulean warblers and Mississippi kite.

The seasons offer a variety of experiences in the floodplain. Spring brings

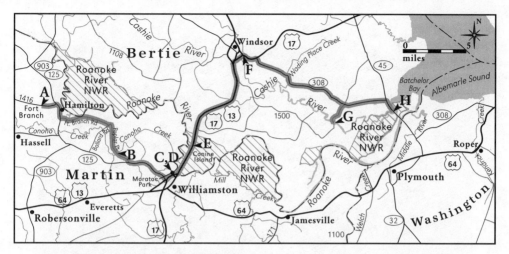

FIGURE 30. Lower Roanoke River tour route

wildflowers, great fishing, and lots of birds. May is the best month for seeing nesting songbirds. Summer offers snakes, turtles, bats, and all kinds of bugs. Fall is a great time for viewing migrating birds. Winter eliminates the bugs, and there are good views and a lower water level for easier hiking. Canoeing and kayaking are the best ways to see this area and its wildlife because much of the land is intermittently under water. Be aware that most of the public lands are open to hunting and that this is a popular hunting area.

The most important lesson you can learn on this tour is how hydrology affects the floodplain landscape and its ecology. For example, natural levees along the channel are better drained than adjacent sloughs and contain a diverse mixture of bottomland hardwood trees, whereas lower areas that are flooded for longer periods of time are dominated by bald cypress and water tupelo. Flooding is the engine that drives this ecosystem. The river waters carry nutrients for the flora and fauna, deposit sediments, and cycle energy.

We encourage you to explore the Roanoke on foot or in a boat, as this offers you the best chance to see the area's abundant wildlife. Early morning and late afternoon are the best times of day for wildlife observation. You can also learn how landscapes like this extraordinary floodplain have been conserved for the enjoyment of future generations. In the Lower Roanoke, for example, a number of public and private groups and individuals, including the Bertie and Martin County Commissioners, the North Carolina Wildlife Resources Commission, the U.S. Fish and Wildlife Service, The Nature Conservancy, and the North Carolina Wildlife Federation, have worked together to protect 50,000 acres in the river floodplain along a 137-mile river corridor. Some major highlights in this protection process

FIGURE 31. Lower Roanoke River and floodplain. (Photo courtesy of North Carolina Nature Conservancy)

include the creation of the Roanoke River National Wildlife Refuge and the state-owned Roanoke River Wetlands in 1990, and a 1994 agreement between Georgia-Pacific Corporation and The Nature Conservancy to jointly manage and protect approximately 21,000 acres in the floodplain that are owned by Georgia-Pacific.

This tour can be made in either direction, but we suggest that you start at Hamilton and work your way down to the mouth of the river so that you travel downstream with the river current and can see how the river floodplain slowly widens toward the mouth (Figure 31).

Please note that all of the sites on the tour are in the floodplain, and some of them are subject to fluctuating water levels. Some of the sites will not be walkable when flooded and some canoeing routes may be shallow or dangerous at various times of year. Please use your best judgment before venturing into these areas. Also, some of the areas are open to hunting, so be aware of hunting schedules before visiting the Conoho Game Lands and the Roanoke River National Wildlife Refuge.

At the time of this writing, there were no public facilities on any of the publicly owned lands on the Roanoke. There are public boat landings at the river crossings on US 258, downstream on US 17 at Williamston, and near the river mouth below Plymouth on NC 45. The Cashie River, Devil's Gut, Gardner Creek, and Conoho Creek offer great canoeing opportunities. The main channel of the Roanoke River has a much stronger current than these streams. Be aware that it can be dangerous to boat in the main channel, particularly during flood stage.

A. Fort Branch

The tour begins at Fort Branch, located on Fort Branch Road (SR 1416), 2.5 miles east of Hamilton. Situated on the outside portion of a large bend of the Roanoke River, this fort was used during the Civil War to defend the upstream towns and plantations from Union gunboats. The strategic importance of the site is readily evident; the high bluffs offer a clear, unobstructed view of the river channel for at least a mile downstream and provided an excellent site for the installation of cannons and earthworks. Today, Fort Branch is owned and operated as a private tourist attraction and is open from April through November on Saturdays and Sundays from 1:30 P.M. to 5:30 P.M.

The fort is located in a natural area distinguished by a series of high (70-foot) bluffs and steeply sloping ravines adjacent to the river channel. These bluffs are remnants of ancient ocean sediments that have been eroded by the river. The rugged topography resembles river bluffs of the Piedmont and mountains. The river channel is actively cutting into the valley wall, causing a series of undercut bluffs and exposing underlying fossil-rich marl deposits.

The streams draining the upland terrace have eroded a series of steep ravines adjacent to a narrow floodplain with natural levees along the river. Natural levees are elevated berms or ridges adjacent to river channels that are formed over years of floods carrying suspended sediments over the riverbanks. This flooding builds successive layers of sediment on the banks, forming levees that are often 10 to 15 feet higher than the lower portions of the floodplain surface.

The ravines at Fort Branch harbor a beech–mixed hardwoods plant community that contains many species more typical of the Piedmont and mountains. Fort Branch is home to an unusually large population of maidenhair fern.

B. Optional Canoeing on Conoho Creek off Poplar Point Road

From Fort Branch, head east on Fort Branch Road. After 2.2 miles, you will intersect Ballard Road; turn left. This road eventually veers to the right and becomes Poplar Point Road. After driving 6.8 miles from the intersection of Fort Branch and Ballard, you will cross a bridge over Conoho Creek. There is a sandy pull-off area on the left side of the road just past the bridge. You can park here and carry your canoe or kayak down to the creek beneath the bridge. This blackwater stream is great for paddling, but during dry spells, submerged and downed trees can present a challenge.

From its headwaters near Hamilton, Conoho Creek flows 30 miles east and south through the 7,000-acre Conoho Swamp before joining the Roanoke River north of Williamston. The lower end of Conoho Creek constitutes an unusual natural community type known as a backwater stream. These deeply flooded swamp forests are created when natural levees along the river act as dams and cause water to back up along the lower reaches of tributary streams.

The north-facing slopes along the creek are covered by mixed hardwood forests that are home to the state's only population of magnolia vine, a rare vine that occurs in a relict population in the southeastern United States. These forests also support other rare plant species and species typically found in the Piedmont region.

The lower section of Conoho Creek is deeply flooded, 6 to 10 feet deep, and contains an extensive cypress-gum swamp distinguished by numerous old remnant tupelo (or "gum") and bald cypress trees exceeding 30 inches in diameter (Figure 32). The area resembles a small version of Merchants Millpond, as the cypress is heavily festooned with Spanish moss and the pondlike area beneath the canopy is covered in dense beds of vegetation. These habitats provide good foraging and nesting areas for mammals such as river otter, mink, and weasel. Wood ducks, wild turkeys, and Neotropical migratory songbirds, including prothonotary warbler, northern parula, and wood thrush, nest here.

FIGURE 32. Cypress-gum swamp. (Photo courtesy of North Carolina Nature Conservancy)

The Wildlife Resources Commission and The Nature Conservancy have worked together to protect over 1,400 acres of Conoho Creek and swamp; these are managed as the Roanoke River Wetlands/Game Lands. Please note that this area is open to hunting.

c. Moratoc Park, Williamston

Back on Poplar Point Road, drive 1.2 miles until the road intersects NC 125; turn left and drive to Williamston. After 3.4 miles you will intersect US 17 North Business at the stoplight; turn left and drive down Main Street in Williamston. After 0.7 miles, turn left at the sign for Moratoc Park and take another immediate left into the parking area. Farther on toward the park, the road splits: the left fork goes to the Roanoke River Game Lands described in the next section and the right fork takes you to Moratoc Park.

Moratoc Park, an 18-acre park owned by Martin County, includes a large riverside banquet hall that is fashioned after the old warehouses once plentiful along the river and a pier overlooking the river. The park is open from sunrise to sunset and features fishing access, picnic tables, and open greenway areas, but there are no public restrooms.

From the park, you can look across the river to a portion of the Roanoke River National Wildlife Refuge containing a levee forest of ash, sycamore, and elm. Farther upstream, the land along the left bank is owned by the North Carolina Wildlife Resources Commission.

A Wildlife Commission public boat landing is located about 0.4 miles east of the park. Adventurous small boaters can put in at the landing and paddle upstream about 1.4 miles and enter Conoho Creek on the left bank. Do not attempt this when the river is flooding!

D. Roanoke River Wetlands/Game Lands

This particular section of the Roanoke River floodplain offers one of the few easy opportunities to explore the publicly owned land in this immense natural area on foot. To get to the game lands, drive down the previously described fork and park in the dirt parking area, making sure not to block the gates.

If you walk past either gate, you will have a chance to walk several miles down old logging roads and see a cross-section of river floodplain habitats, including backswamp deposits and natural levees. This area offers good hiking, birding, and mountain biking. If you visit this popular hunting area during deer season, be sure to wear blaze orange, or best of all, schedule your trip for Sunday, when hunting is not allowed.

Backswamps are usually large, poorly drained, oval-shaped depressions located immediately behind natural levees. They are formed when the finer suspended sediments (clays) carried by river floodwaters are deposited in the slack water ponded between the natural levees and the valley wall of the first terrace. Clays are the last particles to settle out during flooding. Backswamps, being lower than the adjacent levees and sheltered from floodwaters, act as settling ponds for these fine sediments.

Backswamps have very high water tables and are often flooded for six months or more at depths ranging up to 7 feet. They range in size from small bodies several acres in extent, to enormous deposits encompassing several thousand acres. The forest canopy in backswamps is dominated by two species adapted to extreme flooding conditions: bald cypress and water tupelo.

Although backswamps are not accessible to terrestrial mammals during much of the year because of the flooding, they are home to an abundance of birdlife. These game lands are heavily used as feeding and roosting areas by numerous species of waterfowl, including mallard, black duck, and wood duck. Throughout the year, birders will also have a chance to see barred owl, waterfowl, woodpeckers (pileated, red-bellied, and downy), and white-breasted nuthatch. During the spring, the game lands are inhabited by breeding Neotropical migrants such as warblers, tanagers, vireos, thrushes, and flycatchers.

Various aquatic turtles such as painted, yellow-bellied, and Florida cooter are common here, as are several species of water snakes and the poisonous cottonmouth. The game lands are home to bullfrog, southern leopard frog, southern cricket frog, and several species of tree frog.

E. Conine Island, within Roanoke River National Wildlife Refuge

Head out of the Moratoc Park entrance and turn left on the paved road. Drive 0.4 miles and you will see a North Carolina Wildlife Resources Commission boat landing on the left. The road veers to the left and runs into the US 13/17 Bypass; turn left on the bypass. You will drive on a bridge over the Roanoke River (Figure 31) that takes you through the heart of the lower Roanoke River floodplain, which is about 5 miles wide. About 1.8 miles after getting on the bypass, look for a pullout on the right side of the road. There is another pullout about 0.8 miles from the first one, also on the right side of the road.

At either of these pullouts, you can park and walk past a gate about 0.75 miles into Conine Island, which is part of the 17,500-acre Roanoke River National Wildlife Refuge. This area offers good birding and wildlife observation. The roads are sometimes inaccessible because of seasonal flooding, so call the refuge office at 252-794-5326 for the latest information about access.

Conine Island is completely surrounded by the Roanoke River and Conine Creek. This tract contains several different natural communities, including alluvial flats, natural levees, and cypress-gum swamps. Alluvial flats are poorly drained natural communities that occur along the margins of some backswamp deposits and on the lower edges of natural levees. They are often inundated by floodwaters for up to five or six months during the late winter and early spring but are subject to annual summer drydown.

The forest canopy in alluvial flats is dominated by stands of overcup oak and water hickory with a few scattered bald cypress, green ash, and sycamore. There is little or no shrub layer except for scattered ironwood, deciduous holly, and Carolina water ash.

Because of the abundance of mast-producing trees (mast is the nuts of beech, oak, and similar trees), numerous mammals and birds inhabit alluvial flats. Common mammals in the flats include white-tailed deer and marsh rabbit. Wild turkey forage in these areas in the late summer and fall. When the area is flooded, often in the winter and spring, large numbers of wood ducks and other species of migratory waterfowl roost and feed in the flats. Common breeding birds found here include pileated woodpecker, barred owl, tufted titmouse, summer tanager, and white-breasted nuthatch.

F. Windsor Wetlands Boardwalk on the Cashie River

Get back on US 13/17 and head north toward Windsor. After about 8.5 miles, take the US 17 Bypass to the right. After 0.2 miles the road intersects King Street at a stoplight; turn left, then after about 1 mile, turn right on York Street. The road will curve around to the left and you will see a sign for the Cashie Wetlands Walk. You can park in the parking lot in front of the Freeman Hotel and walk out on the boardwalk. This boardwalk takes you through a swamp forest within the Cashie River floodplain. Interpretive signs discuss natural interactions in the forest and label the tree and shrub species.

The Cashie River is a blackwater stream that flows for 30 to 35 air miles diagonally across Bertie County where it joins the floodplain of the Roanoke River as it empties into Albemarle Sound. Southeast of Windsor the river's floodplain is approximately 1 mile wide. Blackwater rivers differ from brownwater rivers like the Roanoke in that their headwaters are located wholly in the coastal plain. They generally carry much less sediment than brownwater rivers and are more acidic.

There is little or no evidence of a natural levee or ridges or swales within the Cashie River floodplain, but there are several floodplain islands in the narrower floodplain of Roquist Creek. These islands feature slightly higher ground and a mixed hardwood forest, as opposed to the cypress-gum swamp that covers the remaining 95 percent of the floodplain.

The Cashie Wetlands Walk takes you through a cypress-gum swamp. Because these natural communities are flooded for long periods, their vegetation is of low diversity, but they may provide important habitat for aquatic animals, like muskrat, and plants, such as pickerel weed. The swamp forest is dominated by a mixture of water tupelo, swamp tupelo, and bald cypress. The subcanopy features water ash, red maple, and American hornbeam.

If you would like to explore the Cashie further, free canoes are available at the beginning of the boardwalk. By paddling downstream, you will pass through land that is protected through an innovative partnership between The Nature Conservancy and Georgia-Pacific Corporation. In 1994, the private conservation group and the forest products company entered into a joint management agreement on 33 square miles (21,068 acres) in the lower Roanoke River floodplain. Through the agreement, the two groups are developing a joint ecosystem management plan governing any activity on the land, including timber harvesting. The agreement protects close to 1,300 acres along the Cashie River.

The Cashie Wetlands Walk is also the starting point for a proposed canoe trail that will have guide markers and camping platforms. The trail would run between Windsor and the Albemarle Sound and would allow people to explore the watery wilderness of the lower Roanoke River floodplain.

G. Sans Souci Ferry

Retrace your steps back on York Street, take a left on King Street, drive up to a stoplight, turn right on US 17 Bypass. Two miles after you merge with US 17/13, turn left on Woodard Road (SR 1500). After about 4.5 miles, you will arrive at the Sans Souci Ferry, which crosses the Cashie River. Blow your horn for the ferry.

The Sans Souci is one of the last surviving two-car inland ferries in North Carolina. The 3-mile trip is free and saves you a 20-mile drive to the other side of the river. The ferry does not appear on state maps and is primarily utilized by locals. Several osprey nests are located along the river near the ferry, and birds can often be seen fishing in the vicinity. The Sans Souci Ferry runs from March 16 to September 15, 6:30 A.M. to 6 P.M., and from September 16 to March 15, 6:45 A.M. to 5 P.M.

H. Mouth of the River and Conaby Creek Boat Launch

Once you cross over on the ferry, drive about 2 miles on Sans Souci Road. At the intersection with NC 308, turn right (east). Drive 3.2 miles, until you intersect NC

45 South/308 East; turn right and after about 1 mile, you will cross a bridge that takes you over the Roanoke, Middle, and Cashie Rivers.

The bridge offers a spectacular view of the lower portion of the Roanoke River floodplain. Numerous channels and creeks bisect the floodplain, making this area a paddlers' paradise. Be sure to bring a topographic map of the area if you plan to canoe here, because it is easy to get lost in the maze of streams.

Immediately after crossing the bridge, you will see a North Carolina Wildlife Resources Commission public boat landing on the right; 4.2 miles after getting on NC 45/308, turn left on Conaby Lane and you will see a smaller boat launch area on the right on Conaby Creek. This canoe and kayak access point for the Albemarle Region Canoe Trail offers you a chance to explore Conaby Creek by boat.

The Conaby Creek natural area is the best example in the Roanoke River floodplain of the swamp-pocosin forest natural community. This community is an interesting assemblage of alluvial swamp forest and pocosin shrub bog floral elements unknown elsewhere in the Roanoke floodplain. Alluvial swamp forest plants such as bald cypress, water tupelo, and swamp tupelo occur in association with typical pocosin species such as pond pine, Atlantic white cedar, sweet bay, red bay, and numerous evergreen shrubs. This is the only known pond pine and Atlantic white cedar population in the Roanoke River floodplain. Both species are more typically found in inland, nonalluvial pocosin wetlands. The natural area has a relatively undisturbed "wilderness" character and contains several old-growth (greater than seventy to eighty years old) stands of Atlantic white cedar and pond pine.

Conaby Creek is a scenic blackwater stream that contains a large population of freshwater fish, including largemouth bass, pickerel, crappie, warmouth, bluegill, white perch, and channel catfish.

Albemarle-Pamlico Peninsula

Pocosin Lakes and Wetlands

B. J. COPELAND
AND LUNDIE SPENCE

This 160-mile tour circumnavigates the central portion of the peninsula that separates Albemarle and Pamlico Sounds. The land of the peninsula lies only a few feet above sea level, and the plants and animals there are all adapted to wet soils and tannic waters. But this is a land of subtleties; only the observant can appreciate its precision, beauty, and mystique. Slight differences in the acidity of water in a lake can make it appear clear or brown tinged. Differences in elevation on the order of inches signal a change in the soil from sandy loam to peaty loam. The Albemarle-Pamlico peninsula is also a land of white-tailed deer, black bear, and river otters and home to the once extirpated red wolves—now reintroduced and making a comeback. It is also home to other unique plants and animals.

On the tour, you will see landscapes and bodies of water that have supported people for thousands of years. Algonquin people lived here for at least five thousand years, as shown by their abandoned cypress canoes just visible in the clear waters of Lake Phelps. Early colonial plantations, like Somerset, left their mark on the land: long canals, dug by slaves, barged rice to Albemarle Sound for international trade.

Along the tour you should contemplate what makes this part of North Carolina unique. Why are some waters in the rivers and lakes brown? What causes the water to be acidic (low pH)? Why do you find insect-eating pitcher plants in only a few places? What trees are uniquely adapted to staying wet around their roots and prized for timber used in houses and boats? What wildlife lives in the thick shrub bogs along the road?

North Carolina is fortunate to have state parks and national wildlife refuges where you can find the answers to these questions. This tour will lead you to Pettigrew State Park and Somerset Place Historic Site on Lake Phelps, Pocosin Lakes National Wildlife Refuge, the Partnership for the Sounds Visitor Center on the Scuppernong River in Columbia, and Lake Mattamuskeet near Fairfield.

The major thing you can learn from this tour is how water and land interact to

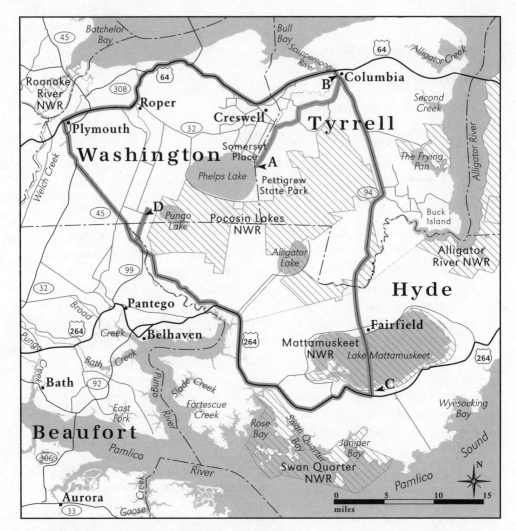

FIGURE 33. Albemarle-Pamlico peninsula tour route

form wetlands, lakes, and water courses that have sustained both wildlife and humans for thousands of years. Lakes dot the landscape of this area, and the best examples are visited on this tour. Adjacent wetlands (pocosins) support unique ecological assemblages. Sometimes called "shrub bogs," pocosins are marshy or boggy areas with poor drainage where peaty soils support scattered pond pines and a dense growth of shrubs (mostly evergreen). The term pocosin derives from an Algonquin word, "poquosin," meaning "swamp on a hill." Pocosins are found on the Atlantic Coastal Plain from southern Virginia to northern Florida. Waters that drain from them are very dark and acidic, due to the decomposition of woody matter, which produces tannin as a byproduct. Tannic acid lowers the pH of the water to acidic levels (pH 4.3 to 4.7—much below the neutral pH of 7).

The production of "swamp gas" is another interesting feature of pocosins. Resulting from the decomposition of organic matter under flooded and anaerobic (oxygen-deprived) conditions, methane gas is released when the water table draws down during prolonged dry spells and the peat is exposed. In some cases, the exposed, dry peat will catch fire and burn for months, deep in the ground. In general, pocosin ecosystems are adapted to fire, and some emergent vegetation, such as pond pine, is not only tolerant of fire but actually depends upon it for the completion of life cycles. Pocosin soils are also slow to release nutrients, which limits the kind of vegetation that can grow here. Insectivorous plants, such as pitcher plants and sundews, actually are adapted to this low-nutrient condition; by attracting, catching, and "digesting" insects, these plants meet their nutritional requirements.

The water levels of lakes that form within pocosins are controlled by the balance between rainfall and evaporation. Because pocosin lakes are generally perched on peat deposits and are often higher than the surrounding area, surface water drains from the lakes—not into them. Groundwater discharge—that is, the subsurface loss of stored water, is rarely significant because water percolates so slowly through peat. However, the use of drainage canals over the past two hundred years has disrupted natural flows enough that sounds and rivers adjacent to the lakes can sometimes affect water levels.

This tour's initiation point is the Lake Phelps pocosin area near the small town of Roper. Roper is on US 64 about 8 miles east of Plymouth or 26 miles west of Columbia. Just east of Roper on US 64, turn south onto Newland Road; follow that road for the next 6.8 miles to the Tyson Farms headquarters area (three-way intersection). Notice the deep canals on both sides of this straight road that separate you from vast expanses of cropland. Shallower ditches entering the large roadside canals subdivide the fields and drain off the water. Depending on the season and year, you will see dark soils or green fields of wheat, corn, soybeans, and potatoes. Installation of these drainage ditches has allowed the conversion of the natural wetland pocosins into farmland. Deep plows have rooted out the pines and maples and gums, and abundant crops are grown in the rich peaty soils.

At the Tyson Farms junction (Shore Drive at mile 6.8, from Roper)—the first turn in the road—you can choose either Pocosin Lakes National Wildlife Refuge to the right or Pettigrew State Park straight ahead.

To explore Pettigrew State Park, drive past the Lake Phelps Volunteer Fire Department at mile 9.7 to the intersection and turn right onto Weston Road (mile 11.9). Turn left onto Mail Route Road (mile 13.6) and then right onto Creswell Road at mile 15.8. Follow the mile of old bald cypress trees on your left that line the Thirty Foot Canal, which drains Lake Phelps. Stop and take a look at the old canal (somewhat filled in now), which once floated barges that transported crops from the plantations around Lake Phelps to market via the Scuppernong River and Albemarle Sound. The bald cypress trees were planted along the canal over 180 years ago. Continue along the canal and turn left onto Lakeshore Drive at mile 16.4.

A. Pettigrew State Park and Somerset Place

Pettigrew State Park hugs the shore of Lake Phelps (Figure 34), which is a prime example of the pocosin lake ecosystem. The lake is surrounded by pocosins, some still in their natural state. Nearby Somerset Place has recently been restored to demonstrate plantation life in the area during the period 1785–1865. The plantation's 100,000 acres of rich soil supported a prosperous rice, corn, and wheat plantation tended by over 300 slaves.

Immediately after crossing the canal and to your right you will see the Pettigrew State Park entrance, office, boat ramp, and campgrounds. Be sure to visit the ranger's office—it is small, cramped, and friendly. Taxidermy specimens of black bear, otter, raccoons, and snapping turtles line the top cabinets. You will find local maps that mark walking paths, bicycle trails, colonial carriage roads, and newer paths. Take some of these hikes (or bring a bicycle) so that you may experience up close the beauty and uniqueness of the pocosin ecosystem. But be prepared for insects and poison ivy along the trails, and do wear closed-toed shoes.

Lake Phelps is slightly elliptical, a typical feature of pocosin lakes. Prevailing southwest winds often create short choppy waves on the 16,600-acre lake, and the shallow water (averaging about 4.5 feet) can be crystal clear in calm weather or full of sediment in summer squalls. Tannins contribute to the black-to-brown color and acidic pH. Near Moccasin Overlook—2 miles from park headquarters—huge buttressed cypress are reminiscent of rainforest giants. These cypress represent some of the oldest and largest specimens of this species in the Coastal Plain. Each season has its beauties. Fern glades are graced by hordes of white Atamasco-lilies during April, and the park superintendent challenges anyone to find a denser or more expansive natural flower garden than these. Backwater ditches hold yellow heads of spatterdock in May and June. Fishing in the summer yields largemouth bass, shellcrackers, and white and yellow perch. Birding is excellent during the fall and winter, when you will also see the varied fruits of the pocosin shrubs. This is a good place to explore during any season.

Over thirty dugout canoes crafted by Native Americans have been discovered in Lake Phelps. Although four have been recovered and are on display, the remainder have been left in their protected graves on the bottom of the lake. Using radio-

FIGURE 34. Lake Phelps and Pettigrew State Park. (Photo courtesy of Pettigrew State Park)

carbon dating methods, scientists have determined the ages of nineteen of the dugouts. The oldest is 4,400 years old and the youngest is 550; the average age is over 1,500 years.

You can easily hike (thirty minutes, or a mile from park headquarters) to Bee Tree Overlook to see one of the six canals leaving the lake via water control structures. These canals drain water from the north side of Lake Phelps, connecting to the Scuppernong River and leading to Albemarle Sound. Bee Tree Canal terminates at the overlook. Because the lake sits higher than the surrounding pocosin, the canals drain water away from the lake.

The buildings of Somerset Place sit on what was the edge of the lake. You can easily see the colonial shoreline in the transition from old cypress trees to relatively young ones. This is a clue that the size of the lake is shrinking. The Collins family, the original, eighteenth-century owners of the plantation, was responsible for the canals as well as the row of bald cypresses lining Thirty Foot Canal. Typical swamp chestnut oaks, sycamores, and shagbark hickories edge the main buildings.

B. Partnership for the Sounds Visitors Center, Columbia

To reach Columbia and be able to explore the mouth of the Scuppernong River, you must leave Pettigrew State Park via Thirty Foot Canal Road. Continue 4.6 miles to the intersection with Spruill Bridge Road, where you will turn left toward

Creswell. At mile 6.5, turn right on 6th Street to meet US 64 in Creswell; drive east on US 64 to Columbia. After crossing over the Scuppernong River bridge (about 8.4 miles from Creswell) you will see the Partnership for the Sounds Visitor Center.

The visitors center is a perfect family stop—clean restrooms, vending machines, maps, and advice on touring the area by car and boat. A concession company rents kayaks for more in-depth exploring.

To explore this pocosin-blackwater river system, follow the boardwalk that skirts the Scuppernong for about 0.5 miles. Nicely spaced signs explain the eco-system and help you focus on essential details of these wetlands. Special programs take place in the classroom built right in the swamp.

C. Lake Mattamuskeet

Lake Mattamuskeet is the largest pocosin lake in the southeastern United States— almost 40,000 acres. You can reach it on NC 94 from Columbia, just past the town of Fairfield. Continue across the causeway bisecting the lake to the refuge's grav-eled entrance on the left at mile 33.8. The causeway has only a few large culverts to allow the winds to push water through. This arrangement limits exchange of materials from one part of the lake to the other. Turn left at mile 36.0 to visit the Mattamuskeet National Wildlife Refuge. The refuge headquarters, auto wildlife trails, and historic Lake Mattamuskeet Pump House/Lodge are worth the drive.

Lake Mattamuskeet supports 10 percent of the East Coast's winter migrating waterfowl. During that season, from November through February, all boats are banned from the lake to ensure that the swans, geese, and ducks can feed with-out harassment (Figure 35). The lake is very shallow (about 4 feet) and con-tains abundant submerged aquatic vegetation (e.g., wild celery, redhead grass, and muskgrass) that provides food for many ducks and geese. It is also home to one of the largest populations of ospreys in the state—about ninety nesting pairs.

The ecology of Lake Mattamuskeet is very different from that of Lake Phelps, Pungo Lake, and New Lake. An infusion of estuarine brackish waters through the four main canals that connect the lake to the estuaries of Pamlico Sound has raised the pH to near neutral. This allows submerged vegetation and other plants to grow. Bald cypress, red maple, swamp cottonwood, and wax myrtle are common trees around the lake.

D. Pocosin Lakes National Wildlife Refuge

Pocosin Lakes National Wildlife Refuge is moving its exhibits and visitors center to Columbia, where they will become part of the Partnership for the Sounds center

FIGURE 35. Geese on a pocosin lake. (Photo courtesy of Pettigrew State Park)

mentioned earlier. The headquarters are currently 3.4 miles down Shore Drive from Tyson Farms headquarters. Actually, the best part of Pocosin Lakes National Wildlife Refuge is on back roads.

One site in the refuge is Pungo Lake, an elliptical, tannin-stained lake surrounded by pocosins. To get there, drive to Plymouth and take NC 32 south to NC 99 to Pungo. Red bay, magnolia bay, and gallberry shrubs are part of the thick, short forest that grows on the nutrient-poor, acidic soils. If you are a real tree fan, the U.S. Fish and Wildlife Service and Weyerhaeuser have established a 12-acre demonstration stand of Atlantic white cedar just south of Pungo Lake. These trees were once abundant and prized for boat building, but have all but disappeared from the area.

To explore the pocosin ecosystem at its finest, drive south from Columbia on NC 94. At the Frying Pan Road intersection (mile 7.0), turn right onto Northern Road (unmarked and unpaved) to explore bear habitat in the well-developed and extensive pocosin. This is reputedly the "largest pocosin swamp in the world." Northern Road should be approached with caution or, better yet, in a four-wheel-drive vehicle; it can become treacherous during wet weather. You can only go about 4 or 5 miles; then return to NC 94.

For those with a sense of adventure and seeking a more intimate interaction with pocosin swamps, try canoeing or kayaking in the Northwest Fork of the Alligator River. You can launch your boat just downstream of the NC 94 bridge (mile 15.0 from Columbia); there is a put-in site for canoes and kayaks to the left. The river twists under the road and meanders through miles of wilderness. A relict barge rots quietly about half a mile upstream of the bridge. We saw a large rattle-snake sunning on the decaying deck and admired the woodwork on the cabin of the vessel.

Just south of the bridge on the left lies extensive habitat for insectivorous pitcher plants. Please just take photos: you can buy plants in nurseries. Leave the wild ones for others to enjoy.

Where Fresh and Salt Water Meet

The Upper Pamlico River Estuary

VINCE BELLIS

This 33-mile tour takes you along and over the upper estuarine portion of the Pamlico River. Along the way you will see Coastal Plain landforms and native habitats such as southern river swamp forest, brackish marsh, open estuary, pocosin, and pine savanna. Look for red-cockaded woodpeckers and see the northernmost native palms along the Atlantic Coast. The tour begins in Washington at the North Carolina Estuarium—an interpretive museum of estuarine environments and their role in local history. You will be on the waterfront in Bath (a town founded in 1705) in time for a picnic lunch before crossing the estuary to drive beside the giant open-pit phosphate mine belonging to Potash Corporation of Saskatchewan (PCS). Watch seagulls dive for their dinner as you cross the Pamlico River by free ferry. Visit the Fossil Museum in Aurora, where you can examine evidence of the marine life that lived here when the today's Coastal Plain was beneath the sea. See an ancient ocean beach now covered by pine forest. Bring a fishing pole, a canoe, or a bicycle so that you can explore coastal creeks and back roads at a more leisurely pace.

The major lesson to be learned on this tour is how an ancient ocean shaped this land as sea level advanced and retreated across it. The sea is never really still. Evidence of the importance of water in shaping the coastal environment is all around you. The land is flat because it has been shaped by waves and flowing water. The soils contain layers of water-deposited sand and clay. Sea level is currently rising and thus is gradually flooding an ancient drainage system that formed when the sea was several hundred feet lower than it is today. The Tar-Pamlico River system represents the main channel of this ancient river. Among its many tributaries are Tranters Creek, Broad Creek, Goose Greek, Bath Creek, South Creek, and Durham Creek.

As the rising sea level raised the freshwater level in upstream river valleys, they were transformed into swamp forests dominated by bald cypress and tupelo gum. The level and poorly drained land remaining between the flooded valleys, known as interstream divides, developed a type of forested wetland called "pocosin" by

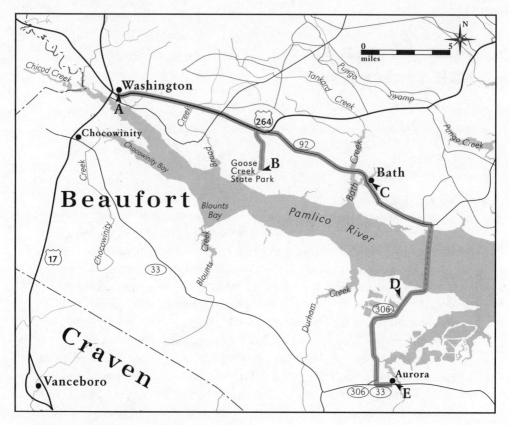

FIGURE 36. Upper Pamlico River tour route

Native Americans or "evergreen shrub bog" by botanists. A rising sea also brings water of higher salt content (salinity) farther up the river, but a river swamp forest cannot withstand saltwater flooding and dies back. Salt-tolerant grasses such as sawgrass, smooth cordgrass, and salt meadow cordgrass hay become established in sunlit openings beneath dead and dying trees. The line of dead trees bordering a coastal creek (locally called a gut) marks the current interface of freshwater/ saltwater environments. Swamp forests will continue to be converted to brackish marshes as long as the sea continues to rise. Peat accumulates in the brackish marsh soils as dead plant matter accumulates. Thus the marsh grows vertically; some marshes in creeks along the upper Pamlico stand on top of 15 to 20 feet of peat. Carbon 14 dates for this peat suggest that it has been accumulating at an average rate of about 3 feet every thousand years.

Eventually even the brackish marsh may succumb to the sea and be washed away, leaving an open estuary. Broad expanses of open water allow the wind to form waves on the river surface and, if the prevailing winds are strong enough, wind tides push water against the shore. Waves undercut the exposed clay or sand walls of the ancient river valley, and great masses of soil collapse onto the beach and are soon sorted into fine clay and coarser sand by wave action. The sand remains behind on the beach while clays are carried offshore to settle out on the river bottom and accumulate as soft mud. Tea-colored tannins and other organic detritus derived from freshwater streams form particles upon contact with salt water. This material also settles to the bottom and contributes to the muddy sediment. Few organisms can inhabit this dark, sometimes oxygen-deficient environment. In contrast, the sediment that remains near shore provides anchorage for beds of submerged aquatic vegetation and a host of invertebrate animals that live there. These weed beds serve as a nursery that provides abundant food and protection from predators for juvenile fish and crabs.

Tens of thousands of years ago sea level was falling and left behind stranded beaches. Geologists call these ancient beaches scarps. In contrast to the interstream divides and their pocosins, the scarps are well drained and were originally covered with pine savanna vegetation.

A. Washington

If you approach Washington from the south via US 17, you must cross nearly a mile of forested floodplain associated with the Tar-Pamlico River system. The road has been elevated to protect it from inundation by wind tides. Note the many large trees blown down by Hurricanes Bertha and Fran. Soft, water-saturated swamp soils do not provide good anchorage for tree roots. Washington is near the upper limit of saltwater penetration, and this river swamp forest exhibits early stages of replacement by brackish marsh. Hurricanes may speed this transition by creating sunny openings in the swamp in which salt-tolerant grasses can become established. The bridge represents the official line of demarcation between the Tar River (fresh water) and the Pamlico River (salty water). The North Carolina Estuarium on the waterfront in Washington has been especially designed to introduce you to the Pamlico estuary and its natural environments. Proceed to the Estuarium to begin your tour (telephone 252-948-0000). There is a nominal entry fee.

B. Goose Creek State Park

Follow US 264/NC 92 8 miles east from Washington. Turn right just before these routes split; brown signs will direct you to the state park. Observe the land as you proceed toward the park. This land lies on a coastal terrace that averages only about 35 feet above sea level. Most of the original upland pocosin and mixed forest has been cleared, drained, and replaced by grain fields and loblolly pine planta-

FIGURE 37. Road through forest—Goose Creek State Park. (Photo courtesy of Goose Creek State Park)

tions. Corn and soybeans provide feed for poultry, swine, and cattle, while south-ern yellow pine timber and pulpwood support a major wood products industry. As you drive along look for sawmills, lumber yards, logging trucks, cattle trucks, and other signs indicating the economic significance of forestry and agriculture to the region.

Goose Creek State Park is an excellent location for observing estuarine shoreline erosion (Live Oak Trail) and for viewing the transition zone between brackish marsh (Ragged Point Trail) and coastal forest. Stop at the visitors center to obtain a trail map and an orientation to the park.

Proceed through the park to the parking lot that serves the swimming beach. Take the short walk to the beach through the picnic area and look for red-cockaded woodpeckers and their nest holes in the pines along this trail (Figure 37). The Live Oak Trail extends east along the river shoreline from the picnic area. It runs on top of a sand berm formed by sand eroded from the river edge and washed up during storms. Place your fingers into the water and touch a drop to your tongue. Is the water salty? Is it as salty as ocean water? In winter look for stringy green or brown seaweeds along the shallow edge. In summer look offshore for floats marking crab pots placed by commercial fishermen.

Compare the width of the river here to the width near Washington. To the east the horizon consists of open estuary; no land is in sight. Look across the river and note the elevated shoreline and row of cottages. As your eyes travel east note a sudden drop in height of the riverbank and the appearance of an industrial com-plex. This is the PCS phosphate facility. The drop in elevation represents the location of an ancient beach ridge called the Suffolk Scarp. This scarp extends from eastern Virginia to Cape Carteret, North Carolina, and now represents the 25-foot contour interval (elevation above sea level). To the east of the former beach lies the Pamlico Terrace where the land elevation is often only 3 to 15 feet above sea level. Although phosphate ore lies under all of the land that you can see, including Goose Creek State Park, it can be mined more economically east of the scarp because there is less overburden (sand and silt) to remove in order to reach the phosphate. Towns and farms located on the low Pamlico Terrace are sometimes flooded by salt water during storms when wind tides can reach heights of 10 feet. The higher land west of the Suffolk Scarp forms the Talbot Terrace.

Proceed along the Live Oak Trail and note the evidence of shoreline erosion: dead and fallen trees, steep riverbank, tree stumps protruding from the water several yards offshore, and fresh sand washed across the trail. Look for patches of black sand on the beach. Pick up a handful and note how heavy this sand is. The black grains consist of particles of heavy metals such as manganese, which erode from the soil and are sorted by the waves. Examine the sand more closely. Along with the dominant black manganese oxide are grains of red garnet, yellow topaz, and other miniature gems.

Look for the Live Oaks that this trail is named for. These majestic trees with their massive trunks and giant curved branches were once harvested to provide strong ribs and planking for tall ships that carried American commerce to the world. Look also for palmetto palms. Abundant from Florida to coastal North Carolina, this is the northernmost location known for this plant.

Return to the swimming beach and take the Ragged Point Boardwalk Trail. You begin your walk through a pine forest. Note the sandy soil. Next you will pass abruptly into a swamp dominated by scattered cedar trees and low shrubs. Greenbrier and poison ivy grow well where the forest canopy has been lost. These vines cover dead and dying trees in this transition zone between forest and brackish swamp. Here the boardwalk will keep you from sinking up to your knees in sulfursmelling mud, but you should still be able to catch the aroma of decay. The bacteria living in this swamp help recycle biologically important elements such as nitrogen, iron, and sulfur. When you reach the end of the boardwalk you will find a superb panorama of all of the views described above.

c. Bath

Return to NC 92 and proceed 5 miles to the town of Bath. Stop at the visitors center for an orientation concerning colonial Bath and information about Blackbeard and other pirates who once lived there. The visitors center museum includes a display showing the importance of forest products to the colonial economy. Note the abundance and variety of stones used in gardens and borders. These stones are not native rock; they were brought here from all parts of the world as ballast to stabilize colonial sailing ships.

Look at a map of the Carolina estuarine shoreline. Why do you suppose pirates selected our coast as a base for their operations? In more modern times this shoreline has provided a haven for bootleggers and drug smugglers. Drive down to the Bath waterfront. Note that each of North Carolina's first three colonial towns—Bath, New Bern, and Edenton—were all located on points of land between two creeks. Was this coincidence or were such locations deliberately chosen?

d. Crossing the Pamlico

Proceed 5 miles along NC 92 to the Pamlico River Ferry landing. (For the ferry schedule call 1-800-BY-FERRY.) Take the free ferry ride across the Pamlico River (Figure 38). You are now east of the Suffolk Scarp. While you ride take a good look up and down river and recall the funnel shape of the Pamlico. Go to the stern of

FIGURE 38. Sunset on the Upper Pamlico. (Photo courtesy of Goose Creek State Park)

the ferry and watch the seagulls searching the wake for food stirred up from the bottom. Does this tell you anything about the water depth? Note the olive color of the water, which results from organic matter suspended in the water. The nearest ocean inlet (Oregon Inlet) through which this water will reach the sea is nearly 30 miles to the east. Water passing beneath the Herbert Bonner Bridge at the inlet is usually clear. What happens to the organic matter? Between here and the inlet sea water mixes with fresh river water, causing the suspended tannins and clays to precipitate and settle to the bottom, where they form a soft organic mud.

E. Aurora and the PCS Phosphate Mine

Drive 7 miles along NC 306 to Aurora. Note the massive open-pit phosphate mine that extends almost to the road. Here phosphate ore is mined from below sea level. The extracted ore is treated with sulfuric acid to produce phosphoric acid and phosphate fertilizer; a byproduct of this process is calcium sulfate (gypsum). The large white mounds of gypsum that you see have accumulated over three decades of mining. Phosphate ore was deposited beneath the sea when this entire area was part of a broad continental shelf. Phosphate ore is a rich source of fossils. Paleo-ecologists can use these fossils to learn what the extremely productive ancient marine environments that produced the ore were like. The Aurora Fossil Museum displays and interprets many of these fossils. Rock material remaining after ore processing is called "reject" by the mining industry. Reject often contains fossil mollusks, corals, and the bones and teeth of ancient sea creatures. Several piles of reject are usually available near the museum parking lot for sifting by fossil hunters.

Aurora is located on the low Pamlico Terrace east of the Suffolk Scarp. Creeks east of the scarp have low banks and are usually bordered by salt-marsh grasses. Drive down to the Aurora boat launch to observe the fringing salt marsh of South Creek. The tallest marsh grass is tall cordgrass. Look also for southern cattail and sawgrass. Note the several fish- and crab-packing establishments in Aurora. Commercial fishing has traditionally been of relatively greater importance than farming on the Pamlico Terrace because well-drained fields are limited while marsh-fringed creeks are plentiful.

Proceed west from Aurora on NC 33. Note the wide, level fields to the south and the fine silty soil. About 2 miles west of Aurora you will observe fields that end abruptly at a band of pine forest. If you look carefully, you will notice a very slight rise in the otherwise level road. The road also bends slightly to the north at this point. This is the Suffolk Scarp. As you move up onto the scarp note that the soil is light-colored beach sand. You are now atop an ancient ocean beach: you have left the Pamlico Terrace and are on the Talbot Terrace. Pine trees with an understory of evergreen trees and shrubs dominate these well-drained, but nutrient-poor sandy soils. Drive south on NC 306 for a mile or two and then turn back east on one of the several dirt roads that lead across the scarp. Here, the transition between forest and open field is even more conspicuous.

Return to US 17 and Washington via NC 33 West. The south side of the Pamlico River has traditionally been more isolated and less densely populated than the north side. Crop land is less abundant than on the north side, while pine plantations are much more abundant. Weyerhaeuser Corporation (a forest products giant) is the largest landowner/manager in several of our eastern counties. Recently Weyerhaeuser has added land development to its list of commercial ventures. Note road signs promoting Weyerhaeuser and other shoreline developments. Most of these developments occur along the upper estuary because this is where houses and marinas can be built directly along the river edge. Most of the native pocosins and pine forests in the region have been converted to farms or pine plantations. Cottages now crowd the shoreline and bulkheads line its beaches. Few places remain along the upper Pamlico estuary where natural vegetation and animal populations can be seen. The lower river, east of the Suffolk Scarp, is less suitable for development because the river edge is more likely to consist of forested wetlands or brackish marsh.

Croatan National Forest
Wetlands and Wildflowers

JEAN W. KRAUS

This tour covers about 80 miles (counting backtracks) within Croatan National Forest where you will see a wide variety of wetlands and wildflowers. The tour also includes a 15-mile extension outside the national forest to Island Creek Nature Trail. Distinct wetland habitats along the tour include longleaf pine savannas, natural ponds and lakes, Carolina bays, hardwood-cypress swamp forests, pocosins, bay forests, pond pine woodlands, and freshwater and saltwater marshes. Observation of dominant plants will aid in identifying each wetland type. Keen observers may also spot unusual plants and wildflowers, such as carnivorous plants. Visitors will also see how the national forest is managed for multiple uses. Management techniques range from timbering and reforestation; prescribed burning to eliminate undergrowth and uncontrollable wildfires, and to encourage plant diversity and wildlife habitat; monitoring of endangered species and other conservation activities; and maintenance of recreation areas. There is plenty of room in which to apply these techniques: the national forest occupies over 150,000 acres between the towns of New Bern, Swansboro, and Morehead City.

The primary lessons to be learned from this tour are how environmental factors and management methods affect vegetation distribution and growth patterns. While you follow the tour, compare and contrast how physical features affect dominant vegetation, and identify dominant or unusual plants that distinguish each wetland type. Wetland type and vegetation is determined by source and type of water, soil moisture and type, nutrients and pH, geological underpinnings, fire regime, and plant succession sequence.

For additional information and maps, contact the U.S. Forest Service, Croatan Ranger District, 141 East Fisher Avenue, New Bern, NC 28560 (252-638-5628). For other guided tours, contact North Carolina Maritime Museum, 315 Front Street, Beaufort, NC 28516 (252-728-7317). For detailed tour descriptions highlighting birds, see John O. Fussell's book, *A Birder's Guide to Coastal North Carolina* (see "Suggestions for Further Reading").

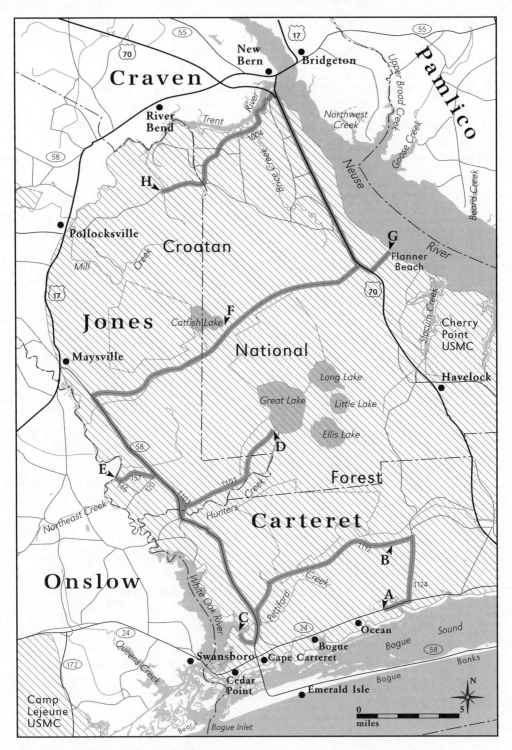

FIGURE 39. Croatan National Forest tour route

A. Patsy Pond Natural Area and Nature Trail

Begin at the North Carolina Coastal Federation office near Ocean on NC 24 about 10 miles west of the NC 24/US 70 intersection in Morehead City, and about 6.5 miles east of the high-rise bridge between Cape Carteret and Emerald Isle. Visit the headquarters for trail information and other coastal learning opportunities. Signs clearly mark the trail loops, which generally follow old sand roads.

The naturally impounded ponds and beach ridge system are of Pleistocene age (1.5 million to 10,000 years ago). The coarse quartz sands are barrier deposits that accumulated on the downdrift side of an ancestral Neuse River. Wind and stream erosion produced gently sloping sand ridges and flats. The ponds are old stream impoundments, possibly remnants of the Neuse River paleochannel. During a cold freeze I observed that while there was a layer of ice on Bogue Sound, no ice appeared on the shallow ponds, implying the presence of warmer spring-fed water. During a drought when the ponds dried out, springs were visible in each pond, which suggests there is a supply of natural artesian water from the underlying Castle Hayne aquifer. The pond bottoms consist of water-saturated organic muck and care must be taken not to sink into it.

The relict dune ridge is dominated by longleaf pine, scrub oaks such as turkey oak, and huckleberries and blueberries. The presence of live oaks and yaupon suggests a link to a former maritime forest on the barrier sand ridge. Past fires are evident on the pine trunks, and holes in the ground reveal where fires burned into the flammable resin at the bases of trees. Herbaceous plants include blazing star, milkwort, asters, sand nettle, and jointweed* (plants whose names are marked with an asterisk are considered endangered or threatened). Concentric zones of emergent and wetland plants formed around the ponds, depending upon water depth. The pond margins are dominated by black gums with a thick understory of rhizomatous shrubs such as titi, fetterbush, and blueberries. Pond spice* and cassena holly*, which are more typical of lime sinks, grow here. A zone of open sand provides habitat for an array of interesting plants with interesting names: sundews, gaywings, meadow beauty, yellow-eyed grass, hatpins, screw-stem, bladderworts, *Burmannia**, and grasses and sedges. Shallow ponds are dominated by grasses, but deeper ponds harbor aquatics such as spatterdock, water lily, pond gentian*, and bladderwort*. These ponds and forest are home to numerous birds, reptiles, and amphibians.

This natural area is recognized by the state through a voluntary "registry" program and is managed for endangered and threatened species. The U.S. Forest Service conducts prescribed burns to clear out the understory—a technique that encourages the presence of the endangered red-cockaded woodpecker (nest trees are marked with blue bands). The unique Patsy Pond area is valuable for scientific research and environmental education.

B. Millis Road

Drive east on NC 24 about 1.5 miles and take Nine Mile Road (SR 1124, "Nine Foot Road" on some maps) north about 3 miles to Millis Road (SR 1112 becomes FR 128). It is worthwhile to stop on Nine Mile Road to see carnivorous plants and wildflowers that grow beneath the power line. You will begin to see longleaf pine savanna on the south side of Millis Road about 1 mile west of Nine Mile Road (Figure 40). The savanna sits on a landscape of ridge-and-swale topography—part of a relict beach system. The ridges are oriented in a northeast-southwest direction. The dry, coarse sands of the ridge, together with a hardpan and low water table, support a canopy of scattered pines. Frequent fires nearly eliminate a shrub layer. Wiregrass dominates the ground cover along with dwarf huckleberries and blueberries and numerous seasonal wildflowers.

The swales support pocosin vegetation with an open canopy of pond pines and rhizomatous, mostly evergreen shrubs such as blueberries, sheepkill, fetterbush, gallberries, wax myrtle, sweet bay (swamp magnolia), titi, and loblolly bay. Pocosin is the Indian word for "swamp on a hill," which may be better defined as a shrub bog. The ecotones, or transition zones, between the savannas and pocosins produces many wildflowers, including some rare plants. The profusion of wildflowers begins in the spring with various lilies, orchids, and carnivorous plants such as Venus flytrap, pitcher plants, bladderworts, butterworts, and sundews. Summer brings meadow beauty, gaywings, yellow-eyed grass, and gentians. Fall is a riot of color—fringed orchids, autumn gentians, false foxgloves, blazing stars and other members of the aster family, and many grasses. In spring listen for the trill of the rare Bachman's sparrow and the high-pitched call of the red-cockaded woodpecker. Search the tall pine trees for a possible sighting of the bird or its nest cavities ringed with tell-tale white sap.

As one of the best examples of pine savannas in this region, Millis Road Savanna is managed as a natural research area. Frequent prescribed burns maintain the open savanna for the woodpeckers and plant diversity. Fire stimulates wiregrass and other species to bloom and encourages wildlife habitat.

Continue along Millis Road through high pocosin and bay forest vegetation. In about 2 miles, the road curves over the sand rim of a Carolina Bay dominated by longleaf pines and turkey oaks. These elliptical depressions, mainly visible from the air, are theorized by geologists as originating by the prevailing winds and receding sea level in ancient estuaries. The bays in the Croatan National Forest are filled with pocosin vegetation rather than standing water.

FIGURE 40. Millis Road longleaf pine savanna. (Photo by J. Kraus)

During the next 2 miles the scenery consists of loblolly and longleaf pine plantations. Note the lack of plant diversity in these managed rows of trees. A stop at a small bridge over Pettiford Creek provides a view of a blackwater stream and swamp, where the black tea-colored water drains from the dense peat in the pocosin. The bottomland hardwoods—oaks, swamp tupelo, sweet gum, maple, ash, tulip poplar—provide excellent habitat for spring warblers and other songbirds. Continue to the end of Millis Road, passing through pine flatwoods, and keep an eye open for interesting flora, such as pitcher plants (Figure 40).

c. Cedar Point Tideland Trail

At the end of Millis Road turn left on Whitehouse Forks Road (SR 1111) and left onto NC 58. In 1 mile or so turn right on VFW Road (SR 1114) and left on FR 153A to continue about 1 mile to the parking lot.

Located near the mouth of the White Oak River, the trail meanders over tidal creeks, mosquito ditches, salt and brackish marshes, and through an upland pine-hardwood forest. A boardwalk allows you to make close-up observations of the marsh without getting your feet wet; you should be able to find fiddler crabs among their burrows, juvenile fish, other crabs, mammal tracks, and shorebirds. Specific viewing platforms offer excellent views of the estuary and river. The new boardwalk replaces one that was destroyed during Hurricanes Bertha and Fran in 1996.

The plants of the marsh and maritime forest are adapted for living in an environment of fluctuating levels of salt water, direct sun, and salt spray. Special adaptations to reduce water loss include succulent leaves (sea ox-eye), succulent photosynthetic stems with reduced leaves (glasswort), grass blades that curl inward (salt meadow hay) or are round in cross-section (black needlerush), small waxy or leathery leaves (yaupon, wax myrtle, live oak), blades that expel excess salt (spike grass and smooth cordgrass), and rhizomes that anchor plants in soft mud or moving sand (smooth and salt meadow cordgrass).

Islands of maritime forest dominated by live oak, red cedar, yaupon, and wax myrtle contain an understory of marsh species, indicating saltwater inundation. Trees on the edge of the maritime forest show signs of dying from exposure to salt water and wind. Hikers can return to the parking lot from this short trail loop (about 0.5 miles) or continue on the long loop (just over 1 mile), which winds along the edge of a pine-hardwood forest that is more protected from salt spray and the effect of tides.

A salt marsh within national forest boundaries is unique. Cedar Point Tideland Trail is managed within a recreation area that offers a campground and boat ramp. The trail illustrates a dynamic ecosystem influenced by tides and the impact of storms. The marsh edge fluctuates with daily tides. There is evidence of sea water encroachment, possibly from rising sea level. The same hurricanes that destroyed the boardwalk also weakened or felled many loblolly pines. Natural succession continually renews the forest with new shrubs and trees.

D. Great Lake

Turn left on NC 58, and in about 5 miles turn right on SR 1103/SR 1100 at Kuhns. In less than 1 mile turn right on Great Lake Road (SR 1101 becomes FR 126). It is about 7 miles to the lake. Geologists theorize that Great Lake was formed by massive peat fires that burned into the mineral soil. The low-nutrient, tea-colored, tannic acid waters drain from the surrounding pocosins and swamp forests. Pocosins developed over the past twelve thousand years as organic materials accumulated in blocked drainage systems, formerly vegetated by cypress and white cedar forests. Prior to being swamp land this area was part of the ancient Neuse River estuary.

The Croatan is considered to have some of the best and largest examples of pocosins, that is, freshwater wetlands dominated by evergreen shrubs, scattered pond pines, and bay trees (Figure 41). Species dominance is determined by the thickness of peat, hydroperiod (how long it is wet), and fire frequency. Low pocosins characterized by a stunted shrub layer and scattered, stunted pines occur on the wettest and deepest peatlands. Rhizomatous shrubs include titi, gallberries, sheep laurel, fetterbushes, bayberry, chokeberry, blueberries, and zenobia. Carnivorous plants, wildflowers, and grasses occur along edges and openings. High pocosins with dense thickets of tall shrubs, scattered bay vegetation, and pond pines occur over shallow peat that is seasonally saturated. Shrub dominance is maintained by fire in both types of pocosin.

Bay forests occur on peat over mineral soils on the edges of domed peatlands or along the headwaters of small streams. In the absence of fire, pond pine, loblolly bay, sweet bay, red bay, swamp tupelo, and red maple grow to maturity. Pond pine woodlands grow along pocosin margins over poorly drained, shallow peat and mineral soils. Seasonally flooded hardwood-cypress swamp forests grow in mineral to mucky organic soils drained by blackwater streams. The bridges crossing tributaries of Hunters Creek are good stops for songbirds. A mature sweet gum–cypress swamp grows along the southern lake shore and is usually dry enough to walk in. The natural lake shoreline characterized by cypresses and grasses is regularly churned by wind over the shallow lake.

Much of the Croatan pocosin is protected as a national wilderness area. Management requires the maintenance of a high water table and occasional fires. Fishing is limited due to the water's acidity and the lack of aquatic vegetation food sources, but the pocosins and lakes provide habitat for black bear and alligator.

FIGURE 41. Pond pine woodland with pocosin understory. (Photo by J. Kraus)

E. Haywood Landing at the White Oak River

Return to NC 58, turn right, and drive 1.5 miles to Long Point Road (FR 120 with sign for Haywood Landing). Immediately turn right on Loopy Road (FR 157) and right again on Haywood Landing Road (FR 146) to the boat ramp.

After the road passes through a managed loblolly pine forest, begin looking toward the right side of Haywood Landing Road as it slopes down to a bottom-land hardwood forest. The canopy of mixed oaks, ash, red maple, sweet gum, tulip poplar, swamp tupelo, walnut, and American elm shades an understory of red cedar, sweet bay (swamp magnolia), swamp dogwood, and dwarf palmetto. Few herbaceous plants grow in this seasonally flooded forest. Outcrops of fossil shell material can be observed here, which makes the soil more basic (higher pH) than the soil of the surrounding area. The slope of upland hardwoods contains maples, hickories, American beech, and oaks with an understory of flowering dogwood, umbrella magnolia, red buckeye, and a variety of herbs like mayapples and wild ginger.

The hardwood-cypress swamp in the floodplain here intergrades with the tidal cypress-gum swamp along the river's edge. Tides at this point in the river are due more to wind than to the sun and moon, as is the case further downstream. Dominant trees include swamp tupelo, bald cypress, ash, and maple. Flooding eliminates most understory plants except some vines such as Carolina jasmine, climbing hydrangea, poison ivy, and catbriar. Stumps and riverbanks support some shrubs such as alder, swamp dogwood, Virginia willow, rose mallow, and swamp rose.

The tidal freshwater marsh along the White Oak River is dominated by cattails, sawgrass, and wild rice. Wildflowers grow on stumps and riverbanks and provide a seasonal display of Virginia iris, golden club, pickerelweed, swamp windflower, duck potato, butterweed, water parsnip, swamp windflower, and ferns. The narrow-leaved cattail usually grows only in circumneutral soil, so clearly the soil is more basic in this area.

The White Oak River is a blackwater stream that originates in the pocosins of Onslow County and thus displays the typical tea color derived from tannins leached from the pocosin. Its origin and course are described in a White Oak River tour earlier in this book. The best way to observe wildlife and plants along the river and its creeks is by canoe. Paddle the slow-flowing stream for close-up views of aquatic plants including parrot-feather, tapegrass, and bur-reed. Glimpse darting songbirds, warblers, ducks, and hawks, as well as frogs, turtles, and snakes. Signs of black bear, deer, river otter, and alligator can be seen by keen observers.

F. Catfish Lake and Impoundments

Go back to NC 58, turn left, and go about 5 miles to turn right on Catfish Lake Road (SR 1105). The drive takes you through wet pine flatwoods and swamp forests, and a good bird stop is at the small bridge over Black Swamp Creek. Then the landscape opens into pond pine woodlands, high pocosins, and finally, low pocosins. Low pocosins grow over the deepest, wettest peat in the Croatan. The Catfish Lake area gives sightseers the best example of this stunted shrub and scattered pine vegetation. Look for yellow pitcher plants among the stunted shrubs and for bladderworts in the roadside ditches. Drive about 8 miles to Catfish Lake Farm Road (FR 158), and turn left. There are several pull-off areas from which to view the lake. The prevailing winds continually erode the shoreline, preventing the development of a marsh. On the north side of the lake stands a remnant Atlantic white cedar forest. Once abundant in eastern North Carolina, white cedar trees were used for boat building and lumber and don't readily regenerate. There is also a good example of a mature bay forest near the lake.

Continue about 2.5 miles, and turn right on FR 3000 to the Catfish Lake Waterfowl Impoundment. The Forest Service is developing the impoundments to attract wintering waterfowl. The road is closed after the impoundment, so return to Catfish Lake Road, turn left, and continue about 7.5 miles to US 70.

G. Neuse River Recreation Area, Flanner Beach

Turn right on us 70, and in less than 1 mile turn left at the sign for the Neuse River Recreation Area, Flanner Beach. Follow the road about 1.5 miles to the parking lot.

The bluffs along the Neuse here are ancient beach ridges formed by the ancestral Neuse River. Trails meander over a varied topography with steep slopes eroded by ancient streams. The Neuse is a brownwater river because it originates in and carries sediment from the Piedmont. Severe erosion is evident along the riverbank where winds have undercut large trees, and cypress trees stand at the mouths of the swamps. Rose mallow and Carolina willow grow along the sandy beach.

Hardwood-cypress swamps composed of bald cypress and swamp tupelo stand at the outlets of small meandering streams that are tributaries of the main river. Regular flooding eliminates a herbaceous layer, except for vines like climbing hydrangea that climb the tree trunks.

Upstream, where flooding is seasonal, bottomland forests with ash, maples, walnut, sweet gum, and tulip poplar tower over an understory of swamp dogwood, Virginia willow, spicebush, and swamp rose. Observe the herb layer made up of water-loving plants such as lizard's tail, Jack-in-the-pulpit, water loosestrife, touch-me-not, cardinal flower, Virginia arum, and pickerelweed.

On the upland slopes a variety of oaks, American beech, hickories, ironwood, umbrella Magnolia, black gum, sourwood, and pines grow over a diverse understory of flowering dogwood, persimmon, strawberry bush, witch-hazel, horse sugar, wild azalea, storax, and silky camellia (the last is rare). The rich herb layer includes orchids, lilies, numerous woodland wildflowers, and ferns.

While Flanner Beach provides a developed campground with a swimming area, both of these facilities are closed between December 1 and March 15. A similar site to visit nearby is Fishers Landing, just north of the Croatan Ranger Station. Go back to us 70, turn right, and go about 2.5 miles. A stop at the ranger station is recommended for maps, brochures, and information. Follow the road to Fishers Landing about a mile to the parking lot. Fishers Landing offers undeveloped camping, hiking trails, and a sandy beach and is open all year. It is the site where a Confederate regiment held the bluff until forced to withdraw by massive Union naval guns during the Civil War.

H. Island Creek Forest Walk

Return to us 70, turn right, and drive about 5 miles before exiting for the drawbridge to New Bern. Turn left before the bridge on Old Airport Road, and in less than a mile turn right on Brice Creek Road (SR 1004, Island Creek Road on some maps). Continue about 8 miles to a parking area just past a small bridge, and look for a large trail sign at the entrance.

The 0.5-mile trail follows the creek along the edge of a hardwood-cypress swamp and loops back through a mature hardwood forest. The stream cuts through limestone as it empties into the Trent River, leaving behind steep banks and rock outcrops. This limestone elevates the soil pH over the surrounding area and provides habitat for plants that are considered rare and unusual for the Coastal Plain. Several species of rare ferns grow on the outcrops.

The hardwood-cypress swamp along Island Creek is dominated by bald cypress and a mixture of hardwoods—swamp tupelo, walnut, swamp chestnut oak, tulip poplar, sweet gum, and red maple. The relatively swift current eliminates most of a shrub and herb layer. Steep banks confine the swamp to a narrow band bordering the stream. The rare shadow-witch orchid occurs on the edge of the swamp along with other wetland plants such as golden club, arum, lizard's tail, cardinal flower, and pickerelweed.

The upland hardwoods on the streambanks are in a relatively stable state and contain several rare species and plants that are more typical of the Piedmont than of the Coastal Plain. There is a rich diversity of species because of the maturity of the forest and the more basic soil conditions provided by the limestone. Trees include hickories, oaks, American beech, walnut, sourwood, American elm, tulip poplar, maples, and sweet gum. A rich understory includes silky camellia (rare), spicebush, dwarf pawpaw, and umbrella magnolia. The diverse herb and fern layer includes orchids like autumn coral-root, rattlesnake plantain, and the rare shadow-witch orchid, as well as liverleaf, turtleheads, false Solomon's seal, columbine, thimbleweed, bloodroot, alumroot, skullcap, and unusual ferns. The walk is also interesting for birdwatchers, who will find a variety of woodpeckers, songbirds, warblers, and wood ducks.

Island Creek Forest Walk is managed as a nature trail. Spring and fall are the best times to enjoy wildflowers and fall color.

Carolina Bay Lakes

Lake Waccamaw
and Bladen Lakes

DIANE LAURITSEN

This 80-mile tour takes you to some of the most beautiful and best-preserved examples of Carolina bay lakes—ecosystems that have been described as exotic, mysterious, and unique. These are all appropriate descriptors of Carolina bay, a landform found in the United States only on the southeastern Coastal Plain. This trip will take you through a part of the state that is little known to tourists, although it contains some of the jewels in the state park system. Lake Waccamaw, the largest bay lake in the area, is home to a number of endemic species and is quite different chemically and biologically from the Carolina bay lakes to the north in Bladen County. This area is worth a visit of at least two days—one day at Lake Waccamaw and another day for the loop trip to the Bladen Lakes and Elwell Ferry, a small inland ferry that crosses the Cape Fear River.

This tour provides an opportunity for visitors to become familiar with the defining characteristics of Carolina bays. These shallow, elliptical depressions—most with their long axes in a northwest to southeast orientation—are perhaps the most distinctive landform on the eastern seaboard. When they are viewed from the air, their uniform shape is particularly striking. Most Carolina bays fill with water only during wet periods; Lake Waccamaw and the Bladen County lakes are among the few bays that qualify as true lakes because they are permanently water-filled. The term Carolina bay refers to the predominant vegetation found in these wetlands—three species of bay trees (red, Virginia, and loblolly)—and the fact that these depressions are most abundant in the Coastal Plain of North and South Carolina. There are, in fact, several thousand Carolina bays in the two states, and although most of them have been altered by human activity, numerous remnants and intact bays can still be observed in aerial photos (Figure 43). Many of the Carolina bays found in North Carolina have elevated sand rims outlining their southern edges, and these rims are occupied by distinctive xeric (dry-adapted) vegetation.

A number of myths and theories are associated with the origin of Carolina bays. South Carolina geologist Michael Toumey first described Carolina bays in 1847. He observed that they were circular depressions, flat and shallow, and likened them to

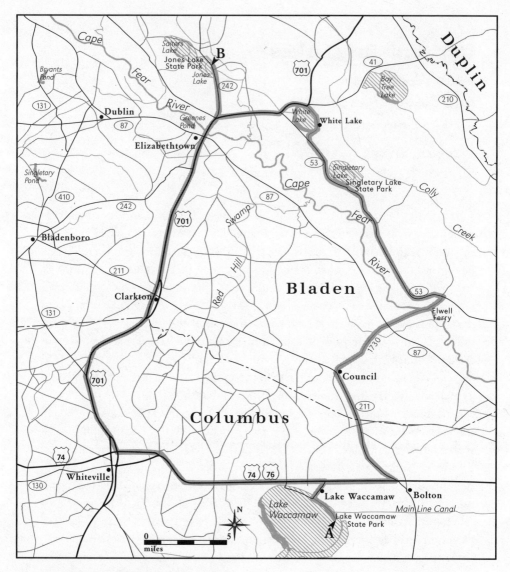

FIGURE 42. Carolina Bay Lakes tour route

racetracks. He began to study them for clues to their origin and concluded that they were formed by springs and wind action.

Toumey's work received little recognition, however, with the result that another geologist, Leonidas Glenn, was given credit for discovering Carolina bays in 1895. Glenn's description of the characteristics of Carolina bays was published in a prestigious journal and attracted attention. Soon a host of theories were proposed to explain the origin of Carolina bays, beginning a flurry of interest that has carried over to the present day.

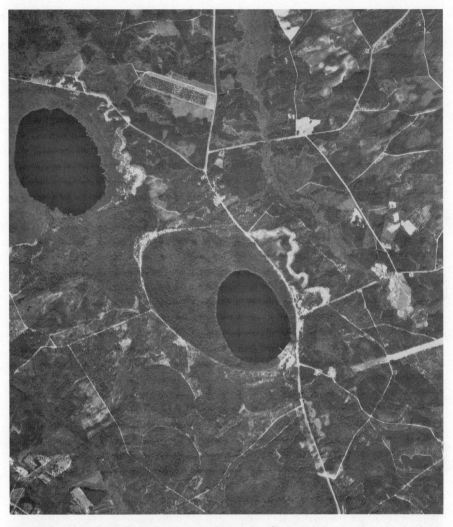

FIGURE 43. Aerial view of Carolina Bays and bay lakes (Salters Lake, top; Jones Lake, bottom). (Photo courtesy of U.S. Geological Survey)

Origin theories have ranged from formation by giant schools of fish, working their fins to create nests, to formation by artesian springs, ancient estuaries, or wind-driven currents. By far the most popular theory of the origin of Carolina bays resulted from examination of aerial photographs of the bays. Inspection of aerial photographs taken near Myrtle Beach, South Carolina, in 1930 led Edwin Corlett to speculate that the strikingly abundant large and small ellipses dotting the landscape were a result of the impact of a shower of meteors.

The meteoric theory of origin soon caught on with the public, especially after popular articles such as "The Comet That Struck the Carolinas" gave it wide acceptance. This idea has remained appealing, even in more recent times; for example, in his 1982 book *The Mysterious Carolina Bays*, Henry Savage outlined his version of the meteor theory, linking the extinction of the dinosaurs with the creation of the Carolina bays.

Although the meteoric theory is glamorous, investigators have found no evidence (such as meteor fragments) to support it. Also, it seems that meteor craters are always circular, not elliptical. A more widely accepted theory was proposed in 1977 by a South Carolina researcher, Raymond Kaczorowski. He used a wind tunnel to demonstrate that wind blowing in a constant direction could cause water-filled basins to take on an elliptical shape (with the orientation of the lake perpendicular to the wind direction) as a result of wind-driven water currents, and argued that similarly oriented lakes are found in the Alaskan Arctic and in Tierra del Fuego, Chile.

Try to allow for at least a two-day visit to the Carolina bay lakes area. If you wish to camp, Jones Lake is the only state park in this tour that provides family campsites, so you could begin your loop around to the other sites from there. My personal preference is to start at Lake Waccamaw and use it as home base. It is a wonderfully relaxing place, and the longer you stay, the more you will appreciate it. There are two bed and breakfasts located there; an additional advantage to staying at one of them is that you may then have access to the northern shore of the lake, which is all privately owned.

A. Lake Waccamaw

Located 35 miles west of Wilmington, Lake Waccamaw is accessed from US 74/76. If you are coming from the east, take the first exit marked for Lake Waccamaw, at Wannish (it will be the second Lake Waccamaw exit if you are traveling from the west). This brings you to the lake via a delightful little road flanked by closely planted pecan trees, which is, of course, named Pecan Lane.

As you reach the lake, you will become aware that you are on a bluff. This is a limestone outcrop, part of the Waccamaw Formation, which is about 4 to 5 million years old. Turn right onto Lakeshore Drive, and after a few miles you will see how the bluff ends abruptly. Turning right at the stop sign will take you back out to US 74/76, while a left turn will put you onto Canal Cove Road (look for alligators in the canal, which begins on your right). You will eventually reach a public boat landing and RV campground; if you wish to see more of the lakeshore, make a right and then a quick left, and you will eventually come to a dam and the start of the Waccamaw River.

To reach Lake Waccamaw State Park, drive along the undeveloped southern shoreline of the lake, and head east on Lakeshore Drive (a left turn at the end of

Pecan Lane); the road will veer to the left, and you will then see signs for the park, directing you to a right turn. State Road 1947 (Bella Coola Drive) will take you to Martin Road, at the end of which is a parking area for the park.

The Lake Waccamaw State Park Visitors Center (located near the entrance to the park) has been designed to show you the unique aspects of the lake and its surroundings. Lake Waccamaw is different from the other Carolina Bay Lakes because of the limestone outcrops of the Waccamaw Formation. This rock buffers, or neutralizes, the water coming into the lake (spring water and swamp water), so that it has a pH of near neutral (compared to the other bay lakes you will see, where the water is acidic). The great abundance and variety of aquatic life found in Lake Waccamaw is a consequence of the neutrality of the water.

The abundance of rooted aquatic plants in the lake provides cover for a diverse fish population, including three endemic species (found here and nowhere else). Microscopic plant life is abundant in the sediments of the lake, particularly in the shallow waters along the northern shore; if you scoop up a handful of sand here, you will be struck by its green color. The algae in the sediments provide food for a fantastic number of invertebrates, including mussels (several of which are endemic), small snails, an introduced species of clam, and many small immature insects. Even freshwater forms of jellyfish and sponges can occasionally be found in the lake.

The drive through the state park offers a good opportunity to see the vegetation characteristic of Carolina bays. The pine forest includes loblolly bay, Virginia (sweet) bay, wax myrtle, titi, and red bay; a visit in midsummer, when the various bays and other small shrubs, as well as wildflowers, are in bloom, can be a delight. Several rare plants can be found in the area, including Venushair fern and green-fly orchid.

Plan to spend some time exploring the park on foot (the parking area is at the end of the road, near the lakeshore). The boardwalk to the lake is short and an easy walk, and it's the best way to see the vegetation up close and to appreciate what an impenetrable mass it forms in wetter areas. At the end of the boardwalk, you will be able to see a long stretch of undeveloped shoreline, characterized by black gum and cypress trees.

The Sand Ridge Nature Trail is an easy 0.8-mile trail through the park that gives you the chance to see the vegetation adapted to life in the dry areas—the sand rim and sand ridges. Here you will see such plants as turkey oak, longleaf pine, wiregrass, and lichens. A variety of birds are often visible on and around the lake, including osprey, cormorants, egrets, and eastern kingbirds. In winter, an abundance of waterfowl establish residence there.

Other things to do while at Lake Waccamaw include exploring Big Creek by canoe (there is a county boat landing nearby, and you will pass it on the way to the state park), and making a visit to the Lake Waccamaw Depot Museum, on Flemington Drive. The depot museum contains a variety of old tools, artifacts, and exhibits that describe the once-important turpentine industry. There are also some fascinating old photographs and a seventeenth- to eighteenth-century dugout canoe on display.

B. Loop Trip to the Bladen Lakes Bays and Elwell Ferry

If possible, try to do this complete loop, in the direction described. The reason for this will become evident. The route covers 85 miles, starting from Lake Waccamaw.

To begin the trip, you must head west, toward Whiteville, on US 74/76. Take the first Whiteville exit and turn north, onto Red Hill Road (SR 1700). At the end of this road, turn left and then right, and you will be on US 701 headed north. Continue on 701 until you cross the Cape Fear River, on the north edge of Elizabethtown. Look for a left turn and get onto NC 242; you will soon see Jones Lake State Park on the left (it is about 2.5 miles north of Elizabethtown).

The park is sited on the sand rim of Jones Lake; note the similarity of the vegetation to what you saw on the sand rim at Lake Waccamaw. Jones Lake is quite acidic and supports a much less diverse population of fish and invertebrates (fishes include chain pickerel, catfish, yellow perch, and sunfish). Canoes and paddleboats can be rented, allowing you to get a closer look at the lake and its shoreline, while the 3-mile Lake Trail loop offers the opportunity to see the area on foot.

It is also possible to visit Salters Lake—a pristine, never developed Carolina bay lake. It is necessary to first obtain a permit from the ranger at Jones Lake, and you must have your own canoe if you wish to explore this one. If getting away from civilization appeals to you, this is one of the best places to do it; you will be able to see and hear an abundance of wildlife. Bald eagles are occasionally spotted in the area, and the uninhabited areas around the Bladen Lakes, as well as around Lake Waccamaw, are one of the few remaining coastal refuges for the once common black bear.

To reach the next lake on the tour, head south on NC 242 until you get back to US 701. Turn left this time and follow the signs for White Lake (it is about 7 miles from Elizabethtown). This will take you on US 701/NC 41, and you will see signs for White Lake directing you south, which will take you along the eastern side of the lake. Follow this road to the end, and it will meet up with NC 53.

White Lake is unusual in not having any significant swamp water inputs; it is a clear, spring-fed bay lake. I can imagine that it was once an extraordinarily beautiful place; and because of that, it is now something quite different. Simply driving past the development along its lakeshore should provide a striking counterpoint to what you have already seen on your tour.

Head south on NC 53 and you will pass another Carolina bay lake—Singletary Lake. Since this state park is used only for group camping, a visit will require calling ahead (during business hours, Monday through Friday). There is a more extensive sand rim along Singletary, and the 133-acre Turkey Oak Natural Area offers the opportunity to see the characteristic Carolina bay sand rim vegetation and glimpses of a wide variety of wildlife.

As you continue south along NC 53, you will be traveling roughly parallel to the Cape Fear River. After a quiet, 14-mile stretch of highway, you need to look for a right turn. This will be SR 1730, and a large sign posting the operating schedule for Elwell Ferry sits at the intersection. The ferry runs from 6 A.M. to 6 P.M. in summer and from sunrise to sunset in winter.

Elwell Ferry was originally a privately run ferry and is now one of two remaining inland ferries operated by the state of North Carolina. In the words of one of the operators, it is used by "loggers, fishermen, locals, and people who get lost." The short ride on the small cable ferry makes crossing the river seem like an adventure, and you may be pleased to know that the state has no plans to replace the ferry with a boring old bridge.

Continuing south on SR 1730, you will pass Oakland Plantation on your right. This was the home of General Thomas Brown, who served in the Revolutionary War, and is not now open to the public (the plantation lands are part of a turf farm).

At Council turn left on NC 211; after about 3 miles you will come to US 74/76. A right turn will take you back to Lake Waccamaw, and will complete your tour.

Southern Lumber River Region

STAFF OF LUMBER RIVER STATE PARK

The Lumber River, a free-flowing blackwater stream, passes through the Sandhills and southern Coastal Plain region of southeastern North Carolina. Many bridge crossings provide easy access for boaters as well as excellent opportunities to view the river by vehicle. Several rare plant species grow along the river; examples include the water elm, Carolina bogmint, and sarvis holly. There is always a chance of seeing river otters, beavers, and many species of songbirds that call the river corridor home.

The southern portion of the Lumber River is part of the 115-mile-long Lumber River State Park. This portion meanders through a rural part of North Carolina's Coastal Plain. As the river snakes its way toward South Carolina, access can be attained at ten locations along the way. Outstanding scenic views include various stands of bottomland hardwoods and cypress gum swamps along the river's undeveloped corridor. A visit to this part of the Lumber River also provides a look into the geomorphic processes and landforms of a free-flowing blackwater river.

The major learning experience available from this tour is an appreciation of the river's role in the natural and cultural history of southeastern North Carolina. A first impression of the river may be that it is just a dark-colored stream flowing through the countryside of Robeson County. As you drive along, however, you will be able to observe this river's impact on the area's ecology and culture. The extensive length of the river corridor also provides opportunities for water-based recreation such as fishing, small-craft boating, and canoeing in an uncrowded natural setting. Cultural features along the tour route date back hundreds of years, from relict bridges and dock pilings to the many old railroad bridges that hint of the importance of lumber and naval store industries in the early development of the region.

This 30-mile tour of the Lumber River can be made starting at either end. We recommend starting at the northern end in the city of Lumberton and heading south. The starting point is within Lumberton's city limits at the intersection of First and Elm Streets. Sixty yards south of the intersection is the Robeson County Museum.

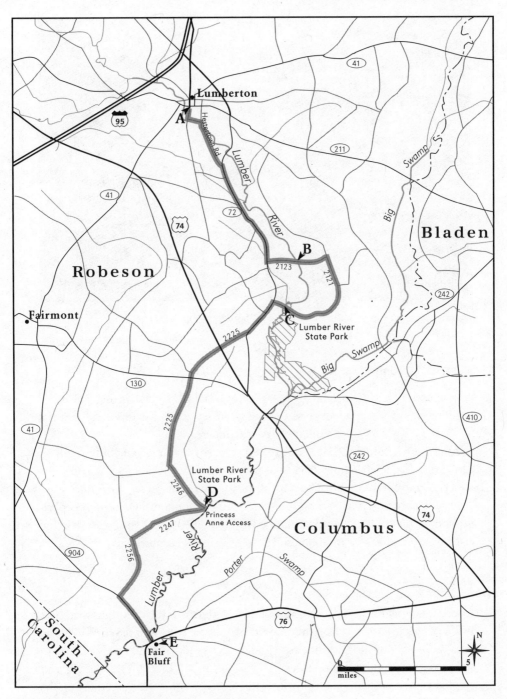

FIGURE 44. Southern Lumber River tour route

FIGURE 45. Lumber River bottomland forest. (Photo by D. Frankenberg)

A. Robeson County Museum

This museum has a little bit of everything to offer. Housed in the old office building of the Railroad Express Company, it depicts the natural and cultural aspects of Robeson County and the City of Lumberton.

After you've viewed the museum's exhibits return to your car and head south on Elm Street. When you come to South Chestnut Street turn right (this is a one-way street). Continue on South Chestnut until you see Noir Street; turn right onto Noir and go approximately 1.25 miles until you come upon the Noir Street playground. At the back of the playground is the Lumber River. As you peer out at the river, be aware that you are still inside the city limits of Lumberton.

B. Mathews Bluff

Continuing east on Noir Street you will find Hestertown Road. A right turn here will take you to NC 72. Turn right onto NC 72, then take the first paved road to the left, Mathews Bluff Road. While traveling on this road, you will have a chance to view a bottomland hardwood forest. The bridge on Mathews Bluff Road gives an excellent view both up- and downstream of one of the wider sections of the Lumber River.

c. Boating Access

Continuing on Mathews Bluff Road, you will intersect with Beulah Church Road; take a right and enjoy a peaceful drive through a farming area of the county. The road will become Willoughby Road shortly before crossing the river near its intersection with NC 72. At this bridge crossing is a boating access site and another prime location to view the bottomland forest along the river (Figure 45).

Turn left onto NC 72 headed toward US 74. A state park directional sign will then put you onto SR 2225 headed south. Following the state park directional signs will take you to the Princess Anne Access Area of Lumber River State Park.

d. Lumber River State Park Access

At the time of this writing, Lumber River State Park was North Carolina's newest developed state park. The Princess Anne Access Area offers picnicking, primitive camping, a nature trail, and a boat ramp for easy access to the river. This part of the park is located on the site of the second oldest town in Robeson County—Princess Anne. Park staff offer interpretive programs on a regular basis. Contact the park office at 910-628-1522 before you leave home. By calling ahead, you can plan your visit around a park program; the staff can also provide information on canoe trips and canoe rentals in the area. This is a good starting and ending point for short canoe trips.

e. Fair Bluff

Leaving the Princess Anne Access Area, you can reach the town of Fair Bluff by taking all left-hand turns at intersections, starting with a left turn at the park gate. The small town of Fair Bluff offers a unique look back into the life of a river town. The Lumber River played an important role in this town's history. Goods from the surrounding areas were shipped on the river to many parts of the East Coast and the world. Of interest in Fair Bluff is the Depot Museum located in an old train depot building. The museum houses several projects of the local historical society, such as train memorabilia from the early 1900s and displays depicting life in the county through the decades.

Land of the Longleaf Pine

Weymouth Woods and the Sandhills

KIM HYRE
AND SCOTT HARTLEY

This 35-mile tour takes you to longleaf pine savannas in half of North Carolina's Sandhill counties. The majestic longleaf pine with its 12- to 18-inch-long green needles and large cones is the predominant tree species to be seen as you drive along. Evidence of recent fires can be seen on the trunks of the trees, or there may be a controlled burn in progress during your visit. Most of these fires have been conducted under strict control measures, but they are a natural part of the longleaf pine forest ecosystem. You will visit several habitats in a state nature preserve, a federal military reservation, a state game land and fish hatchery, a local historical farm, and on private lands. Several miles of hiking trails can be found, but hiking should take place only in designated sites because hunting or military exercises take place during certain times of the year. You can stop at a visitors center/ museum to gain a better understanding of the role of fire in the native forest's survival. Possibilities for wildlife viewing in the region include sighting of the endangered red-cockaded woodpecker, the fox squirrel, wild turkey, and white-tailed deer.

The primary learning experience of this tour will be an understanding of the essential role of fire in maintaining the longleaf pine forest ecosystem. You will also be exposed to the unique geology of the Sandhills and can learn something about the people and animals that make their homes in the area. Driving along, the first thing that will be very striking will be the longleaf pines, wiregrass, understory oak trees, and white sandy soils along the roadside. You can't help but notice the 10-inch-long cones that fall from the longleaf pines. With a little closer look, you may notice evidence of a past fire—blackened tree trunks. Europeans have always viewed fires as destructive, but in the land of the longleaf pines you will find that it is not only beneficial but necessary to maintaining a healthy forest. This once-vast region burned in its natural state as a result of lightning strikes during the dry spring and summer months. Today in the Sandhills fires are orchestrated by well-trained forest managers.

Visiting this region you will get a sense for the topography—the hills of white sandy soils give the region both its character and its name. The Sandhills region formerly was believed to have been an ancient sand dune system, but more current understanding of its origin asserts that it is an ancient delta plain, formed by sediment-laden streams flowing from the mountains across the Piedmont and emptying into the sea that once covered the Coastal Plain.

Today it is hard to imagine that this land was useful for anything other than the golf courses that dot the landscape; however, Native Americans and, later, Scottish immigrants found this region rich in wild game and a good place to build home-steads and small towns. The Native Americans visited the region following the migrating wild bison, whereas the Scots came to find sanctuary away from the turmoil of their homeland. The Scots found profit in the land from such activities as farming, harvesting naval stores from the forest, and, later, logging the timber.

A. Walthour/Moss Foundation and Yadkin Road

This tour begins at the Manly exit of US 1, which is reached by taking US 1 south from the large metropolitan areas of the Triangle to the Southern Pines area. Four miles south of Vass at a sign stating, "Southern Pines Next 4 Exits," take the first exit to Manly (Figure 46). You will cross the northbound traffic. The land just to the left of the US 1 exit is owned by the Walthour/Moss Foundation and is part of approximately 4,000 acres preserved for traditional equestrian use by the effort of two local families. There are hiking trails that can be accessed from the first left on Equestrian Road. A small information board about the trails sits on the right side of the road.

You can also continue to travel by car on North May Street into Southern Pines. There are several horse farms along the road to admire. In about 1.5 miles you will cross an intersection with Yadkin Road. On the left there is a historical marker that sits parallel to Yadkin Road and which may be hard to see. "The Yadkin Road" is the title, and you will be able to read a brief narrative about the historical signifi-cance of the road.

B. Weymouth Center and the Boyd Tract

Continue south on North May Street for another mile into town to the first stoplight and make a left turn onto Connecticut Avenue. A block and a half later, there will be a sign on your left: "Weymouth Center." The house that you see from the parking lot is the former home of James Boyd, a noted author in his day. The home is open to the public Monday through Friday, 10 A.M. to 4 P.M. Weymouth Center has an artist-in-residence program and is the cultural center for the South-ern Pines area. The grounds and gardens are open daily. As you walk away from the

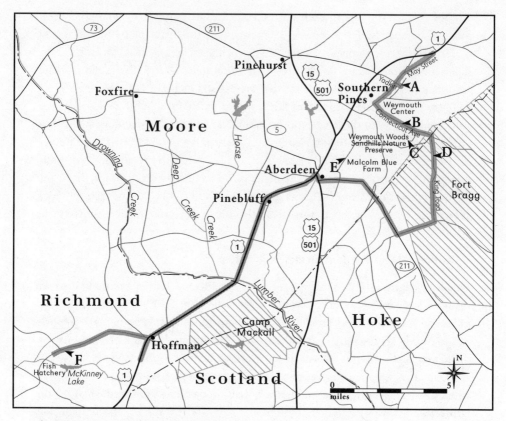

FIGURE 46. Weymouth Woods tour route

back of the house into an open meadow you are now on lands operated by Weymouth Woods–Sandhills Nature Preserve. Following the edge of the meadow and heading away from Connecticut Avenue is a loop trail blazed in orange (approximately 1 mile) through an old-growth forest of longleaf pines (Figure 47). These trees are at the maximum age for the species: 400 to 500 years old. Boyd was instrumental in preserving this land from the timber industry, which clear-cut most of the area where the town of Southern Pines sits today.

c. Weymouth Woods–Sandhills Nature Preserve

The next stop on the tour is the visitors center and nature museum. Follow Connecticut Avenue east and away from town for approximately 2.5 miles; you will see a North Carolina State Park sign for Weymouth Woods. Turn right onto Fort Bragg Road and follow the signs to the entrance gate. The park road will lead to the visitors center and museum. This is also a starting point for several hiking trails.

FIGURE 47. Longleaf pine forest. (Photo by D. Frankenberg)

Maps and trail descriptions are available at the visitors center; the preserve maintains 4.5 miles of hiking trails. Stop in at the office and the staff will be able to
provide specific information on where to see certain plants and animals at the
preserve (Figure 48). Animals that can be seen include red-cockaded woodpeckers,
fox squirrels, several uncommon butterflies including King's streak, Edwards hair-
streak, pine elfin, frosted elfin, Meskes skipper, to name a few. Plants and wildflowers that can be seen include sundews, three species of pitcher plant, orchids,
numerous composites, pine barrens gentian, and pocosin shrubs like titi, inkberry,
staggerbush, and witch alder. Most of the longleaf pine trees bear small square
scars that are the results of the harvesting of resin to produce turpentine. Museum
exhibits depict and explain how important the longleaf pine was for the naval
stores industry in the 1700s. Park staff provide interpretive programs every Sunday
at 3 P.M. April to October. Organized groups can request a program by contacting
the park office.

Weymouth Woods–Sandhills Nature Preserve was donated to the North Carolina Division of Parks and Recreation by Mrs. James Boyd in 1963. The Boyds
acquired the property in the early 1900s. Mrs. Boyd's father-in-law, James Boyd,
was traveling by train through Southern Pines in 1903. He heard the sound of axes
and saws felling trees east of town from his open train window. Evidently the
uncontrolled cutting of the trees disturbed Boyd enough that he bought land
southeast of Southern Pines to protect the longleaf pine from logging. He built a

FIGURE 48. Wildflowers and butterflies on forest floor. (Photo by D. Frankenberg)

house on the land and named his estate "Weymouth" because the pines reminded him of the pines he had seen on a visit to Weymouth, England. The pines that Boyd had seen in England were called Weymouth pines, but they were actually our native white pine, *Pinus strobus*. The white pine was brought to England in 1605 from what is now the state of Maine by an officer of the British Royal Navy; his name was Captain George Weymouth. At this time in England there was a very serious lack of trees suitable for masts for the British Royal Navy's ships. The white pine was the answer to their problem and was declared a national treasure and given the name Weymouth pine in honor of Captain Weymouth.

D. Fort Bragg Military Reservation

Please note that while you are on military lands, it is necessary that you remain only on the paved roads. All other areas are off-limits to the public without an escort.

A short backtrack on Fort Bragg Road will be needed to get to the entrance gate of the military reservation. From the front gate of Weymouth Woods make a left and follow the road back to the stop sign. A right turn will take you through the gates and onto the reservation. At the top of the rise there is an intersection and flashing warning light; make a right turn onto King Road, from which you will gain an overall view of the local topography and a clear view of the pine forest. If you stop on one of the higher ridges you will find a very scenic view. Fort Bragg Military Reservation is managed for the training of troops, but the Department of Defense is also actively preserving the endangered red-cockaded woodpecker by regularly conducting prescribed burns of their native habitat. The white bands you will see around the longleaf pines along the way indicate the presence of red-cockaded woodpecker colonies. Some but not all of these are active at any one time. After about 7 miles you will come to a "Y" intersection; you need to stay right of the "Y" to exit Fort Bragg Military Reservation. Cross the railroad tracks, and NC 211 will be the road that you intersect. This intersection is across from the Sandhills Youth Center at McCain. Turn right and head for Aberdeen on NC 211 North.

E. Malcom Blue Farm

After traveling north for 7 miles on NC 211 toward Aberdeen, you will approach a sign for the Malcom Blue Farm; make a right turn. Once you are off of NC 211 make another right onto Bethesda Road (also known as NC 5), and this will lead past some of the historical buildings of Aberdeen, such as the Bethesda Presbyterian Church, founded in the 1700s. The Malcolm Blue Farm is past the church on the left. An annual festival is held on the grounds of this private farm during the last weekend of September. At other times there is a small farming museum open to the public on Thursday through Saturday, from 1 P.M. to 4 P.M.

F. Sandhills Game Lands

Backtracking once again on NC 5/Bethesda Road South (right turn from Malcom Blue Farm), follow the signs through Aberdeen until you get to the intersection of US 1. As you drive through Aberdeen look for the historical placards on each of the homes. Turn left on US 1 South to Hoffman, where there is a state fish hatchery. Turn right at the sign and follow additional signs to the hatchery on your left. Some of the land on both sides of the road is part of the Sandhills Game Lands and is managed by the North Carolina Wildlife Resources Commission. This is a good place to see birds of many types—land birds in the savanna, water birds and fish eaters around the hatchery.

Once you have visited the fish hatchery you will need to backtrack to US 1. Make a right turn onto US 1 South and travel about 3 miles to Old Laurel Hill Road on the left. This is the starting point for Alan Weakley's tour beginning on page 193. As you cross the railroad tracks you will be in Scotland County. These lands are managed for both endangered species and hunting. It is advisable that you stay on the main roads during hunting season. There are signs along the way to the three different sites along this road. Site 3 is the first one you will find on the right, and it is a typical longleaf pine–scrub oak forest that is being burned on a three-year burning rotation (winter burns only). Site 2, on the right approximately 2 miles down the road, is an area that was thinned in the mid-1980s using both chemical and mechanical methods of removing the understory. It is burned on a three-year rotation during winter and growing seasons. The last site is about 1 mile farther down the road and is located on the left. This area is an International Paper Company holding that was once a slash pine plantation but now is planted in the native longleaf pine and is burned on a winter rotation.

The Piedmont

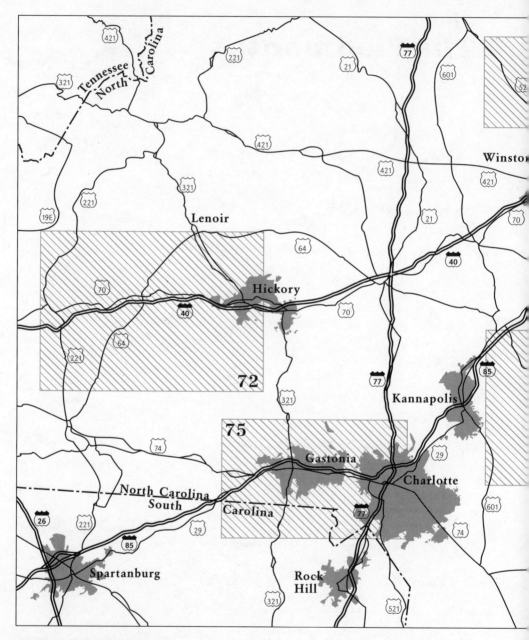

FIGURE 49. Piedmont tour routes
Numbers in boxes indicate figure numbers for individual tour route maps.

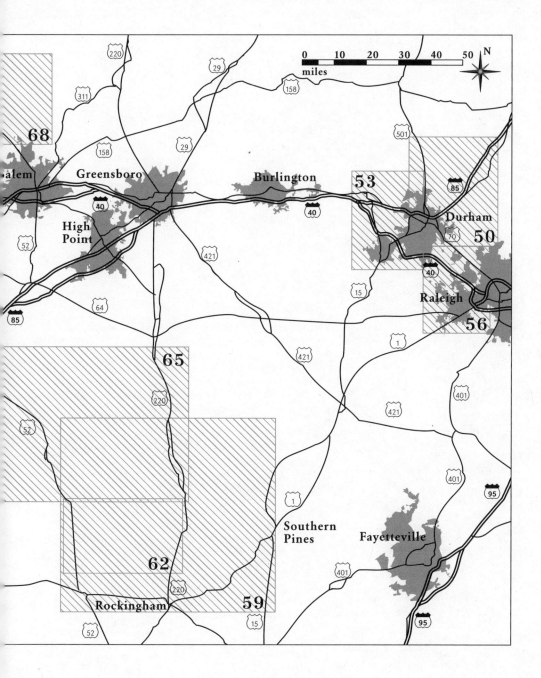

0   10   20   30   40   50   N
miles

68

Greensboro   **Burlington**   53

Durham   50

High
Point

Raleigh

65   56

Rockingham   62   59

Southern
Pines   **Fayetteville**

álem

Rocks, Soils, and Plant Life in the Central Piedmont

HARRY LEGRAND

This 56-mile tour takes the motorist through a cross-section of the central Piedmont, from the northern edge of the city of Durham, to Hill Forest in northern Durham County, then eastward to Butner and Falls Lake in Granville and northern Wake Counties. This tour is designed for persons interested in rare plants and unusual natural communities, especially vegetation growing on basic (above neutral in pH) soils. North Carolina State University's Hill Forest comprises typical vegetation for the central Piedmont, as it lies in the geologic province known as the Carolina Slate Belt. Farther west there are unusual rock formations in the Durham and Butner areas, which lie in a Triassic basin. Within the basin, there are several places where a horizontal layer of rock that is rich in magnesium, and which weathers to a high pH soil, are found. These diabase sills are very rare, and many rare plants grow on them. Finally, the tour leaves the Triassic basin and heads east into the Raleigh Belt, which consists of older, metamorphosed rocks.

The tour can be made either from Durham or Raleigh, in either direction. It is easiest to start from the intersection of Interstate 85 and NC 55 (Roxboro Road, Exit 177) in northeastern Durham. The trip is best done in the warmer months, when the wildflowers are in bloom and the leaves are on the trees. Both of these factors help in the identification of plant species and natural community types. If you are interested in birding, for instance at Falls Lake, you might want to drive the route in the winter months, when more birds are present.

This tour offers opportunities to learn about the geology and biota (plants and animals) of the central Piedmont and, most important, about the intimate relationship between the two. The causal linkage between soil type and biota is easily seen along this tour route as it takes you past soils formed from three different types of rock. These rock types meet one another where they were fractured apart by the stresses of continental collision and fragmentation (see the section on geology in the Introduction). The openings between the two widespread rock types (Carolina Slate Belt and Raleigh Belt) were filled with molten material that intruded upward from deeper in the crust. These intrusion materials had a dif-

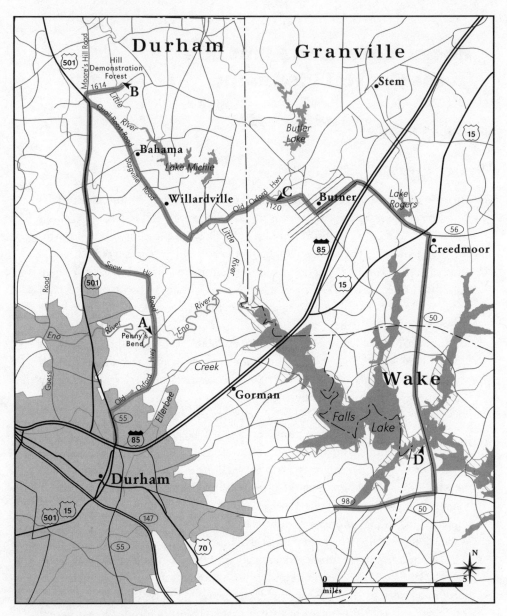

FIGURE 50. Central Piedmont tour route—Durham to Falls Lake

ferent chemical composition than the granite and sandstone that form the upper layers; and, predictably enough, these chemically different parent rocks formed different types of soil as they weathered. These different soils now sustain different types of plants and animals. This tour of Durham, Granville, and Wake Counties takes you through acidic (low pH) soils typical of most of the Piedmont and into the Durham Triassic basin with its basic (high pH) soils formed from magnesium-rich mafic rock that intruded into overlying layers of granite. Such intrusions occur in many places in the Piedmont, but they are usually much smaller and less well defined biologically than those you will see along the edges of the Durham Triassic basin.

A. Penny's Bend Nature Preserve

From Interstate 85 travel north on NC 55 for 1.5 miles and turn right onto Old Oxford Highway (SR 1004). Follow this road across the Eno River (3.1 miles) and immediately turn left onto Snow Hill Road (SR 1631); then make another immediate left into a parking area for the Penny's Bend Nature Preserve. This natural area is part of the Falls Lake Project owned by the U.S. Army Corps of Engineers, but it is managed by the North Carolina Botanical Garden Foundation. Penny's Bend is named after a sharp, horseshoe bend in the Eno River, and it lies over a diabase sill where the rock is very close to the surface. A diabase sill is a thin horizontal rock layer of intrusive (diabase) rock wedged between older rocks. Over time, the overlying rock beds eroded away, leaving the diabase (magnesium-rich mafic rock that forms high pH soils) exposed at or near the surface. There is a foot trail paralleling the Eno River, leading from the right corner of the parking area, where in March and early April you can see Dutchman's breeches in bloom in a rocky forest at the southern end of the loop trail. There is also a series of pathways mowed into the field adjacent to the parking area, where rare herbaceous plants (most of them are typical of prairies) grow on the high pH soils. Plants along this field trail include prairie dock, tall larkspur, blue wild indigo, and the federally endangered smooth coneflower (Figure 51).

B. Hill Demonstration Forest

Continue northward along Snow Hill Road for 4.5 miles and turn right onto US 501. You have now left the Triassic basin and are in the hillier topography of the Carolina Slate Belt. After 5.5 miles turn right onto Moores Mill Road (SR 1601), and in 0.2 miles take another right onto State Forest Road (SR 1614). Within 0.6 miles you will come to Hill Demonstration Forest, a state-owned facility administered

FIGURE 51. Wildflowers in Penny's Bend Nature Preserve. (Photo by D. Frankenberg)

by North Carolina State University. A map of Hill Forest can be found on the left-hand side of the road, 0.2 miles inside the forest boundary. This map not only shows you where forest roads/trails are located, but it also portrays the forest's stands, with age and type of trees (loblolly pine, upland hardwoods, etc.) indicated. There are forest roads (most are gated) that can be hiked at several points along State Forest Road, both before and after the low-water bridge crossing the Flat River. Make sure you sample a few of the trails/roads (park only along SR 1614); you might want to make a sketch of some of the roads, trails, and forest stands when you are studying the map of the forest. Just before the river, on the left, is Slocum Camp, where courses, workshops, and training in forest resources and management are conducted by N.C. State University staff. The Flat River is one of the more scenic rivers in the central Piedmont, with a number of large rocks protruding from the water (Figure 52). Rare freshwater mussels are found in this river, an indication of its very good water quality.

Unfortunately, no trail parallels the river, but a few of the forest roads reach it, particularly the first on the right after you cross the river. The forest road on the right before you reach the river only passes mature stands of upland hardwoods, although some of the side trails on the left lead to the river. You will see a variety of forest types in Hill Forest, ranging from mesic stands with beech, to upland oak-hickory forests, to natural stands of loblolly and shortleaf pines, to recent clear-cuts. There are even some stands of planted trees such as white pines.

FIGURE 52. Flat River in Hill Demonstration Forest. (Photo by D. Frankenberg)

c. Butner Natural Areas

To continue the tour, backtrack to US 501, then turn left and go 0.3 miles, turning left onto Quail Roost Road (SR 1615), which takes you through the quaint community of Bahama (pronounced buh-HAY-muh) in 2.5 miles. Continue south through Bahama on SR 1615 (now called Stagville Road) for another 3.7 miles, and turn left at Old Oxford Highway (SR 1004). This latter road runs along the northern edge of the Triassic basin, so the land (especially on your right side) is very flat. You will pass a federal prison on your left as you cross into Granville County. A mile after the prison, turn right onto Veazey Road (SR 1120). A diabase sill lies under the surface in this region. The soil is rich brown in color and is almost a sticky brown-black when wet; the local residents call this soil Butner Gumbo. The U.S. Army Corps of Engineers owns land adjacent to Veazey Road, as this is the upper reaches of Falls Lake. You are free to traverse the countryside here, as the lands in the Butner area are owned by either the State of North Carolina or the Corps of Engineers. However, be aware that these are game lands, with hunters present at certain times of the year (mainly fall and winter). The best places to walk—there are no hiking trails here—are sewerline clearings that traverse several habitats.

After crossing a bridge on Veazey Road at 0.2 miles, park at a pullover spot on the left. There are sewerline clearings on both sides of the road. The sewerline to the right (southwest), adjacent to the bridge, parallels two large beaver ponds inhabited by a great array of wildlife—things such as wood ducks, prothonotary warblers, turtles, and frogs. These clearings might not be recently mowed or cleared, so use your best judgment about whether to walk along them and into the nearby woods. You will note a much larger percentage of red cedar and redbud in the forest (on your left) over the diabase than over the typical granite- or sandstone-derived soils elsewhere. You might also see the diabase rock in the streams near the sewerline; the diabase weathers rather evenly, so rocks made of it are generally rounded and heavy, reminiscent of bowling balls!

Continue on Veazey Road toward Butner and turn left onto Westbrooke Street (SR 1174) after 1.3 miles; then make a quick right onto Central Avenue (SR 1103). Drive 0.8 miles and turn left onto C Street, in the middle of Butner. Follow C Street for 1.7 miles to a powerline crossing just before the road bends. You might want to walk in the powerline clearing on both sides of the road to look for rare plants such as prairie dock (blooms in July and August), hoary puccoon (blooms April and May), and blue wild indigo (blooms May and June), as this site lies over diabase. The diabase soils in the Butner and Durham areas support over two dozen rare plant species, probably the highest concentration of rare plants in the Piedmont of North Carolina. Ironically, most of the rare plants are found in artificial openings, such as powerline and sewerline rights-of-way. These unusual plants probably favored natural openings once created by wildfires and possibly by large native grazing mammals such as bison.

D. Falls Lake (Falls of the Neuse Reservoir)

The tour now heads southeast to Falls Lake, a reservoir constructed by the U.S. Army Corps of Engineers. The Corps has left a wide and wooded buffer around the entire shoreline, making it a good place for naturalists. The western half of the lake lies in the Triassic basin, and the eastern half is in the Raleigh Belt. Thus the western half has wide expanses of water that filled the broad Triassic basin flood-plain of the Neuse River, whereas the eastern half consists of narrow coves in the more dissected Raleigh Belt. Continue on C Street (which becomes NC 56) over Interstate 85, and in 3.2 miles (in Creedmoor) you will intersect US 15. Go straight across the intersection, and at the top of the hill, in two blocks, turn right onto NC 50. Follow NC 50 southward for 7.4 miles to Falls Lake. Just before reaching the lake you will see an area of open pines that formerly served as habitat for the federally endangered red-cockaded woodpecker. Unfortunately, the woodpeckers disappeared from the area around 1980. The Army Corps of Engineers has continued to burn and thin the stand in hopes that the woodpeckers will return.

Just past the lake, on the left, is a turn to the North Carolina Division of Parks and Recreation office, where you can obtain maps and other information about trails in the area. This agency manages most of the public lands on the eastern shore of Falls Lake (the North Carolina Wildlife Resources Commission manages most of the lands on the western shore of Falls Lake as state game lands.)

To visit several of the more significant natural areas at Falls Lake, continue south on NC 50 from the parks office and turn left at NC 98 in 1.5 miles. After 0.6 miles, turn left again onto Ghoston Road (SR 1908). Go 0.9 miles and park on the road shoulder next to where the Falls Lake Trail crosses the road. On the left (west) the trail passes through the Old Still Creek Registered Natural Heritage Area. Walk along the trail for several tenths of a mile. You will see some trees that were blown down during Hurricane Fran in September 1996. This is one of the more mature examples of the Mesic Mixed Hardwood Forest type in the northeastern Piedmont of the state. American beech trees are common, and umbrella magnolias are numerous in the understory. Broad beech fern is a conspicuous component of the herb layer. In the spring, there is an impressive wildflower display.

Return back to NC 98 on Ghoston Road; turn right onto NC 98 and travel 3.9 miles until you reach a floodplain with a guard rail along NC 98. Park just past the guard rail and walk north (right) into the floodplain, which should be dry during most of the year. This is part of the Lick Creek Bottomland Forest Registered Natural Heritage Area—a good example of Piedmont bottomland forest. Trees such as swamp chestnut oak and cherrybark oak are present; the rare Douglass's bittercress blooms in March in the floodplain.

For those interested in birding at Falls Lake, the best places are at the upper end, in the Triassic basin, where the lake is wider and shallower. When the lake is low, often in summer and fall, large numbers of shorebirds and waders may be present. In the winter large numbers of gulls are always present, along with a scattering of waterfowl. A few bald eagles can be seen year-round, and the ever-increasing double-crested cormorant abounds in the warmer months.

To best view the lake, visit Cheek Road and the Hickory Hill Boat Ramp. Cheek Road can be reached from the east by turning west off NC 50 onto Old Weaver Road (SR 1901), just south of the Granville–Wake County line. Follow the road for 4.5 miles to the lake, where you will come to the Cheek Road bridge (Cheek Road is the name of this road once it reaches Durham County.) You can see a large expanse of the upper part of the lake, both upstream and downstream. To reach the Hickory Hill Boat Ramp, continue west across the bridge and in 1 mile turn right onto Hereford Road (SR 1800). After 0.6 miles turn right at a T-intersection onto Redwood Road (SR 1637); drive 0.6 miles to the entrance of the boat ramp. From the ramp area you can scan the upper part of the lake north to Interstate 85. Unfortunately, you cannot stop along the interstate to look for birds. One other area popular with birders is reached by continuing back to Redwood Road, turning right, and going beneath the Interstate 85 overpass to park at a small pullout where Redwood Road makes a sharp bend to the left, about 0.6 miles past the overpass. Walk ahead to the railroad tracks, and walk along the tracks or in adjacent fields to your right for views of marshes and shallow waters near the head of the lake.

From the Durham area or areas to the west, these viewing spots are best reached by taking Interstate 85 east and turning onto Redwood Road at Exit 183. The boat ramp and the Cheek Road bridge will be to your east and the railroad tracks to your west.

Other popular viewing areas are at the Division of Parks and Recreation facilities—Sandling Beach, Beaverdam Lake, and the NC 50 Access—all of which are located off NC 50 in Wake County just north of the NC 50 bridge. A fee is charged at these facilities during the warmer parts of the year. Obtain a map of the lake and facilities at the park office just off NC 50, south of the lake.

Ecological Succession and Old-Growth Forests of the Central Piedmont

PHILLIP MANNING

This 30-mile tour takes you to natural areas preserved by two universities (Duke and the University of North Carolina at Chapel Hill), a state park (Eno River), and a state natural area (Occoneechee Mountain). Along the way you will pass through developed parts of Chapel Hill, Durham, and Hillsborough. The route takes you past examples from what might be called a "what-not-to-do manual" of Piedmont forest ecology. From the earliest days of colonial America, the Piedmont's moderate climate, abundant timber, and numerous rivers brought in wave after wave of European settlers. First came trading posts, then mills, farms, and towns and cities like those you will pass through. Today, from New Jersey to Alabama, hardly a patch of virgin Piedmont forest remains.

Fortunately, many of these destroyed forests have since regenerated, through the process of ecological succession, on abandoned farmland. This tour will take you through some of North Carolina's old-growth Piedmont forests and through younger forests in earlier stages of succession. Although these forests can be glimpsed from your car, I suggest you walk a short trail or two at each stop. As with most natural areas, these forests are best appreciated on foot.

The old-growth forests you will see on this tour resemble those encountered by the earliest Europeans. Although these were practical men, primarily interested in timber and soil, they were impressed with the beauty of the Piedmont. When John Lawson, who became surveyor-general of North Carolina, traveled through the region in 1701, he called it "extremely pleasant" and a "delicious country."

Our tour of this delicious country starts at the North Carolina Botanical Garden in Chapel Hill and passes through parts of Duke Forest and Eno River State Park, to end at Occoneechee Mountain in Hillsborough.

Learning experiences on this tour are similar to others in the Piedmont. You will witness the resilience of nature as it restores itself through natural processes after being disturbed by the footprints of humans. The forests on this tour illustrate both this resilience and the process of succession that produced them.

Ecologists define succession as "the nonseasonal, directional continuous pattern

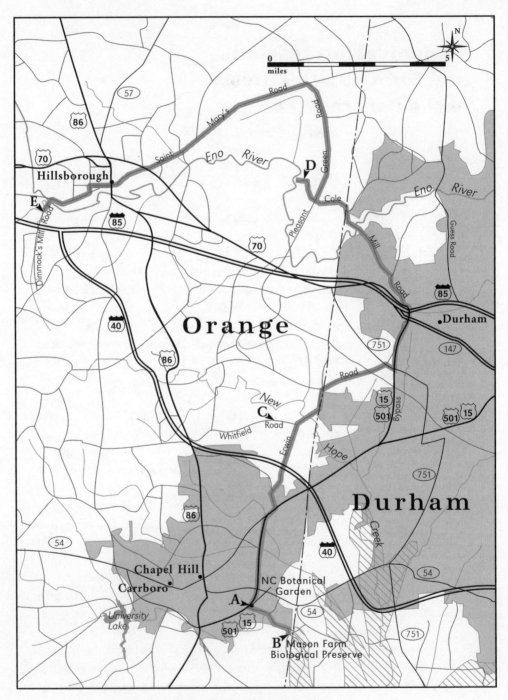

FIGURE 53. Central Piedmont tour route—old-growth forests

of colonization and extinction on a site by populations." Happily, this process is not as complicated as it sounds. Put simply, it means that when vegetation is destroyed by fire or hurricane or humans, nature will fill the void. We have all witnessed this process. Take, for example, an abandoned farm. Vines and shrubs have swarmed over the deserted farmhouse and will finally obliterate it; weeds poke through cracks in the driveway, which tree roots will eventually destroy; and pines have begun their scraggly march across the untended cornfields and will gradually turn them into forests.

In the Piedmont, as elsewhere, succession is so predictable that ecologists can tell when a plot of land was last disturbed from the types of vegetation that grow there. First comes crabgrass, then broom sedge and horseweed, pines, and pioneer hardwoods. The end point of succession in the Piedmont is a forest of hardwoods and wildflowers that is self-perpetuating—at least until the next disturbance comes along.

In the last few centuries, humans have disturbed almost all of the land in the Piedmont. On this tour you will see plant communities in every stage of succession, including a few climax forests. But even these forests are not identical to the ones that greeted the early settlers. The chestnut trees that once supplied their abundant nuts to deer and squirrels have succumbed to a blight. And the trees in today's young forests have yet to attain the girth of those of yesteryear. Nevertheless, a climax Piedmont forest is a lovely place, and it's no wonder that many of our forebears chose to settle here.

A. North Carolina Botanical Garden

The parking lot for the garden is on Old Mason Farm Road, just off us 15-501 Bypass on the southeastern side of Chapel Hill. The garden's visitors center, the Totten Center, is across Laurel Hill Road. The hiking trails start from the parking lot.

There is no better place to begin a tour of North Carolina's natural areas than the Totten Center at the North Carolina Botanical Garden. The center sells field guides that will help you identify the state's flora and fauna. Surrounding the center are living collections containing over 2,500 species of plants and trees found in North Carolina's major ecosystems, from the coast to the mountains. A stroll through these collections is a perfect introduction to the state's natural areas.

Across Laurel Hill Road from the Totten Center, two nature trails lead into a Piedmont forest. Loblolly and shortleaf pines dominate the 0.3-mile-long Streamside Trail. Less than a century ago, this was farmland; after it was abandoned, grasses and goldenrod reclaimed the old fields, beginning the successional process. Loblolly pines soon followed. So routine was this sequence that farmers gave loblollies another name: old-field pine.

Beneath the pines along this trail grow the future: red maples and sweet gums, tulip poplars, oaks, and hickories. These hardwoods tolerate shade better than sun-loving pines. In fact, pine seedlings cannot survive on a shady forest floor. And as the older pines fall, from age or lightning or disease, hardwoods will replace them. The end result will be a hardwood forest, the mature stage of Piedmont succession.

Such a forest can be seen on the 1-mile Oak-Hickory Trail (which branches off from the Streamside Trail), parts of which have not been logged in over one hundred years. The path leads into a stand of mature oaks, ashes, gums, and beeches. Dogwoods and sourwoods flourish beneath the canopy, and in early spring, trilliums and other ephemeral wildflowers bloom in the duff on the forest floor. In the fall, the prettiest time of the year to me, the forest glows with the reds and oranges of maples and scarlet oaks.

You will almost certainly see gray squirrels along this path, as well as an assortment of forest birds such as chickadees, titmice, and thrushes. I have rarely walked this trail without seeing or hearing red-bellied woodpeckers.

B. Mason Farm Biological Reserve

From the North Carolina Botanical Garden, proceed south on Old Mason Farm Road past the Finley Golf Course club house and driving range. Continue on an unpaved road into the reserve. About 1.3 miles from the end of the paved road, an unnamed dirt road goes off to the right. Follow it over a ford across Morgan Creek. The parking lot is just beyond the ford.

Mason Farm is managed by the North Carolina Botanical Garden. The 367-acre tract is part of an 800-acre farm left to the University of North Carolina by Mary Elizabeth Morgan Mason and the Reverend James Mason in 1894. Mason Farm is not a park; it was set it aside as a place for ecological research and nature study. Permits are required to enter it and are available for no charge at the Totten Center.

The reserve's loop trail passes fields of goldenrod and broom sedge. The university periodically harrows these fields, so they can be used to illustrate the process of succession to biology students. The path then circles Big Oak Woods. These woods were made famous by John Terres (Figure 54), the former editor of *Audubon* magazine, who wrote a Burroughs Award–winning book about Mason Farm. *From Laurel Hill to Siler's Bog* detailed the author's adventures on Reverend Mason's old farm. In the early 1990s I was privileged to walk this trail with Terres. Although he was in his eighties at the time, he identified the calls of all the birds we heard, including the almost inaudible cry of a great horned owl.

Bobcats still roam this remnant forest, and over two hundred species of birds

FIGURE 54. John Terres at Mason Farm. (Photo by P. Manning)

have been spotted at Mason Farm over the years. The southernmost part of the trail passes through swampy ground where hardwood snags stud the damp landscape. The quiet walker can usually find pileated and red-headed woodpeckers there.

c. Duke Forest

Return to us 15-501 Bypass via Mason Farm Road and proceed north to Erwin Road. Go left on Erwin Road and follow it north for 2.3 miles to Whitfield Road (sr 173). Turn left and watch for trailheads on the right (north) side of the road; there are two within 0.3 miles, but the second, 0.9 miles from Erwin Road, will take you to New Hope Creek.

Duke Forest is owned by Duke University and consists of six management divisions and 8,300 acres of land with over 35 miles of roads and trails. The university began acquiring the land in the 1920s to buffer its campus from the outside world. Today Duke's faculty and students conduct research projects in the forest, but it is open to the public for recreational use. Before entering the forest, visitors should obtain the brochure "Duke Forest," which lists ten simple rules that the university asks all recreational users to follow. To obtain this brochure and trail maps contact Duke's Nicholas School of the Environment (919-613-8013).

Although each division of Duke Forest has something to offer, I prefer the Korstian Division, which was named for Dr. Clarence F. Korstian, the forester Duke brought in to manage its newly acquired land. At the time, the land didn't amount to much. It was, Korstian said, "farmed out." Today, Duke Forest is healthy, as a walk along its trails will show you.

A good place to start is along New Hope Creek. The above-mentioned trail from Whitfield Road crosses and parallels the creek and leads you upstream through a mature Piedmont alluvial forest, thick with sycamores, oaks, and hickories. In these bottomlands grow an occasional black walnut, a rare tree these days because of the value of the wood. A single straight-grained mature walnut tree can bring its lucky owner $20,000 or more.

You can continue along the New Hope Creek Trail for over 3 miles, but I prefer to take one of the many dirt roads that intersect it. They lead upland into Dr. Korstian's farmed-out lands. Plantations of white pine and loblolly pine, some planted by Korstian himself, are spaced along the way and intermingle with un-managed stands of hardwoods (Figure 55). If you leave the road and venture into one of these tracts, you will notice a texture of low ridges to the land that is as regular as the beat of a metronome. The texture represents old furrows where rows of cotton or corn once stood. Stop and look at the forest around you and marvel at the recuperative powers of nature—and at Dr. Korstian's healing hands.

FIGURE 55. Pine plantations in Duke Forest. (Photo courtesy of Duke Forest)

D. Eno River State Park

Return to Erwin Road and turn left (north). At its intersection with NC 751, jog right to US 15-501 Bypass. Take a left and go north on the bypass; exit at US 70 Business (Hillsborough Road) and proceed west. Make a right turn on Cole Mill Road; Few's Ford Access, a division of Eno River State Park, is at the end of the road.

Except for a few coastal towns, some of the longest settled land in North Carolina is in the Piedmont. Of course, even the earliest settlers were newcomers compared to the Native Americans, who had lived there for centuries. When John Lawson passed through here in the early eighteenth century, his guide was Enoe-Will, a chief of the Eno Indians.

The Enos treated Lawson well, feeding him "fat bear" and "barbekued . . . venison." Enoe-Will reappeared in William Byrd's *Journey to the Land of Eden*. According to Byrd, Enoe-Will tried to sell him a silver mine. Byrd didn't buy the mine but instead slipped the old man a bottle of rum. By the mid-eighteenth century Enoe-Will and his entire tribe were gone, displaced by European settlers moving into the region. Like the Indians before them, they were attracted by the clean waters of the fast-flowing Eno River, which at one point had as many as thirty mills operating along it.

Nowhere is the history of Piedmont forests painted more vividly than at the

2,064-acre Eno River State Park. The park has multiple access points, but Few's Ford is a good place to start. Several hiking trails (a free map is available at the park office) take off from the parking lot into the Piedmont forest. These trails take you through every stage of Piedmont succession, from overgrown fields with fence posts still in place, to scrubby stands of cedars and pines and, finally, along the river to a mature hardwood forest.

Be sure to cross the river on the swinging bridge that spans Few's Ford. You will find the water is still fast-flowing and clean. Many people—especially the recently deceased Margaret Nygard—fought hard to preserve this river after the city of Durham proposed to dam it and turn it into a reservoir. The evidence of their vision and hard work is all around you.

E. Hillsborough and Occoneechee Mountain State Natural Area

Return down Cole Mill Road to its intersection with Pleasant Green Road; turn left for about 6 miles to Saint Mary's Road, which is built along the route of a Native American trading path. Turn left (west) on Saint Mary's Road toward Hillsborough. Cross US 70 into downtown Hillsborough and bear right onto King Street just past Saint Matthews Episcopal Church. The Orange County visitors center is in the Dickson House, a restored eighteenth-century Quaker plan building at the intersection of Saint Mary's Road and East King Street.

Hillsborough is worth a visit for those interested in history and the early development of the Piedmont. The town was founded in 1754 and is the seat of Orange County—a county that once stretched west into unsettled lands in Tennessee and Kentucky but now contents itself by being home to Chapel Hill and its University of North Carolina campus.

The place to start a tour of Hillsborough is at the Dickson House. The Dickson House was the building (then located over a mile away) in which Confederate officers determined conditions for the truce they would sign with General Sherman. The visitors center housed there now provides information and guides to Hillsborough, including a self-guided tour of seventy-four historic houses and landmarks, as well as brochures describing nearby house museums, the county museum, and places to eat and spend the night.

Hillsborough and Orange County carried formidable political power during the Revolutionary War and for several decades thereafter. An early, and notoriously unsuccessful, tax revolt was held here in 1771 (the graves of six hanged participants are just uphill from the visitors center). The third Provincial Congress was held here in 1775, and so were five meetings of the General Assembly and the Constitutional Assembly of 1788. Hillsborough almost became the state capital in 1791, but the present site in Raleigh was chosen instead. Much physical evidence of the town's early history, including the street plan, houses, schools, churches, and public buildings, remain in place and accessible to visitors.

To reach Occoneechee Mountain State Natural Area, continue west on King Street until its intersection with Nash Street at a top-of-the-hill traffic light. Turn left past the textile mill, right onto Dimmock's Mill Road beyond the shops of West Hillsborough, and follow it as it veers left under the railroad tracks. Pass the Hillsborough Business Center (another old mill) on your left, then turn left onto Eno Mountain Road, which crosses the Eno River within 0.25 miles of the intersection and then swings over the eastern end of the mountain and passes the Piedmont Minerals mine. At the stop sign turn right onto Orange Grove Road; then take the first right onto Virginia Cates Road and proceed about 200 feet to the new state-parks-managed parking area and trails. (Note: the Division of Parks and Recreation discourages parking in the "traditional" places along Eno Mountain Road: these are on private property.)

The Occoneechee Mountain State Natural Area, like both Hemlock Bluffs and Swift Creek Bluffs southeast of Raleigh (see the Wake County tour), preserves plant communities that were established in an earlier, colder climate and which are persisting today on steep north-facing slopes. The mountain is one of the last of a series of monadnocks that run in a northeasterly direction through the southwestern portion of the county. Capped with a rock that is more resistant to erosion than the surrounding countryside, these "mountains" project above the Piedmont peneplain. At Occoneechee Mountain you will find laurel and rhododendron thickets comparable to those found typically in the mountains hundreds of miles west and hundreds of feet higher in elevation. These can be seen along the trail leading down on the east side of the abandoned quarry, reached by trails from the parking lot.

Nature amidst Development

Wake County Natural Areas

LAURA WHITE
AND MARK JOHNS

This 16-mile tour takes you to three unique and interesting natural areas in the developed Wake County area of North Carolina. The tour starts at William B. Umstead State Park, located off Interstate 40 near Cary, and includes stops at Cary's Hemlock Bluffs Nature Preserve, a dedicated North Carolina nature preserve, and the Triangle Land Conservancy's Swift Creek Bluffs Nature Preserve. The significant impact that humans have had on the natural environment, both historically and recently, will be obvious at and around all of the tour stops. Also impressive are the unique opportunities available in the county to explore and enjoy the nature that still exists in this rapidly urbanizing area.

The major learning experience of this tour will be insight into the tremendous impact that humans have had on the landscape and, thus, on natural communities and plant and animal species of the central Piedmont. You will see both natural and developed areas within 10 miles of downtown Raleigh. The natural areas you visit have been preserved as investments for future generations. They are areas rich in natural heritage, and they demonstrate the processes of ecological succession and some of the unique natural features of Wake County. Lands encompassed by William B. Umstead State Park superbly illustrate the processes of ecological succession: what was once eroded farmland and timbered forests is now beginning to resemble the former natural communities of this part of the Piedmont. Visitors to the park can also learn something about the history of settlement in central North Carolina and about the culture of eighteenth-century European settlers. Hemlock and Swift Creek Bluffs are north-facing bluff systems whose cooler temperatures support disjunct plant communities more typical of climates of 18,000 years ago. These bluff systems also preserve floodplain alluvial forests and upland oak-hickory woodlands more typical of the Piedmont before European settlement, over 300 years ago.

A. William B. Umstead State Park

This tour begins at William B. Umstead State Park at the park entrance off of Interstate 40 (North Harrison Avenue, Exit 287) near Cary. Park hours vary with

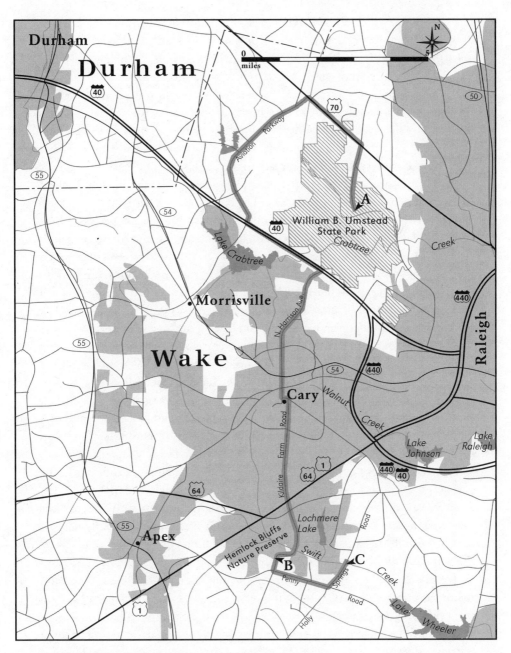

FIGURE 56. Wake County natural areas tour route

the season, so visitors should call 919-677-0062 for information on hours or programs. There is ample parking, and picnic facilities with restrooms are available (the restrooms are closed during winter). Over 17 miles of hiking trails provide a daylong experience within the 5,330-acre park; shorter loops are available as well. There is another entrance to the park off of US 70, 6 miles northwest of Raleigh. It is considered the main entrance to the park and provides public access to the new visitors and environmental education center, the public campground, recreational lakes, and group meeting and picnicking facilities. There are also three artificial lakes with seasonal boat rentals on the US 70 side of the park.

Within the park are pine forests, various hardwood communities, and mixed forests that demonstrate the process of old-field succession. The biota of the park is fairly diverse for the central Piedmont, with over 1,100 plant species and diverse populations of amphibians, reptiles, birds, mammals, and fish in the park's streams. Much of the land is covered by second- or third-growth woodlands that have developed since the land was abandoned by farmers in the 1930s. A mosaic of different forest types grow here, ranging from the last-abandoned farm sites, which are dominated by pines, to older forests consisting of a variety of hardwoods like oaks, hickories, tulip poplar, red maple, and black gum. Steep slopes along creeks harbor interesting disjunct species, like Catawba rhododendron; and 50 acres along Crabtree Creek hold forest dominated by what is believed to be virgin beech trees and southern maples. This particular area is included in the National Registry of Natural Landmarks. Spring wildflowers are abundant; species include bloodroot, trout lily, mayapple, yellow lady's slipper, spring beauty, and Jack-in-the-pulpit. A powerline right-of-way crossing the park allows the visitor to observe full-sun species typical of old fields. Pond edges are occupied by a variety of wetland plants.

There are excellent opportunities to study animals of all types and sizes in the park. Over sixty species of reptiles and amphibians occur within park boundaries, as do at least thirty species of mammals. One hundred eighty-five species of birds have been observed within the park. Fourteen warbler species currently nest, or have historically nested, within the park, and wild turkeys are established breeders. The park also serves as an important breeding area for many migratory birds and as a vital stopover for transient migrants in the spring and fall. Less common mammals of urban Wake County still sporadically occur here, such as mink, river otter, and long-tailed weasel. White-tailed deer are abundant and are often seen during the day by hikers. Good butterfly viewing opportunities can be found along the powerlines and along service road edges.

Prior to its agricultural use, the park was most likely a magnificent forest dominated by oaks, hickories, beeches, and many other deciduous trees. For about 150 years, trees were cut, farming was commonplace, and grist mills were built and operated along streams. Poor land-use practices led to massive erosion and eventual abandonment of most farms by the 1930s. In 1934 federal and state agencies bought 5,000 acres and earmarked them for a recreation area. The Civilian Conservation Corps (CCC) worked in the late 1930s, until the start of World War II, constructing buildings and other structures, planting trees, and controlling erosion. In 1943 the land was deeded to the state to meet public recreational purposes. The price for the property was $1, and the park was established as Crabtree Creek State Park. The name was changed in 1955 to William B. Umstead State Park to honor a former North Carolina governor.

After much restoration work by humans and even more by the natural processes of ecological succession, the park is on its way to being adequately forested again. Interestingly enough, a tornado in 1988 and a hurricane in 1996 downed trees and created large openings in the forest canopy. These events set succession back to the beginning of the natural cycle in several sections of the park. With its diverse plant and animal biota, large trail system, and scenic woodlands, streams, and lakes, William B. Umstead State Park is an important natural area. This is one of the most frequently visited state parks in North Carolina due to its recreational opportunities and its proximity to heavily populated urban areas.

B. Hemlock Bluffs Nature Preserve

To continue the tour, proceed south on North Harrison Avenue toward and through Cary (left onto Chapel Hill Road, right onto Academy Street, then left onto Kildaire Farm Road). Take Kildaire Farm Road south to eventually reach the nature preserve 1 mile south of the Tryon Road intersection. Watch for the highway directional signs (binocular image and "Wildlife Viewing") and large signs on the right for Hemlock Bluffs Nature Preserve. Be sure to call 919-387-5980 to determine the preserve and nature center hours, which vary seasonally.

The Stevens Nature Center, located near the parking lot, offers nature exhibits and a gift shop for visitors to enjoy. The restrooms are available only when the center is open. No picnic facilities are available at this site. The nature preserve contains 150 acres with over 2 miles of well-maintained trails, which include two self-guided nature trail loops. One of the loops includes an extensive boardwalk along Swift Creek, which flows through the preserve. The trail is situated along an impressive north-facing bluff system and incorporates several scenic overlooks and connecting stairs. Parts of the trail are handicapped accessible, and all trails are routed through heavily wooded areas and are well maintained. The preserve is actually a dedicated state nature preserve with about half of the property owned by the Town of Cary and the other half owned by the state but leased to the town. The Town of Cary has provided year-round staffing, maintenance, and nature programming for the site since 1992.

FIGURE 57. Forest along Hemlock Bluffs beside Swift Creek. (Photo courtesy of Hemlock Bluffs Nature Preserve)

The preserve includes a disjunct population of eastern hemlocks along the bluffs overlooking Swift Creek (Figure 57). These relics from colder times during the last ice age, over 15,000 years ago, combine with other more montane plant species to make this an unusual Piedmont site. Hemlock Bluffs is famous for its spectacular spring wildflower displays—one of the best in Wake County. The most attractive displays can be easily viewed along the Swift Creek loop trail; the bloom progression starts in late February and continues through May. Upland areas of chestnut oak along the west end of the preserve contrast with the alluvial floodplain in the east, with its rich diversity of deciduous trees, shrubs, and herbaceous plants. Overturned and blown-down trees impressively illustrate the power of nature and are obvious throughout the preserve. Most of the damage was done during Hurricane Fran in 1996. This once-contiguous woodland is now pockmarked with gaps in the canopy created by the hurricane's powerful winds.

This nature preserve is devoted primarily to the protection of natural communities and their associated biota, thus stringent rules and regulations govern visitation. Staying on designated trails at all times makes observation of animal life more difficult but is necessary to reduce human impact on the environment. Plant life is very diverse for such a small area and is easily seen from boardwalks and trails. The north-facing bluffs support the most unique natural community in the preserve. This community can be studied from the convenient overlooks. The eastern hemlocks along the bluffs are separated from their typical mountain range by almost 200 miles. Significant populations of galax (also a typical mountain plant) grow on the bluff face, and chestnut oak dominates the ridgetops. The upland oak-hickory forests merge into mixed mesic hardwoods along the more gradual slopes at the east end of the preserve, and an alluvial floodplain forest is rich in species. Loblolly pine, shortleaf pine, Virginia pine, and longleaf pine all occur within the preserve.

This site is an impressive area in which to bird watch, especially during spring migration. Over 160 species have been sighted within the preserve property. Forty-two species of birds have been documented as breeders on the property. Temporary pools provide breeding habitat for several frogs, as well as spotted and marbled salamanders. The preserve also shelters an impressive population of red-backed salamanders in the uplands. Raccoons, opossum, deer, and both species of fox are occasionally spotted. Beaver and muskrat frequent Swift Creek at night. The nature center gardens provide opportunities for butterfly and bird watching during warmer weather.

Obvious signs of past human settlement are visible along the trails throughout the preserve. Intensive farming occurred throughout the flatter uplands, and selective timbering took place in the upland areas and along the slopes after settlement in the late 1700s. Many nonnative plant species are found in the western end of the preserve; they serve as reminders of past home sites and of the negative horticultural impacts of previous landowners. A grist mill operated in the eastern part of the preserve beside Swift Creek, and part of the Swift Creek Loop Trail is actually routed along the mill dam. Old crop rows are noticeable in the floodplain of Swift Creek, reminders of past uses from over eighty years ago. The natural communities of the preserve are continuing to go through the processes of succession, and visitors will observe these processes for years to come. The value of this site will increase in the future, for it serves as a peaceful reminder of the past and is protected for generations to come.

c. Swift Creek Bluffs Nature Preserve

To reach Swift Creek Bluffs, continue South on Kildaire Farm Road by turning right as you exit Hemlock Bluffs Nature Preserve. Turn left at the first stoplight onto Penny Road. Turn left onto Holly Springs Road and proceed downhill. Watch for a small brick municipal pumping station on the left, before the Swift Creek bridge. You will turn left and park in a small gravel lot to access the Swift Creek Bluffs Nature Preserve trail system. Do not block the service road to the Town of Cary pumping station, or your vehicle will be towed. This preserve is open year-round for walking and nature study.

FIGURE 58. Swift Creek when not very swift. (Photo courtesy of Hemlock Bluffs Nature Preserve)

Swift Creek Bluffs Nature Preserve includes a series of north-facing bluffs that can tower 100 feet above Swift Creek. The preserve is about 2 miles downstream from Hemlock Bluffs Nature Preserve and is now owned and managed by the Triangle Land Conservancy. The local land trust has established foot trails with interpretive markers describing the natural history of the preserve. Shady ravines and slopes are home to tremendous beech trees. This tract of trees is probably the most extensive native beech stand remaining in the Piedmont of North Carolina. This site also contains massive northern red oaks and white ash trees. The unique 28-acre site has an extensive loop trail system traversing several habitats, with spectacular views from the top of the bluff system. Within 5 miles of downtown Cary, this area is a green haven for Wake County citizens.

The overall landscape of the area can be viewed as four different habitats—two associated with the Swift Creek floodplain (Figure 58) and two associated with the bluff system and uplands above. The highlight of this unique natural area is the series of north- to northeast-facing bluffs above the floodplain of Swift Creek. The floodplain varies in width from a few meters to several hundred meters, so some areas have markedly more floodplain habitat than others.

The plant life of the area reflects a combination of the various rock types and unusually contrasting local relief. A fair amount of old-growth timber still exists on this site, a feature that is rare for this part of the Piedmont. Spring wild-flower displays rival even those at Hemlock Bluffs, and some of the soils are circumneutral and support high herbaceous diversity on the lower slopes along the bluff system. Species more typical of the mountains and Piedmont mix with some species more common in the Coastal Plain. The small group of overcup oaks dominating a small swamp forest along the base of the bluffs is an example of the latter.

Even though this is a small forested area, the bird, amphibian, reptile, and mammal life is substantial. A good day in the spring can easily lead to observation of a dozen warbler species. Barred owls commonly call in the later parts of the day in spring or fall. Though the Swift Creek Bluffs area is more famous for its unique botanical traits, a careful observer can see quite a lot of wildlife here, especially in the spring and fall. River otters were observed along the creek a few years back, and temporary pools provide breeding habitat for several species of amphibians in the early spring.

As at Umstead Park and Hemlock Bluffs, Hurricane Fran altered the forest here by opening up some parts of the canopy. This disturbance adds an interesting bit of early successional flair to the woodlands. For the last few years, eastern towhees and indigo buntings have moved in to those openings, and early successional, sun-loving plants now occur along the streamside trail. This type of dramatic habitat change has occurred historically for thousands of years in our area and is probably more of an inconvenience to humans than to local wildlife. To end this driving tour, simply retrace your route back to Hemlock Bluffs Nature Preserve and continue past the preserve to access US 64 or Interstate 40 by turning left at Tryon Road.

Coastal Plain to Piedmont Transition

Natural Communities of the Sandhills and Uwharrie Mountain Regions

ALAN WEAKLEY

This 80-mile tour takes you across the transition from Coastal Plain sandhills to the Piedmont plateau. Along the route you will see forests and natural communities typical of both regions, and will learn to recognize the ecological characteristics of both and of the transition zone that separates them.

On the first part of this tour, you will see one of the largest remnants of the longleaf pine ecosystem remaining in the Atlantic Coastal Plain. The once-vast longleaf pine ecosystem, stretching from southeastern Virginia south to southern Florida, and west to eastern Texas, dominated the southeastern Coastal Plain and provided habitat for a distinctive flora and fauna, including thousands of species found nowhere else. This fire-dependent landscape was almost completely destroyed during the nineteenth and twentieth centuries, and now less than 5 percent of it remains. The Sandhills Game Land, about 60,000 acres administered by the North Carolina Wildlife Resources Commission, is one of the larger and better-managed remnants of this once-vast resource. The tour will visit a variety of dry-soil and moist-soil longleaf pine communities, as well as other communities, such as upland ponds, seepage bogs, and streamhead pocosins, that are embedded in the longleaf woodlands. You will visit a colony site of the endangered red-cockaded woodpecker, and see a tarkiln, a reminder of the historic exploitation of longleaf pine for naval stores such as tar, pitch, turpentine, and rosin.

On the second part of the tour, you will see a Piedmont landscape in more natural condition than most. The Uwharrie National Forest contains forest communities typical and representative of the Piedmont, as well as a number of unusual communities and geologic features. Because of its more rugged topography, it has some features reminiscent of mountainous western North Carolina, yet its proximity to the Sandhills region of the Coastal Plain is responsible for the presence of longleaf pine communities and other Coastal Plain features. The tour

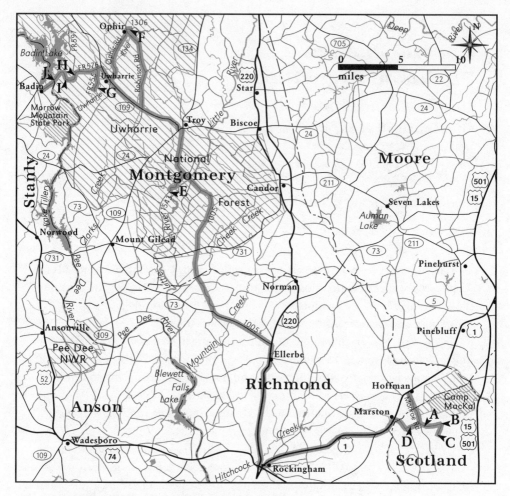

FIGURE 59. Sandhills and Uwharrie Mountains tour route

is interesting in all seasons; while plants and communities can be better studied during the growing season, geologic features and landforms will be more visible in the winter.

Be aware that both the Sandhills Game Land and the Uwharrie National Forest are popular hunting areas and can be heavily used by hunters in the fall. If you prefer to visit the area when hunting is not taking place, you can visit on Sundays, or check the North Carolina Wildlife Resources Commission regulations for the dates of annual hunting seasons. During the growing season, ticks and chiggers can be common, so take appropriate precautions. For additional information and maps, contact the Sandhills Game Land or the Uwharrie National Forest office, 2 miles east of Troy on NC 27 (Route 3, Box 470, Troy, NC 27371; phone 919-576-6391).

While feasible to complete in a long day, this tour is long and is probably best divided into two portions, allowing you to take a more leisurely and exploratory approach. Instructions are included for dividing the trip into two one-day tours (though this may lessen, somewhat, the impact of the striking juxtaposition of the very different forests visited in the first part and the second part of the tour). Alternatively, you can overnight in Rockingham, Ellerbe, or Troy and do the two parts of the tour on consecutive days.

The major learning experience on this tour is to gain an appreciation for the diversity of natural communities that occupy the Sandhills and Piedmont regions of our state, and the wide diversity of forests in the transitional regional between these major geographic parts of North Carolina.

A. "Extreme Sandhill"

The tour begins at the crossroads town of Hoffman, about midway along US 1 between Southern Pines and Rockingham. Turn southeast off US 1 in Hoffman on Butler Drive and continue straight on Monroe Road. After Broadacres Lake, the paved road will turn to loose sand but is passable by a normal passenger car. In 1.6 miles after Broadacres Lake, turn left on an unmarked sand road, Scotland Lane. The road traverses a treeless clearing (a "drop zone" used by Fort Bragg Army base for parachute training). Stop 50 to 100 yards past the end of the clearing, and walk into the woods to the left.

You are in an area referred to by geologists and physiographers as the fall-line Sandhills. The fall-line Sandhills are the innermost and oldest portion of the Coastal Plain, extending from south-central North Carolina south through South Carolina to near the Georgia-Alabama border. The Sandhills consist of sediments eroded from the Appalachian Mountains long ago and deposited in the Cretaceous and early Tertiary periods. In North Carolina these sediments are largely coarse quartz sand, with some interbedded clays and silts.

At this first stop, the soils consist of deep, coarse sands through which rain drains rapidly. These conditions present considerable challenges for plant growth. The longleaf pine sandhill natural community in which you are standing is one the hottest and driest environments in the state. In this driest, most extreme form of longleaf pine sandhill, the longleaf pines (*Pinus palustris*) are often widely scattered, turkey oaks (*Quercus laevis*) are abundant, few herbaceous plants are present, and bare white sand is obvious (Figure 60). Here and at later stops, study the longleaf pines, once the primary tree of the southeastern North American Coastal Plain, dominating most upland sites from southeastern Virginia south to southern Florida and west to eastern Texas. A relatively slow-growing pine, longleaf starts life in a "grass stage," first putting its resources into developing a strong, deep root

FIGURE 60. Longleaf pine–turkey oak vegetation. (Photo by D. Frankenberg)

system to access water and nutrients, before suddenly elongating into a somewhat comical-looking unbranched stem, and then branching sparingly and eventually developing its mature form.

In dry situations, turkey oak is a nearly constant associate of longleaf pine, from southeastern Virginia south to Florida and west to eastern Louisiana (it does not cross the Mississippi). Note that the leaves are often held in a vertical plane to avoid excessive light radiation, especially on seedling individuals. If you search around, you will be able to find other plants, all of which will show specializations to the extremely hot and dry conditions that prevail in the Sandhills in summer. Many of the other species have reduced leaves, often with a waxy texture or densely hairy. The most extreme example (and readily findable) is wireplant (*Stipulicida setacea*), a 3- to 6-inch-tall plant in the Pink family with a very narrow forking stem and leaves reduced to tiny scales.

Along the sandy roadside, you may see trailing clumps of Pickering's dawn-flower (*Stylisma pickeringii* var. *pickeringii*) flowering from June to August, with its small tubular white flowers and resembling a miniature morning-glory. This species is a rare plant, found in only a few dozen deep, sandy sites in New Jersey, North Carolina, South Carolina, Georgia, and Alabama.

B. Longleaf Pine Flat, Red-Cockaded Woodpeckers, and Tarkilns

Continuing in the same direction on Scotland Lane, descend a long hill, cross a stream, proceed uphill to an intersection with another sand road, and turn right. Proceed about 0.6 miles to a broad flat with no oak trees.

This "oak-free" flat demonstrates the effects of soil differences. Apparently soils in this area become too moist for turkey oaks and the other sandhill "scrub oaks" to tolerate. To the right (west) of the road are several old longleaf pines—often known as "flattops" because of the gnarled, flattened crown that develops only after about a century. Trees marked with white bands of paint are so-called cavity trees used by a family group of red-cockaded woodpeckers, an endangered bird that was once common in the southeastern United States. These birds live in Coastal Plain longleaf pine forests but also further inland in longleaf, shortleaf, and other pine species. Do not tarry long immediately below the trees (especially during the breeding season), but you can walk over toward the cavity trees and look at the "resin wells" chipped into the bark to maintain the flow of sap, which forms a white shield around the roosting and nesting cavities. Cavities are maintained and used by the colony for long periods of time. The population of red-cockaded woodpeckers in the Sandhills Game Land, nearby Fort Bragg, and adjacent areas is one of the largest and healthiest in existence. You may be lucky enough to see a group of the birds foraging in this area; the constant familial chatter the group makes as they feed can help alert you to their presence.

To the left (east) of the road, walk into the woods about 50 yards and look for two subtle roundish mounds, rising about a foot above the normal ground level. These are "tarkilns," a reminder of an important North Carolina industry, the production of naval stores, including tar, pitch, rosin, and turpentine, from the sap of longleaf pine. Tarkilns are remnants from the production of tar from longleaf pine logs. Logs were stacked in a circular mound, set smoldering, and covered over with sand; over a period of several days, tar was extracted from the trunks and collected in a channel and pit on one side of the tarkiln. Through much of the nineteenth century, North Carolina was a world leader in the production of naval stores, which made up a large and critical part of the state's economy. North Carolina's nickname, the Tar Heel State, and the official state toast, "Here's to the land of the longleaf pine, the summer land where the sun doth shine . . . ," both refer to the importance of longleaf pine to the psyche and economy of North Carolina.

c. Seventeen Frog Pond

Continue about 0.3 miles farther, to where a faint sand road turns off to the right. Park off the road and walk down this faint sand track to Seventeen Frog Pond, a treeless, and seasonally water-filled depression surrounded by longleaf pine woods.

Seventeen Frog Pond is named for the abundance of frog species that use it as a breeding site, seventeen anurans (frogs and toads) having been recorded as calling at this sight in a single night. Other, more colloquial names are Grassy Pond and the Bog Hole. Most years, the pond dries out by late summer, leaving an expanse of cracked mud, which is quickly covered over by a wide variety of plants. This nearly annual drying makes the site particularly desirable for breeding frogs and salamanders, since it keeps the pond free of predatory fish. Additionally, the pond supports a diversity of plant species, including a number of rare species. It is fascinating to return to Seventeen Frog Pond in different seasons and different years to observe its constantly shifting appearance.

d. Scotland Lane Annual Burn Area

Walk back to your car. Turn the car around (carefully—do not get stuck in the soft sand) and backtrack: back past the oak-free flat, take first left, pass the "extreme sandhill," cross the drop zone, and return to Marston Road. Cross Marston Road and proceed about 1 mile. Park on the edge of the road and walk into the Scotland Lane Annual Burn, to the left (south).

This site has been burned nearly every year for two decades. Fire is a critical and natural ecological process in longleaf pine ecosystems, including those of the Sandhills. Fire is necessary to maintain ecosystem health and to provide habitat for most of the plants and animals associated with longleaf pine. Humans have now interfered with the natural regime of fires caused by lightning, and fire is now often excluded from the natural landscape. On some areas where the longleaf pine ecosystem remains, land managers now conduct prescribed burns to replace and mimic the natural process. This site has been burned very frequently, and in the growing season, as an experiment to study the response of the community and its component species to this particular burning regime.

Note that the application of frequent fire has changed the appearance of this area, compared to other parts of the game land, through which you have been driving. Scrub oaks are fewer, and many have been reduced to shrubby sprouts. Grasses and legumes are more abundant, denser, healthier, and flower and fruit more vigorously. The streamhead pocosins (evergreen shrub thickets along small streams that interfinger through the Sandhills) are lower and support a mixture of shrubs and herbaceous plants, rather than merely forming almost impenetrable, dense shrub thickets.

Walking downslope, one can see two very different communities. One, with longleaf pine, overlies sandy soils that support dense tussocks of wiregrass (*Aristida stricta*) and other grasses and diverse upland herbs, including abundant native legumes, which provide important food for quail and other wildlife species. The other, with shorter-needled pond pines (*Pinus serotina*), has moist sandy or mucky soils that support switch cane (*Arundinaria gigantea* ssp. *tecta*, a native bamboo), insectivorous plants, orchids, shrubs, and peat moss (*Sphagnum* species). Look for pitcher-plants—the upright, slender red pitcher-plant (*Sarracenia rubra*) and the reclining, stout, purple pitcher-plant (*Sarracenia purpurea* ssp. *venosa*). Spring, in April or May, is a particularly good time to see flowering pitcher-plants and various species of native orchids; it is also the time at which burns are conducted in this area, so you may find the area recently blackened—but either will make for an interesting visit.

E. Pleasant Grove Church Longleaf Pine Stand

The second part of the tour begins just southwest of Pleasant Grove Church, south of Troy, in Montgomery County. *To continue the tour from Stop D*, continue forward on Scotland Lane from the Scotland Lane Annual Burn. You will come to a sand road intersection; turn right and proceed to the intersection with us 1. Turn left and proceed west through Marston, then bear right (staying on us 1 and avoiding nc 177). Proceed west to Rockingham, where lunch can be had. On the west side of Rockingham, turn north on us 220 and go about 10 miles to Ellerbe; about a mile north of Ellerbe, turn left on nc 73. This section of nc 73 is part of the Uwharrie Grassy Island/Indian Heritage tour that appears in the next chapter of this book. In about 5 miles, after entering nc 73, turn right on sr 1005, which you will follow for more than 10 miles through the crossroad communities of Coving-ton, Ex-way, Pekin, and Onvil, to sr 1543 (Pleasant Grove Church Road). Pass Pleasant Grove Church within a few hundred yards. After passing a low spot in the road (an intermittent stream), park on the roadside.

To start the tour at the beginning of the second part (Stop E), start in Troy, North Carolina. Turn south on sr 1005 in the center of town, and proceed south about 4 miles, then turn right on sr 1543 (Pleasant Grove Church Road), passing Pleasant Grove Church within a few hundred yards. After passing a low spot in the road (an intermittent stream), park on the roadside.

On both sides of the road is an unusual longleaf pine community. While largely restricted to the Coastal Plain (including the fall-line Sandhills) of the south-eastern United States, the original distribution of longleaf pine extended inland into the Piedmont or low mountains in a few areas. This was true most extensively in Alabama and Georgia, but was also true in North Carolina in and around the Uwharrie Mountains.

Longleaf pine is a fire-dependent tree, reproducing well only following ground fires that remove undecomposed leaf litter, low shrubs, and herbaceous plants, which might compete with the seedlings. Young longleaf pines remain "hunkered down" in a grass stage for three to ten years while they develop an extensive root system and save resources for vertical growth. If you walk into the site you should see grass stage longleaf seedlings, as well as young trees that have begun apical growth. These young trees may not be branched at all, or may just have a few lateral branches, and have an outline almost like a saguaro cactus.

Actually, if you look closely and walk around a bit (particularly to the right or northwest of where you parked), you will notice that there are several species of pine present. Longleaf pine lives up to its name—it has the longest needles (some-times as much as 18 inches long, but more usually about 12 inches long), borne in pom-pom-like clusters at the ends of the branches. The branches are also conspic-uously thick, about as large in diameter as a man's finger, and the cones are large. Loblolly pines can be recognized by the needles, which are mostly 5 to 7 inches long, and intermediate-sized cones. Shortleaf pines have short needles and small cones. A few Virginia or scrub pines may also be seen, with very short and twisted needles and bark flaking into small, purplish flakes.

This community was once probably dominated by longleaf pine, with some admixture of shortleaf pine. Fire exclusion in forests of the Piedmont changed successional patterns and allowed trees less tolerant of fire to invade this community; less tolerant species include loblolly pine, Virginia pine, and a variety of hardwood species. The U.S. Forest Service has been restoring this site to a forest community more similar to that which was once here. They began by cutting out hardwood species that had invaded, as well as by opening the canopy through removal of loblolly pines, to let more light reach the ground-layer vegetation. The Forest Service then conducted prescribed fires every few years to simulate the ground fires that formerly spread through this landscape as a result of lightning strikes and fires set by Native Americans to drive game toward hunting bands.

Soils here are highly acid, derived from metamorphosed volcanic and sedimentary rocks, and you will see an abundance of quartz pebbles on the ground surface. Fire, gentle topography, and acid soils in this part of the Uwharries create conditions relatively similar to those found in the Sandhills and Coastal Plain to the east (the Sandhills begin only about 5 miles east of here, just west of Candor), and many of the plant and animal species found at this stop are characteristic of the Coastal Plain and not at all typical of the Piedmont.

F. Dark Mountain and Barnes Creek

From Pleasant Grove, return northward to Troy on SR 1005 and turn west on NC 109. Proceeding about 3 miles northwest of Troy, turn right on Robinson Road and follow it until it makes a T-intersection with Ophir Road. Turn right, and then in just a few hundred yards turn right again, onto Flint Hill Road (SR 1306). Follow this to a U.S. Forest Service parking area on the right. From here you can take an optional out-and-back hike on the Uwharrie Trail or just investigate the immediate area.

The area on both sides of the road within a few hundred yards of the parking lot encompasses a diversity of landforms and corresponding forest types. The landscape is a complex one, with Barnes Creek and smaller streams dissecting the area, and gentle and steep slopes exposed in different directions. North- and east-facing slopes have moister conditions, and south- and west-facing slopes have drier conditions. Steeper slopes exacerbate this effect. On moister slopes (such as north of the road) beech dominates—a characteristic community seen throughout the Piedmont on steep and moist slopes associated with streams. Drier slopes show more dominance by oaks, especially white oak, red oak, and rock chestnut oak, sometimes with a dense undergrowth of mountain laurel (*Kalmia latifolia*). Careful exploration by the botanically inclined can reveal several unusual shrub species, including mountain witch-alder (*Fothergilla major*), which occurs here disjunctly from the lower portions of the mountains of western North Carolina, with its conspicuous white bottlebrush flowers in April, and mountain camellia (*Stewartia ovata*), with its spectacular white camellialike flowers borne most years in early July. Another unusual shrub—at least for its location here—is titi (*Cyrilla racemiflora*), which grows along stream banks and forms an attractive, gnarled small tree with reddish bark. It is more typical of coastal areas and surprisingly ranges south through the West Indies into northern South America.

For those with more time and an inclination to hike a bit, following the Uwharrie Trail to the south will reveal some obviously and other subtly different forest communities. Oaks generally dominate the canopy, but the mixture of oaks changes on different slopes and elevations, and the understory varies as well. You can walk a few hundred yards or several miles, and then turn around and return to your car.

G. Uwharrie River and Adjacent Slopes

From the parking lot, return in the direction from whence you came (on SR 1306) until you reach the church at Ophir. Turn left, and follow Ophir Road until you reach the T-intersection into NC 109 at the town of Uwharrie. Turn right, proceed about 1 mile, cross a bridge over the Uwharrie River (Figure 61), and turn left at a sign for the Uwharrie Hunt Camp. Proceed past the picnic area, turn right on FR 576, and then turn left on FR 555 and proceed about 1 mile, until the Uwharrie River first appears immediately on your left (and you see a steep slope on your right). Park in a pullover area, making sure to leave room for vehicles to get around you.

Here, steep slopes provide a variety of microhabitats above the river floodplain. Steepest convex slopes have oaks and dense mountain laurel (*Kalmia latifolia*), while a steep concave slope (allowing the accumulation of moisture, soil, and soil nutrients) provides the setting for a forest reminiscent of the rich cove forests of the mountains. This is an exceptional site for a diversity of spring wildflowers.

H. Schweinitz's Sunflower

Turn around and return to FR 576, and turn left. Note that this gravel road is narrow and surprisingly heavily traveled, so drive with caution. After a right turn, remain on FR 576 by turning left rather than proceeding straight on FR 597; stop and park carefully out of the way on the road edge.

On the road shoulder at this intersection is a small population of Schweinitz's sunflower (*Helianthus schweinitzii*), an endangered species that occurs only in a small number of populations in the Piedmont of southern North Carolina and northern South Carolina. It can be recognized by its narrowly lance-shaped leaves, which are very rough on the upper surface and velvety whitened below, and can grow from 1 to 3 yards tall. The actual sunflowers are less than 2 inches across, and the plant flowers primarily in September. This attractive plant was first discovered in the early 1800s by the North Carolina Moravian botanist Lewis David von

FIGURE 61. Uwharrie River and forests. (Photo by Watts Hill)

Schweinitz; the species was named for him by the preeminent North American botanists of the time, John Torrey and Asa Gray. Like most sunflowers, this species requires open or semiopen habitats. Its natural habitat was in Piedmont woodlands (open-canopy forests) and prairies, which were kept open and sunny by periodic fires. As European settlers moved into the Piedmont, fire suppression became more and more effective and wildland fires became rare. Prairies and woodlands closed in (one historic account from the 1800s states that "the woods in latter days have become so dark and intricate"), and habitat for Schweinitz's sunflower and other sun-loving plants was lost or reduced. Today's remaining populations of Schweinitz's sunflower hang on in powerline rights-of-way and on road shoulders, where bush-hogging maintains suitable habitats.

Another interesting plant growing with Schweinitz's sunflower at this site is eastern false-aloe (*Manfreda virginica* or *Agave virginica*). It can be recognized by its somewhat fleshy, agavelike leaves (2 to 10 inches long) and tall branchless flowering stalks. It is the only agave native to eastern North American, and it also grows primarily in a variety of open habitats, including rock outcrops, glades, and barrens. Eastern false-aloe flowers primarily in June.

I. The Rock Maze (Optional Stop)

Turn right, staying on FR 576. Set your odometer and proceed 1.8 miles, parking in a pull-off area to the right just before a sharp left bend in the road. This stop requires a hike of several hundred yards (each way) and there is no trail, so keep careful note of your bearings.

Hike north uphill. The forest community is an unusual one, caused by the unusual soils derived from unusual rocks. This part of the Uwharries is dominated by "mafic" metavolcanic rocks. These rocks originated as volcanic basalt flows and ejected tuffs of "mafic" chemical composition (that is, with an abundance of magnesium and iron minerals). Later these volcanic rocks were subjected to metamorphosis. After being exposed, they have weathered to create soils with pH unusually high for the Piedmont and a clayey texture and purplish color. These soils support unusual forests, with abundant pignut hickory (*Carya glabra*), southern shagbark hickory (*Carya carolinae-septentrionalis*, Latin for "North Carolina hickory"), white ash (*Fraxinus americana*), few heath species, and common viburnums, especially rusty black-haw (*Viburnum rufidulum*). The southern shagbark hickory is an unusual and interesting tree, obvious from the shaggy gray bark, hanging from the trunk in long strips. The rusty black-haw is also interesting, forming small trees with dark, rough bark; the opposite leaves are glossy above and smaller than a dogwood's, and the buds are conspicuously reddish brown.

Further upslope, you will see large outcrops of rock. These outcrops rise as much as 10 yards out of the ground. Note that the outcrops are aligned in a northeast-southwest direction, forming corridorlike features between the adjacent "fin-like" outcrops. This alignment is characteristic of rock outcrops in much of the Uwharrie Mountain region and can also be seen at the North Carolina Zoological Park south of Asheboro.

This is the Rock Maze. Explore the area, but make sure you keep your bearings; backtrack downslope to your car.

J. Mafic Slope, Upland Depression Swamps, and the "Canyon of the Yadkin"

Continue on about another 2 miles. Park in a pull-off area along the road, where there is a steep slope to your right (due west, down to the Yadkin River) and a steep slope to your left (due east). A short but moderately vigorous walk upslope will reveal some very interesting forests, scenic rock outcrops, and peculiar upland depression swamps—all on a steep slope overlooking the "canyon of the Yadkin." Bushwhack directly upslope, due east (a compass will help ensure that you will return safely to your car).

A hundred yards upslope notice that the forest canopy consists of trees such as post oak (*Quercus stellata*, with rounded leaf lobes like white oak, but with an overall cross shape), blackjack oak (*Quercus marilandica*, with leathery, barely lobed leaves widest toward the tip), southern shagbark hickory (*Carya carolinae-*

septentrionalis), and pignut hickory (*Carya glabra*). A striking and conspicuous understory tree is chalk maple (*Acer leucoderme*), a smaller southern relative of the sugar maple (*Acer saccharum*) of the Southern Appalachian Mountains and the northeastern United States and adjacent Canada, from which maple syrup is made. The chalk maples on this slope have whitish bark and are small trees, usually with several main trunks. In autumn, chalk maple's leaves turn a bright orange, and in winter many of the leaves turn tan and remain attached to the twigs.

The ground is unusually grassy for a Piedmont forest and includes various grasses and herbs more typical of prairies and woodlands of drier climates to the west of North Carolina. Two of the common grasses on this slope are little bluestem (*Schizachyrium scoparium* or *Andropogon scoparius*) and black needlegrass (*Piptochaetium avenaceum* or *Stipa avenacea*), the latter with glossy black-awned seeds borne in late May or June. Shrubs of the heath family (such as blueberries, huckleberries, azaleas, rhododendrons, and mountain laurel) are hard to avoid in North Carolina, because of its typically acid soils, which are particularly conducive to the growth of most heaths. On this slope with circumneutral soils, however, heaths are few, primarily represented by a few farkleberries (*Vaccinium arboreum*). Instead, typical shrubs here include rusty black-haw (*Viburnum rufidulum*), painted buckeye (*Aesculus sylvatica*), and fragrant sumac (*Rhus aromatica*), a shrub which resembles poison ivy (*Toxicodendron radicans*) but has no poisonous properties. Farther upslope, the forest's unusual structure and composition becomes more exaggerated, and "fin-like" rock outcrops (similar to those at the Rock Maze but not as large) become prominent. Enjoy the rare pleasure of walking through a nearly shrub-free North Carolina forest!

Rather abruptly, the steep slope will end and the ground levels off. Continue in the same direction (due east) across the flat. The trees on this flat are much the same as on the upper slope—post oak, blackjack oak, southern shagbark hickory, and pignut hickory being prominent, joined by a few shortleaf pines (*Pinus echinata*). These gnarled trees, growing in heavy clay soils, may be older than you think—some of the post oaks here are three hundred years old, even though few exceed a foot in diameter. A hard life builds character!

In the middle of this upland flat is a surprise: two oval depressions that hold water in the winter and early spring (and after heavy rains at other times of the year). Tree species more characteristic of Coastal Plain swamps form the canopy of these upland depression swamps—willow oak (*Quercus phellos*, with narrow unlobed leaves resembling those of a willow), swamp chestnut oak (*Quercus michauxii*, with sinuous-margined leaves), sweet gum (*Liquidambar styraciflua*, with star-shaped leaves), and overcup oak (*Quercus lyrata*, with deeply lobed leaves reminiscent of white oak). Water-tolerant grasslike plants, sedges (*Carex* species), are abundant. If you visit in the early spring, you may see two special sights—one botanical and one zoological. The white flowers of Atamasco lilies (*Zephyranthes atamasca*) look like small Easter lilies and are usually visible in early April. At about the same time, these depressions are filled with the clear to milky, gelatinous egg masses of various breeding salamanders, frogs, and toads, which seek out these isolated, fish-free pools to lay their eggs.

Retrace your steps (now proceeding due west) back toward your car. Take time to notice that you are now nearly 300 feet above the Yadkin River—not a breathtaking elevation, but certainly a notable topographic feature for the Piedmont. In winter you will be able to readily see the Yadkin River and the Badin or Narrows Dam, constructed in 1917 to provide electric power for the aluminum facility at Badin. With leaves on the trees, only glimpses can be had of what was described in 1896 by botanist John Kunkel Small as "the cañon at the falls of the Yadkin River."

Once you reach your car, turn around at a convenient and safe location and return back along Forest Service roads to NC 109.

If you did both parts of this tour, beginning in the Sandhills Game Land at Stop A, you have now completed a tour that shows a tremendous variety of geology, soils, and forests—from the fall-line Sandhills of the Coastal Plain to acid and circumneutral clay soils of the Piedmont. Although you are now only about 40 miles (as the crow flies) from your first stops in the Sandhills, you have crossed a fundamental natural boundary that has profound historic and modern effects on North Carolina.

Uwharrie Lakes
Scenic Loop
Grassy Island Crossing
and Indian Heritage Trail

ALEX COUSINS

This 50-mile tour takes you along two of North Carolina's newest scenic byways (Grassy Island Crossing and Indian Heritage Trail). Together, they form a scenic driving tour that takes about one and one-quarter hours to travel, not counting stops. Travelers along this route will see native flora and fauna of upland pine forests, bottomland hardwood forests, Pee Dee River and associated tributaries, private and national wildlife refuges, farms, and the communities of Cedar Hill and Ellerbe. The landforms in this region are characterized by the fall line where the Piedmont plateau gives way to the Sandhills, and by the Pee Dee River valley. The area also lies along a major inland flyway for migratory songbirds of North and South America. You will pass through portions of the Pee Dee National Wildlife Refuge, over the Pee Dee River bridge on NC 109, past the Grassy Island section of the Pee Dee River and Blewett Falls Lake, into Ellerbe, and up to the Town Creek Indian Mound.

This tour provides opportunities to learn about the flora and fauna and associated habitats of a central North Carolina river system and about Native American history. Much of the observable land mass at the beginning of the tour is U.S. Fish and Wildlife Service property of the Pee Dee National Wildlife Refuge, or private farms working in cooperation with the refuge. One of about five hundred federal refuges in the nation, the Pee Dee Refuge is the only inland wildlife refuge in North Carolina. About 75 percent of the refuge is in pine woods. Trees are selectively cut, and controlled burns are used to control wildfires and provide habitat for fire-dependent plants and animals. The refuge provides a home for the endangered red-cockaded woodpecker, which lives and roosts in cavities of living pine trees. The refuge permits deer and small game hunts, as well as fishing in more than 55 acres of ponds. It is bisected by the Pee Dee River (Figure 63), which separates Anson and Richmond Counties.

Before federal designation in 1965, the refuge was known as Gaddy's Wild Goose

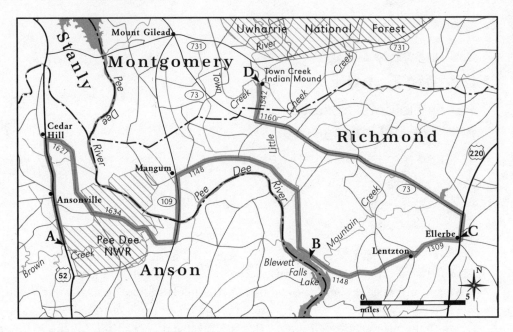

FIGURE 62. Uwharrie Lakes tour route

Refuge. Lockhart Gaddy used live goose decoys to hunt during the 1920s and 1930s before deciding he would provide food and sanctuary for the wild geese. In 1934 Gaddy used decoys and feed to attract nine geese to his ponds. The annual migration grew to 10,000 geese by the early 1950s. Hazel Gaddy continued to feed the wild geese after her husband's death in 1954, and the migration continued through the mid-1970s. Today, the refuge works in cooperation with area farmers who utilize best management practices such as buffering fields and streams, no-till farming, low pesticide use, and organic farming methods, including rotation of crops such as corn, soybeans, wheat, and other small grains. The Pee Dee refuge currently serves a wintering habitat for more than 7,500 ducks and 500 geese.

The Yadkin–Pee Dee River system is along the Atlantic flyway for migrating Neotropical songbirds, and the refuge is a good place to spot some of these occasional visitors. Among the resident and visiting species are loons, cormorants, anhingas, bitterns, ibises, ducks, geese, swans, various raptors, cranes, cuckoos, owls, goatsuckers, hummingbirds, kingfishers, woodpeckers, flycatchers, swallows, wrens, thrushes, vireos, warblers, finches, and tanagers. Wooded habitats range from mast-producing hardwood areas to pine plantations. Interspersed in the wooded areas are numerous low-growing shrubs, vines, and wildflowers that are attractive to some of the most readily seen wildlife, such as white-tailed deer, rabbit, raccoon, squirrel, opossum, reptiles, and songbirds. Open areas such as cultivated farmland, pastures, and grassed areas also attract wildlife. Raptors,

FIGURE 63. Pee Dee River. (Photo by Watts Hill)

rodents, songbirds, deer, crows, and many smaller mammals can be seen from area roadways. Many of these species are accustomed to humans. However, some are secretive and will not be observed as easily.

The abundance of wildlife living in the Pee Dee River valley also made the area attractive as a place to live for Native American tribes. The rich bottomland of the Pee Dee River was occupied by the Catawbas, Waxhaws, Cheraws, Pee Dee, and Saponis. Although none of the tribes have ancestors remaining in the area today (the nearest tribe is the Lumbees in Robeson County), there are many vestiges of this rich Native American heritage. There are several important archaeological sites along the Pee Dee that are closely guarded by the North Carolina Department of Cultural Resources, including Indian fish traps that are visible when the river is low. Two places that can be visited to learn more about the area's early culture are the Rankin Museum of American Heritage in Ellerbe and the Town Creek Indian Mound State Historic Site near Mount Gilead.

A. Pee Dee National Wildlife Refuge

Before starting out, you may want to stop at the headquarters of the Pee Dee National Wildlife Refuge, located on us 52, 2 miles south of Ansonville and north of the county seat in Wadesboro. There are interpretive displays that reveal the refuge offerings, including driving and hiking trails and wildlife-watching areas. Wildlife Drive is a 2.2-mile vehicle or hiking trail that begins at the refuge office.

Interpretive signs for the area's wildlife (habitats, behaviors, etc.) are located along the route. Another 0.25-mile trail leads to an impoundment and a waterfowl observation blind, affording up-close views of area resident and migratory bird species, especially wading birds. Be on the lookout for pine trees with white painted bands that mark the nesting areas for the refuge's red-cockaded wood-peckers. Other roads in the refuge are not as well marked; there are 10 miles of dirt and gravel roads that can be used as hiking or biking trails. Pets are not allowed here, and officials ask that you keep noise to a minimum.

The tour continues north on US 52 for 5 miles to the historic Cedar Hill community. The Cedar Hill United Methodist Church, with its stone-walled antebellum-era cemetery, is located here. Turn right from US 52 onto Pinkston River Road (SR 1627) and head southeast for 4.8 miles to enter the Pee Dee National Wildlife Refuge lands. Take a left to head east on Grassy Island Road (SR 1634). The road winds and you will cross Brown Creek, a tributary for the Pee Dee River. Travel 4.6 miles and then turn left (north) on NC 109 North. Go 1 mile and cross the broad and tranquil Pee Dee River. Your view from the bridge reveals one of the few glimpses of the Pee Dee River in its free-flowing, undammed state. Because of the many dams that have been built along the Yadkin–Pee Dee, there are actually relatively few places to cross the river. Years ago numerous ferries transported travelers back and forth, and many area road names are still called Ferry Road. Upon crossing the river, you will leave Anson County and enter Richmond County.

B. Grassy Islands

After crossing the Pee Dee River, travel 2.6 miles and turn right onto Richmond County's Grassy Island Road (SR 1148) near the community of Mangum. Proceed 10 miles on this winding country road, past woodlands and cotton fields, until you approach the shore of Blewett Falls Lake. Blewett Falls Dam is operated by Carolina Power and Light Company. There are boat ramps and fishing access points for the lake, including a handicapped-accessible fishing pier attached to the back of the Blewett Falls power house. At 11 miles on the left there will be a lake access area for boats and a put-in point for the newly expanded Yadkin–Pee Dee River Canoe Trail. This part of the lake is referred to as the Grassy Islands, so named for a group of earthen masses and small islands in the river. Follow Grassy Island Road for 5 more miles to the crossroads community of Lentzton. Turn left onto Page Street Extension (SR 1309) and follow it for 2 miles into Ellerbe.

c. Ellerbe

Ellerbe has two claims to fame. It is home to the Rankin Museum of American Heritage, and it is the final resting place for wrestler-turned-actor, Andre The

FIGURE 64. Town Creek Indian Mound. (Photo by D. Frankenberg)

Giant. From Page Street Extension, turn left onto Fourth Street and then make an immediate right onto Church Street. The Rankin Museum is one block down on the right. The museum possesses one of the best holdings of Native American artifacts in the state. An excellent grouping of baskets, pottery, implements, effigy pipes, vessels, and arrowheads is displayed. One of the most impressive holdings in the Rankin Museum is its Woodland period collection of Pee Dee artifacts from Richmond County and vicinity. The museum also has an impressive display of vintage nineteenth-century Americana, such as early farm implements, tools, blacksmithery, barrel-making instruments, and artifacts from the turpentine industry. Richmond County was on the edge of the vast longleaf pine forest that made North Carolina a major producer of naval stores in the eighteenth and nineteenth centuries. The museum is open Tuesday through Friday from 10 A.M. to 4 P.M., and weekends from 2 P.M. to 5 P.M. There is a modest admission fee.

Upon leaving the Rankin Museum, continue down Church Street and then turn left onto US 220. Head north out of town and go past several roadside fruit and vegetable stands. This is North Carolina's prime peach growing region, and there are several local produce stands that are open in season. At 1.2 miles, take a left on NC 73. There is a Department of Motor Vehicles rest stop on the right, with picnic tables and restrooms. If you like instead, continue on US 220 for another 0.5 miles to see historic Ellerbe Springs Inn and Restaurant. This grand bed and breakfast inn was originally a turn-of-the-century mineral springs resort. Turn left at the highway rest stop and continue along NC 73 for another 11.4 miles. This winding road leads you past several large plantation homes, which are reminders of the area's antebellum past. Take a right on Indian Mound Road (SR 1160), go 0.5 miles, and cross into Montgomery County.

D. Town Creek Indian Mound

Indian Mound Road (SR 1160) becomes SR 1542 in Montgomery County. After about 2 miles, you will see the Town Creek Indian Mound on your right. Town Creek is the oldest of North Carolina's State Historic Sites and the only Native American archaeological site that is open to the public. The site is situated at the confluence of Town Creek and the Little River, and it features an ancient ceremonial center for Indians of the Pee Dee culture. In addition to being a settlement, the Indian mound was a setting for significant religious ceremonies and a place for the discussion of matters important to the collective clans of the tribe some four hundred years ago. The site contains an earthen mound (the major temple), plus a minor temple and a reconstructed stockade. Excavations at Town Creek began in 1937 and continued for fifty years. The property became a state historic site in 1955. A visit to Town Creek Indian Mound offers a glimpse of pre-Columbian life in the Piedmont of North Carolina (Figure 64). The visitors center contains interpretive exhibits, as well as audiovisual programs that bring alive a rich cultural heritage from the buried past. Self-guided tours of the rebuilt structures, the mound, a nature trail, and other group activities are available. Town Creek Indian Mound is open April through October Monday through Saturday 9 A.M. to 5 P.M. and Sunday 1 to 5 P.M., and November through March Tuesday through Saturday 10 A.M. to 4 P.M. and Sunday 1 to 4 P.M. Admission is free.

The driving tour ends a few miles up the road from the Indian Mound at the intersection of NC 731 just east of Mount Gilead.

Uwharrie Minerals and Landscapes
Origins and Use

JEFF MICHAEL

This 65-mile tour will take you through the Uwharrie Mountain's scenic rural landscapes to important natural areas and significant historic sites, all of which owe their existence to the region's unique geology. As you visit historic gold-mining areas, Native American sites, and manmade reservoirs along the Yadkin–Pee Dee River system, you'll discover a rich heritage of human existence within a landscape of subtle and gentle beauty.

This tour will be a pleasant discovery for many North Carolina travelers, as it introduces you to the unique features of one of the state's lesser-known regions. The Uwharrie Mountains are located in the south-central Piedmont of the state, just to the south of the urban crescent along well-traveled Interstate 85. The most prominent peaks of this ancient mountain range can be found in the four counties of Stanly, Montgomery, Davidson, and Randolph, all of which are covered in this tour.

Compared to the state's better-known regions, the Uwharries are somewhat of an enigma. With no major interstates passing through the heart of these smallest of North Carolina mountains, many first-time visitors are surprised when they stumble upon the subtle beauty of the region. Its bucolic landscape of small farms framed by rugged hills is at times reminiscent of Virginia's Shenandoah Valley. But visitors should not be led by the Uwharries' self-effacing charm into thinking that little of human achievement has occurred here. For throughout this region are many natural and geologic gems and a remarkable history of humankind's relationship with them.

A. Reed Gold Mine

The tour begins 20 miles to the west of the Uwharries at Reed Gold Mine. This state historic site is found 2 miles up Gold Mine Road to the north of NC 24/27 in Cabarrus County. The road to the mine is 1.5 miles east of the NC 24/27 intersec-

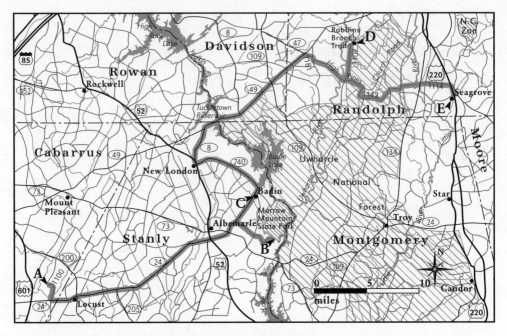

FIGURE 65. Uwharrie minerals and landscapes tour route

tion with US 60 North and 2.5 miles west of the town of Locust. This is the best preserved of the gold mines that once dotted the Uwharries, and as a state-run historic site, it provides an outstanding introduction to the important role that gold played in the region's early years. In 1799 twelve-year-old Conrad Reed found an unusual stone in Meadow Creek. The family used the stone as a doorstop for three years before his father sold it to a silversmith in Fayetteville. After this discovery, a gold rush soon established the southern Piedmont as one of America's earliest important gold-producing areas.

In addition to seeing Reed's historic mine shafts, you'll also have the opportunity to see the impressive work of an old stamp mill that was actually salvaged from the abandoned Coggin Mine in Montgomery County, not far from the Uwharrie River. These stamp mills used their powerful crushing force to separate gold from the rocks mined in the shafts. As the awesome power of the stamp mill displays, the gold found in the Uwharries did not easily yield to the eager hands of miners; it had to be extracted with considerable effort and cost. This lesson characterizes the history of the Uwharrie Mountains (which some people say are named from an old Indian term for "rocky soil"). Miners were not alone in having to work hard to earn a living from these rocky soils. Hard work has been required by all the humans who have established a fruitful relationship with this rugged land.

B. Morrow Mountain State Park

From Reed Gold Mine, follow NC 24/27 east to Albemarle and follow the directional signs (via NC 740 and Morrow Mountain Road) to Morrow Mountain State Park. As the third oldest park in the state park system, Morrow Mountain has long been the primary introduction to the Uwharries for many North Carolinians.

In the heart of what is known as the Carolina Slate Belt, the Uwharrie Mountains are not really mountains at all, but rather what geologists refer to as monadnocks, or the remnants of harder rock that have survived millions of years of erosion. More precisely, geologists refer to the Uwharries as "inselbergs," left over from the erosion of the ancient Miocene peneplain. The rocks of the Uwharries themselves date to the Precambrian period, when they were formed by the lava and ash of ancient volcanoes and later metamorphosed by the changing energy and force of the earth's movement. Only after these more dramatic forces had created the raw materials for the Miocene peneplain did the artistry of millions of years of erosion create the subtle beauty of the landscape we now know as the Uwharries.

Morrow Mountain provides an accessible view of this landscape, with expansive vistas of the Uwharrie Mountain range and of the Yadkin–Pee Dee River that has played no small part in the shaping of this region. However, like Reed Gold Mine, Morrow Mountain State Park also provides a history lesson of humankind's ongoing attempts to develop a symbiotic relationship with the geology of this land.

You will get a first hint of this relationship upon entering the main entrance to the state park, with its beautiful gate and visitors center made of native slate stone. Morrow Mountain State Park was created during the Great Depression and was built, in part, with Works Progress Administration and Civilian Conservation Corps labor, reflecting a maturing philosophy among early-twentieth-century park developers that emphasized the use of native materials and the harmonious blending of recreational facilities into the landscape. With its roots in the work of Frederick Law Olmsted and Frank Lloyd Wright, it seems only fitting that this philosophy found such full expression at Morrow Mountain, with its rich history of human resourcefulness in using native stone.

The Native Americans of this region were particularly adept at using the strong but malleable rhyolite at the top of Morrow Mountain for the making of stone tools and weapons. For years, archaeologists have been aware that the many shards and slivers of stone found at the summit of Morrow Mountain (and still visible today [Figure 66]) were the result of thousands of years of quarrying by Native Americans. However, only recently has research shown that Morrow Mountain stone implements, from arrowheads to stone tools, were used extensively throughout the Piedmont of North Carolina and even in some neighboring states. This

FIGURE 66. Rhyolite shards at the summit of Morrow Mountain. (Photo by D. Frankenberg)

evidence suggests that rhyolite found at Morrow Mountain and at other quarry sites in the Uwharries was of such high quality that the quarries became "manufacturing centers" for the rhyolite, which was then traded along now-forgotten trading paths by the region's earliest humans.

European settlers continued this tradition of using the native stone and particularly favored the same slate used in building the state park for the building of the foundations and chimneys of their own pioneer log homes. In fact, it is likely that the quarry sites used during the construction of the state park had already been in use for more than a hundred years by local settlers. Today, one can get a glimpse of life during this early period of European settlement at the park's reconstructed Francis J. Kron historic site, which features a rustic home and idyllic setting.

As one would expect, though, Morrow Mountain State Park also contains a treasure of natural areas. Perhaps none is more important than the Biles Mountain Natural Area. Running along a north-south ridge on the park's western boundary, this natural area was identified in a 1995 inventory of mafic rock areas conducted by the North Carolina Natural Heritage Program as one of only a handful of mafic sites of "national significance" in the Piedmont. The botany of mafic sites is described by Harry LeGrand (Durham Triassic Basin) and by Alan Weakley (elsewhere in the Uwharries) in earlier chapters of this book. Strewn with massive mafic volcanic rocks, the ridge to some people resembles an ancient ceremonial site such as those at Stonehenge, England, or on Easter Island. But its real value lies in the undisturbed quality of its three upland depression swamp forests and several significant areas of xeric hardpan forest, the latter characterized by an open and grassy forest floor. Other examples of upland depression wetlands in Uwharrie National Forest are also described by Alan Weakley in "Coastal Plain to Piedmont Transition," above.

For those knowledgeable about the botany of these unique ecosystems, a trip to this site can be a real treat. However, you should first check with park rangers about access to the site as there are no designated trails into the area. Also, part of the ridge remains in private ownership, and it is not recommended that one venture into this area during hunting season.

c. Badin and the Narrows of the Yadkin

Upon leaving the state park on Morrow Mountain Road, turn right onto Valley Drive, a state-designated scenic byway. This pastoral drive will take you north through an area of rolling countryside dotted with small farms that reflects the typical development pattern of the region. The poor, rocky quality of the soil in the Uwharries never leant itself to large-scale cultivation of the land (as in the plantation-dominated eastern part of the state), and for this reason the early agricultural economy of the region was dominated by small yeoman farmers.

With the dawning of the twentieth century, however, industrialization had created a new vision of the potential for drawing upon the earth's geologic resources for human advancement. Nowhere is this story so dramatically told as in the town of Badin, listed on the National Register of Historic Places, where the region's most unique geologic feature, the Narrows of the Yadkin, was transformed into the power source for a major manufacturing facility.

It is appropriate that you enter Badin from the rural countryside of Valley Drive, for at the turn of the century, this scene of neat, small farms surrounded by hardwood forests was typical of the land where the town now sits. A few miles away along the Yadkin River were two of the Piedmont's natural wonders—the Narrows of the Yadkin and the Great Falls. After flowing along at a wide, leisurely pace, the Yadkin River was suddenly transformed into a rushing torrent of water as it was forced through a narrow, natural gorge known as the Narrows of the Yadkin. Several miles downstream, this spectacle culminated with the crashing roar of the water falling over a series of rocks known as the Great Falls.

This had long been a significant gathering spot for local residents. For thousands of years, Native Americans fished along the banks of the Yadkin (particularly for the plentiful shad) and a succession of native cultures had inhabited one of the strategic high points at the beginning of the gorge (the internationally known

Hardaway site). Early Europeans also fished along these river banks but visited even more often as tourists for weekend picnics to admire the natural beauty of the gorge and falls.

After the turn of the century, a French aluminum company recognized the tremendous hydroelectric potential of the Narrows of the Yadkin, which could serve as a cheap source of energy for the electrolysis process that turned alumina into aluminum. After beginning to carve out of the rural countryside a town and manufacturing facility that would become dependent upon the emerging dam facility being built at the Narrows, the French company was forced to abandon the project in 1914 when World War I cut off the flow of capital and recalled many of its most talented engineers. Andrew Mellon then bought the project from the French, and his Aluminum Company of America has had a presence here ever since.

The French did not depart Badin before leaving a distinctive mark on the town's character. While typical of an early-twentieth-century company town in its paternalistic institutions and structures, Badin is unique in its progressive architecture and urban design, which reflected not only European tastes in building styles but also some of the new ideas in city planning then being incorporated into new developments. Like the design of Morrow Mountain State Park, these ideas incorporated a philosophy of using the existing landscape to design streetscapes. Today, Badin is one of the earliest examples in North Carolina of the use of curvilinear streets working in harmony with the topography of the land, as opposed to the traditional grid system.

After touring the town in its picturesque setting between Badin Lake and the Uwharries, drive up Falls Road, which will take you out of town and on to a public access landing for the Falls Reservoir. Be sure to bring a canoe or kayak to explore one of the Uwharrie's most delightful, as-yet-undiscovered spots. The Falls Reservoir is the smallest of the reservoirs constructed along the Yadkin–Pee Dee River system; it was completed around 1919, when the Falls Dam was built at the site of the Great Falls to supplement the power being generated at the Narrows Dam. You can easily canoe the entire 3-mile-long reservoir, which is protected from development by the shared management of the shoreline by ALCOA and the Uwharrie National Forest.

While one can no longer experience the rushing waters of the Narrows of the Yadkin and the Great Falls, the steep slopes of the reservoir's shoreline reveal a sense of what the Narrows Gorge must have been like (Figure 67). Keep your eyes open for bald eagles as well, as the Falls Reservoir has become one of the primary feeding areas for these birds along the Yadkin. Also, if you visit the reservoir in autumn, be on the lookout for the elusive Yadkin River goldenrod in bloom along the reservoir's banks. This plant is found nowhere else in the world. Although it

FIGURE 67. Narrows of the Yadkin, Falls Reservoir. (Photo by Watts Hill)

was recently thought to be extinct (last sighted in the late nineteenth century), this species of goldenrod was rediscovered by botanists in the early 1990s.

As you leave Badin, follow NC 740 to the town of New London. There follow NC 8 to NC 49, and then proceed on NC 49 toward Asheboro. This stretch of NC 49 is also a state-designated scenic byway, as it takes you through the heart of the Davidson County and Randolph County segments of the Uwharrie Mountains. After entering into Randolph County, you will eventually turn right onto SR 1181 (New Hope Church Road). After a few miles, turn left onto High Pines Church Road, another state scenic byway, and perhaps one of the most beautiful roads in the Uwharries. Rolling fields of farmland are framed by a silhouette of blue mountains, instantly reminding one of the Shenandoah Valley of Virginia.

D. The Birkhead Wilderness Area

Just a few miles down High Pines Church Road is Lassiter Mill Road (SR 1107), which will take you to the trailhead for the Robbins Branch Trail of the Birkhead Wilderness Area. Birkhead is the only federally designated wilderness area in the Piedmont. It offers a more rugged and pristine Uwharrie experience than can be found at some of the more developed recreation areas at Morrow Mountain State Park and the Uwharrie National Forest's Badin Lake Recreation area. Even so, the trails of the Birkhead Wilderness Area continue to reveal glimpses of a pioneer past for hikers with a keen eye. The stone remains of house foundations and chimneys provide physical evidence of a past agricultural society, while earthen works near streams point to long-abandoned gold-mining enterprises.

There is even an interesting legend related to the Civil War in this part of the Uwharries, which developed a reputation during the war as a haven for deserters and Union sympathizers. Once again, the landscape and geology of the Uwharries contributed to this reputation, as its rugged country discouraged efforts on the part of the Home Guard to seek out these deserters.

E. Seagrove Potters

After leaving the natural beauty of the Birkheads, get back on High Pines Church Road and follow it east to Hopewell Friends Road (SR 1142), which will take you (via SR 1114) just a short distance to US 220, south of Asheboro. You can then follow US 220 South to a community that has received international acclaim as a pottery center. With that reputation tracing its roots through the Piedmont clay back to the pottery traditions of England, this is a fitting end to a tour that has had as its theme the history of one region's unique relationship between humans and the land.

Seagrove's history as a pottery center dates back to the eighteenth century, when immigrants of English descent brought with them some of the pottery traditions of their native lands. Originally producing utilitarian jugware from the indigenous clay, these potters targeted the local farming community as a market for their wares. Over time, outside influences combined with these native traditions to develop a unique reputation for Seagrove as an enclave of artisan potters producing products prized as much for their aesthetic beauty as for their functional utility. Today, you can visit over a hundred individual potters in their studios, or get a more comprehensive overview of Seagrove and its potters at the newly opened North Carolina Pottery Center.

Lonely Mountains

The Sauratowns
from Hanging Rock to
Pilot Mountain State Parks

MARSHALL ELLIS

This 32-mile tour of the Piedmont region of the state will take you through an ancient mountain range known as the Sauratown Mountains. Sometimes called "the mountains away from the mountains," this low-elevation range was formed as an outlier to the Blue Ridge Mountains, which are approximately 30 miles to the north. The scenery and ecosystems found among the ridges and valleys of the Sauratown range are extremely varied and are most notable for their unusual combinations of mountain and lowland plants and animals. Although much of the vegetation might be familiar, the setting is not. The highest peaks of the Sauratowns reach elevations of around 2,500 feet above sea level in a prominent series of steep, erosion-resistant quartzite ridges and pinnacles that have survived millions of years of weathering. These dramatic quartzite outcrops, known geologically as monadnocks, frequently include vertical cliffs that exceed 200 feet in height.

The ecological lesson to be learned from this tour is that some mountain plants exist as "relicts" in Piedmont settings that share topographic features with the mountains further west. As with any trip into mountainous terrain, this tour will offer opportunities to observe the effects of elevation on vegetation patterns. The surrounding plateau averages only 800 feet in elevation, and trips to the highest points in either state park will result in elevation gains that approach 2,000 vertical feet.

On the lowest elevation of this trip, you will encounter the floodplains of the Yadkin River as it flows along the Piedmont plateau. Here the vegetation will be typical of the Piedmont and will be dominated by pine species, sycamore, beech, and river birch. As you gain elevation, you will pass through a variety of plant communities, beginning with oak-dominated forests along the moist lower slopes. These will give way to pines and heath-dominated communities on the higher and drier slopes and ridges. Vegetation along the highest ridges will be dominated by sparse, sometimes stunted vegetation. Along the highest ridges, look for dwarfed

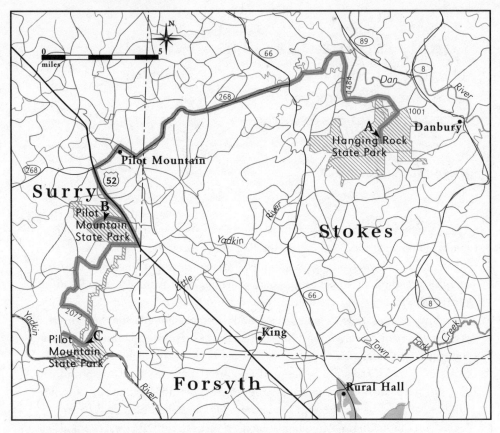

FIGURE 68. Sauratowns tour route—Hanging Rock to Pilot Mountain

examples of pitch pine, Table Mountain pine, and bear oak; all of these species are recognized by ecologists as indicators of ecosystems that are shaped by frequent disturbances, such as fire, ice, snow, and high winds.

The slopes of these mountains are dissected by steep, cold mountain streams that produce spectacular cascades in narrow canyons. The spray-soaked plant communities that occur near these waterfalls are dominated by lush assemblages of mosses and ferns. These so-called spray cliff communities are rare in the Piedmont, but they are particularly well developed along the canyon formed by Cascade Creek at Hanging Rock; these are, in fact, among the best examples found in the state.

This tour will also provide a close-up view of the Sauratown range's geology. The rocks that make up these mountains were formed over one billion years ago, and although they have been greatly eroded, this tour will take you through an area of arched, uplifted rocks that will reveal clues about rock deposition, composition, and weathering. Connections between the geology and ecology of this area will be readily visible, as the species composition of the resident plant communities is directly related to the thin rocky soils that have developed from chemical and physical weathering of the rocks. Many of the most spectacular quartzite cliffs and outcrops are easily visible from numerous vantage points, and most are reached via moderately difficult hiking trails. Quartzite, gneiss, schist, muscovite, and a rare form of sandstone, known as itacolumite, are among the rocks and minerals that can be encountered on this tour.

The primary destinations on this tour will be Hanging Rock State Park and Pilot Mountain State Park. Both of these parks protect large, undisturbed landscapes that support high quality examples of the region's vegetation. These parks also protect much of the Sauratown range's most extensive and representative rock outcrops and pinnacles.

This tour can be taken in either direction, and there are numerous locations in both parks that will allow you to see and experience the region's geology and ecology. Although the panoramic vistas from the summit area of Pilot Mountain are more easily reached, the vantage points at Hanging Rock will probably be less crowded. Both parks have extensive trail systems as well as observation points that will require little more than a casual stroll from your car. This tour will include recommendations for particularly high quality areas in each park.

A. Hanging Rock State Park

Hanging Rock State Park was established in 1936 as North Carolina's fifth state park. The park's facilities were constructed as a Civilian Conservation Corps project spanning the years 1935 to 1942, and today the park protects approximately 6,500 acres. The park is located in the center of Stokes County, approximately 4 miles west of Danbury. Danbury can be reached from the north or south via NC 89. The park is reached by following directional signs and then taking Hanging Rock Road (SR 1001) west from its junction with NC 89 at the Danbury Hospital.

Hanging Rock sits in an unusually steep region of the Sauratown range. The park's most prominent ridges, which include Moore's Wall on the west, Cook's Wall on the south, and Hanging Rock on the east, are easily visible from the surrounding countryside. As you view these ridges and outcrops, notice that each is capped by a prominent ridge of quartzite—rock that has proven to be highly erosion resistant. Vegetation atop these exposed ridges will sometimes be quite sparse, and the vertical cliffs, which are generally vegetation-free, offer excellent bird nesting habitat.

The following areas provide excellent opportunities to see the park's geological and biological features, and all are reached via park trails originating at the park's visitors center or bathhouse, which are located approximately 2 miles inside the park. Many of these features can also be observed from observation points in and around the park that require little or no hiking.

Moore's Knob

At 2,579 feet above sea level, the top of Moore's Wall is the highest point in the region. It is reached via the strenuous, 4.2-mile-long Moore's Wall Loop Trail, which starts from the bathhouse and is reached via the Chestnut Oak Nature Trail. One side of the loop passes through the campground and leads to the observation tower at the wall's northwest end; the other side leads toward Huckleberry Ridge and then ascends the wall's southwest end. Watch for trail signs, and be sure to carry a park brochure and map.

The lower slopes of this hike pass through extensive hardwood forests that are dominated primarily by chestnut oak. Look for red maple, sourwood, hickories, and dogwood, among others, in the understory. In the shrub layer, look for heath species, including blueberry, mountain laurel, and rhododendron. On higher, drier slopes, particularly those that are south-facing, the hardwoods will be less prominent and will be replaced by more pines and heath species.

Moore's Knob's rocky summit features large open areas, with sparse vegetation found growing out of rock crevices. The vegetation is dominated by pines, hemlocks, and the occasional oak, many of which will be stunted from exposure to the wind. As you hike the ridge, look for the shrubby bear oak; this diminutive species is known from only five sites in North Carolina, and the population at Moore's Wall is the state's largest. This species thrives in areas that are exposed and frequently disturbed by fire, wind, snow, and ice. Look for blown down and broken trees and other signs of the extensive ice storm that hit the park in March 1994; openings created by this storm provided much-needed light and space for the bear oaks.

To get an ever better sense of the Sauratown range's isolation, climb the tower at Moore's Knob for tremendous views of the Blue Ridge escarpment to the north, Sauratown Mountain to the west, and beyond it, the huge, distinctive quartzite hump of Pilot Mountain. Similar vegetation patterns can also be seen along the less strenuous 2.2-mile trail that leads from the bathhouse to Cook's Wall, on the park's south side.

Upper and Lower Cascade Falls

These falls occur at opposite ends of the steep 2-mile canyon that has been carved by Cascade Creek. Look for this impressive canyon off to your right as you ascend the park's entrance road. These falls are extremely picturesque and offer easily reached examples of how the park's ridges have been heavily dissected by the region's fast-flowing streams. The upper falls drop off at an elevation of approximately 1,600 feet and can be reached from the visitors center via an easy 0.2-mile trail. The lower falls are at approximately 1,000 feet and can be reached via an easy 0.3-mile trail that starts from Hall Road. You can find the trailhead by exiting the park and turning left onto Moore's Springs Road (SR 1001). After approximately 0.5 miles, turn left onto Hall Road (SR 2012). The trailhead will be approximately 1 mile ahead, on your right.

The Cascade Creek canyon area features highly unusual combinations of soil and habitat types that result in some interesting plant associations. For instance, look for Canadian and American hemlock growing side-by-side near the upper falls (Figure 69). The seepage and spray from the cascades support lush populations of ferns, mosses, and liverworts, including several species that are rarely seen. Look for gray birch growing in the rocky soils above the falls; in the finer alluvial soils below the falls, look for black birch. Much of the understory in this rugged area will be covered with dense thickets of rhododendron and mountain laurel. Although the majority of the canyon is extremely rugged and receives little visitor use, the falls areas are popular destinations. Remember to walk with care and to stay on the trails and boardwalks.

Other dramatic and picturesque streams and cascades that illustrate the cutting action of the area's steep streams can be found along Indian Creek at Hidden Falls and Window Falls. The Indian Creek Trail provides access to these falls, which are no more than 0.6 miles from the trailhead at the visitors center.

Hanging Rock

The park's namesake geological feature reaches an elevation of approximately 2,100 feet. It is reached via a moderately difficult 1.2-mile trail that begins at the visitors center. For those who do not wish to make the ascent, an overlook that provides a clear view of the rock is located on the south side of the visitors center parking lot. The vegetation patterns that you will encounter along this trail will be similar to those seen along both Moore's Wall and Cook's Wall, but bear oak will be missing from the summit ridges.

The view from the summit is spectacular, but will require a scramble over approximately 200 vertical feet of quartzite outcrops (Figure 70). This peak is another classic example of an open, rocky summit. Vegetation is sparse and much of it stunted. Once you are atop the summit, look for sprouts of American chestnut among the larger crevices; these are all that remain of the mighty chestnut forests that dominated much of the Appalachian Mountains before being overwhelmed by a fungal disease early in this century. Also look for ravens flying overhead—a common sight in this part of the park. The quartzite cliffs here and at Moore's Wall provide excellent nesting habitat for this species.

FIGURE 69. Cascade Creek Upper Falls. (Photo courtesy of N.C. Division of Parks and Recreation)

FIGURE 70. Moores Wall. (Photo courtesy of N.C. Division of Parks and Recreation)

The view from the summit will give you an excellent perspective on the location of the park's other ridges. Notice how they form the natural bowl that holds the park's facilities. This is also an excellent vantage point from which to observe sections of the park's higher elevation forests that were affected by the 1994 ice storm. Surveys conducted after the storm estimated that as much as half of the park's trees were affected. Look for telltale signs of these effects, which include snapped trees, large blowdowns, and small gaps. While rare, such large-scale disturbance is a well-documented feature of these mountain ecosystems. You will also be able to see isolated stands of dead pine trees; many of these were killed by the southern pine beetle, a native species whose outbreaks affect pines that are stressed by lightning, dense stands, or drought.

Hikers with much ambition can get the grand tour of the park's ridges and rocky summits by departing the Hanging Rock summit and then taking the Wolf Rock Loop Trail south to the Cook's Wall Trail. From Cook's Wall, descend to the Moore's Knob Trail and then ascend to Moore's Knob. The trail from Moore's Knob takes hikers past two excellent overlooks at Balanced Rock and Indian Face before descending through oak forests to the campground area.

Tory's Den and Falls

This area is located in the park's extreme northwestern corner. It is less visited than the main park areas and is reached via a moderate 4.2-mile loop trail that begins at a trailhead located on Charlie Young Road (SR 2028). To reach it, exit the park and turn left onto Moore's Springs Road, and then left onto Hall Road (SR 2012). Drive approximately 5 miles and turn left onto Mickey Road (SR 2011). After approximately 1.5 miles, turn left onto Charlie Young Road; the trailhead will appear on your left after approximately 0.75 miles. This drive will take you along the park's northwestern perimeter and will provide excellent points from which to observe the slopes and cliffs of Moore's Wall.

The Tory's Den Trail connects with the Sauratown Loop Trail and the Huckleberry Ridge Trail. The moist, north-facing slopes in this area go from the summit of Huckleberry Ridge to the gorge below Tory's Falls and span a change in elevation of nearly 1,400 vertical feet. Look for the familiar quartzite outcrops at both extremes in elevation.

The soils throughout the area are quite thin and rocky, but they support extensive forests dominated by chestnut oak over a dense understory of blueberry, mountain laurel, and other heath species. Clues to the acidic nature of these thin, rocky soils are given away by the presence of such herb species as galax and trailing arbutus.

In this area you can see evidence of the extensive logging that occurred throughout the region in the early 1900s. Many of the canopy trees are relatively small, perhaps 10 to 12 inches in diameter; but look for remnant stands of large trees.

B, C. Pilot Mountain State Park

Pilot Mountain State Park was established in 1968 as North Carolina's seventeenth state park. It is located in the southeastern corner of Surry County, approximately 24 miles north of Winston-Salem, and approximately 3 miles south of the town of Pilot Mountain. Like Hanging Rock, the namesake pinnacle is the park's most familiar and frequently visited feature. Pilot Mountain was designated as a National Natural Landmark in 1976, and today the park protects approximately 3,700 acres.

The park is approximately 20 miles west of Hanging Rock and can be easily reached from Hanging Rock by taking Moore's Springs Road (SR 1001) north; turn right onto Georges Road (SR 1484) for approximately 2 miles, and then left onto Lynchburg Road (NC 268). Follow NC 268 west for approximately 12 miles to the town of Pilot Mountain, where US 52 South leads to the park entrance after approximately 2 miles. The landscape along this drive is rural and features scattered farms.

The park is divided into two sections: the Pilot Mountain Section, reached by following the above directions, and the Yadkin River Section, which is located approximately 10 road miles south. The two sections are connected by the Corridor Trail, a 5.5-mile-long moderately to strenuously difficult hiking trail. This tour will highlight features in both sections. Refer to Figure 68 for more specific information regarding the park's trails and other visitor facilities.

Pilot Mountain Section

As with the quartzite outcrops found at Hanging Rock, Pilot Mountain is an erosion-resistant remnant of the Sauratown Mountain range. It is capped by two pinnacles, the prominent Big Pinnacle, for which the park is named, and the Little Pinnacle, which provides a dramatic view of the Big Pinnacle and the surrounding plains. The two are connected by a prominent, but narrow, saddle that runs from east to west. The Big Pinnacle served as a navigational landmark for European settlers as well as local Indians, who named it *Jomeokee*, which means "great guide."

The park road ascends for approximately 2.5 miles to the summit parking area, which has several overlooks. You will gain approximately 1,500 vertical feet during this ascent, and the plant communities will mirror those seen across the slopes of Hanging Rock's escarpments. Forests dominated by chestnut oak occur along the south-facing slopes; notice that the canopy is quite open in many places, allowing understory species such as sourwood and black gum to thrive. On the moister north- and east-facing slopes, look to see where heath species have occupied the understory beneath the dominant oaks and pines. The slopes and ravines along the east side of the mountain are dominated by the familiar chestnut oaks, which are joined by other oaks, including white and red, and several species of hickory.

Most of the hardwood-dominated forests you will see are second-growth stands. The park's forests were heavily logged during the early twentieth century, and large fires, fueled by the resultant logging slash, were common through the 1920s. As elsewhere in the Sauratown range, these forests have a distinctly mountain composition and are able to survive in isolation largely as a consequence of elevation and the thin soils that result from the weathering of the underlying rocks.

Perhaps the best lessons to be learned here are geological. This cone-shaped mountain is unique in the Sauratown range, and it provides superb displays of the area's geology. Pilot Mountain, which rises more than 1,600 vertical feet above the surrounding plateau to an elevation of more than 2,400 feet above sea level, is capped with a stunning quartzite pinnacle with vertical cliffs more than 200 feet tall (Figure 71). There is much to see and learn at this park and most of it requires little effort.

As you ascend the park road to the summit area, you will cross the geologic intersection between two distinctly different rock types. Look for this change by finding the light gray to tan-colored quartzite over the darker gneisses and schists. Another clue to this change in geology will come from the more rounded edges

FIGURE 71. Pilot Mountain. (Photo by D. Frankenberg)

found on weathered quartzite; they will stand in contrast to the chemical scouring and decomposition that are more typical of the gneisses and schists.

During the short walk from the parking area to the Little Pinnacle observation point, look for small, steplike surfaces along the rocks. These sections are usually thin (less than one inch thick), and comprise sections of the quartzite beds that were deposited during the Sauratown range's formation. On sunny days, look for sparkles in these beds; they are caused by a mineral known as muscovite.

The Big Pinnacle can be reached via an easy 0.8-mile loop trail that leaves the parking area. As you approach the base, you will pass through forests largely dominated by oaks; thickets of rhododendron and mountain laurel will extend down the mountain's slopes, particularly on the moister north slopes. You will also encounter the rare bear oak as you circle the Big Pinnacle. On reaching the Big Pinnacle, notice that many of the rock surfaces are rounded or spherical in shape. These shapes occur as a result of weathering and are commonly seen at joints and fracture points. On the southwest side of the Big Pinnacle, look for well-developed examples of what geologists call cross-bedding, in which layers of sediment were deposited at different angles in response to changes in wind direction.

The summit of the Big Pinnacle is closed to pedestrian traffic in order to protect its plant and animal communities. With binoculars, you will be able to see that the mesalike top is covered with a dense growth of chestnut oak, pitch pine, and Table

Mountain pine. The understory supports the by-now-familiar cohort of heath species, including rhododendron, mountain laurel, and blueberry. Bear oak is also present, and, as noted in the Hanging Rock description, it serves, along with pitch pine and Table Mountain pine, as an indicator of a plant community that is adapted to frequent disturbance from snow, ice, wind, and fire.

The vistas from the overlooks can be spectacular, particularly on clear days. They provide excellent views of the quartzite ridges and caps on Sauratown Mountain, Moore's Knob, and Hanging Rock to the east. The Blue Ridge escarpment will be visible to the north, and on occasion, views to the west will yield a sighting of the high country toward Grandfather Mountain.

The Little Pinnacle and its associated east-west quartzite ridge line are separated from the Big Pinnacle by a prominent saddle. This saddle provides further insight into the mountain's historical geology. The mountain's northwest slopes are concave, indicating that the upper surface of the quartzite deposits have been scooped out. The southeast slopes are more convex and exhibit the parabola-shaped profile of a talus slope formed by the deposition of blocks that have been cleaved from the pinnacle. The talus slope landform is quite rare in the Piedmont.

Yadkin River Section

The Yadkin River Section of the park is south of the Pilot Mountain Section and is reached by taking US 52 South approximately 2 miles to the Pinnacle Exit. From there, follow directional signs to the River Section and the Horne Creek Farm, a state historic site operated at the River Section. The park entrance is on SR 2072, approximately 0.4 miles from the historic site entrance. The unpaved park road leads to a picnic area and small camping area, and terminates at a cul-de-sac just above the Yadkin River. Visitors should be aware that reaching any of these facilities will require three crossings of Horne Creek. These are low-water fords without bridges. Prudent visitors will call ahead to the park office (910-325-2355) to inquire about water levels and road conditions. Additional access to the area is provided by a series of trails that lead visitors to the river as well as the interior of this section of the park.

This area is bounded on the south by approximately 2 miles of the Yadkin River. The river is broad and shallow in this section, and there are numerous riffles. The vegetation in this low-lying area is more Piedmontlike than that encountered elsewhere on this tour. In the floodplain areas you will encounter sycamore, river birch, sweet gum, and ash. As you move toward the uplands, you will see former agricultural land being reclaimed by several species of pines. For an interesting look at the park's cultural resources in this area, take the Bean Shoals Canal Trail from the parking area and turn west (right) along the river. Keep an eye out for the massive remnants marking one wall of the Bean Shoals Canal, an ambitious, if unfinished, water-control project that was undertaken between 1820 and 1825. Exercise caution when crossing the railroad tracks that parallel the river in this area of the park.

One of the most interesting areas in this section of the park occurs near the entrance, where Horne Creek occasionally leaves its banks to form shallow pools along its floodplain. The slopes above this floodplain support a well-developed oak-hickory forest whose species span an unusually wide range of soil and moisture gradients. Look for beautiful examples of smooth-barked American beech that are mixed with various oaks and hickories on these generally open slopes. The floodplain pools that form here are widespread in North Carolina, but they are uncommon in the Piedmont. The Horne Creek floodplain is well shaded by the adjacent slopes, and the pools frequently hold water for extended periods of time. These pools provide breeding habitat for numerous amphibian species, several of which are at the limits of their ranges.

The South Mountains Area

ANNE L. MAKER

This 90-mile tour takes you through the South Mountains, a rugged foothill range in the upper Piedmont that stretches across six North Carolina counties. Though they are separated from the Blue Ridge by a fairly flat valley, the South Mountains reach elevations of nearly 3,000 feet and are as rugged as most of the land in the Blue Ridge. The unbroken forests across the South Mountains stand as a biological reservoir of exceptional size, quality, and importance.

The South Mountains are located in the Catawba River watershed. The Catawba River valley and the gaps across the mountain range to the west were major routes of travel for Native Americans, explorers, and early European settlers. The first permanent settlements in the area were along the fertile river bottomlands. The South Mountains at one time separated the Cherokee and Catawba Indian tribes.

The South Mountains are known for large areas of unbroken forest, wildlife, and numerous rare and unusual plants. Mammals that inhabit the South Mountains include deer, squirrel, raccoon, bobcat, black bear, and boar. Some of the birds of the South Mountains are ruffed grouse, turkey, hawks, owls, ravens, wood warblers, and mourning dove. Along forest-pastureland boundaries there is ample habitat for rabbit and quail. A host of other animals are less frequent but nevertheless significant—centipedes and millipedes, stoneflies, caddisflies, moths and butterflies, beetles, arachnids, fish, salamanders and other amphibians, turtles, and snakes. Plant species also abound in the South Mountains, from trilliums, Jack-in-the-pulpit, rhododendron, mountain laurel, cardinal flower, and ferns.

The South Mountains' geographic location is in large part responsible for the array of plant and animal species living here. Because this area lies in the transition zone between the mountain and Piedmont provinces, range limits of both northern and southern species can be found here.

On this tour you can learn about the aquatic ecosystem of a river, forest succession, geology of the region, and plants and wildlife in the Piedmont transition zone. By observing the plants and animals that live in the transition zone you can learn how physical factors affect organism distribution.

To view the Piedmont-to-mountain transition, drive south of Morganton on NC 18 to the junction of NC 10. Take NC 10 west to Polkville, then NC 226 north to Marion. You will see glimpses of the South Mountains on this drive. Enjoy the

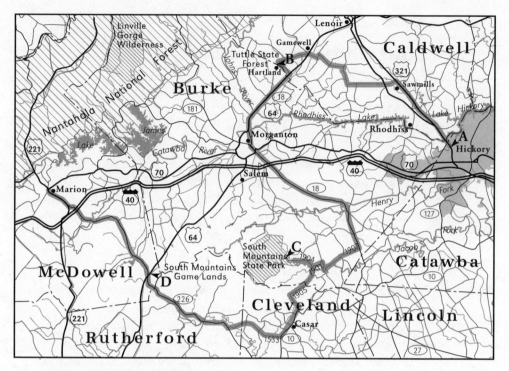

FIGURE 72. South Mountains tour route

upper Piedmont farmlands and spectacular views of the mountains. Look for the apple and corn crops that may be seen from the road. As you approach Marion, you will begin to see North Carolina's Appalachian Mountains.

The clear, cold, highly oxygenated, and turbulent streams are good habitat for trout and other cold-water fishes. Native brook trout along with introduced rainbow and brown trout thrive in the Jacob Fork and Henry Fork Rivers. Minnows, darters, and other small fishes also occur in these rivers.

A. Catawba Science Center

This tour begins at the Catawba Science Center in Hickory. Take Interstate 40 to Exit 125, then follow the brown directional signs to the Science Center at 243 Third Avenue NE, Hickory, NC (telephone 828-322-8169).

Catawba Science Center offers visitors of all ages hands-on fun as they learn about the natural and physical sciences through participatory exhibits and programs. The center provides educational programs, exhibits, teaching collections, and activities that emphasize the active participation of individuals to further their understanding of science and technology. Exhibits include a Hall of Life Science, which takes the visitor from the North Carolina coast to the mountains and includes a living mountain stream. You can also visit the Physical Science Arcade, BodyWorks, KidSpace (for toddlers), RaceWays, and special traveling exhibits. A wide variety of fun, educational programs are offered for all ages, including summer and after-school sessions, fieldtrips, teachers' workshops, and camp-ins.

B. Tuttle Educational State Forest

Tuttle Educational State Forest is located at 3420 Playmore Beach Road in Lenoir, NC 28645 (telephone 828-757-5608). To get there from Morganton, drive north on NC 18/US 64. Playmore Beach Road will be on your right 10 miles from Morganton.

At this facility you can learn how to tell the age of a tree, how forests influence wildlife, and how important North Carolina's forest resources are to the state's citizens. You may also learn about the different parts of a tree, investigate the environmental factors that affect tree growth, and discover the many common and uncommon products that come from trees. Did you ever stop to consider that trees, unlike coal or oil, are a renewable natural resource? Trees can be planted to replace those cut and tree products can be recycled.

Tuttle Educational State Forest was designed to teach the public about the forest environment. Classes conducted at Tuttle help visitors understand that forests are complex, interdependent ecosystems that can be managed for a diversity of uses on a sustainable basis. All programs are presented in outdoor amphitheaters and feature hands-on activities. The forest features self-guided trails that include exhibits, tree identification signs, a forest education center, and a talking tree trail. Forest rangers are available to conduct classes for school and other youth groups. You can choose from a selection of thirty-minute programs that cover all aspects of the forest environment from soil, water, and wildlife to timber and forest management.

c. South Mountains State Park

South Mountains State Park is located in southern Burke County, on 3001 South Mountains Park Avenue, Connelly Springs, NC 28612 (telephone 828-433-4772). It can be reached from Morganton by taking NC 18 (14 miles), then turning right on Rhoney Road for 5 miles (see Figure 72).

The park comprises approximately 13,000 acres and is part of the approximately 100,000-acre South Mountains range. The South Mountains, eroded outliers of the Blue Ridge, are a broad belt of peaks and knobs that rise abruptly from a valley floor (Figure 73). The peaks are steep and rugged, averaging 2,000 feet in elevation. The highest point, at Buzzard Roost, reaches 2,980 feet above sea level. Elevation

FIGURE 73. South Mountains and the Catawba River valley. (Photo courtesy of South Mountains State Park)

in the park ranges from 1,200 feet along the Jacob Fork River to 2,894 feet at Benn's Knob on the park's southern boundary. The park superbly illustrates the Piedmont-mountain transition zone, as it harbors plant and animal species of both the Piedmont and mountain regions—a true natural history treasure.

South Mountains State Park protects a large part of the contiguous and wildest portion of the South Mountains and includes the Jacob Fork and Henry Fork Watersheds. The streams in the park have excellent water quality, and both Jacob Fork and Henry Fork have been designated as "outstanding resource waters." Within the park are extensive examples of natural communities typical of the mountain region and nearly absent in the Piedmont: chestnut oak forest, montane oak-hickory forest, and acidic cove forest. Smaller areas of rich cove forest, pine-oak/heath, and spray cliff natural communities also occur.

You can visit the South Mountains State Park during all seasons of the year for hikes, exploration, nature study, and other activities. There are five marked hiking trails, as well as equestrian trails and a loop trail for mountain bike riders. Most of the trails here can become loops that return you to the parking area. The hikes offer splendid scenery as the Jacob Fork River and Shinny Creek flow over and around huge stones in the riverbed and create countless waterfalls (Figure 74) and rapids. There are also several primitive backpack camping areas, each with several campsites.

FIGURE 74. High Shoals Falls in South Mountains State Park. (Photo courtesy of South Mountains State Park)

D. South Mountains Game Lands (Rollins Tract)

You can reach the South Mountains Game Lands from NC 64 south of Morganton.

These 17,000 forested acres surround South Mountains State Park on the north, west, and south and provide dramatic landscapes critical for wildlife, rare plants, and the environmental integrity of the South Mountains region. Stretching across three counties (Cleveland, Rutherford, and McDowell), the South Mountains Game Lands feature the regions's most extensive low-elevation rocky summits, a rare community type, and its most extensive montane oak-hickory forests. There is more acreage in acidic coves, pine-oak/heath forests, chestnut oak forests, and dry to dry-mesic oak-hickory forests. There are also rich cove forests with beeches, basswoods, and buckeyes. Bluffs harboring the unusual Carolina hemlock crown magnificent rocky summits.

The South Mountains Game Lands support a beautiful old mountain hardwood forest (there is some old growth) and provide valuable habitat for deer, turkey, bear, squirrel, and other wildlife. In addition to old growth there is mixed-age hemlock, mixed hardwoods, and pine forests. Several rare plant species distinguish it as well. The tract will be used for environmental education, hiking, hunting, and bird watching.

Parks, Forests, and Geology of the Southwest Piedmont

DEIDRI SARVER

This 56-mile tour will take you to natural areas and historic places. It begins at a Revolutionary War battleground in South Carolina at Kings Mountain National Military Battlefield, and a nineteenth-century historic farm at the adjacent Kings Mountain State Park. Heading north into North Carolina, the tour continues along the ancient Kings Mountain Range where you will see remnants of these once mighty peaks. Hiking trails, picnicking, and other recreational opportunities abound in Crowders Mountain State Park. Driving eastward toward Gastonia and the Charlotte area, a myriad of other opportunities await the day-tripper or weekend excursionist. Enjoy the world-class Schiele Museum of Natural History and Planetarium in Gastonia; stroll through a "Garden of Eden" at Stowe Botanical Gardens; observe close-up the rehabilitated birds of prey protected and cared for by the Carolina Raptor Center in Charlotte.

The learning opportunities here focus on forest succession as you tour the battlefield and the two neighboring state parks in South Carolina and North Carolina. Landscapes where virgin forests were cleared in the eighteenth and nineteenth centuries are gradually returning to the forested state. You will see various successional stages that followed the clear-cutting and overgrazing of the past. Some wildlife species, such as turkey and deer, are increasing in population size here, while others (for example, bear and bobcat) are becoming so uncommon they are rarely, if ever, seen. You will also learn about the cultural origins of the southwestern Piedmont when you visit an eighteenth-century backcountry farm and a Catawba Indian village. You can learn about the effects of settlement on the environment, economy, and culture, and gain an understanding of the lasting effects of each. Learn about subterranean geologic forces that shape our landscapes constantly and the slow but tremendous changes that have occurred over the last 500 million years. You will also learn about different plants suitable for cultivation that can enhance and help preserve habitats crucial for many bird species, both migratory and resident. Finally, in the city of Charlotte you will have a chance to stargaze in a world-class planetarium or travel, museum style, to other continents, or even view native flora and fauna from ages past.

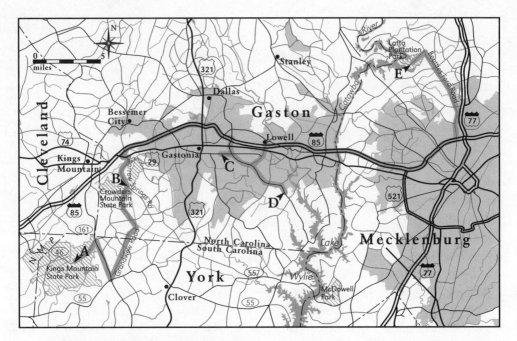

FIGURE 75. Southwest Piedmont tour route

A. Kings Mountain State Park and Kings Mountain National Military Park

The tour begins off of Interstate 85 at SC 161 south of the town of Kings Mountain. Take NC 161 South into South Carolina approximately 5 miles to the Kings Mountain State Park entrance road, Main Park Drive, on the right. This park is part of an 8,882-acre tract purchased in 1934 and created under President Franklin D. Roosevelt's administration. During this period of the Great Depression many unemployed people were put to work here. Thus the seeds were planted for an ever-increasing effort toward conservation and protection of our nation's most beautiful and unique resources.

The immediate upcountry of South Carolina was once part of Tryon County, North Carolina, and retains strong ties to the history and culture of the North Carolina foothills. York County, South Carolina, where both the military battlefield and the state park are found, played a role in the pioneer movement of Scotch-Irish immigrants. These early settlers of the mid-1790s traveled from the North into the Piedmont by way of the Great Philadelphia Wagon Road, which extended from Pennsylvania southward through the Maryland, Virginia, North Carolina, and South Carolina Piedmont.

Kings Mountain State Park offers a living history farm of the 1850s and an impressive collection of well-preserved log and timber structures from this region. A visitor to the farm and the adjoining national military battlefield will make the connection to those who fought or supported the American Revolutionary war effort. Many were the early Scotch-Irish and German settlers whose descendants later farmed the Piedmont and established many of the enduring traditions of the South.

Kings Mountain State Park provides the visitor with a variety of recreational opportunities, from boating to swimming and camping (equestrian, trailer, and tent). There is a 15-mile bridle trail through both the national and state parks for those who own horses. Hikers can enjoy approximately 20 miles of woodland trails, some of which connect the two parks. There are rustic cabins for rent for those desiring a stay with more homelike amenities.

Because of its large size, the state park is an important nature preserve. It provides a safe haven for migratory bird species and is a transition zone between mountain and Piedmont plant species. Mountain laurel and galax—two common plant species of the mountains—can be found growing among exposed rocks.

There is no admission for day use at Kings Mountain State Park. Lake York (65 acres) and Lake Crawford (15 acres) are available for water recreational activities. Swimming and boating concession fees vary according to craft and length of rental.

After your state park visit, continue along Main Park Drive until you leave the state park and enter Kings Mountain National Military Park. This attraction features a beautiful visitors center, open year-round, and is the site of an important turning-point battle during the Revolutionary War. A visitor to the 4,000-acre park can relive these moments in history on the paved, self-guided tour (forty-five minutes to an hour). As mentioned above, 20 miles of trails span the two parks, and for the hardy camper, backpack sites are available in the national military park.

B. Crowders Mountain State Park

Exit the state park entrance onto SC 161; proceed south for approximately 2.7 miles until you reach Grandview Road (a church and cemetery are on the corner). Turn left and go 7.3 miles along the back roads and into North Carolina until you come to the Crowders Mountain State Park entrance gate (State Park Road) on your left. If you approach from Interstate 85, take Exit 13 onto Edgewood Road and follow brown park signs to the entrance. The first right off Sparrow Springs Road after entering the park will take you to the park visitors center, where directions and information can be obtained.

Crowders Mountain State Park was originally formed in 1974 as a result of

FIGURE 76. Rainbow over Crowders Mountain. (Photo courtesy of Crowders Mountain State Park)

determined efforts by a local conservation group called the Gaston County Conservation Society. Lobbying for the mountain's protection, the group succeeded in stopping mining to extract a valuable mineral (kyanite). The nearby Henry's Knob (in South Carolina) had been virtually stripped of its lush vegetation a few years earlier and now stood barren and scarred from the mining of this mineral.

The park has grown from its humble size of just over 400 acres to its present 3,024 acres. It is surrounded by highways: US 29/74, US 321, and NC 161 to the north, east, and west, respectively. Interstate 85 lies approximately 3 miles north, and the impressive cliffs of the park can be seen by the interstate traveler (Figure 76). Two remnant peaks of the ancient Kings Mountain Range, part of the Appalachian chain, showcase the park. Crowders Mountain, with its sheer vertical profile, reaches an elevation of 1,625 feet. Kings Pinnacle, the higher of the two peaks at 1,705 feet, offers a more rounded knoblike appearance (Figure 77). Both peaks are recognized as North Carolina Registered Natural Heritage Areas, and both support a variety of flora and fauna that are considered rare in the Piedmont. Some examples are the reclusive Carolina pygmy rattlesnake and the rare Bradley's spleenwort fern, which grows among the exposed rock of cliff tops. Other species include bear oak, here occurring at southern limits of its range, ground juniper, and Biltmore carrionflower.

The peaks at Crowders Mountain are geologically classified as metamorphic

FIGURE 77. King's Pinnacle. (Photo courtesy of Crowders Mountain State Park)

kyanite-quartzite monadnocks. Only the erosion resistance of quartzite has allowed these pinnacles to withstand the wind, water, and other forces that wore
down areas of less-resistant rock. As you hike up the mountain trails, notice the
terrain and vegetative changes. A pine-hardwood forest trail becomes a steep
incline with boulder fields. Stunted growth and only the hardiest species of vegetation cling to the rugged cliffs and ridgetops. Large sprouts of the American
chestnut tree, some bearing fruit in the fall, can be found scattered on Kings
Pinnacle (Figure 77). Pockets of Catawba rhododendron tucked among cliff-top
crevices can be seen in bloom during April and May.

Recreational and environmental education opportunities abound at Crowders
Mountain State Park. Over 15 miles of hiking trails, from easy to strenuous, connect throughout the park and its two peaks. Rock climbing is a popular recreational activity here, but it is allowed only in designated areas; scenic views from
the peaks await all outdoor enthusiasts.

You can fish for largemouth bass, bream, and crappie from the shoreline or
floating dock of the park's more than 9-acre lake, which is handicapped accessible.
A North Carolina fishing license is required and all state fishing regulations apply.
Try your paddling skills with one of the park's six rental canoes, available daily
from May through September 8 A.M. to 5 P.M.

There are no fees for day-use visitation to Crowders Mountain State Park.
Camping is available at primitive pack-in sites; family sites are $8 each per night.

There is also a group campground with a minimum fee of $8 per site per night. Reservations can be made for groups by calling the park office at 704-853-5375.

The park's new visitors center houses exhibits, a learning lab, and a theater-style auditorium. This building provides information on the environment and conservation ethics for all who visit the park. Hours of operation vary depending on the month. Call the park office for further information.

c. Schiele Museum of Natural History and Planetarium

As you exit Crowders Mountain State Park, turn left onto Sparrow Springs Road and then left again (still Sparrow Springs Road) at the next intersection to US 29/74. Heading east toward Gastonia, continue 1.8 miles to the Interstate 85 sign. Take the interstate highway north to Exit 20–New Hope Road. Follow signs to Schiele Museum on Garrison Boulevard.

At the museum there are winding pathways across the grounds where a leisurely stroll can take you back in time. Visit the on-site Catawba Indian village and the Eighteenth-Century Back Country Farm to view demonstrations of daily life in the Piedmont of long ago. Events and special programs are offered, indoors and out, year-round and cover many topics. Inside lies a treasure trove of educational exhibits, arts and crafts, wildlife exhibits, cultural displays, and archaeological artifacts; and a planetarium awaits those interested in our universe and its wonders.

Admission to the museum is free, but donations are accepted. Fees of $2.50 a person ($1 for senior citizens) are charged for planetarium presentations, and some workshops require a registration or materials fee. The museum is open from 9 A.M. to 5 P.M. Monday through Saturday, and from 1 P.M. to 5 P.M. on Sunday. Planetarium programs are presented on Saturdays at 11 A.M., 2 P.M., and 3 P.M. and on Sundays at 2 P.M. and 3 P.M. Call 704-866-6900 for more information.

D. Daniel Stowe Botanical Garden

Leaving the Schiele Museum, backtrack from Garrison Boulevard back to New Hope Road. At that intersection turn right and go south for 9 miles. Look for signs and the white gate for the garden on the right.

In 1991, from a small 10-acre tract planted in ornamentals and perennials, Daniel Jonathan Stowe established his Botanical Garden. The future holds great promise for nature lovers and horticulturists alike as the garden continues to grow. Phase I of its development is a 110-acre area completed in October 1999. Eventually, over the next 40 years, the garden will cover 450 acres. Mr. Stowe committed $14 million to complete his dream of this one-of-a-kind garden. Phase I includes ponds rimmed with 60,000 spring-flowering bulbs, nature trails, and wildflower meadows. A variety of tended thematic gardens and a visitors pavilion, complete with meeting areas, classrooms, and gift shop, are also available to visitors. The goal of this botanical garden is to promote the Piedmont physiographic province. Conservation measures will protect and preserve natural flora and fauna of the area. As a learning destination the garden will give unique study opportunities for students, interns, scientists, and visitors from around the world.

Currently the garden hours are 9 A.M. to 5 P.M. Monday through Saturday and noon to 5 P.M. on Sunday; it is closed on Thanksgiving, Christmas, New Year's Day, and bad-weather days in the winter (call ahead: 704-825-4490). There are no admission fees to the garden; however, donations are accepted. During special events there may be a parking fee.

E. Carolina Raptor Center, Latta Plantation Park

After leaving the Daniel Stowe Botanical Garden, backtrack to Interstate 85 and head north approximately 20 miles to Beatties Ford Road. Go approximately 5 miles and then turn left on Sample Road. Watch for signs for the Raptor Center, which is located on 57 acres in Latta Plantation Park.

The Carolina Raptor Center is a nonprofit, tax-exempt organization that exists to provide public education on environmental issues and about the importance of raptors to our environment; to care for sick, injured, and orphaned raptors; and to conduct and contribute to research about birds of prey. Often after a few weeks of treatment and recovery a bird can be released back to the wild. Efforts are made to release the bird near or at the location where it was found. The center has received more than five thousand raptors in need of care and has released thousands of them back to nature.

Over six thousand programs have been presented by staff and volunteers at the Raptor Center since 1980. More than one million individuals have attended various kinds of presentations, all featuring live birds of prey.

The Eagle Aviary houses eight resident injured, nonreleasable bald eagles. Two golden eagles also reside in the aviary, at the center of which is the second largest raptor facility in the United States. Research is ongoing at the center. Annual hawk watches in North Carolina and annual midwinter bald eagle population surveys keep staff and volunteers busy. Food requirements and other aspects of bird physiology are also studied.

When visiting the center you can learn how to help a resident raptor through the Adopt-a-Bird program and enjoy close-up encounters with magnificent live birds. The center is open Tuesday through Saturday 10 A.M. to 5 P.M. and is closed

Mondays. Admission fees are $2 per student and $4 per adult. Groups of 10 or more get in for $1.50 per person with advanced notice to the center.

On Saturdays and Sundays, educational programs with live birds of prey are presented for the general public. Times for these programs are noon, 1:30 P.M., and 2 P.M. Programs are approximately twenty minutes long. Call for further information: 704-875-6521.

The Mountains

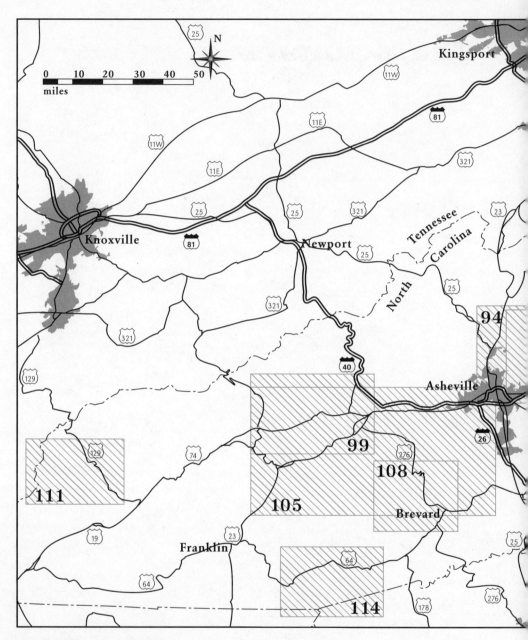

FIGURE 78. Mountain tour routes
Numbers in boxes indicate figure numbers for individual tour route maps.

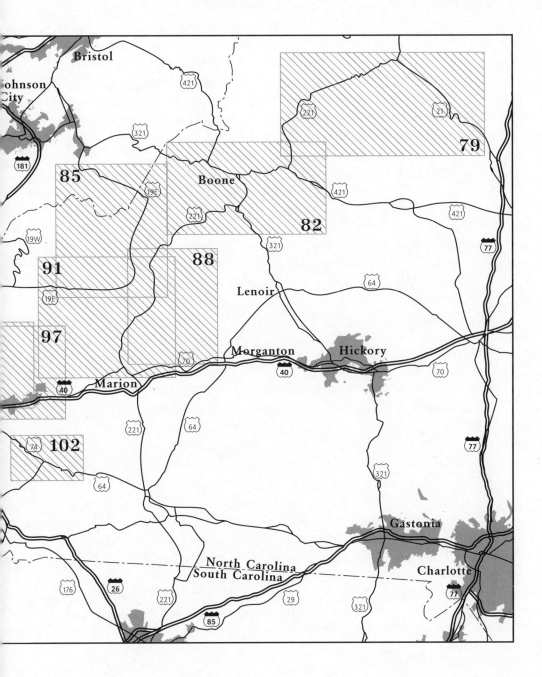

Northwestern Mountains

Stone Mountain, Mount Jefferson, and New River State Parks

MARSHALL ELLIS

This 46-mile tour focuses primarily on three units of the North Carolina State Parks System and takes you through some of the most scenic and diverse areas of the Blue Ridge Province. At Stone Mountain State Park you will learn about the area's unusual geology by visiting a massive granite dome that is the largest of its type in the state. The steep escarpment region surrounding the park displays examples of several different plant community types, and the sparse, stunted vegetation along the exposed summit of Stone Mountain shows the effects of exposure.

From Stone Mountain, you will travel up the Blue Ridge escarpment to the Blue Ridge Parkway. The drive south on the parkway takes you through pastoral country and examples of high-elevation natural communities for approximately 20 miles before you turn north to reach New River State Park. The New River has been designated as a National Scenic River. Along this exceptionally beautiful river you will view evidence of the geological processes that produced its deep entrenchment. From the New River, you will travel west to Mount Jefferson State Natural Area. This mountain outlier of the Blue Ridge is another place to explore mountain plant communities and geology.

This tour will enable you to observe and learn about the biology and geology of the Blue Ridge Province. You'll be able to see how elevation affects vegetation patterns, and at each stop of the tour you will observe landforms that are unusual in this region and that illustrate a variety of geological processes.

A. Stone Mountain State Park

Stone Mountain State Park is located in Wilkes and Alleghany Counties, approximately 15 miles north of Elkin. After passing through the hands of a succession of mining companies that attempted unsuccessfully to market the mountain's granite for commercial use, the park was established in 1969 when the land was donated to the state by the North Carolina Granite Corporation of Mount Airy, North Caro-

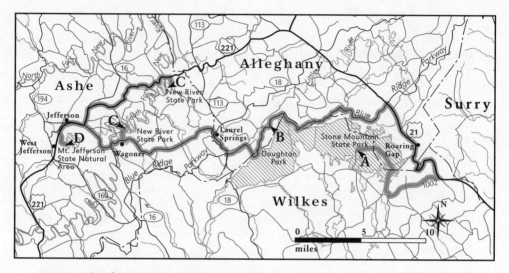

FIGURE 79. Northwestern mountains tour route

lina. At nearly 14,000 acres, it is one of the state's largest and most undeveloped state parks.

To reach the park, travel north from Elkin on US 21. Following directional signs, turn west (left) onto SR 1002 just beyond Thurmond. Drive 4.3 miles and turn right onto the John P. Frank Parkway (SR 1784); the park entrance will be 2.5 miles ahead. Brochures, maps, and complete information on the park can be obtained at the park office, which will be on your right approximately 0.25 miles beyond the gate.

The park sits at the base of the steep, heavily forested Blue Ridge escarpment, and its most prominent feature is its namesake granite dome, which rises almost 700 feet above the valley floor (Figure 80). Trails to the summit, the meadow on the mountain's south side, and the nearby Stone Mountain Falls begin at the parking lot located at the picnic area directly opposite the visitors center, as well as at another parking area located approximately 2 miles from the visitors center.

Formed 200 million years ago, Stone Mountain is composed of a light-gray, medium-grained biotite granite. It became visible as a dome on the landscape after erosion and weathering had removed overlying material. Similar, smaller domes formed just across the valley at the areas known as Wolf Rock and Cedar Rock. All three of these are monadnocks, as described in the Lonely Mountains tour in the Piedmont section of this book. Short hikes of moderate to strenuous difficulty provide access to these other domes and afford spectacular views of the huge south face of Stone Mountain, which was designated as a National Natural Landmark in 1974.

FIGURE 80. South face of Stone Mountain. (Photo courtesy of N.C. Division of Parks and Recreation)

As you view Stone Mountain's south face from the meadow, you will see that except for two prominent ridges, or arêtes, the familiar cracks and crevices normally associated with cliffs are absent, and the face is quite polished in many places. You will also notice that sections of the face are stained from top to bottom with long black streaks. These streaks are water channels, usually less than one inch deep, that have been cut through weak sections of the granite's veneer. Toward the southern (right) end of the face, look for the prominent railroad-track-like rills that run from lower right to upper left. Although it is difficult to tell from the ground, some of these tracks are quite wide and are large enough to walk on. There is a scattered talus field along the base of the south face, and several of the blocks are fairly large. A short trail leads into this area. Look for the largest block off to your right; it is an easily identified huge boulder with a broad, level surface. This rock is known as the Threshing Rock and is said to have been used by early settlers as a place to separate the chaff from their grain crops.

These low-elevation granitic domes, known geologically as plutons, are an unusual occurrence along the Blue Ridge escarpment. Their steepness varies considerably, and except for scattered shallow patches, soils are absent over much of their areas. Stone Mountain can be climbed from the north and south ends via the Stone Mountain Trail; this 4-mile loop has strenuous sections that cross steep, exposed sections of the face. Hikers should exercise great caution, particularly in wet weather. As you move about, always be aware of your location on the face; it is deceptively easy to wander too far down the face onto steeper sections. All of the features and vistas described here are found along the flat sections of the mountain's summit. Once atop the mountain, you will have numerous opportunities for truly spectacular views of the Blue Ridge Escarpment, and on exceptionally clear days the high country around Mount Mitchell will be visible to the west.

As you gain elevation, notice that the vegetation changes from well-developed hardwood-dominated forests to scattered patches of pine- and heath-dominated forest. This change is a reflection of the effects of elevation and the loss of a suitable soil layer. The stunted and gnarled vegetation along the broad summit superbly illustrates the effects of exposure. You'll see that the vegetation on the drier, more exposed south side of the summit is noticeably more stunted and less well developed than on the moister, more shaded north side.

As you traverse the summit, look for the narrow drainage channels that have been cut through sections where the granite veneer is weak. These channels can be extremely slippery, even when dry. Use great caution when approaching and crossing these areas. You will also notice numerous areas with vast arrays of shallow circular potholes. Like the drainage channels, these pits are formed in areas where the veneer is weak. Deeper pits contain deposits of scouring sediments. These pits are often places for plant colonization; look for pioneering mosses and lichens that have established in these areas.

The slopes surrounding the dome support a variety of mountain plant communities. In the western section of the park, you can visit an excellent example of a cove forest on the acidic soils around the Garden Creek area. Look for tulip poplar, red maple, red oak, Canada hemlock, black locust, and sweet birch in the canopy. Look for a shrub layer dominated by rhododendron and mountain laurel. The more open upper slopes and ridgetops are dominated by chestnut oak forests. Also, look for pitch pine along the lower slopes and Table Mountain pine at the higher elevation slopes; these species are distinguished by their heavily armored, tightly closed cones.

To the east, in the area toward Widow's Creek, look for examples of pine-oak/heath communities along the upper slopes. The canopy here is composed of chestnut oak, red oak, and dwarfed specimens of pitch and Table Mountain pine. The dense shrub layer contains familiar heath species, including mountain laurel, rhododendron, and flame azalea.

Rich cove forest—one of the park's most diverse natural community types—can be found along the East Prong of the Roaring River, Big Sandy Creek, and Garden Creek. The canopy of these forested areas is diverse and includes Canada hemlock, American beech, tulip poplar, mountain basswood, sweet birch, yellow birch, red oak, red and sugar maples, cucumber tree, and ironwood. Rhododendron dominates along the stream margins but decreases as you move away from a stream.

B. Blue Ridge Parkway

From Stone Mountain, retrace the route to US 21. Turn north and continue up the escarpment. Pass through the town of Roaring Gap and at the Blue Ridge Parkway turn south, toward Doughton Park. The Blue Ridge Parkway is a unit of the National Park Service, and with 17 million visitors annually, it is the most visited park unit in the country. Construction of the parkway began in 1935, as part of President Franklin D. Roosevelt's depression-era economic recovery program. This scenic route is widely known and appreciated for its rural essence and extraordinary vistas and has been designated by the National Scenic Byways Program as an All American Road. You will pass through pastoral country as well as undisturbed natural communities, and there are numerous scenic overlooks, including the pullout at milepost 232, which provides a fantastic view of the escarpment and Stone Mountain. This overlook definitely merits a stop.

Built largely by the now famous Civilian Conservation Corps, the parkway hugs the crest of its namesake mountain range for 469 miles and connects Shenandoah National Park in the north with Great Smoky Mountains National Park in the south. Although the elevations along the section of parkway traversed by this tour reach only around 3,800 feet above sea level, along its distance the parkway crosses extraordinarily wide elevational and ecological gradients, approaching 6,000 feet in the area around Mount Mitchell State Park at milepost 355. Over 1,250 species of vascular plants have been documented along its route, and as you ascend its heights, look for transitions from oak-hickory forests at the lower elevations to conifers and more typically northern species, such as beech, buckeye, and hemlock. Above 5,000 feet, the deciduous forests will give way to spruce-fir forests that are much battered and gnarled from exposure to wind, rain, snow, and ice. Visitors to Doughton Park can expect to see such high-elevation species as bigtooth aspen, Carolina hemlock, and Fraser magnolia. The area is famous, as is much of the parkway, for the dazzling spring and early summer displays of rhododendron and mountain laurel, and there are numerous flower species, including blazing star, mayapple, fire pink, violets, and bluets.

The Doughton Park area was originally known as The Bluffs, a reference to nearby Bluff Mountain. It was renamed in 1961 to honor Congressman Robert L. Doughton, who was an ardent supporter of the parkway. Today, at 6,000 acres, Doughton Park is one of the largest tracts along the entire parkway. Visitor facilities include backcountry camping, car and RV camping, a motel called the Bluffs Lodge, a gas station and coffee shop, and picnic areas. Doughton Park is open year-round and offers excellent opportunities for hiking, camping, cross-country skiing, and photography.

There are over 30 miles of trails of varying length and difficulty, and detailed trail maps are available at the Bluffs gas station. Some of the most popular trails include the 15-mile-long (round-trip) Bluff Mountain Trail, which parallels the parkway for 7.5 miles to milepost 244.7. This can be a long day's journey, but the gradient is generally easy. Shorter hikes include the Fodder Stack Trail, a 1-mile-long trail starting at milepost 241 that takes the hiker along a ridge through a variety of plant community types. The Basin Creek Trail, at milepost 243.7, is accessed from the backcountry campground and covers 3.3 miles over moderately difficult terrain. The Flat Rock Ridge Trail, at milepost 244.7, is a 5-mile hike of moderate difficulty that rewards the hiker with spectacular vistas. This trail, along with the nearby Cedar Ridge Trail and the Grassy Gap Fire Road, is highly recommended for those who enjoy bird watching.

c. New River State Park

Exit the Blue Ridge Parkway at the intersection with NC 18, near milepost 249. Turn north and drive toward the town of Laurel Springs. New River State Park, located in Alleghany and Ashe Counties, was established in 1977 following efforts to save the river from development as a hydropower source. It includes 22 miles of the South Fork and 4.5 miles of the North Fork; this entire 26.5-mile stretch was designated in 1975 as both a National and North Carolina Scenic River.

There are three access areas for the park. The park office at the Wagoner Road Access is located 8 miles southeast of Jefferson. It is on SR 1590, which is 1.2 miles east of the intersection of NC 16 and NC 88. Maps, brochures, and complete information on the park are available at this location. The US 221 Access Area is located 8 miles northeast of Jefferson and can be reached directly from US 221. The Alleghany County Access Area is just south of the North Carolina–Virginia border; it is accessible only by canoe.

The New River is located in the New River Plateau of the Blue Ridge Province. The region is mountainous, and the average elevation along the plateau is around 2,500 feet. The headwaters for both forks of the New originate in the Blue Ridge Mountains, and they merge just south of the North Carolina–Virginia border. The river and its tributaries cross the plateau in winding courses that combine exaggerated meanders with long straight reaches. The river's course is contained by steep, heavily forested valley walls, and it flows to the northwest, which is at right angles to the trend of the plateau's bedrock formations. This tight course is unusual for a river with such a moderate gradient and can be attributed to geological uplift and tilting, which produced the entrenched valleys through which the river flows.

Although the river is bordered by mountains along its length, many sections have a well-developed floodplain. Agricultural crops thrive in the fine alluvial soils, and many of the areas adjacent to the river have been altered. One of the most common crops you will see in this region is Christmas trees. Undisturbed sections of the floodplain are not numerous, but when you find them, look for bottom-land hardwood forests dominated by American beech, sycamore, willow, and red maple.

This is an exceptionally scenic river that follows a deeply entrenched, meandering course over some of the oldest rocks in the Appalachian range. The granitic gneisses that occur along the plateau are part of what is known as the Elk Park Plutonic Group; they are believed to be over one billion years old and were originally formed as the core of a long-eroded mountain range. This is certainly an old river, but although popular consensus touts the New River as the oldest river in North America, and the second oldest in the world (behind the Nile), in fact, geologists have yet to establish a reliable age for it. Another misconception concerns its northward flow. Although this has been deemed highly unusual by many and is, in fact, not common among North Carolina's rivers, it is not geologically or hydrologically unusual.

Much can be learned from glimpsing the river from the shore and from vantage points at various bridges and roads; however, the best way to observe the river's geology is from the river itself. Look for the following features at the park's three access areas.

Wagoner Road

This area occupies a narrow floodplain on the South Fork's southwest bank, just opposite a large sandbar. Islands of sand and gravel are created when the water's velocity slows and is no longer able to carry these sediments suspended in the water column. Just downstream, near the camping area, look for outcrops composed of muscovite biotite quartz gneiss that strike across the river. Here you'll be able to observe differential weathering and erosion in these outcrops, whose components possess different degrees of hardness.

There is also a fine example of a rich cove forest at this site; you can reach it via the short nature trail. Although the site has a long history of disturbance, over 120 species have been documented in the forest. Look for American beech, yellow buckeye, sugar maple, black walnut, butternut, and red oak in the canopy. The herb layer is particularly rich, and in it you will find ginseng, maidenhair fern, walking fern, showy orchis, black cohosh, blue cohosh, mayapple, and ragwort.

US 221 Access Area

This site is located on the South Fork along the northwest side of a large meander. The camping area is on the inner, or depositional, side of the meander in an area of low water velocity. The far side of the river is much steeper, with rocky cliffs in some areas. These cliffs are composed of amphibolite and layers of muscovite biotite gneiss. Look for riffles and rapids, which are formed as a consequence of differing rates of erosion on the river's substrates. Along the New River, the most erosion-resistant layers, and hence the rocks of most rapids, are composed of quartz-rich gneiss. Look for the silver streaks left by low-riding aluminum canoes that scrape over these hard outcrops.

Alleghany County Access Area

This site is reached only by canoe and is located across from a granite wall that rises nearly 200 feet above the river. Known locally as The Bluffs, these cliffs are composed of granitic gneiss that is over one billion years old. As with the US 221 site, the camping area is located on the depositional side of a meander, where stream velocity is relatively low. The bluffs are located in an area of high water velocity and offer an example of the dynamics of stream channel development. At numerous places along the river, you will be able to observe this process, in which water being carried at high velocity is cutting into steep slopes on the outsides of meanders and bends. You will also see a large sandbar on the northeast side of the picnic area.

D. Mount Jefferson State Natural Area

To reach Mount Jefferson from the New River, take NC 88 west toward Jefferson to its intersection with US 221. Follow the signs to SR 1152, which leads to the park entrance and office.

Mount Jefferson is a steep, isolated peak located in Ashe County (Figure 81). It sits at the edge of the New River Plateau in the drainage between the north and south forks of the New River. Mount Jefferson State Natural Area was established in 1956 and covers approximately 550 acres. Surviving as a remnant of a long-eroded mountain range, it is composed mainly of amphibolite and gneiss. The peak reaches an elevation of 4,684 feet above sea level and rises 1,600 feet above the surrounding valleys. The plant communities found here are in excellent condition, and they exemplify many of those that are found in the Blue Ridge Mountains. Most of the slopes above 4,000 feet have never been harvested, and they support outstanding plant communities. The condition of these natural communities was a major factor in the mountain's designation as a National Natural Landmark in 1974.

As you ascend to the summit via the park's 2-mile-long road, you will have an opportunity to stop at two overlooks to take in spectacular scenery and to view the park's features up close. From the parking area, you can hike easy trails to the summit area and to Luther Rock, which is reached via the self-guided Rhododendron Trail. The Luther Rock area provides excellent vistas and supports a number of natural community types.

Much of the forested area below 4,000 feet was dominated by American chest-

FIGURE 81. Mount Jefferson. (Photo courtesy of N.C. Division of Parks and Recreation)

nut until its abrupt disappearance from the landscape after the introduction of a nonnative fungus early in this century. Massive chestnut stumps and logs still linger in the area, but the species survives today only as stump sprouts that grow into stunted shrubs; look for these shrubby trees with their distinctively toothed leaves. Today, much of the area has been reforested by stands that are dominated by oak and hickory species.

You will be able to observe several different plant communities in the summit and Luther Rock areas. The southwest-facing slopes west of Luther Rock support a well-developed chestnut oak forest that is dominated by chestnut oak, red and white oaks, and red maple. A shrub-dominated heath bald can be found on the southern part of the summit at Luther Rock. Look for Catawba rhododendron, mountain laurel, black chokeberry, deerberry, mountain highbush blueberry, and mountain sweet pepperbush. The trees here will be scattered and stunted from exposure to severe winds, ice, and cold. Look for dwarfed red and white oaks, black locusts, mountain ash, and American chestnut sprouts.

Much of the summit and ridgetops of Mount Jefferson are covered by high-elevation red oak forest. This community occurs in a harsh environment, and although some trees are quite large, many of them are stunted and are older than they look. Notice the open canopy in this community; it is believed to have resulted from the loss of the chestnut, which formed a tighter, more closed canopy. You will encounter rocky outcrop communities at the overlooks and at Luther

Rock. These exposed areas have little soil, and vegetation is generally limited to shrub or herb species that occupy protected crevices. Also, from the overlooks, look down and try to see the stands that are dominated by the bigtooth aspen, whose leaves waggle and flutter in the breeze. This mountain species is rare in North Carolina, having been documented in only four counties.

Blue Ridge Parkway
Grandfather Mountain Region

CURTIS SMALLING

The story of the Appalachian Mountain region is a story of change. Through seasons, history, and each day, the mountains change. Indeed, probably the most striking feature of the mountains, especially in the Blue Ridge, is their variety of expression. Elevational gradients, weather, abundance of habitats, aspect (or the compass direction of slope) all combine to create a mosaic of microhabitats, each with its own group of plant and animal inhabitants.

This 32-mile tour of the high country from Deep Gap to Grandfather Mountain takes us to some of the best of the "wild" areas left in the region. It should be remembered, however, that one visit is simply a snapshot. The same route traveled in another season will yield an entirely different experience. I encourage you to return time and time again to learn about these sometimes subtle and sometimes dramatic changes in the landscape.

A. E. B. Jeffress Park

Our tour begins at the intersection of US 421 and the Blue Ridge Parkway at Deep Gap. A quick trip north on the parkway will bring you to E. B. Jeffress Park (milepost 272, hereafter MP). This middle-elevation park sits on the edge of the Blue Ridge escarpment. The escarpment is the transition zone between the generally higher elevation Blue Ridge Province and the Piedmont. Throughout most of this tour, the Blue Ridge Parkway hugs the escarpment, providing stunning vistas. The escarpment here falls some 2,000 feet on average, usually within 1 mile of horizontal distance. This steep grade creates active streams that sometimes tumble down wonderful falls and cascades. Indeed, the primary attraction at Jeffress Park is the Cascades Trail, a moderate 1.2-mile round-trip to the Cascades, a jumble of rocks and waterfalls tumbling some 500 vertical feet, with excellent views of the valley below. Interpretive labels will help you identify the common plant life. This trail can be an excellent place to bird watch in the spring, with elusive cerulean warblers reported in most years. Jeffress Park also has restroom facilities and a picnic area. The restrooms are only open from May through October.

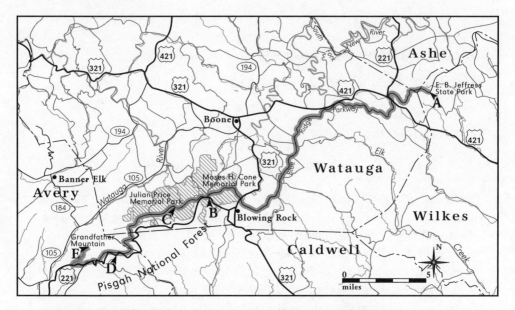

FIGURE 82. Blue Ridge Parkway tour route—Grandfather Mountain area

Returning to the parkway and heading south this time, you will pass back over the junction with US 421 and continue to Grandview Overlook (MP 281.5). This aptly named scenic overlook provides a spectacular view of the escarpment in any season, and on cool August and September mornings, fog often blankets the valley below. The view is to the south, and winter sunrises here are marvelous. This overlook also has the advantage of being adjacent to US 421 at Parkway Elementary School, and so it is accessible even in snowy weather when the parkway is impassable. There is a North Carolina Department of Transportation rest area (with restrooms) in front of the school, and on snowy days when parkway access is bad, you may park there and cross the road to the parkway on foot. From the rest area, Grandview is 0.25 miles to the west (your right). Watch for traffic, as this section of roadway is heavily traveled. The viewshed below the overlook has recently been protected through a conservation easement and should remain intact for years to come.

Continuing south to MP 285 and pull off at an overlook on your left. While the parkway has left the edge of the escarpment by this point, this area is ripe with local history. The hemlocks around this overlook often harbor interesting migrants in spring and fall as well as birds of more open country, since the surrounding area is composed largely of residential and agricultural land. Nearby is the place where Daniel Boone reportedly came into the mountain region in the 1760s on his way into east Tennessee and, finally, Kentucky. A sheltering rock outcrop near here was supposedly used by Boone and other early explorers in the region. The first recorded white visitor to the area, Bishop Auguste Spangenburg, crossed here as well. Spangenburg, looking for land on which to found a colony of Mennonites, visited the area in 1752. After a hard day's climb up the escarpment in December, he arrived here to find snow on the ground and more coming. Although he loved the scenery and explored for a number of days in the Blue Ridge, he finally settled on land that became known as the Wachovia tract, where present-day Winston-Salem was founded. A small stone marker here erected by the Daughters of the American Revolution after World War I marks the historic Boone's Trail into the high country.

Continuing south on the parkway, note that the road rejoins the escarpment for several miles. Each overlook and break provides scenic views into the Piedmont. While these views are sublime and spectacular, this section of the parkway can be treacherous in bad weather, with fog in spring and fall, and ice and snow in the winter. Indeed, at Aho Gap (MP 288.4), the Park Service has installed gates to close this section of the parkway in bad weather. Keep this in mind during the winter months. The silver lining to these closings is that this makes for wonderful areas for cross-country skiing and snowshoeing during those times. Always remember to park your vehicles off of the road and do not block the gates at any time.

An interesting stop along this section is the Raven Rocks Overlook (MP 289) on your right. This overlook is one of the few along this section of the parkway with views to the west. The vista in front of you at this overlook includes good views of the four highest peaks in the area. Grandfather Mountain (your final destination) is on your far left, and the trio of peaks in the northwest corner of Watauga County are on your right; they are, from left to right, Rich Mountain, Snake Mountain, and Elk Knob. All of these mountains are over 5,400 feet in elevation, and each supports its own unique history and ecology. The large white home visible just to the left of center of the view is the Cone Manor House, a later stop along this tour.

The next notable stop is Thunder Hill Overlook (MP 290.2). Here the full sweep of the escarpment is visible. This is a wonderful place from which to watch the march of the seasons across the face of the mountains, particularly in spring and fall. It is said that spring travels north 15 miles a day or up 100 feet in elevation. From here, the traveler can see spring approaching even though the parkway may be wintry under a mantle of snow. Gradually, as the season progresses, the light green color of buds and new herbaceous growth inches its way up the slope, eventually overtaking the Blue Ridge. The reverse happens in the fall, with brilliant colors splashed across the mountains by mid-October and peak color often not arriving in the foothills until a month later. Standing at Thunder Hill, you can be surrounded by trees already bare for winter and look down on brilliant oranges, reds, and yellows far in the valley below. The overlook is aptly named, for a visit on a stormy summer's eve can reveal some spectacular lightning shows down in the Piedmont. Summer storms often gather strength over the escarpment as super-heated air rushes up the slopes. Keep that in mind when hiking in the region, as storms can develop quickly on the high ridges.

Return to the parkway now and proceed to the US 321 intersection for access to Boone and Blowing Rock. Blowing Rock is 2 miles southeast of here, and Boone is about 7 miles to the north. Each has gas, food, lodging, and attractions, some of which are available seasonally, others year-round, if you want to extend your stay in the area.

The long pull uphill after crossing US 321 on the parkway brings you back onto the leased agricultural land along the parkway. Cattle grazing is the most common use of these tracts, and these cattle pastures often support good flocks of wild turkey, which have recently returned in large numbers to the region. This area around MP 292 is especially good for turkey, as well as open-country birds such as bluebirds, robins, and blackbirds.

B. Moses H. Cone Memorial Park

Moses Cone Memorial Park and Manor House is at MP 294. Look for the manor house access point on your left and continue around to the parking area behind the house and old stable building. The park is named for the denim king, Moses H. Cone, who built and lived on this estate in the late nineteenth and early twentieth centuries. The estate originally included some 3,500 acres and was a working farm with over 25,000 apple trees planted on the grounds. The park boasts some of the best hiking and cross-country skiing in the area on its over 25 miles of original carriage roads that meander through the park. The manor house (Figure 83) was considered second only to Biltmore Estate when it was first constructed; today it is home to an information center/bookshop run by the National Park Service, as well as a nice craft shop run by the Southern Highland Handicraft Guild. Here artisans demonstrate their trades throughout the summer and fall. Restrooms are also available at the manor house from April through October.

The Cone estate includes two important bodies of water. Trout and Bass Lakes usually harbor some of the best numbers and variety of migrating waterfowl in the region. The views are often excellent too, as both lakes are small. Winter regulars at these lakes include ring-necked ducks, pied-billed grebes, hooded mergansers, occasionally a ruddy duck, and buffleheads. Summer breeders include Canada geese, mallards, and substantial numbers of beautiful wood ducks. Green herons are also common in summer. Both lakes are surrounded by good habitat for nesting northern bird species that reach their southern range limits in the Appala-chians, including brown creeper, Canada warbler, blackburnian warbler, veery,

FIGURE 83. Manor House, Moses H. Cone Memorial Park. (Photo by D. Frankenberg)

golden-crowned kinglet, red-breasted nuthatch, and yellow-bellied sapsucker. Beaver are common on Bass Lake. An old-growth hemlock forest with massive trees grows around the 16-acre Trout Lake. Fishing is allowed on both lakes, although single hooks and artificial lures only are to be used on Trout Lake. Neither lake allows boating or swimming.

To access Bass Lake and its easy 1-mile walking trail, continue from the manor house south on the parkway to the junction with US 221 (MP 294.6). Turn left toward Blowing Rock and proceed 1 mile to the Moses Cone Park Car Access Road on your left. There is also a small parking area just past the access road for a leisurely walk down to the lake. This park is the most heavily used in the area, with most days seeing lots of joggers, hikers, and fishermen. Parking on holiday weekends can be tight. Note that there is a year-round-accessible Porta-Potty here for visitor use—one of just a few open all year. To access Trout Lake from the Cone Manor House, turn south on the parkway, then turn left at the junction with US 221, as described above, but take an immediate right before 221 and follow the signs under the parkway for Shull's Mills and Flannery Fork Roads. At the intersection under the parkway bridge, take a left and an immediate right onto a one-way paved road to the parking area.

Return to the parkway at the junction with US 221 and proceed south to the Sims Creek Overlook (MP 295.3). This overlook connects with the Green Knob Trail. This trail passes through many habitats including hemlock cove forest, mixed hardwood forest, and active as well as idle agricultural lands. One of the best areas for owling, the Sims Creek Overlook has produced screech owl and barred owl observations with great regularity, as well as an occasional winter sighting of saw-whet owl and great horned owl.

c. Julian Price Memorial Park

Continuing south, you will next enter Julian Price Memorial Park. This 4,300-acre tract was given to the National Park Service by the founder of the Jefferson Pilot Insurance Company. Originally intended as a recreational retreat for the employees of Jefferson Pilot, the park now hosts abundant seasonal visitors at its large picnic area (MP 296.5), campground with amphitheater (MP 297.1), and lake access with canoe and boat rental. Campsites are available from May through October, although full staffing and boat and canoe rentals occur only from Memorial Day through Labor Day. A leisurely 2-mile hike around the Price Lake Loop is enjoyable at any season. This lake (Figure 84) often hosts migrating waterfowl, including common loons and double-crested cormorants in the spring and fall. Fishing is also available, and a nice added feature is a wheelchair-accessible fishing deck to the right of the dam parking lot (MP 296.7). From the campground or picnic area, the Boone Fork Trail is an enjoyable 5-mile loop that passes through mixed hardwood forest for most of its route. One interesting spot along this trail is Boone Fork Bog, adjacent to the Price Park picnic grounds. This ancient lake bed supports a mix of wetland vegetation including mosses, ferns, willows, and alders. It also supports a healthy beaver population and one of the rarest nesting birds in the mountains—the alder flycatcher, which is reported from here most summers. It is also an excellent spot to see the mating flights of the American woodcock. Beginning about dusk on warm, late-winter evenings (February through March), look and listen for the birds' high flights beginning with their buzzy calls as they ascend and the tinkling sound of air through their feathers as they fall the 100 or so feet back to earth. About 1 mile from the bog area is The Rocks, a jumble of rocks along Boone Fork Creek that makes for tremendous bouldering and wading possibilities. This is a favorite spot along the parkway for the younger crowd and tends to be busy on warm spring and summer days.

After leaving Price Park and continuing south on the parkway, you will begin a long, relatively steep climb up the "back side" of Grandfather Mountain. The parkway may be closed by gate at the Holloway Mountain Road intersection (MP 298.6) in winter. This section can be glorious for on-the-road hiking in winter; snow and rime ice often convert the surrounding landscape into one of the most wintry scenes in the Southeast. Remember not to block the parkway gate at any

FIGURE 84. Lake at Julian Price Memorial Park. (Photo by D. Frankenberg)

time you come here to hike or ski. The parkway winds its way for 5 miles up to the Linn Cove Viaduct, and then, at MP 305, you will come to another junction with US 221 and access to the privately owned sections of Grandfather Mountain.

Grandfather Mountain is one of the jewels in this section of the Blue Ridge Parkway. It is the highest peak in the Blue Ridge Mountains at 5,964 feet above sea level. It is also the world's only privately owned International Biosphere Reserve (as designated by the United Nations Man and the Biosphere Program). Much of the mountain has been protected by conservation easements that the owner has donated to The Nature Conservancy, and it is bounded on its southern edge by Pisgah National Forest. The mountain is home to some thirteen endangered animal species and thirty rare and endangered plants. Some of these rare residents include peregrine falcon, Virginia big-eared bat, Carolina race of the northern flying squirrel, and spruce-fir moss spider. Rare and endangered plant species include Heller's blazing star, Blue Ridge goldenrod, and bent avens.

D. Hiking Trails: Tanawha and Others

The parkway provides many overlooks between Price Park and Grandfather Mountain. There are scenic vistas into the Catawba River basin and trail access to more than 30 miles of interconnected trails. Some are moderate to easy, like the

13.5-mile Tanawha Trail, which runs from the Price Park campground up the southeastern flank of Grandfather to the Beacon's Heights Overlook (MP 300.5). This trail, especially if you hike it from top toward bottom, can provide an easy all-day hike encompassing the whole range of habitats that are easily accessible along the parkway. Over eighty species of birds nest on Grandfather, including some twenty warbler species.

The Tanawha, a National Park Service trail, also provides connections to some of the backcountry trails of Grandfather Mountain. Some of the overlooks with access to the Tanawha and other Grandfather trails include the Boone Fork Overlook (MP 299.9), Raven Rocks Overlook (MP 302.4), Rough Ridge Overlook (MP 302.9), and the Wilson's Creek Overlook (MP 303.7). Because Grandfather Mountain is a privately held property, a hiking permit is required and a small fee is charged for hiking the backcountry. Check at the entrance to Grandfather for permits, fees, and information on hiking and camping in the backcountry; staff there can provide you with a brochure-sized trail map that contains up-to-date information on trail closings and so on. Call Grandfather Mountain at 800-4MT-PEAK to order information on the trails and programs, or visit their web site at http://www.grandfather.com.

One of the most popular hikes in this area is the trail up Rough Ridge. Park at the Rough Ridge Overlook (MP 302.9) and walk to your right to the end of the parking area. Proceed uphill, bearing to your left for 0.2 miles to a boardwalk area. This area, a heath bald covered by huckleberry, mountain ash, and Catawba rhododendron, is a marvelous spot to watch the autumn hawk migration. It is typified by very dry conditions with sand myrtle, turkeybeard, and galax providing contrast to the low shrubs. Winter wrens, dark-eyed juncos, catbirds, and others nest here and along the spruce-fir edge to this bald. Continue up the mountain to Ship Rock for more spectacular views and then an easy 0.5-mile hike back to the Rough Ridge Overlook and your car.

At MP 300 the most famous section of the Blue Ridge Parkway, the Linn Cove Viaduct, meanders its way around the side of the mountain. This bridge, completed in 1987, is formed of individually precast concrete sections. The viaduct's design enabled construction of this part of the parkway with very little damage to the existing mountainside. This was the last section of the Blue Ridge Parkway to be built, and it was completed fifty years after construction of the roadway began. The Linn Cove visitors center (MP 304.4—open late-April through October) provides restrooms, a bookstore, and exhibits on the construction of the viaduct. At the far end of the paved parking area here is a wheelchair-accessible portion of the Tanawha Trail that stretches 0.5 miles into the forest and under the viaduct before becoming a dirt and gravel path. This is an excellent spot at which to find saw-whet owls in the spring, as well as numerous veerys and red-breasted nuthatches.

E. Grandfather Mountain

Return to the parkway and proceed south to the intersection with US 221 (MP 305.1). Follow US 221 to your right for 1 mile to the entrance to Grandfather Mountain. A fee is charged for entrance to the mountain property, which is open year-round, weather permitting. About halfway up the mountain (approximately 1 mile), stop at the nature museum for programming information, exhibits, restrooms, restaurant, gift shop, and natural animal habitats. These habitats are home to black bears, river otters, cougars, white-tailed deer, and bald and golden eagles. Be on the lookout for native birds like common raven, peregrine falcon, and broad-winged hawk flying overhead. The feeders at the museum often host large numbers of dark-eyed juncos and pine siskins, and in "finch winters," you are likely to see evening grosbeaks and purple finches.

Continue up the mountain to the visitors center and swinging bridge at 2.4 miles. Be prepared for switchbacks and breathtaking views as you approach the highest portions of the mountain. Trailheads can be found at parking areas along the road up the mountain; the trails they lead to traverse some of the roughest terrain in eastern North America. Weather can be deadly at this elevation, with winds in excess of 190 miles per hour recorded at the weather station at the top of the mountain (and those winds were not associated with major storm centers like hurricanes). Even in summer, the weather can turn in an instant. Hypothermia is possible even in the warmer months, so if you plan to hike the backcountry, come prepared for weather extremes. Lightning can also be deadly here as summer storms approach. A little caution, respect for the mountain, and preparation can make your time at Grandfather Mountain one of the most enjoyable parts of your visit to the high country. Trailheads at the uppermost parking area lead to the famous "mile high swinging bridge" and Calloway Peak, the highest point on the mountain.

As you leave Grandfather Mountain, you may rejoin the parkway and head south to the Linville Falls and Linville Gorge Wilderness areas, where another tour in this book awaits you, or you can turn right on US 221 and head to Linville, North Carolina, and an intersection with NC 105. A right turn on NC 105 North leads you toward Boone (17 miles) and Banner Elk (7 miles). Straight across the intersection has you on your way to the Roan Mountain area along NC 181 to Newland, NC 194 to Elk Park, and US 19E to Roan Mountain (33 miles), where yet another tour found in this book awaits.

Remember that your visits to the North Carolina high country are mere snapshots of an ever-changing region. Whether you enjoy warm springs days and the flood of avian migrants, or the chill of a quiet winter afternoon spent cross-country skiing, this area of the Blue Ridge is an exquisite part of our natural state.

Roan Mountain Highlands

Ecology, Geology, and Cultural History

ELIZABETH HUNTER

This 68-mile driving tour begins in Bakersville—the Mitchell County seat and the "Gateway to the Roan." It climbs to Carvers Gap atop Roan Mountain on the North Carolina–Tennessee state line, then makes a 5-mile loop on a Forest Service road to the old Cloudland Hotel site, Rhododendron Gardens, and the trailhead to Roan High Bluff Overlook. It descends the mountain on the Tennessee side to Roan Mountain State Park and the town of Roan Mountain, Tennessee, then swings back into North Carolina, winding through the communities of Elk Park, Cranberry, Minneapolis, and Plumtree before terminating at the Blue Ridge Parkway's Museum of North Carolina Minerals near Spruce Pine. Excluding stops, allow approximately two to two and one-half hours to drive this route. A shorter alternative, a loop tour that begins and ends in Bakersville, follows the same route to Roan Mountain State Park's visitors center, then retraces its steps to the community of Burbank, Tennessee, takes Cove Creek Road across Hughes Gap, descends to the community of Buladean, North Carolina, and returns to Bakersville (Figure 85). The alternate route is approximately 58 miles (46 miles if you skip the visit to Roan Mountain State Park). Both tours cross the mountain, but the main tour circles the eastern end of the Roan Massif, offering glimpses of Round and Jane Balds, Yellow Mountain, and Big and Little Hump; the alternate route circles the western end of the massif, with good views from Buladean of the spruce-fir forest on Roan High Knob and Roan High Bluff.

The tour's highlight is the summit of Roan. The Roan Massif is a large mountain mass with a central ridge—a 12-mile-long series of rounded peaks and gaps—that trends in a northwest-southeast direction from the Blue Ridge to the Unaka Mountains, along the Tennessee–North Carolina line. The term Roan Mountain refers to the westernmost 5-mile portion of the Roan Massif (from Roan High Bluff to Grassy Ridge, and including Roan High Knob, Round Bald, and Jane Bald). Elevations range from 6,286 feet at Roan High Knob to 5,512 feet at Carvers

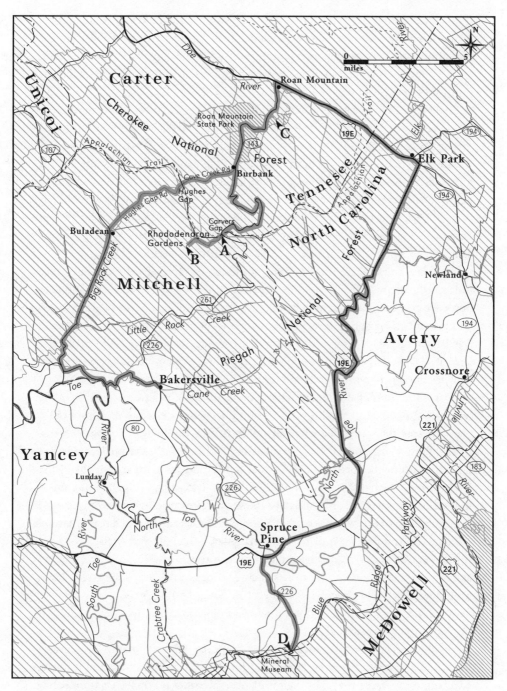

FIGURE 85. Roan Mountain Highlands tour route

Gap. Outstanding natural features of Roan Mountain are the grassy balds, spruce-fir forest, and 600 acres of natural rhododendron gardens. All are visible from the road, but each is worthy of an exploratory hike via the Appalachian, Cloudland, and Rhododendron Gardens Trails. Pack a picnic lunch and plan to spend the day exploring Roan Mountain and environs.

Roan Mountain has long been recognized as one of the most scenic mountains in the Southern Appalachians. Professor Elisha Mitchell, for whom the highest mountain east of the Mississippi is named, reserved his greatest praise for Roan Mountain. "It is the most beautiful of all the high mountains," he noted in his journal in 1836. "The top of the Roan may be described as a vast meadow without a tree to obstruct this prospect, where a person may gallop his horse for a mile or two with Carolina at his feet on one side and Tennessee on the other, and a green ocean of mountains rising in tremendous billows immediately around him." A century and a half later, the effect is still as Dr. Mitchell described.

There are four major learning opportunities on this tour. The first is the chance to learn the characteristics of a threatened spruce-fir ecosystem; the second is to observe examples that support scientific theories about the origins of grassy balds and current management practices designed to perpetuate them; the third is to learn how high-elevation protected lands provide habitat for relict plant and animal species; and the fourth is to understand how Roan Mountain's natural history has influenced the cultural and economic development of its surroundings.

Roan Mountain's balds and relict spruce-fir forests, the latter a survivor of the Ice Ages, support a highly diverse flora and boast a greater concentration of rare plant species than any area of comparable size in the Southern Appalachians. Many of the species found on the Roan evolved in the Southern Appalachians, but others are disjunct "northern" species that were common in the region during the Ice Ages, but which disappeared in the Southeast—except on the high mountains— as the climate warmed. Unfortunately, the spruce-fir ecosystem is now threatened by infestations of the balsam woolly adelgid (and insect) and by acid precipitation.

Plant community types of the Roan Highlands include Fraser fir forest, red spruce–Fraser fir forest, northern hardwoods forest, rocky summits, and grassy and shrub balds. Rare plant species include Gray's lily, spreading avens, Roan Mountain bluet, and Greenland sandwort. Among the Roan's most unusual resident wildlife are southern pygmy shrews, Carolina northern flying squirrels, and the New England cottontail.

Many theories have been advanced to explain the origins of the treeless, grassy balds that are one of the Roan Highlands' most distinctive and beautiful features. Early explorers were puzzled by their presence, since they occur at elevations below the timber line. One of the theories purports that the balds are a result of natural phenomena and date from the early Pleistocene, and that their presence has been perpetuated since by human activity. Some believe that large grazing and browsing animals—nearly two dozen large herbivore species ranged through the Southern Appalachians during the last million years—are responsible for the balds' creation; others believe that they are the result of physical factors such as catastrophic fires or climate changes. Still others think the balds are of more recent origin and attribute their presence to the use of fire by Native Americans, or to grazing herds of bison, deer, and elk that once populated the region. After European settlers moved into the Roan Mountain area, they used the balds for grazing livestock (cattle, sheep, goats, horses, mules, and hogs), a practice that maintained and in many cases enlarged the grassy areas. The U.S. Forest Service's balds management plan calls for a variety of techniques—including hand-mowing, grazing, limited herbicide use, and controlled burns—to halt encroachment by invasive species like hawthorn and thornless blackberry.

The biological diversity of the Roan Highlands has attracted botanists and travelers for more than two hundred years. Among its most famous visitors, in addition to Dr. Mitchell, were Andre Michaux, who collected botanical specimens there for the French government between 1789 and 1795, and Englishman John Fraser (the Fraser fir bears his name), who discovered a "new plant"—the Catawba rhododendron—on Roan's summit during explorations in the latter part of the eighteenth century. Asa Gray, the father of American botany, in 1841 discovered the beautiful Gray's lily that grows in scattered colonies on the balds. Like Mitchell, Gray considered the Roan "without doubt, the most beautiful mountain east of the Rockies."

General John Thomas Wilder, who in 1885 built the 166-room hotel that operated for twenty-five years near Roan High Knob, extolled the Roan's scenery: "magnificent views above the clouds . . . a most extended prospect of 50,000 sq. miles in six different states, 100 mountaintops over 4,000 feet high in sight." But Wilder himself was attracted to the area initially not by the mountain's scenery, but by a seam of magnetic iron ore that cuts through the Roan Highlands from the community of Cranberry, on its eastern end, to Buladean. Cranberry was the site of extensive iron ore mining from before the Civil War to 1929.

Wilder bought about 7,000 acres on the summit and slopes of Roan Mountain around 1870; by the time the U.S. Forest Service began acquiring land in the Roan Highlands—including the Wilder tract, from the general's heirs in 1941—all merchantable timber had been cut and truckloads of rhododendron had been carried away. The forests and rhododendron balds you see today have grown back since that time. Forest Service holdings on Roan Mountain are part of the Pisgah National Forest on the North Carolina side and the Cherokee National Forest in Tennessee. Of the nearly 15,000 acres of protected lands in the Roan Highlands, the U.S. Forest Service is the largest landowner. But the state of Tennessee began developing the 2,006-acre Roan Mountain State Park, 10 miles from the top of the mountain, in the 1970s; and the Southern Appalachian Highlands Conservancy and The Nature Conservancy own and manage several smaller tracts. About half the land above 4,000 feet is currently protected.

Begin this tour in the town of Bakersville (population four hundred), a community that bills itself as "the Gateway to the Roan." If you follow the main tour route, keep an eye out throughout the day for signs of damage from a one-hundred-year flood that roared through Bakersville, Roan Mountain, and other small communities on the slopes of the Roan Massif in January 1998. The raw, rocky aspect of creeks on both sides of the mountain is a result of the flood.

Bakersville has only two traffic lights; at the second, bear straight ahead on NC 261. The scenic highway passes through forested areas, agricultural lands, and pastures as it gradually ascends Roan Mountain. Note particularly the Christmas tree plantations on the higher slopes, where Fraser firs ("the Cadillac of Christmas trees") are grown. The spruce-fir forest atop Roan Mountain is a primary source of seeds and seedlings (the Forest Service allows cone harvests in the fall of "good cone years" and annual pulling of seedlings) for this burgeoning, multimillion-dollar industry, which provides income for many part-time and a few full-time growers. If you are planning to picnic along the tour, you may want to buy your supplies in Bakersville—there will be very few other opportunities for many miles.

A. Carvers Gap

The 13-mile drive from Bakersville takes you through the small communities of Glen Ayre (at 6.4 miles) and Roan Valley (9.5 miles) before your final ascent to Carvers Gap, on the North Carolina–Tennessee state line. At the Gap, Roan Mountain's "bald complex" (Round and Jane Balds, and Grassy Ridge) is to your right (Figure 86), accessible by the Appalachian Trail (AT), which crosses the highway and continues into the spruce-fir forest to your left. For the kind of view Professor Mitchell was talking about, park in the paved parking area to the left and follow the AT for 0.5 miles to the summit of Round Bald (elevation 5,826 feet). The rock you will walk over is 1.2-billion-year-old Precambrian gneiss—the oldest rock a hiker encounters on the 2,150-mile AT, which runs from Maine to Georgia. This trail is a major route for avid hikers. At the top of the bald is a small stand of Fraser firs planted in the 1930s by Professor D. M. Brown of East Tennessee State University, then a teacher's college. Brown, who is credited with conducting the first thorough vegetational study of Roan Mountain, planted the seedlings "to help explain the past and future of this grassy bald," according to a sign that once stood at the plot.

From the top of Round Bald, looking east, Jane Bald is in the immediate fore-

FIGURE 86. Roan Mountain Highlands. (Photo by Robert W. Harvey)

ground, with Grassy Ridge stretching to the southeast and the balds of Little Hump and Big Hump in the distance. To the southwest, look for the Black Mountain range (of which Mount Mitchell is a part) among the myriad North Carolina mountains. The Valley and Ridge Province of east Tennessee and southwest Virginia is visible to the north. Its predominantly sandstone ridges and the shales and limestones of its valleys are much younger (400–550 million years old) than the Precambrian rock of the Blue Ridge. Just beyond the top of Round Bald, before the AT begins its descent to the saddle between Round and Jane Balds, look for a dike of black rock (Bakersville gabbro) cutting across the grain of the lighter-colored gneiss. This is a remnant of the molten material that flowed into deep cracks that formed in the earth's crust 750 million years ago, during a period of continental rifting. Erosion has since exposed these basalt dikes to view.

The clumps of shrubby vegetation rising from the grasses and sedges of Round Bald include Catawba rhododendron, flame azalea, blueberries, and mountain ash, each of which lends a splash of color to the balds as the seasons progress. Flame azalea blooms range from golden to a deep red-orange, followed by the purple rhododendron bloom in late June. The foliage of the blueberries turns gradually to red and burgundy as the berries ripen in the fall; and scarlet berries cling to the mountain ash for months, providing food for migratory and resident birds.

B. Rhododendron Gardens

Returning to your car from Round Bald, follow the paved Forest Service road toward Rhododendron Gardens (Figure 87). The road is gated and is open, weather permitting, from early May through October. There is a fee station—$3 per vehicle or $1 per person for vans or buses carrying twelve or more people—before you reach the first (of four) parking lots on this 5-mile round-trip from Carvers Gap. The old Cloudland Hotel stood at the top of the low rise at the east end of the parking lot just past the fee station. Roan High Knob, the highest point (6,286 feet) on the Roan Massif, is a little to the east of the hotel site. At the west end is the first of several trailheads for the Cloudland Trail, an easy 1.2-mile-long walking path linking this parking area to the Roan High Bluff Overlook on the Roan's westernmost prominence. (The Cloudland Trail is also accessible from the other parking areas.) There are restroom facilities at this parking lot and a few picnic tables.

Continue along the Forest Service road to the end of the loop, where there is a parking area for the half-mile walk to Roan High Bluff Overlook. The first part of this trail is paved, and there are picnic tables scattered throughout the grassy area at the beginning of the trail. For a good look at Roan Mountain's relict spruce-fir forest, hike at least part of this trail. If it's a clear day, the view from the overlook is gorgeous. Rock crags and dense forest surrounding the wooden platform drop steeply to the valley floor, with its fields and the little community of Buladean laid out below. Rising beyond the valley are the Unaka Mountains, whose summits mark both the route of the AT south of Roan Mountain and the North Carolina–Tennessee state line.

Return to your car, continue around the loop, and stop at the Rhododendron Gardens before retracing your route to Carvers Gap. A 0.3-mile handicapped-accessible paved loop trail winds among huge clumps of rhododendron, a sea of purple-pink bloom in late June. A second loop, which together with the first forms a figure 8, is paved, though not handicapped accessible, and leads the stroller deeper into the gardens and through small stands of spruce-fir and grassy glens. A wooden viewing platform in the gardens opens onto vistas to the south; the gardens are equipped with restrooms, a picnic area, a small visitor information station, and a bus parking lot.

No food is sold anywhere on the mountain, and some areas are closed to human activities because of the presence of rare plant communities. Visitors are asked to stay on trails and refrain from picking any plants because of the extreme sensitivity of the entire area. In addition to restroom facilities in the gardens and at the old hotel site, there are primitive facilities at the Carvers Gap parking lot. When the gate at Carvers Gap is closed, restroom facilities at the gardens and the hotel site are locked. When there is snow on the mountain, the gated road is a popular

FIGURE 87. June rhododendrons on Roan Mountain. (Photo by Ed Schell)

sledding and cross-country skiing spot. Birding is a year-round activity in the Highlands of Roan. Snow buntings have been spotted on Round Bald during the winter months; alder flycatchers haunt the alder stands in late spring and summer and have nested on the Roan in the past. Ravens squawk as they ride the air currents, and you may glimpse a peregrine falcon (the North Carolina Wildlife Resources Commission began peregrine falcon reintroduction on the Roan in the summer of 1997).

From Carvers Gap, begin your descent via TN 143 (the highway changes route numbers when it crosses the state line); 4.1 miles from the top of the mountain is Twin Springs (picnic area and restrooms). At 7.5 miles from the top, you will come to the community of Burbank. Descending the north slope of the Roan, you leave the grassy balds and spruce-fir forest behind and enter the hardwood forests of the lower elevations. Those who plan to follow the alternate loop route back to Bakersville should note the turn off to the left (Cove Creek Road); you will take that road after visiting Roan Mountain State Park (a few miles further down TN 143) and retracing your route to Burbank.

Approximately 2 miles beyond Burbank on TN 143, a turnoff to the left leads to a bird's-eye view of a typical mountain farm of a century ago. The Dave Miller Farmstead occupies a small cove 1.4 miles off TN 143. It is open Wednesday through Sunday from Memorial Day to Labor Day, 9 A.M. to 5 P.M.; walk around it if you have time. The picturesque farmstead includes a number of outbuildings—a chicken house, root cellar, corn crib, smokehouse, cow barn, and hay barn, in addition to the main house—designed to make isolated holdings in rugged terrain all but self-sufficient. An interpretive sign at the parking lot overlooking the farmstead identifies the buildings. Across the lot, a trailhead connects the farmstead to the state park's network of trails.

c. Roan Mountain State Park

From the Dave Miller Farmstead parking lot, retrace your route to TN 143 and continue north 3 miles to the state park visitors center. Open year-round, the park offers camping, rental cabins, a seasonal restaurant, picnic tables and pavilions, a swimming pool, hiking, and a wide range of additional recreational activities. (For information or reservations, call 800-250-8620.) The visitors center is open from 8 A.M. to 8 P.M. from Memorial Day to Labor Day (except Wednesdays, when it closes at 4:30 P.M.); at other times of year, it is open from 8 A.M. to 4:30 P.M. The visitors center has some historical and wildlife exhibits, trail maps, and other information. More than 180 species of wildflowers have been identified in the park; a short hike along one of the trails will give you a good idea of what grows on the Tennessee side of Roan Mountain at lower elevations.

After visiting the state park, those opting for the main route should continue north on TN 143 to its intersection with US 19E at the town of Roan Mountain. (To take a look at General Wilder's home in Roan Mountain, follow the signs to the Wilder Bed and Breakfast; the white frame house is on the National Register of Historic Places.) Turn right onto US 19E and proceed toward Elk Park. You will pass several turn-of-the-century frame store buildings that once stood alongside the East Tennessee and Western North Carolina Railroad track. The railroad was constructed in the 1880s to connect Johnson City with the Cranberry iron mines, but it also carried tourists to the town of Roan Mountain, where they boarded hacks to ride to the Cloudland Hotel. In addition to the ore it carried to Johnson City for processing, the railroad hauled out the timber harvested in the region. Driving toward Elk Park, you traverse a broad, scenic valley at an easy grade; 3.9 miles from the TN 143/US 19E intersection, a sign notes the crossing of the highway by the AT. From this point (on foot) to Carvers Gap is 13.4 miles. Lying between the two points the trail crosses five Roan Massif summits with elevations in excess of 5,400 feet.

The Appalachian Trail is one of two noteworthy trails associated with Roan Mountain. The other is the Overmountain Victory Trail (OVTA)—the route traveled in 1780 by the Overmountain Men, a frontier army that mustered at Sycamore Shoals near Elizabethton, Tennessee, before setting out for Kings Mountain (described in the earlier Crowders Mountain tour), near Charlotte, where they helped win a battle that was a turning point in the defeat of the British in the Revolutionary War. Their march led them through Yellow Mountain Gap. The point at which the AT and the OVTA intersect is 8.7 miles from the AT crossing on US 19E. Yellow Mountain Gap was on Bright's Trace—the route followed by the first Europeans to settle in Avery and Mitchell Counties.

Continue on US 19E. In the 30 miles between the North Carolina state line and the Museum of North Carolina Minerals, you will pass through the communities of Elk Park, Cranberry, Minneapolis, Plumtree, and Spruce Pine. A historical marker at Roaring Creek (between Minneapolis and Plumtree) notes the Yellow Mountain Road and Overmountain Victory Trail, which follow much of the remainder of the route to Spruce Pine. Immediately after crossing the bridge over the North Toe River in Plumtree, note the old Tarheel Mica Company buildings, constructed of handmade cement blocks in 1912. You are now entering the Spruce Pine Mining District, a major commercial supplier of feldspar and ultrapure quartz. The pegmatite from which the quartz and feldspar are extracted is 390 million years old and was first mined for the mica (prehistorically by aboriginal miners, who used stone tools to free mica "books" or blocks from the matrix). Mining of sheet mica by white settlers began shortly after the end of the Civil War and ended in 1962, when the federal government stopped stockpiling the material as a strategic mineral. Ground mica (used in paints, makeup, and as a lubricant in oil drilling) is still a byproduct of local feldspar and quartz operations.

D. Museum of North Carolina Minerals

The Spruce Pine Mining District has yielded fifty-seven different minerals, including small quantities of gem-quality aquamarine and emerald. For more information about the area's mineral wealth, visit the minerals museum at the end of your trip. To reach it, turn left at the intersection of US 19E and NC 226 at Spruce Pine. The museum is located at Gillespie Gap, where NC 226 passes under the Blue Ridge Parkway before beginning its descent of the Blue Ridge escarpment. (The Overmountain Men spent a night here before setting off toward Linville Mountain and Morganton.) The museum is open from 9 A.M. to 5 P.M. daily, May through October; the winter schedule varies.

Alternate Route

It is approximately 20 miles from the intersection of Cove Creek Road and TN 143 to Bakersville. Follow Cove Creek Road through a picturesque community (the stone building housing Cove Creek School, 1.3 miles from the intersection, is particularly noteworthy), ascending through a hardwood forest toward Hughes

Gap. When faced with a question as to which is the main road, bear to the right all the way up to the gap. Hughes Gap is 3.1 miles from the intersection. The AT crosses the road at the gap (no sign), which marks the point at which the Highlands of Roan terminate and the Unaka Mountains begin. The first 0.5-mile section of the road (which changes names, to Hughes Gap Road, as you drive into North Carolina from Tennessee) is unpaved on the North Carolina side; the remainder has been hard-topped. Hughes Gap Road ends at its intersection with NC 226 in Buladean. Turn left, and follow NC 226 approximately 13 miles to Bakersville. Roan High Bluff rises above the Buladean valley to the left for the first couple of miles on NC 226. Between the communities of Red Hill and Loafers Glory, the North Toe River is visible to the right below the highway. Cane Creek empties into the North Toe near Loafers Glory at Toecane, a bustling early-twentieth-century trade center in Mitchell County, created when the Clinchfield Railroad carved a route along the Nolichucky/Toe River from Erwin, Tennessee, to Spruce Pine. With the coming of the roads, the community has shrunk in size and now has no commercial establishments. From Loafers Glory to Bakersville, NC 226 snakes along the left bank of Cane Creek, a site of major flooding in January 1998 and in the locally famous "May freshet" of 1901, when much of Bakersville was washed away.

Linville Gorge

Deepest Wilderness Area
in the Eastern United States

ALLEN DE HART

This 56.6-mile tour circles Linville Gorge, where you can see one of the deepest cuts in the earth's surface east of the Grand Canyon. You will see Linville Falls, outstanding views from the Kistler Memorial Highway on the canyon rim, and a view of Shortoff Mountain from NC 126 and will have access to a dozen foot trails that take you to the rim or the bottom of the gorge. There is even a short paved trail for the physically handicapped at Wiseman's View. Your tour will cross the Mountains-to-Sea Trail near The Pinnacle on the west rim of the gorge and will pass near, but south of, the parking area for the Spence Ridge Trail on the east rim. Among the high peaks you will be able to see from the western rim, north to south, are Sitting Bear Mountain, Hawksbill Mountain, Table Rock Mountain, The Chimneys, and Shortoff Mountain. From the eastern rim you can see, south to north, The Pinnacle, Dogback Mountain, Rock Jock Escarpment, Green Mountain, Wiseman's View, and Laurel Knob.

This tour (Figure 88) will stimulate the ear as well as the eye: the faint roar of splashing white water on the Linville River is usually audible from the gorge rim. From The Pinnacle there are views of Lake James and the Catawba River valley between Marion and Morganton, and from Table Rock you will look southeast toward Morganton and east toward the Brown Mountain range. You may catch glimpses of deer, hawks, songbirds, lizards, and squirrels, but black bears, raccoons, grouse, owls, copperheads, and rattlesnakes may be nearby, yet unseen. Brown and rainbow trout are the major fish in the Linville River. A wide range of conifers, hardwoods, and wildflowers are commonplace. You may even see one or two of the few rare species that live in the nearly 10,975-acre wilderness if you carry some specialized field guides with you.

The major learning experience of this tour will be an understanding of wilderness. From the beginning you will sense that this is not going to be an ordinary day of motoring. The landscape will not let you forget that people are only visitors here and that even the Cherokee who roamed this wilderness long ago never found it hospitable. Elevation ranges from 1,300 feet to 4,500 feet above sea level; such a wide range in altitude creates a wonderful situation for observing nature's variety.

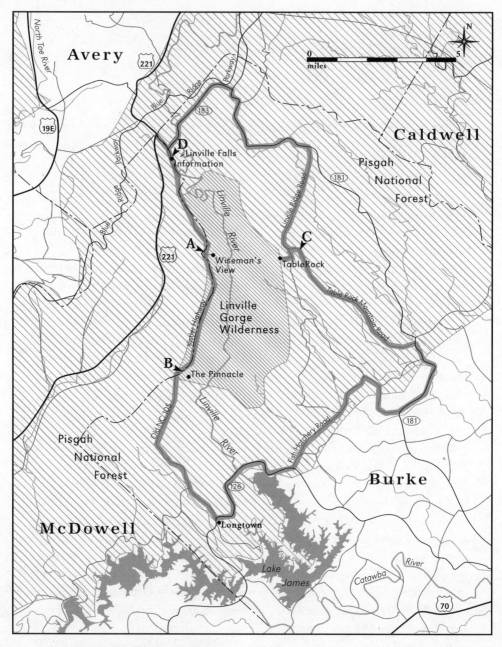

FIGURE 88. Linville Gorge tour route

A diversity of plants and vegetation types will surround you—four species of rhododendron, mountain ash, red chokecherry, flame azalea, mountain laurel, yellowroot, wild orchids, sand myrtle, and many more. Different species of pine, silverbell, and Carolina and Canadian hemlock, grow in patches or mix with black, red, chestnut, and white oaks, maple, ash, tulip poplar, hickory, and many other hardwoods. Considered rare, threatened, or endangered, either federally or by the state, are the following plant species: Heller's blazing star, rough blazing star, mountain golden heather, white camus, large witchalder, roundleaf serviceberry, and deerhair bulrush.

The biological diversity of the Linville Gorge area makes this tour exciting, but the rock formations on the gorge's rim and along the rugged river are the area's most striking features. The rocks are remnants of Precambrian granite gneiss formed nearly a billion years ago and Cambrian quartzite only about half that old. These mountains, which were once nearly four times their present height, were broken apart by complex shifts in the earth's crust. The action was violent enough to force younger layers of rock underneath older formations. Through the millennia softer layers were eroded by the river to create sand and gravel, much of it deposited near the floor of the gorge. Also on the valley floor is debris from the weathered cliffs and peaks above—boulders of varying size and shape.

The Cherokee called the deep gorge of the Linville River *Eeseeoh*, meaning "cliffy river," or "river of many cliffs." They hunted in the area, but they particularly explored the canyon rims. Their favorite and most sacred site was the peak that white settlers dubbed Table Rock. This granite monolith is not as flat as its name suggests. In fact, depending on your angle of view it appears to be a cone, a slanted knob, or square. Dense bunches of heath shrubs cling to Table Rock's west-face fissures and add to botanists' long-standing interest in the mountain.

European settlers began exploring the nearby Catawba and Yadkin valleys late in the seventeenth century. Among the earliest of these explorers was William Linville, for whom the wilderness, river, mountain, town, and nearby cavern are all named. Considerable folklore exists about Linville's travels, and about the site where he and his son were murdered by Cherokee Indians. Different writers locate the ambush "below the falls," "in the gorge," and "near the headwaters" above the falls. One story claims that the "Linvilles went to hunt on the Wataga [*sic*] between 1760 and 1770. They employed John Williams, a lad of 16 to go with them, keep camp and cook for them. They were sleeping in the camp, when the Indians came on them and killed them." Although Williams had a broken leg from gunshots, he was able to mount a horse and ride for five days through "the Hollows in Surry" to a frontier house. There he was nursed to recovery.

During the nineteenth century settlers established home sites near the south end of the gorge and on a few flat areas north of the falls. Other families—Franklins,

Wisemans, Conleys, Childes, and Aubreys—settled around the rims to graze cattle, plant orchards, cut timber, and trade furs. In the early twentieth century Malcolm Pierce organized the Linville Electrical Company. His plan was to dam the entire gorge and build a hydroelectric power plant. Fortunately, his plans failed. By the 1930s the U.S. Forest Service began to purchase large tracts of land in the area, and in 1951 Congress declared the gorge a wilderness area.

This tour begins at the intersection of us 221 (22 miles north of Marion) and nc 183 in the community of Linville Falls. Here you will find a motel (800-634-4421), restaurants, service station, and post office. Drive southeast on nc 183 for 0.7 miles and turn right on Old nc 105, which is also called Kistler Memorial Highway—a gravel road into the Grandfather Ranger District of Pisgah National Forest. Immediately to the left is a parking area for a trail that descends to Linville Falls. (You may wait to visit the falls, because there is another option on your return route from the Blue Ridge Parkway.) Proceed another 0.3 miles to the Linville Falls Information Cabin on the right. You might want to pick up a copy of the forest map of the Linville Gorge area; it contains information on no-trace camping (the rule here), dangers in the gorge, backpacking essentials, and what to do if you become lost. A permit is required to camp in the gorge on weekends (Friday through Sunday) and on holidays from May 1 through October 31. Permits are issued at the district ranger's office, located at the Interstate 40 Mount Nebo Exit, or may be obtained by mail (P.O. Box 519, Marion, nc 28753) or in person at the Information Cabin (828-765-7550), which is open April 1 to October 31. Only fifty campers are allowed in the gorge at any one time, and there is a three-day/two-night limit. There are no facilities in the gorge. Be aware that the trails are not blazed and it is easy to become disoriented without a guidebook or map. If you plan a hike on the Linville Gorge Trail, you will have a cloistered route with unexpected wind drafts, unpredictable temperature changes, ubiquitous fog, and the ever-present sound of the river to add a wild feeling to the atmosphere. You will not have any views of the west rim, but there are occasional views of mountain peaks on the east rim.

For road egress and ingress on this journey it is advisable that you have a detailed map, such as the DeLorme *North Carolina Atlas and Gazetteer*. (For information on how to obtain this book of maps call 207-865-4171.) Either before you leave home or during on-site planning, carefully determine your time schedule. If you choose one day, mainly to ride the distance, leave early and finish before dark. If you plan to hike some of the trails or to take time for nature study, photography, or simply to soak in the atmosphere, plan for two days. And if you want to leave your vehicle at the rim and camp in the canyon, you will need to plan for additional days.

About half of this tour is on gravel roads, so you should schedule this trip in dry weather. For 10 miles of the Kistler Memorial Highway the road is very rough, steep in sections, and not passable with low-axle vehicles. The higher the axle the easier will be your control over the ditches, rocks, mud holes, and eroded areas. Repair and reconstruction of sections of the road are being planned. After you pass The Pinnacle you will find the road in good condition.

A. Wiseman's View

For the first 4 miles you will pass five parking areas on the left with trail access for a descent into the gorge to connect with the 11.5-mile Linville Gorge Trail. In order of your trip they are Pine Gap Trail (0.7 miles, the easiest of all trails into the gorge), Bynum Bluff Trail (1 mile), Cabin Trail (0.8 miles), Babel Tower Trail (1.2 miles), and Sandy Flats Trail (1 mile). Just beyond the Sandy Flats Trail is a fork in the road. To the left it is 0.3 miles to a parking area for Wiseman's View and an asphalt trail for the physically handicapped. For some visitors this is enough. The views are so overwhelming and mesmerizing that you may wonder what else there is to see. This is a great place to view sunrises over Table Rock across the chasm (Figure 89), or sunsets against Hawksbill and Table Rock. If you are here for autumn leaf colors, you may have difficulty describing the magnificent beauty. Garnishing the granite platform at Wiseman's View are mosses, ferns, trailing arbutus, galax, mountain ash, and bristly locust among the rhododendron and mountain laurel.

You may remember that a few years ago two women fell to their deaths at Wiseman's View. And within the past ten years three men in separate incidents lost their lives in the canyon. One of those was a hiker who became separated from his companion on the Devil's Hole Trail (from northeast of rim). The gorge has no mercy on those who attempt to make a new trail, risk entering in bad weather, wade in the rapids, or stand on precipitous ledges.

B. The Pinnacle

The tour continues on Kistler Memorial Highway, passing the Conley Cove Trail (1.4 miles) on the left at 5.8 miles and Pinch-in-Trail (1.4 miles) at 8.8 miles. At 11.1 miles park in a small space at the entrance to The Pinnacle. You are not likely to see a sign here, but look for two white dots on a tree. The dots are the blaze for the Mountains-to-Sea Trail, which meets you here and follows the 0.2-mile old jeep road to the left. You must walk on this road/trail to reach The Pinnacle. As at Wiseman's View, you will be gazing at an awesome canyon. This time you will be able to see the largest stone wall in the chasm—Shortoff Mountain. Upstream you may see some five-story-high stacks of layered quartzite, known as The Chimneys.

FIGURE 89. Table Rock (right) and Hawksbill Mountain. (Photo by Allen de Hart)

You may remember seeing them in the movie *Last of the Mohicans*. The endangered peregrine falcon has been seen in the rocky crevices of The Chimneys, which is now closed to rock climbers.

After 0.7 miles on the Kistler Memorial Highway, you will notice a small parking area on the right. Here is a portion of the famous Overmountain Victory Trail, the route taken by the frontiersmen who marched to victory in a battle with the British at Kings Mountain—a site in the southwestern Piedmont included in a tour in this book—on October 7, 1780. This is also where the Mountains-to-Sea Trail continues west to its western terminus at Clingmans Dome in the Great Smoky Mountains National Park. From where you just were at The Pinnacle, the Mountains-to-Sea Trail continues on a descent to ford the Linville River, cross the top scenic rim of Shortoff Mountain, and will meet you again at the parking lot at Table Rock.

c. Table Rock and Hawksbill Mountain

You can now pick up some speed on your tour. Descend and level out on a paved road among some homes in a pastoral area and pass Paddy Creek Road to the right. Connect with NC 126 at a road triangle at 15.9 miles in the community of Longtown. Turn left and enjoy the rolling hills northeast of Lake James. But drive slowly and keep an eye northeast at 17.5 miles because a stunning view of Shortoff Mountain can be seen up the gorge. You may also see it again as you approach the Linville River bridge at 18.3 miles. Pass a boating and fishing access point to Lake James; then after 1 mile turn off NC 126 onto Fish Hatchery Road, left, at 20.8 miles.

For the next 6.3 miles stay on Fish Hatchery Road, where you will pass through meadows and forests and by scattered homesites. If you look up, northwest, you may have a glimpse of Table Rock. You will pass Fish Hatchery Avenue, Table Rock Road, Pleasant Grove United Methodist Church, Rose Creek Road, and arrive at paved NC 181 at 27.1 miles. Turn left, pass through a grassy valley, cross a creek, and pass by Table Rock Nursery and Rose Creek Family Campground. Watch carefully for a narrow gravel road to the left at 30.3 miles; there will be a small sign saying "Table Rock" (it may also say "Simpson Creek Road"). Turn left and then after 0.2 miles turn right. You now have a long climb weaving in and out of dozens of coves. It is a beautiful area in the fall, with all the colors of a hardwood forest. Ignore all roads to the right until you come to an intersection at 39.5 miles. Here a Forest Service road goes right, and if you look ahead a second one also goes right. The second one is Linville Ridge Road, but you turn left. There should be a sign that points toward Table Rock, and a sign for the North Carolina Outward Bound School may be there as well. At 40.1 miles there is a sign for a right turn to the school. Come onto road pavement at 41.0 miles, and after steep switchbacks arrive at the Table Rock parking area at 42.3 miles.

There are no views of the gorge here, nor are there facilities except for a restroom. To view the gorge you may go to the south end of the parking area, enter a grove of rhododendrons on the Mountains-to-Sea Trail (also Shortoff Mountain Trail), and walk about 0.4 miles. On this trail you can see chinquapin and blueberry. The scenery is reminiscent of Wiseman's View, except you will have a closer view of The Chimneys and the rugged Rock Jock Escarpment nearby. If you hike north from the parking area, you will see a Mountains-to-Sea Trail sign. As you begin to climb, ignore all trails right made by exploring visitors. Also ignore the first trail left. Turn sharply up and soon you will notice that the Mountains-to-Sea Trail descends left. Over rocks and some steps with a few switchbacks, the trial reaches the top of Table Rock at 0.7 miles. To your north are the rocky crags of Hawksbill Mountain. Plan to stay awhile; the magnificent views are hypnotic, and the shadows of the gorge and the changing hues of the horizon show nature in action.

On the drive down the mountain from Table Rock, take the first turn left, Linville Ridge Road, after passing the Outward Bound School. You are now 45.2 miles on your tour. After 1 mile there is a parking area on the left where you can find the trailhead for the Spence Ridge Trail (1.7 miles), the most used trail from the gorge's east rim down to the Linville River and the Linville Gorge Trail. After another mile there is a parking area on the right for a climb, left, up the Hawksbill Mountain Trail (1.4 miles round-trip). If you climb this peak you will have a different perspective of the upper Linville River. You will notice that trails have been made among the boulders by visitors. It is easy to get lost on these trails. Randy Wayne White, a contributing editor of *Outside* magazine and professional outdoorsman, described in the magazine his panic-stricken experience when he became lost on this mountain.

At 49.7 miles the forest road becomes a paved residential road among homes with lofty vistas. Arrive at NC 181 at 50.9 miles and turn left. Pass a Chevron service station at 53 miles, and at 53.9 miles turn left on NC 183. Follow it to cross the Linville River bridge to complete your circuit auto tour at 56.6 miles to the left.

D. Linville Falls

At the beginning of this tour description I indicated that you had another option for visiting the 90-foot Linville Falls from the Blue Ridge Parkway. (Although you passed under the parkway only 1 mile before completing your circle, there are not any official connections there. There are, however, some one-lane accesses to NC 183 and NC 181.) From the end of your circle continue 0.7 miles to the intersection

FIGURE 90. Linville Gorge below Linville Falls. (Photo by Allen de Hart)

with US 221 and turn right in the community of Linville Falls. After 0.3 miles go under the Blue Ridge Parkway and turn right on an access road; then turn left on the parkway. After 1.4 miles turn right on a spur to pass a parkway campground and to a parking area, drinking water, and restrooms. You are in a 440-acre recreation area acquired by the National Park Service through the philanthropy of John D. Rockefeller Jr. in 1952.

Trails are available from both the right and the left. The wide and easy right trail first crosses the Linville River bridge to the Upper Falls, where you will see part of the falls as the water plunges into an unseen channel. From here you can ascend south 1 mile or less to overlooks for more supreme views of the falls and gorge (Figure 90). If you choose to hike the trail left of the parking area, you will ascend and descend for a 0.5-mile round-trip on Plunge Basin Overlook Trail. From the platform you will be able to view the falls, the gorge, and the surrounding Carolina, Catawba, and rosebay rhododendrons on weather-sculpted walls of the gorge. Connecting with this trail is the 1.4-mile round-trip Linville Gorge Trail, which descends to Lower Falls. Here you can be close enough to the falls to feel the spray. This is a good place to take a moment to reflect on the unforgettable tour of one of the state's most priceless natural wonders you have just finished.

Mountain Touring

Linville Falls to Mount Mitchell
through Gorges, Peaks, and Forests

MICHAEL P. SCHAFALE

This 20-mile tour takes you through spectacular mountain scenery, showing you the full height of the Southern Appalachian Mountains. You will see a spectacular waterfall, a deep gorge, the steep Blue Ridge escarpment dropping to the base of the mountains, and the highest peak in the eastern United States. You will see landforms typical for the Blue Ridge Mountains and also some unusual ones. Along the way you will pass by a wide array of natural vegetation and will be able to observe the effects of elevation on plants and weather.

Lessons you can learn on this tour include the ways that elevation and topography affect natural plant communities. You will be able to see the different vegetation zones, from the lower cove forests, to oak forests, to the spruce-fir forests of the highest ranges. Depending on the weather the day you are there, you may dramatically experience some of the climatic differences that are responsible for the vegetation zones. You will also be able to see the drastic effects that some human actions have had on the natural vegetation and scenery. Along the way you may observe some of the different landforms of the southern Blue Ridge Mountains and get a sense for how they are shaped by geology. If you are inclined, you will also learn of opportunities to explore mountain natural history in greater depth.

This tour can be traveled in either direction. The dramatic ending at Mount Mitchell, running in the direction described, will probably appeal to most people. The starting point is Linville Falls. A spur road to Linville Falls leaves the Blue Ridge Parkway at milepost 316.3. It runs past the National Park Service campground to a paved parking area and visitors center near the falls. From Interstate 40 it can be reached most directly by taking US 221 from Marion or NC 181 from Morganton. From US 221 you will go north along the parkway several miles; from NC 181 you will go south.

A. Linville Falls and Gorge

From the visitors center well-marked, easy-to-moderate trails run to a series of overlooks. The following description follows the Erwins View Trail.

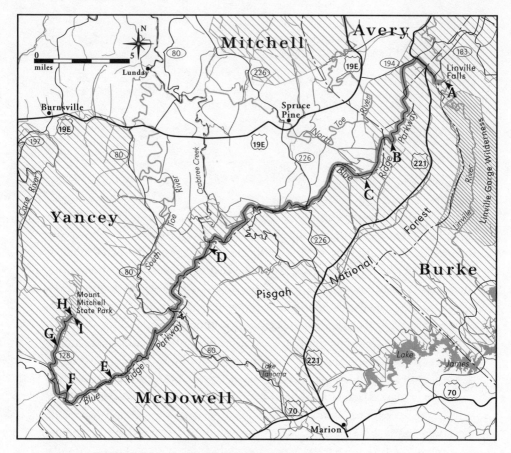

FIGURE 91. Linville Falls to Mount Mitchell tour route

The Linville River has its headwaters near Grandfather Mountain and flows some 15 to 20 miles through high valleys before plunging into its deep gorge. It is unusual in flowing to the Atlantic Ocean; most major rivers in the North Carolina mountains flow to the Mississippi River and Gulf of Mexico. The upper part of the Linville River once also flowed to the Mississippi, but it was diverted to the Atlantic by a geologic process known as stream capture. A smaller Atlantic drainage stream with a lower bed eroded its way into the upper Linville River and captured the Linville waters into its own course. Where you cross the Linville River on the Erwins View Trail, it is fairly placid and gives little hint of the abrupt change just downstream.

Along the trail, especially on the left nearer the river, is a good example of an acidic cove forest, one of the common plant community types of gorges and valley bottoms throughout the North Carolina mountains. You can see large Canada hemlock, tulip poplar, red maple, black birch, and white pine trees, with dense thickets of rhododendron beneath them. The long deep-green leaves of great rhododendron, under dappled sunlight or dripping with rain, are one of the characteristic scenes of the mountains. Parts of the acidic cove forest along the trail are quite mature and give a hint of the majesty of the old-growth forests that once were abundant.

At the falls, the Linville River (Figure 92) plunges over 100 feet in two steps, making one of the largest and most dramatic waterfalls in the South. Upper Falls Overlook, 0.4 miles from the visitors center, lets you view the smaller upper falls and the narrow curving flume leading to the lower falls. The cliffs around Linville Falls, lining the gorge, and making up the overlooks themselves are quartzite, a rock created by metamorphism of ancient sandstones. Quartzite is among the most erosion-resistant rocks in the world and supports steep cliffs even where rain and time have broken other rocks down into gentler slopes. The rocks have been folded and tilted by the forces that raised the Appalachian Mountains. You can see tilted beds in the cliffs around the falls, and a small fold is visible in the floor of the overlook itself. A sign at the overlook explains some of the geologic processes that caused quartzite to be exposed here.

Along the side of the spur trail to the Upper Falls Overlook is a good place to view mosses. These simple plants, which lack roots and water-conducting tissue, can grow on tree trunks, rotting wood, and rocks as well as soil in this climate. If you look closely at the moss along the trail, you will see a diversity of species, including several different upright and horizontal forms. You may see some with the brown, stalked capsules that produce the spores.

Chimney View Overlook offers good views of the lower falls and the bare quartzite cliffs that line the gorge. The short-needled conifers growing around the overlooks and on the cliffs are Carolina hemlocks. Compared to the Canada hemlocks along the trail, they have longer needles that surround the twig more rather than occurring in a flat plane. Carolina hemlock is one of many plants and animals that are Southern Appalachian endemics, occurring in North Carolina and the mountains of adjacent states but nowhere else in the world. In contrast, Canada hemlock is more widespread in the northern United States and Canada than it is in the South. The oval-leaved evergreen shrub around the overlooks is Carolina rhododendron, a relative of the longer-leaved great rhododendron and also a Southern Appalachian endemic.

Erwins View Overlook has another view of the falls, plus a good view of Linville Gorge. From here the Linville River flows through a remote, cliff-lined gorge to the flatter land of the Piedmont. Looking down the gorge, you can see several large bends in the river. In fact, the river forms a large bend around Erwins View, so that it is on three sides of the overlook. This is an excellent example, perhaps the best in

FIGURE 92. Linville Falls. (Photo by D. Frankenberg)

North Carolina, of the geologic phenomenon known as entrenched meanders. These meanders follow the pattern you would expect from a lazy river winding over flat land, not a racing mountain torrent. They indicate that the river established its course in a gentle valley, before it began to cut the gorge.

Several kinds of plant communities are visible from the overlooks. The cliffs themselves support a sparse collection of herbs and mosses that can live without much soil. Where there are cracks in the rocks, shrubs or trees are able to take hold, but such places are too few to give more than a scattering of woody plants. Where the cliffs are kept wet by spray from the waterfall, the community includes a larger number and variety of the simple plants such as mosses and liverworts. In the depths of the gorge, wind and sunlight are limited and the soils are moist. These conditions support acidic cove forests and forests dominated by Canada hemlock and with a dense understory of rhododendron. In somewhat higher and drier locations, the slightly different Carolina hemlock and pines prevail. Elsewhere on the upper slopes, forests dominated by oaks prevail, as they do over most of the middle elevations of the mountains. The interior of Linville Gorge is one of the few places in North Carolina where the forests have never been logged. Trees three to four feet in diameter are common. Because of its remoteness and lack of roads, Linville Gorge was one of the first designated wilderness areas in North Carolina. For the sturdy and well-equipped hiker, a trip down into the gorge on one of the rugged trails brings a spectacular close-up view of the deep forests and cliffs, as well as its solitary world filled with the roar of water. More of the gorge may be seen from above at Wiseman's View, accessible by a gravel Forest Service road off of NC 183 in the town of Linville Falls. A driving tour that circumnavigates Linville Gorge precedes this one.

On your return walk to the parking lot, take note of the fork in the trail; the right fork leads to the paved parking lot connected to the Blue Ridge Parkway.

B. Chestoa View Overlook

Return to the Blue Ridge Parkway via the Linville Falls spur road and proceed south to milepost 320. The valley below this overlook is the headwaters of the Catawba River, one of the major rivers of central North Carolina. Like the Linville, it has cut down to the level of the Piedmont and its valley is lined by quartzite cliffs. But different kinds of rock in the bottom of the valley have allowed processes of erosion to make it wider and less of a gorge. One of these kinds of rock is dolomite, a limestonelike rock that is extremely rare in North Carolina. Like limestone, it is water-soluble, and percolating rainwater has dissolved parts of it away. The largest solution cave in North Carolina, Linville Caverns, occurs in this valley. If you wish to take a detour, or to return to this area, you can visit the private park and take a tour of the caverns. There is a fee to enter, but it includes a half-hour guided tour of the amazing underground formations created by alternating periods of dissolution and precipitation of dolomitic limestone, and a chance to visit fifty-two-degree temperatures anytime of the year. Linville Caverns is the largest of more than six hundred limestone caves in the state. While not distinguishable from above or from within the cave, the vegetation on the few outcrops of dolomite in the valley is distinctive, and supports several rare plants.

Beyond the Catawba River valley is the west rim of Linville Gorge, with the ridge that forms its east rim behind that. This overlook offers a good view of Table Rock Mountain on the east rim of Linville Gorge. This peak and the adjacent Hawksbill get their distinctive shape from the tilted beds of quartzite that form their tops. They are distinctive landmarks, which you will see from several other overlooks on this tour; you can also see both from a great distance out in the Piedmont. While not visible in this view, the ledges of these peaks are home to a plant found virtually no place else in the world, the mountain golden heather.

The forest type around this overlook is called montane oak-hickory forest. It includes white oak, red oak, black oak, and mockernut hickory, with smaller numbers of other trees. Montane oak-hickory forest is one of the most typical community types on open slopes in the mountains at low to middle elevations. You will see it at several other of the overlooks, as well as when you drive along the Blue Ridge Parkway.

c. Hefner Gap Overlook and The Loops Overlook

Once again, proceed on the parkway 6 more miles and stop at the Hefner Gap Overlook (milepost 326). Such overlooks and the land along the Blue Ridge Parkway near them show some of the effects that people have had on the mountain vegetation. Openings that are, or once were, pastures and orchards are common. The areas that remain, or that have become, forested contain large numbers of white pine, with its pale, soft needles, and black locust, with its small, oval leaflets. Both tree species occur in virgin forests but become more common in places that have been cleared or heavily logged in the past.

Across the parkway from the Hefner Gap Overlook is an old apple tree, marking a place where a cabin once stood. At The Loops Overlook (milepost 328), a large, active apple orchard is visible. This overlook also has a display about the railroad that climbed into the mountains through the valley below.

D. Three Knobs Overlook and Black Mountain Overlook

Farther along the parkway, these two overlooks (mileposts 339 and 342) and several unnamed ones offer good views of the Black Mountains, which you will shortly be

FIGURE 93. Black Mountain forests. (Photo by D. Frankenberg)

seeing up close. The Black Mountains are the highest range in North Carolina and also the highest range in eastern North America. They are a narrow range that is extremely rugged and steep in parts.

Several different plant community types of higher elevations are visible on the face of the Black Mountains. You should be able to see the darker green forests composed of spruce and fir that cover the top of the range (Figure 93). They are punctuated by rock outcrop communities along the ridge line and slightly below. Below that, northern hardwood forests of beech, yellow birch, and buckeye alternate with high-elevation red oak forests. Lower down, rich cove forests occur in ravine bottoms, while various oak forests occur on the slopes. The rich cove forests consists of a variety of trees that includes tulip poplar, buckeye, basswood, and magnolia. In midsummer these hardwood forests may all be a uniform green, but if you come in fall or spring they will be different colors. The brilliant golden yellow of the northern hardwood forest and deep red of high-elevation red oak forest in the fall can be a striking contrast. The yellow of tulip poplars, combined with their slender pointed shape, makes the rich cove forest stand out.

A sign at the Black Mountain Overlook identifies the peaks. You can see the small square observation tower at the top of Mount Mitchell and several broadcasting towers on the summit of Clingmans Peak. On the upper slopes below these peaks, you can see the dark spruce forest give way to a zone of paler and visibly smaller hardwoods, shrubs, and grass. This zone is not natural but is the result of particularly destructive logging in the 1910s. Logging of spruce from railroads, followed by devastating slash fires, destroyed the evergreen forest canopy and also its ability to regenerate. You can see the horizontal line of the railroad grade cutting across the slope in places. The northern half of the range was too steep to allow the building of a logging railroad and was not logged, so it offers a view of natural vegetation patterns. Also visible are the results of a dramatic natural process. Several debris avalanche (landslide) scars are visible as vertical lines on the face of the mountains.

The rock cuts at these overlooks and elsewhere along this part of the parkway show the dark gray mica schist that makes up much of the Blue Ridge. Similar rocks compose the Black Mountains. The shapes of peaks visible near and more distantly are typical of the forms that develop on this kind of rock, and these contrast with the sharper and odd-shaped forms of the quartzite peaks around Linville Gorge.

E. Singecat Ridge Overlook, Licklog Ridge Overlook, and Green Knob Overlook

These three overlooks, at mileposts 345, 350, and 351, and other overlooks on the left side of the parkway offer the best views of the Blue Ridge escarpment and its plant communities on this tour. The eastern (actually southeastern) face of the mountains is much steeper than the western side, plunging down to the Piedmont within a few miles. "Escarpment" is a geologic term for a large, very steep face. If you entered the mountains from the east any place in North Carolina or Virginia, you climbed the escarpment on a steep winding road. From here at the top you can see the sharp spur ridges and deep, narrow ravines eroded by small streams into the escarpment. Beyond that the rolling low land of the Piedmont stretches into the distance. If you view the escarpment near sunrise or sunset, the terrain often has a wrinkled look to it. This pattern is the result of the many narrow, V-shaped streams and is characteristic of mountains that have been shaped by running water in rocks of uniform hardness. It is quite different from the smoother slopes and U-shaped valleys in mountains that have been shaped by glaciers.

Looking to the left off the Singecat Ridge Overlook, you can see Singecat Ridge on the skyline and the lower and closer Beartree Ridge. On both you can see a band of pine trees along the top. They will be most dramatically visible in the fall and winter, but will show up even in summer by their distinctive shapes. These pine-dominated forests typically occur on narrow ridgetops, of the sort that are common along the escarpment. They have a dense shrub layer of mountain laurel, and other broadleaf evergreen shrubs beneath them, and may have some oaks in the canopy. The open slopes below them are generally covered with chestnut oak forest. The Mountains-to-Sea Trail crosses the parkway at this overlook and offers an opportunity to hike in the oak forests.

At the Licklog Ridge Overlook the pine community is visibly closer, on a knob just across the parkway. A couple of fine specimens of the characteristic pine occur right next to the overlook. This species is called Table Mountain pine. Like the Carolina hemlock, it is a Southern Appalachian endemic. It is well adapted to the environment of sharp ridges, which includes rapid runoff of water after rains, leaching of nutrients with the runoff, strong exposure to wind and sun, and relatively frequent fires.

The Blue Ridge Parkway climbs substantially in this stretch. At Green Knob Overlook the adjacent forest is high-elevation red oak forest. The Snooks Nose Trail, which runs downhill from this overlook, offers views of this plant community and its transition to the pine community on the ridge below. If you desire, you can follow this trail several miles down to obtain good close-up views of the plant communities of the Blue Ridge escarpment. On the other side of the parkway, just a couple of hundred feet up the road (north) from the overlook, is the Green Knob Trail. It climbs steeply to the old lookout tower. Green Knob is one of the highest peaks along the top of the Blue Ridge escarpment, and the climb offers spectacular mountain views as well as a close-up look at plant communities and many interesting plants.

F. Ridge Junction Overlook

Proceed, again, on the parkway and pull off at the overlook at milepost 355. The Blue Ridge Parkway has now climbed to over 5,000 feet elevation and into the higher vegetation zones. Next to this overlook you can see red spruce trees, with their sharp, short needles. Looking out from here you can see the gradational boundary between the spruce forest and the northern hardwood forest.

G. Mount Mitchell State Park Road

In a few more miles you will come to the junction of NC 128. Turn onto NC 128 and follow it to the parking lot near the top of Mount Mitchell. Along the way, the road continues to climb. At first you will pass through some of the logged spruce-fir forest, now covered with grass, shrubs, small hardwoods, and scattered spruce trees. A display along the road describes efforts to reforest the mountain slopes by planting a variety of trees from other regions. About forty different kinds of trees were planted, but in the end most of them died. The study led to the conclusion that the native Fraser fir was the best tree to plant, but most of the logged area was not planted.

Farther up, the road does pass through conifer forest. The top of Mount Mitchell itself was naturally dominated by fir, with little spruce. Part of it was saved from logging to become North Carolina's first state park. As you drive or look around, you will see areas with many standing dead tree trunks. In fact, the forest on the top of Mount Mitchell and Clingmans Peak is not, at this time, much of a forest. The trees are all small, and in many places there are blackberry thickets and no trees at all. You see standing dead snags and fallen logs of large trees, but almost no living large trees. The old Fraser firs, which dominated the mountaintop forest, all died in the 1960s and 1970s. The immediate cause of their death was an aphid-like insect that was accidentally introduced into the United States from Europe, called the balsam woolly adelgid. Fraser fir proved particularly susceptible to it, and virtually no older tree was able to survive its onslaught. Young trees are not susceptible, and the seedlings that had already become established beneath the old forest canopy have grown up to form the patchy young canopy you now see. These trees are just beginning to produce cones now, and it is unclear if they will establish a new crop of seedlings before they are old enough to be susceptible to the balsam woolly adelgid. Besides introduced insects, the mountaintop forests are under particular stress from air pollution. The high rainfall and frequent fog brings with it acids, excess nitrogen, and toxic metals put into the air by human activities far beyond the mountains. These pollutants "fall out" throughout North Carolina but are concentrated on the mountaintops. The air pollution causes a variety of problems and may be partly responsible for the extreme damage done to these forests.

H. Mount Mitchell Parking Area and Trail

This is a popular tourist attraction, and the parking lot can be quite busy in the summer. Good views of the surrounding mountains and the Fraser fir forest can be seen from the parking lot and concession stand, but the best view is from the summit observation tower, a short climb up a smooth trail. Along the way is a museum that can teach you much about the mountain's plant and animal life, climate, and history.

You should notice that the air is quite cool up here, and you may experience some unusual and dramatic weather. The wind may be very strong. There is a good chance that it will be foggy or raining, even if it was (and probably still is) hot and sunny in the lower areas where you came from. You might see clouds climbing up the side of the mountain, dissipating as they cross the top. Or you might have the opportunity to look down on the tops of clouds in the valleys below you. If it is fall, you might even see snow. High mountains of this kind generate their own weather. The average rainfall on Mount Mitchell is over 70 inches a year, compared to around 50 inches in most of North Carolina. The fog that often bathes the mountain and leaves the vegetation dripping wet contributes additional water, perhaps as much as falls as rain. If you come on a cold foggy day in the late fall, you might even see rime ice, frozen fog that coats the windward side of upright objects with a frosting or long needles of ice. Although the average temperature may be comparable to that in Canada, the large amounts of moisture, the high winds, and other aspects of climate make it quite distinct.

There is another difference to be aware of: the air is significantly thinner at this elevation, and the sun is more intense. If you are prone to sunburn, you will need to take precautions. You can get sunburned even on cloudy days, especially if the clouds are thin.

As you hike the trail or look around the edge of the parking lot, the most abundant tree you will see is Fraser fir. It is distinguished by its flat needles. You may see a few spruces, which have short, sharp needles. You may also see mountain ash, a small hardwood tree with pinnate leave (featherlike, with pairs of leaves along a central rib and a single one at the end). Fraser fir is now widely grown in the North Carolina mountains for Christmas trees, but its native range is confined to the highest six ranges of the Southern Appalachians, most of it in North Carolina. The red spruce, in contrast, extends into the Northern Appalachians. The less obvious plants and animals here follow the same patterns, with some occurring only in this small area (endemic) and others having most of their range in the north. Particularly interesting are those that are disjunct—that is, occurring in the north and here but not in between. Some species in the Southern Appalachians are disjunct hundreds of miles. Such patterns are the result of species moving around in response to the dramatic climate changes that accompanied the Ice Ages. While we may speak of a species as being "a northern disjunct," with most of its range in the north and small remnant populations in the south, in fact the southern populations were once larger and were the source for colonization of the north after the glaciers melted.

1. Summit of Mount Mitchell

At 6,684 feet, this is the highest mountain in eastern North America. Though it is higher than New Hampshire's Mount Washington, its southern location means it does not have areas of alpine tundra, as the mountains of New England do. The nearest higher peak is in the Black Hills of South Dakota. If the weather is clear, the view from the observation tower is one of the most spectacular in North Carolina. You are surrounded by a sea of mountains, almost all clothed in lush green vegetation. If it is really clear, you can see most of the other high peaks of the Southern Appalachians from here, from Grandfather Mountain and Roan Mountain to the north, to the Balsam and Great Smoky Mountains to the southwest. Note that tours in this book describe all three of these areas. Signs on the tower help identify some of the peaks and ranges you can see. You may be able to see, in the nearest ridges, traces of the vegetation patterns you saw in your distant view of the Black Mountains.

Nearer at hand you can see the rugged peaks that stretch north along the crest of the Black Mountains. Most of the vegetation in view near the tower is Fraser fir forest or former fir forest now dominated by blackberries or shrubs. The peaks to the north have some bare rock outcrops, which support a distinctive sparse vegetation. These high-elevation peaks are home to a number of rare plants. You may also see some shrub-dominated areas, known as heath balds.

The rugged trail that runs along the crest of the Black Mountains from Mount Mitchell is an excellent hike for the hardy, as is the climb to Mount Mitchell from the South Toe River valley. The old railroad grade running out from near the park entrance is a much easier hike that will show you the effects of the logging and offer good views. Mount Mitchell has been a popular destination for a long time. Even before the Civil War, tourists came to the mountain on horseback. The sunrise on Mount Mitchell was said to be one of the most beautiful sights in the world. After the logging was completed, the railroad was used to carry tourists and later was converted to a toll road for the first automobiles.

This is the end of this tour. The only practical way back to the starting point is the same way you came, along the Blue Ridge Parkway. If you continue south along the Blue Ridge Parkway to Asheville, you will pass through more spectacular mountain scenery where you will see similar vegetation patterns. In the Craggy Mountains you can see some of the best heath balds in North Carolina, along with northern hardwoods forests. Beyond them you will descend through the lower oak forests to the much warmer, drier Asheville Basin. The next tour covers the natural history of this descent.

Forest Communities of the Southern Appalachians

Asheville to Mount Mitchell

CARLETON BURKE

This tour takes you along a 35-mile stretch of the Blue Ridge Parkway—a scenic highway administered by the National Park Service. In its entirety, the parkway runs for 470 miles, linking Shenandoah National Park in Virginia with the Great Smoky Mountains National Park in North Carolina. It is the most visited single unit of the U.S. National Park System. The section described in this driving tour begins with the parkway's crossing of us 70 in Asheville, North Carolina, near the Folk Art Center located on the parkway, and ends at Mount Mitchell State Park just off the parkway. Several short hikes are described that demonstrate the ecological variations found along this section of the parkway. The entire driving tour, including suggested stops and hikes, can be completed in about six hours. Please note that during the winter months, this section of the Blue Ridge Parkway is sometimes closed due to ice and snow. If you are traveling at this time, be sure to call the Blue Ridge Parkway office (828-298-0398) for current road conditions. Because of the probability of bad weather during winter, I recommend that you travel this route sometime during the period April through October.

The major learning experience on this tour is to understand the close relationships among plant distribution, life form, and elevation. The tour begins in Asheville at approximately 2,200 feet above sea level and extends north along the Blue Ridge Parkway to Mount Mitchell State Park (6,684 feet). You will learn how the plant communities change along this elevation gradient, but may be surprised to know that you would pass through many of the same ecological zones if you were to drive northward, at a constant elevation, from North Carolina through the New England states and into southern Canada, a distance of approximately 1,500 miles. This much shorter tour will allow you to observe a variety of unique forest communities that change with elevation, but which are also influenced by differences in rainfall amounts and exposure to wind and sun. Temperatures at the higher elevations are typical of the northeastern United States and southern Canada, so visitors should plan on bringing along a light jacket, even in summertime. Some of the plant and animal communities encountered on this tour include mixed decid-

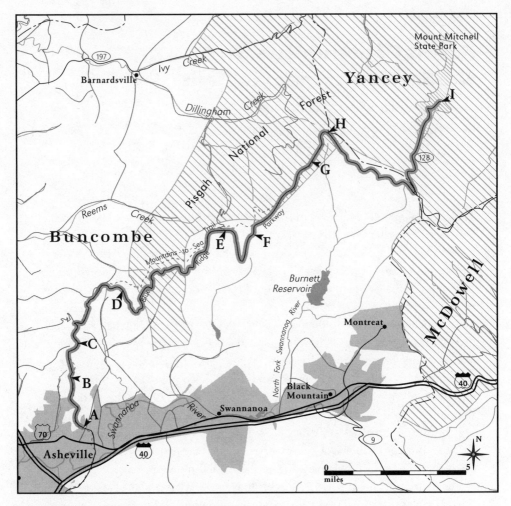

FIGURE 94. Asheville to Mount Mitchell tour route

uous forest, northern hardwood forest, "orchard" vegetation, heath balds, and spruce-fir forest.

The many different ecological zones found in the Southern Appalachians make this region one of the most diverse of any found in North America. Many researchers consider this region to be the most diverse temperate ecosystem on earth. Over 2,300 species of vascular plants, more than 2,000 species of fungi, and over 500 species of mosses and lichens are known to occur in these mountains. Portions of the Southern Appalachian Mountains can be technically classified as temperate rainforest, since they receive over 100 inches of precipitation annually. The natural communities found here reflect this diversity. Forest communities at the lowest elevations in the Appalachians may resemble those of the Carolina Piedmont lowlands, but with a climb in elevation and the subsequent cooler temperatures found there, the forest communities quickly change. At 6,684 feet in elevation, Mount Mitchell, the final stop on this driving tour, is the highest point in eastern North America. The spruce-fir forest community here is a type that is found in northern Maine and southern Canada. Between the highest and lowest points of the mountains, many different forest types overlap and grade into each other, creating a quiltlike mosaic of natural communities and a diversity that offers the visitor unending sources of study. To better understand the information covered in this driving tour, the visitor can bring along one or more field guides, especially one to the trees of this region.

It is easy to get on the Blue Ridge Parkway at Asheville from Interstate 40. Take Exit 55 in East Asheville onto us 70, and turn left toward Asheville. The Blue Ridge Parkway crosses us 70 approximately 1 mile ahead. Turn right onto the parkway entrance and then left onto the parkway itself going north. The Blue Ridge Parkway is marked along the shoulder of the road with milepost markers that indicate distance traveled; these reference points will be used in this tour description. The tour begins as you enter the parkway; proceed approximately 0.5 miles and look for the Folk Art Center on your left at milepost 382. Turn at the access road for the Folk Art Center and park for a short hike along the Mountains-to-Sea Trail.

A. Folk Art Center and Mountains-to-Sea Trail

The Folk Art Center is an excellent stop at which to see mountain crafts and other exhibits and to get general information about the parkway. There is also a gift shop where books, field guides, maps, and crafts can be purchased. From here you can take a short (ten- to fifteen-minute) hike along a portion of the Mountains-to-Sea Trail. The trail entrance is directly across from the visitor entrance to the Folk Art Center at the edge of the parking lot. Proceed along the trail, crossing over the access road into the Folk Art Center, and down the trail for a few hundred yards until it parallels the parkway and you cross over a highway that tunnels under the parkway.

Along this section of trail is a typical low-elevation forest community (Figure 95). Elevation here is approximately 2,200 feet. This oak-chestnut forest is a subtype of the more broadly defined mixed deciduous forest. One of the formerly dominant tree species here, the American chestnut, is now largely absent. A fungal blight that was accidentally introduced around the turn of the century effectively killed almost all of the American chestnut trees in eastern North America. Some small chestnut saplings can still be found scattered along this trail and elsewhere in the mountains. They arise from still-living root systems that send up shoots, which

FIGURE 95. Oak-chestnut forest at ca. 2,200 feet above sea level. (Photo by Carleton Burke)

eventually are killed by the blight. Occasionally a chestnut sapling will grow large enough to flower, but it is seldom effectively cross-pollinated and therefore produces few if any nuts. The chestnut was once one of the most important forest trees in the Southern Appalachian forests. Its nuts were a major food source for wildlife, and it was also heavily utilized by the early settlers for its nuts and as a source of building materials. Many cabins, barns, and other buildings were made of chestnut logs, which are strong, durable, and resist rot. Even today, split-rail fences made of chestnut persist in many locations including areas along the Blue Ridge Parkway. The American chestnut has now been largely replaced in the forest community by other tree species such as chestnut oak, red oak, and black oak. Other dominant species to be found on this site include white oak, black gum, red maple, and white pine. This forest type is also home to the sourwood, a somewhat smaller tree, growing here in great numbers. Sourwood trees seldom grow straight but instead often bend and curve as they twist their way upward through the forest canopy in search of sunlight. Understory shrubs here include the shiny evergreen mountain laurel, flowering dogwood, blueberries, and flame azalea.

Farther along the trail you may notice the presence of tall shortleaf pine trees that are dead or dying. Where these occur, the forest is in a transition from a pine-dominated forest to a hardwood-dominated forest. Forest succession, the orderly progression of plant and animal communities on a given site, is an ongoing event in these mountains. Most of the Appalachian landscape was logged during the 1800s and is now in various stages of succession. Most of the forests encountered along the parkway will be a century old or less. "Climax" forest communities composed primarily of hardwood species will eventually dominate most sites in the Appalachians if they are left undisturbed. After a site is cleared or logged, small grasses and other herbaceous pioneer species of plants will sprout and grow. Within a few years, fast-growing woody vegetation, primarily various types of pines, will take over and be dominant for fifty to seventy-five years. Most pines are shade intolerant and generally short-lived. They are eventually shaded out by various hardwood species, which then become the climax forest community. Forest succession is occurring throughout this region, but, as is the case everywhere, species that grow on any given site are determined by topography, exposure, rainfall, elevation, and other factors.

Retrace your steps back down the trail to the parking lot of the Folk Art Center. Exit the parking lot and turn left onto the parkway heading north.

B. Haw Creek Valley Overlook

The next stop is the Haw Creek Valley Overlook on your left at milepost 380, approximately 2.8 miles from the beginning of the tour. Pull off the parkway to your left and look at the rock face to the right of the roadway.

Geology plays an important role in the development of plant and animal communities in these mountains. Throughout much of the Appalachians, only a thin layer of soil covers the bedrock. Combined with the steep topography, this makes mountain habitats extremely fragile and very vulnerable to damage from erosion, especially if the ground cover is absent or removed. The exposed rock face at this stop provides a look at a typical cross-section of what much of the mountain landscape is like beneath our feet. Notice the thin mantle of soil and overlying mat of vegetation on the top of the rock face. Most of the rock in the Southern Appalachian Mountains is metamorphic. Metamorphic rocks have been changed in their structure through extreme heat and pressure. Because of this restructuring, fossil remains of plants and animals have been destroyed and are rarely encountered in the rocks of the Southern Appalachians.

C. Tanbark Ridge Overlook

The next stop is between mileposts 377 and 376; turn right into the Tanbark Ridge Overlook. Park your vehicle and walk to the far left end of the parking area as you face the overlook. On the right side of the roadway you will notice a wooden guardrail. Carefully cross the highway at this point then walk about 100 feet along the grassy roadbank on the left side of the road. Look carefully for a small trail leading into the woods at the base of the road shoulder. Enter the woods at this point and follow the trail, which turns to your left and leads uphill. Walk for about 100 feet and then stop.

The forest community at this stop has a much different look and feel than the forest you just visited adjacent to the Folk Art Center. Although some of the same tree species are present here, you will notice many more herbaceous plants growing on the forest floor. As you climb in elevation (you are now at 3,175 feet), not only does the temperature change but rainfall amounts generally increase as well, resulting in lush plant growth, depending, of course, on the orientation of the particular site. The tall, straight trees here are members of the magnolia family known as the tulip tree or yellow poplar to many mountaineers. When left to grow, they are one of the Appalachian's largest and tallest trees. Specimens 22 feet in circumference and more than 150 feet tall are still found in isolated areas. Trees of this size used to be common before the area was logged during the last century. The tulip tree is a favorite of loggers due to its quick growth pattern and tall, straight trunk. On moist sites like this, tulip trees along with other hardwood species often attain immense proportions. The soil here is also very rich and supports many plants other than trees: small shrubs, ferns, and herbaceous plants grow here in profusion. These plants have adapted to the low light levels found in these shady woodlands. Woodland wildflowers are particularly common here, but primarily bloom in early spring before the overhead trees leaf out. By early summer, they have stored enough food in their root systems to last the rest of the season. Look here for various wildflower species such as bloodroot, wild geranium, trillium, Jack-in-the-pulpit, Solomon's seal, false Solomon's seal, mandarin, baneberry, and many others. Ferns found here include the cinnamon fern, Christmas fern, grape fern, and maidenhair fern. Understory shrubs and smaller trees include the spicebush, wild hydrangea, sassafras, and dogwood. Hardwood forests on moist sites with rich soil are among the most diverse of the Appalachian forest communities.

D. Tanbark Ridge Tunnel, Rattlesnake Lodge Trail: Transition to Northern Hardwoods

Just past milepost 375, approximately 8 miles into the driving tour, you will approach the Tanbark Ridge Tunnel. Pull off the road onto the gravel parking area on your right just before the tunnel entrance. Carefully walk across the highway and you will notice a trail alongside the streambank. Follow this trail uphill for approximately 100 to 200 yards or more to view a forest in transition to a northern hardwoods forest community.

At this elevation, approximately 3,300 feet, various species of northern hardwoods will begin to appear, especially if the exposure is northerly. Northern hardwood tree species include sugar maple, beech, yellow birch, yellow buckeye, striped maple, mountain maple, and northern red oak. Look closely along the trail and you may see scattered small trees with a distinctive vertical striping; these are the striped maple, which will be seen much more commonly at higher elevations. The stream to the right of the trail is a good site to see the rosebay rhododendron, one of the most distinctive and characteristic evergreen shrubs of the Southern Appalachians. It typically grows along moist streambanks or anywhere there is abundant moisture yet well-drained soil. The mountain laurel, another common and distinctive evergreen shrub with smaller leaves, is usually found growing on drier sites but often intermingles with the rhododendron. It too can be found along this trail. Other streambank shrubs here include wild hydrangea, spicebush, and witch-hazel. Small rocky streams, springs, and seeps abound in this area and are home to one of the most numerous of Appalachian wildlife groups, the salamanders. These delicate, moist, and smooth-skinned amphibians are particularly common in these mountains due to the abundant rainfall, high humidity, and cool conditions that exist in forested areas with a ground cover of mosses, herbaceous plants, and fallen logs. More species of salamanders are found in this region than anywhere else on earth. Although many are very colorful, the most common species, such as the dusky salamanders, sport mottled colors of gray, tan, and brown.

E. Craggy Gardens: Forest Succession from Grassy Bald to Northern Hardwoods

Continue driving north along the parkway. Just past milepost 368, approximately 14.2 miles into the driving tour, look for the sign to Craggy Gardens Picnic Grounds on your left; turn left here on a paved road that leads uphill then makes a sharp right-hand curve. At approximately 0.3 miles up the road, you will notice a circular turnaround on your left and a gravel road with a gate adjacent to the turnaround. Pull off here and park.

You will be taking a short fifteen- to twenty-minute hike to a small grassy bald and then into a surrounding forest area to observe forest succession. Look for the entrance to the trail on the hillside to the left of the gravel road entrance, immediately adjacent to the circular turnaround. A plaque on the trailhead post should indicate that this is a portion of the Mountains-to-Sea Trail. Walk into the woods on the trail about 100 feet to where the trail forks. Turn left and stay on the Mountains-to-Sea Trail. Almost immediately you will enter a small grassy field or bald. Proceed about 100 feet to the small rock outcropping in the center of the bald, climb to the top for a better vantage point and stop.

You are standing in the middle of a forest opening or mountain bald. From a distance these mostly treeless areas look like slick, smooth bald patches when compared with the surrounding forest. Mountain balds are covered, however, with many different types of herbaceous vegetation, such as grasses and wildflowers, and by shrubs, such as rhododendron, mountain laurel, and blueberries. These balds can be extensive, sometimes covering many acres, or, as in this case, very small. What causes balds to form is somewhat of a mystery and a subject of much debate. Treeless areas are usually found at the higher elevations of very high mountain peaks, but there is no treeline in these mountains as there is in the western United States. Severe weather and exposure may be somewhat responsible for keeping larger trees from being established on the balds. It is also thought that early Native Americans might have cut back and burned the vegetation in order to attract browsing game such as deer and rabbits. Early settlers to this region were known to graze livestock and grow vegetable crops such as potatoes on the cool mountain balds. Whatever their origin, it is now clear that these mysterious balds are currently disappearing. Forest succession is eliminating many of them. At this site we have the unique opportunity to view forest succession in action and to observe, with a short walk away from the bald, what this area will eventually become.

If you look around the outer edges of this forest opening you will notice many small shrubs and trees, some of which are also found as small scattered islands within the bald itself. Mountain ash, hawthorne, fire cherry, deciduous hollies, and blueberries are some of the common shrub and tree species in and around the bald. All of these are berry-producing and normally spring up around the edges of the surrounding wooded areas, where birds are most likely to perch. Seeds contained in bird droppings may sprout, starting the process of forest succession on the bald. Slowly, over a period of years, the bald begins to fill in with these trees and shrubs, starting usually with the edges. Scattered vegetative islands within the bald eventually meet, and the bald becomes covered with shrubs. This effect can be seen in the next section of the trail.

From the rock outcropping, follow the trail through the center of the bald and then into the wooded area at the rear of the bald. As you enter the wooded area notice that you are now standing under an almost pure stand of hawthorne, a species of shrub previously seen in the bald—it is easily identified by the numerous sharp spiny projections or thorns along the twigs and trunk. Hawthorne, at this site, grew faster than the other surrounding shrubs and eventually shaded out many of the grasses, wildflowers, and other plants that once grew in the bald where you are now standing. Within the past one hundred years, this stand of hawthorne has replaced this section of the grassy bald.

To view more forest succession and to get a sense of what the bald will look like in perhaps another century or two, continue on through the hawthorne stand about 100 feet to where a faint trail forks off to the right. Follow this trail for about 50 feet and it will dead-end into another trail. Turn left on this trail and begin walking uphill. As you walk this trail you will begin to notice various species of hardwood trees replacing the hawthorne. These trees include black locust, sugar maple, cucumber magnolia, yellow birch, and beech. Look closely to the left of the trail as you begin walking and you may notice an old fence post or two in this now wooded area. These are remnants from the early 1800s when this was an open field and there was a fence here to keep in livestock.

As you crest the hill continue along the trail for another 100 to 200 yards and the trees become larger. As you begin to descend you are entering a northern hardwoods forest. Typical dominant trees here include sugar maple, yellow buckeye, beech, and yellow birch. These are all species of trees commonly found in the forests of the New England states, yet they exist here in the Southern Appalachians hundreds of miles south due to the cooler climatic conditions found at the higher elevations. Also note the dense herbaceous cover on the forest floor.

Retrace your steps to the parking area for the next stop of the driving tour. At this point you can follow the paved road back downhill to the Blue Ridge Parkway or continue on up the paved road for a little less than a mile to the Craggy Gardens Picnic Grounds at Bearpen Gap, elevation 5,220 feet. There are restroom facilities here as well as picnic tables and grills. This is your chance to eat and relax in the cool atmosphere of the northern hardwoods zone. Red squirrels, residents of this northern forest, which replace the common gray squirrels found at lower elevations, may often be seen around the picnic area foraging for handouts. Visitors may also hear the deep guttural call of the raven soaring nearby. Ravens, like the red squirrels, are typically found only at the higher elevations. At the right rear of the parking area is access to a section of the Mountains-to-Sea Trail that parallels the parking area—an opportunity for a short hike to view more northern hardwoods forest.

F. Craggy Flats Trail: Orchard Vegetation and Heath Bald

Drive back downhill on the Craggy Gardens Picnic Grounds roadway to the Blue Ridge Parkway. Turn left heading uphill and north along the parkway. Between mileposts 365 and 364 look for the parking area for the Craggy Gardens Visitors Center, approximately 18 miles into the driving tour. Pull off to the left and park in the far left parking area. You may wish to cross the highway for a grand view of the Asheville Watershed below. The large body of water is Burnett Reservoir, the city of Asheville's main source of water. The watershed is off-limits to the general public, and 15 miles of the parkway pass along the upper perimeter of the watershed's boundaries. You may have noticed the signs previously along the roadway instructing you to stop only at overlooks while in the watershed. Rainfall within the watershed feeds the numerous springs and streams in this area, which eventually drain downhill into the reservoir. The natural forests in the entire Asheville Watershed (more than 17,000 acres) are permanently protected by a conservation easement dedicated by the City of Asheville.

Take the Craggy Flats Trail located at the far left end of the parking area. This a short ten-minute hike through a wooded area and then into a heath bald with great views of the surrounding mountains. Begin walking down the trail and look to your right. You will begin to notice a number of smaller trees, about 10 to 15 feet in height. Many of these trees are stunted and pruned back from a combination of harsh conditions found in this area, winter wind and ice in particular. This constant pruning results in trees that resemble fruit trees in an orchard—hence the name "orchard vegetation." Most of the "orchard" trees along this trail are yellow birch and beech, but other northern hardwood species, depending on the location, can also be found growing in this condition. Sometimes one species may predominate, resulting in an "oak orchard," for example, where the northern red oak is found. Although these orchard trees are small and stunted, some are two hundred years old or older.

Continue along the trail, which heads uphill through a combination of orchard hardwoods and rhododendron. The rhododendron along this trail is a different species than that encountered at the lower elevations. This is Catawba rhododendron, or purple laurel as many mountain folks are known to call it. It grows in profusion at the higher elevations, often in pure stands known as rhododendron slicks or hells because of the difficulty humans encounter trying to pass through them. The thick cover of these thickets provides important habitat for nesting birds and other animals. Continue along the trail and you will exit into an open area. Immediately ahead you will notice a large trail shelter. This was constructed in 1935 by the Civilian Conservation Corps out of American chestnut logs. The great chestnut blight hit the Southern Appalachian Mountains in the 1930s, and even though many chestnuts were killed, the still standing dead trees were often harvested for lumber.

You are now entering a combination heath and grass bald at an elevation of 5,526 feet (Figure 96). Turn left at the trail shelter and use any of the small trails to explore the bald. Heath balds are composed primarily of various shrubs and plants of the heath family, including rhododendron, mountain laurel, and blueberries. Other plants of these high mountain balds include various species of grasses, wildflowers, blackberries, and others. The shrubby vegetation and berry-producing plants attract rodents, rabbits, and birds, which in turn make these areas good hunting grounds for many predatory animals as well. Predators that could occur

FIGURE 96. Heath and grass bald at 5,500 feet above sea level. (Photo by Carleton Burke)

here include timber rattlesnakes, bears, and bobcats. Retrace your steps back to the trail and return to the parking area. Restroom facilities are available at the visitors center, and you may wish to visit the gift shop and view the exhibits there as well.

G. Glassmine Falls Overlook: Spruce-Fir Forest Community

From the Craggy Gardens Visitors Center continue north along the parkway toward Mount Mitchell State Park. Between mileposts 362 and 361 pull off on the right at the Glassmine Falls Overlook. Take the very short paved path at the left of the overlook to a scenic vantage point just up the hill. Notice the split-rail fence along the trail and around the overlook: it is made from chestnut logs.

At the overlook you will probably notice that the mountains in the distance are covered along their upper ridges and slopes by dark trees. These are mostly red spruce, one of the major tree species in the spruce-fir forest. This forest community is normally found only around 5,000 feet in elevation or higher. At around 5,500 feet, the spruce becomes mixed with Fraser fir. Fraser fir may occur in pure stands along the very highest mountain peaks, such as those at Mount Mitchell. From a distance, the dark green needles of these evergreen trees give the appearance of black, from which the Black Mountain range derives its name. Notice that the spruce trees in the distance descend further down the mountain sides in the coves and other protected sites along the mountain slopes. Mingling with the spruce-fir farther downslope is the northern hardwoods forest, in which you are still standing at an elevation of 5,200 feet.

H. Balsam Gap Overlook, Big Butt Trail:
Transition from Northern Hardwoods to Spruce-Fir Forest

Continue along the parkway to just past milepost 360 and turn left into the Balsam Gap Overlook at an elevation of 5,317 feet. To your far left and behind the overlook, the Big Butt Trail descends into a mixed forest of northern hardwoods and spruce-fir forest. Walk along this trail for five to ten minutes and you will see, especially on your right, examples of the spruce-fir forest community. The forest community here is a true northern forest—a remnant of the ice age when forests like this were found throughout much of eastern North America. During this period, some 10,000 to 12,000 years ago, glaciers covered much of the northeastern United States. Although the glaciers ice did not extend as far south as the Southern Appalachian Mountains, the effects did, creating a cool northern forest through-out much of the South. When the glaciers receded and the climate warmed, the northern forest communities gradually disappeared, except for isolated remnants that remained on these cool, high mountain peaks.

I. Mount Mitchell State Park and Spruce-Fir Forest

Continue northward along the Blue Ridge Parkway and turn left between mile-posts 356 and 355 at the sign for Mount Mitchell State Park. Proceed uphill along this road for 4 miles until you reach the parking area just below the summit of Mount Mitchell, the highest peak in eastern North America (6,684 feet). Northern hardwoods and red spruce finally give way to almost pure stands of Fraser fir trees as you approach the summit. Also notice along the highway the numerous dead trees. Forest decline on the slopes of Mount Mitchell and other high-elevation peaks in the Southern Appalachians is a serious threat—in fact, this fragile eco-system is considered to be one of the most endangered in the world. At this elevation, many of the trees are bathed almost daily in a constant mist from rain and passing clouds. Pollutants from automobile exhausts and factory emissions are carried in the rain and clouds and deposited here. In recent years, an intro-duced pest insect known as the balsam woolly adelgid has also been attacking the weakened trees. A combination of all these factors seems to be causing the decline and death of the fir trees here.

Restroom facilities are available at the concession stand adjacent to the parking area. A short but steep trail leads up from the parking area to the summit of Mount

Mitchell. An observation tower at the summit provides spectacular views in all directions on a clear day. Halfway up the summit trail is a small museum with exhibits about the plants and animals in this high-elevation forest and telling the fascinating story of Dr. Elisha Mitchell, for whom this mountain is named. In 1857 he lost his life in a fall while trying to prove that this peak was indeed the highest mountain in the East. His grave is located at the base of the observation tower. Also recommended is the Balsam Nature Trail, a short trail that begins just past the museum, giving the visitor a closer look at the spruce-fir forest community. An interpretive guide for the trail is available at the concession stand adjacent to the parking area.

Big Ivy Road to Craggy Mountain Scenic Area

RON LANCE

This 8.7-mile tour, following well-maintained gravel roads, begins at the entrance to Pisgah National Forest east of Dillingham, North Carolina. The tour will take you past several scenic and noteworthy examples of mountain natural communities. You will also pass clear mountain streams and cascades, high rock outcrops, deep forests of old trees, lush herbaceous cover, and vista points giving glimpses of distant ridges and coves of the Craggy Mountains. Pull-off areas along the way allow visitors to park their vehicles and walk into the forests for closer viewing of plant and animal life. At one end of this route, a developed picnic area (Corner Rock) is available. At the terminus of this dead-end road, a relatively easy foot trail leads to a 70-foot-high waterfall.

This tour will help you learn to observe and enjoy Southern Appalachian plants in pristine natural communities. Such visual recreation is made possible by a slow drive on a gravel road through diverse forests. These natural communities include the oak forests of ridgetops and sunnier slopes, which display a canopy rich in chestnut oak and northern red oak. The great American chestnut trees that once grew here are gone now, but you can still find smaller remnants of these trees that continue to struggle for growth amidst constant attack by the chestnut blight fungus. Other oaks that are common in lower elevations, such as white oak, scarlet oak, and black oak, are not so common in the forests along this route, which stays above 3,000 feet in elevation. These elevations receive progressively greater amounts of precipitation and have shorter growing seasons and a cooler climate. This combination has an effect on plants similar to the effect obtained when you travel northward in latitude: with rise in elevation there is a shift in forest composition to types resembling the forests of northern regions. The two previous tours in this book demonstrate the elevation-forest type relationship across elevation gradients along the Blue Ridge Parkway.

The understory of these oak forests generally contains acid-loving plants, that is, plants that prefer acidic soils. The great abundance of mountain laurel, rhododendron, azalea, blueberry, and sourwood all attest to the acidic soils of these mountains. As the acidity decreases, you may notice a shift of the type and abun-

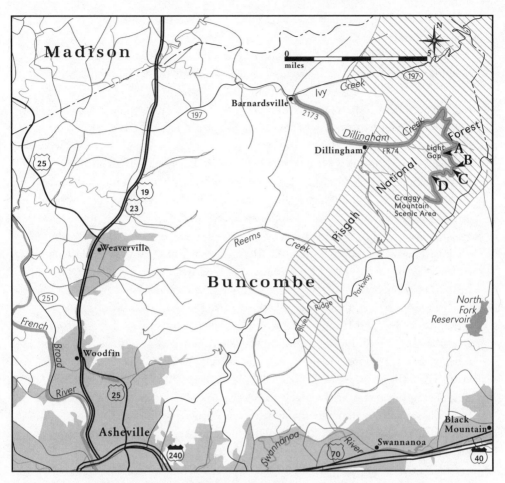

FIGURE 97. Big Ivy Road to Craggy Mountain tour route

dance of certain trees and understory shrubs and herbs. Our richest wildflower displays and most diverse forest cover are usually found in "rich coves," where the soils are less acidic and even approach a basic condition.

A so-called rich cove will support many types of hardwood trees. At elevations of over 3,800 feet, as in some coves along this route, there may not be as many oaks and tulip poplars as there are in lower coves, but you will find sugar maple, yellow buckeye, basswood, white ash, beech, bitternut hickory, and black cherry. Occasional trees of red maple, cucumber tree, Fraser magnolia, hemlock, black birch, and yellow birch will also be visible. The yellow birch, beech, and hemlocks will become more dominant at elevations above 4,000 feet. Smaller trees such as striped maple and hop hornbeam dot the understory, and below these grow diverse herbaceous layers. The stinging nettle is a common herb of this area; take care when walking near patches of this plant—though the annoying rash is fortunately of short duration.

Along with the forests, you will pass rock outcrops, streamsides, and roadside openings that offer such a diverse assemblage of plants that a field guide will be useful to help you identify some of your finds. Please be mindful of those who follow you, leaving flowers for their enjoyment and education, too.

Begin this tour by traveling north on US 19/23 from Asheville to the NC 197 exit to Barnardsville. Take this exit, and upon reaching the Barnardsville Post Office and Fire Department, visible on your left, turn right onto Dillingham Road (SR 2173). Dillingham Road weaves its way along Dillingham Creek, a major drainage of the Great Craggy Mountains. In this valley are numerous small family farms and homesteads nestled at the feet of slopes and stony hillsides. Oaks, hemlock, basswood, buckeye, tulip poplar, birch, and maple dominate the strips of forests along meandering streams. After approximately 5 miles and four crossings of Dillingham Creek, the pavement ends at the boundary of the Pisgah National Forest and the beginning of Big Ivy Road (FR 74), a U.S. Forest Service maintained gravel road.

This road is part of the Toecane Ranger District of the Pisgah National Forest, and it passes through lands owned and administered by the U.S. Forest Service. Near the gate toward the end of Dillingham Road, Corner Rock Picnic Area offers a peaceful semiwooded site for a recreational respite near the sound of rushing water. From this point onward, Big Ivy Road climbs steadily, but not steeply, for 8.7 miles along the slopes of the high mountain spine that separates this watershed from the Cane River and Swannanoa River watersheds to the east and south. By keeping up with your vehicle's odometer readings, starting at the gate near Corner Rock, you can locate the following sites of interest.

At 1.7 miles from the gate, the road crosses Little Andy Creek. This branch courses through a forest of hemlock, ash, buckeye, basswood, birch, and tulip poplar. The moss-covered rocks bordering this scenic stream are also shaded by wild ginger, creeping euonymus, nettle, and bee-balm.

A. Ridgetop Oak Forests and Rock Outcrops

At 3.1 miles the road passes through Light Gap, on Big Andy Ridge, where you may view a typical ridgetop oak forest. There is also a parking area. Nearby, the large trees are chestnut and northern red oaks. Smaller trees are blackgum, sourwood, and hop hornbeam, with mountain laurel in the understory. If you carefully inspect the woodlands in the vicinity of the parking area, you might find living examples of American chestnut. Also in the vicinity are examples of both types of hemlock found in the eastern United States—the common eastern hemlock and the uncommon Carolina hemlock. Carolina hemlock is endemic to the Southern Appalachians, which means it grows naturally nowhere else but in this region.

At 3.4 miles a rock outcrop towers 80 feet above the road. This rock face may be dripping with rivulets of water during wet weather, but when rains cease and sunlight heats and dries the stone, drought comes quickly to the pockets of thin soil perched among the small ledges. Plants that grow in these soil pockets and rock crevices are adapted to extreme conditions and differ from the flora of adjacent forested communities. If you look closely, you will notice the Carolina hemlock making its home here, illustrating that it possesses greater drought tolerance than the eastern hemlock. Some of the clumped shrubs that jut out from the rock are hairy mock-orange, a species that frequents sunny rock outcrops such as this. You may also notice various grasses, sedges, and wildflowers that grow in this habitat and nowhere else along this road.

B. Walker Falls and Walker Cove Natural Area

At 3.8 miles the road crosses Walker Branch. The beautiful waterfall known as Walker Falls is visible above the road to the left. This cascade has been proposed as a National Natural Landmark.

At 4.0 to 4.1 miles you may notice a junction where an old roadbed branches off and ascends Walker Cove, on your left. Walker Cove Natural Area, a 53-acre tract of old-growth hardwood forest, begins here and covers much of the north-facing slope on the side of Walker Ridge in front of you. Logging operations are not allowed in this research natural area, which is protected according to National Forest regulations. This is one of the region's best remaining examples of an old-growth mixed hardwood forest that has been untouched by the extensive logging that took place over most of this region. The dominant canopy trees here are sugar maple, yellow buckeye, basswood, yellow birch, and beech. Some of the sugar maples are well over three hundred years old. The spacious forest understory consists of verdant carpets of ferns and herbs under the high canopy of the old trees. Other trees that you might notice in this cove are hickory, oak, cherry, cucumber tree, white ash, and eastern hemlock.

As you continue your motorized journey toward the bend around Walker Ridge, notice the vines hanging from some of the tall trees of the forest. Those with gray bark and twining habit are Dutchman's pipe, and those with brown, shreddy bark are wild grape. Both of these vines are native species that normally begin their attachment to adjacent trees when they are young; hence, the vines grow up with the trees and ultimately hang down from their high canopies. This means the vines can be close to the ages of the trees to which they are attached.

FIGURE 98. Douglas Falls. (Photo by Ron Lance)

At 4.7 miles you will notice a relatively pure stand of sugar maple on the left. This is a maturing forest, not an ancient one like the forest in Walker Cove—it was logged in the past.

c. Orchard Creek Natural Area

At 6.1 miles you will come to another old-growth hardwood forest similar to that in Walker Cove, except that this one spans both sides of the road. See if you can spot the large ash, cherry, and sugar maples with their accompanying Dutchman's pipe vines.

D. Douglas Falls Trail

At 8.7 miles Big Ivy Road ends in a widened parking area. You must turn around here, but before you retrace your steps, consider hiking the trail that begins at this point. Forest Service Trail No. 162 leads slightly downhill for about 0.5 miles to Douglas Falls, where old hemlocks border a view into an arenalike cove and a creek cascades over a rock face above the trail and falls 70 feet onto the rocks below (Figure 98). You will pass numerous large, old trees on the trail, which next continues up the left side of the falls and proceeds for several more miles into the Craggy Mountain Scenic Area. This scenic area is administered by the Pisgah National Forest, and the trail ultimately ends at the Craggy Gardens Area of the Blue Ridge Parkway. On this delightful walk through hemlock and boreal forest, the old hemlock stands mingle with the mosaic of hardwood forests, where yellow birch, beech, and maple gradually give way to shrub balds on the high ridges.

The driving tour ends at the terminus of the Big Ivy Road, and you must backtrack to Dillingham and paved roads.

Great Smoky Mountains National Park

DIRK FRANKENBERG

Although slightly more than half of Great Smoky Mountains National Park is in North Carolina, the park is an entity unto itself with roads, trails, streams, and campgrounds all managed by the National Park Service and their concessionaires. The park can be used as part of a driving route between North Carolina and Tennessee, but it's a slow trip and a nearly criminal waste of the park's resources. The national park contains over 520,000 acres, more than one-fifth of which is old-growth forest in close to its primeval state. The geology and climate of the park is similar to that described in the overview chapter and in other tours of North Carolina's high mountains, although an area of valley and ridge topography, created by the same continental collision that formed the Appalachians, occurs in 300- to 500-million-year-old sedimentary rocks at the western end of the park. The bulk of North Carolina's part of the park is metamorphic rock formed earlier than the valley and ridge province. These old, erosion-resistant rocks make up some of the most stunning mountain scenery in the country—an attribute that brings close to ten million visitors a year to the park. The mountains, valleys, streams, and floodplains in this scenic area support the richest and most diverse assemblage of plants and animals in any single holding in the state. The natural history of these assemblages is reasonably well known as a result of decades of study by scientists from Tennessee, North Carolina, Georgia, and elsewhere. These efforts have identified over 1,600 species of flowering plants, 200 species of birds, 48 types of fish, and 2,000 fungi. There are more than 500 black bears included among the 60 species of mammals found in the park. A 650-pound bear was shot in the park by a poacher in late 1998. Many of the bears are used to humans, which makes them even more dangerous. Take precautions when hiking, touring, or camping, and never approach a bear, especially with food in your hands.

Great Smoky Mountains National Park is such a treasure house for naturalists that it is better suited as a destination for a long visit rather than as day-trip territory. I recommend devoting time to visiting and learning from the park's magnificent natural resources—in more detail than can be effectively described in a statewide compendium of natural area tours such as this one. Begin your search

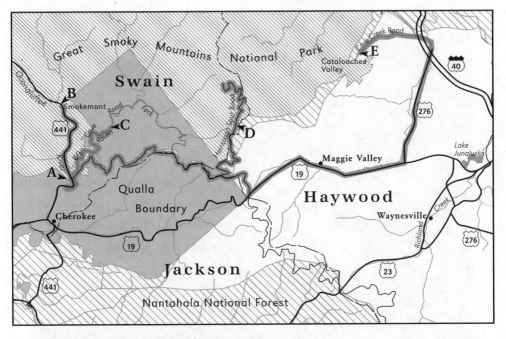

FIGURE 99. Great Smoky Mountains tour route

for background materials with Lynda McDaniels's *Highroad Guide to the North Carolina Mountains* (see "Suggestions for Further Reading" at the end of this book). McDaniels devotes more than thirty pages to the park and covers both North Carolina and Tennessee halves of it. For those who wish to learn more than McDaniels provides, I recommend *Great Smoky Mountains National Park: A Natural History Guide* by Rose Houk, published by Houghton Mifflin (1993). If you can't find time to get these books in advance of your visit, you will find copies in the well-stocked bookstores at the park visitors centers or in the park-focused tourism towns of Cherokee and Gatlinburg.

If you are determined to have a one-day drive in the North Carolina section of the park, I recommend starting at the Oconaluftee Visitors Center 2 miles north of Cherokee on US 441. The visitors center building contains exhibits and park information, and has working mountain farm and gristmill exhibits nearby (see A in Figure 99). Next you may drive 3.2 miles farther north to Smokemont, where you will find a short, self-guiding nature trail, the longer Smokemont Loop Trail, and the still longer Chasteen Creek Trail (B in Figure 99). The loop trail begins at the back end of the campground and follows Bradley Fork for about 1.2 miles to the intersection of Chasteen Creek Trail, then heads up and down Richland Mountain (the latter is a strenuous climb).

FIGURE 100. Mountain Creek. (Photo by D. Frankenberg)

FIGURE 101. Cataloochee Valley. (Photo by D. Frankenberg)

I then suggest you return to just south of the visitors center and drive up Big Cove Road (C in Figure 99) to see the cove forests along Raven Fork. When you have had your fill of the creeks and forests (Figure 100) return to the Blue Ridge Parkway and follow it east for about 6 miles to milepost 458.2 and the Heintooga Spur Road (D in Figure 99). Take this north into Smoky Mountains National Park and to Balsam Mountain Campground. You will pass park trail access points about 6.5 miles down the spur road as well as at the campground about 8.6 miles from the parkway.

Finally, if you want a close-up view of the least-visited valley in the park, return to the parkway and follow it 2 miles east to Soco Gap and turn left onto US 19 East. Go through Maggie Valley to Dellwood, then left onto US 276 toward Interstate 40 and Suttontown. One-tenth of a mile beyond the Interstate 40 entrance, turn right on Cove Creek Road (NC 284) and follow it into the national park at Cove Creek Gap (E in Figure 99). A paved road leads up the Cataloochee Valley (Figure 101), where there is a ranger station, a primitive campground, and 37 miles of trails, including one, the Boogerman Loop, that is both popular and frighteningly named. Once you have arrived in Cataloochee Valley you will understand why it is visited less often than other places in the park—it takes a little more effort to get here. We hope you enjoy it, and remember, you are only about 10 miles from Interstate 40.

Hickory Nut Gorge
A Scenic Approach to the
North Carolina Mountains

ELISABETH FEIL

This tour takes you through Hickory Nut Gorge, one of several valleys cut into the Blue Ridge escarpment—the steep rise that separates the Piedmont from the mountains. Some of the escarpment gorges are well known, especially the Jocassee Gorges, located west of Rosman, and Linville Gorge, northwest of Morganton, both of which are described elsewhere in this book. Hickory Nut Gorge is less well known, but its location southeast of Asheville has made it a thoroughfare for over two hundred years. It is the only escarpment gorge accessible by car for its entire length.

The major features of the gorge are the tremendous cliffs near the mouth of the valley, created by the power of the waters of Hickory Creek and the Broad River. Bat Cave, the largest fissure cave in the world, is hidden in the dense forest. A 400-foot waterfall drops from a hanging valley high up on the cliffs. The Bottomless Pools present interesting creek formations. Lake Lure, created in 1926 to provide electricity for the fledgling town of the same name, adds to the outstanding beauty of the gorge. Chimney Rock Park, an example of a well-managed ecotourism destination, offers hiking trails with outstanding views, a nature center, and interpretative literature. The valley is heavily traveled by tourists, especially near the mouth of the gorge. Most of the land is in private ownership, and public access is generally restricted to commercial enterprises.

Hickory Nut Gorge provides a concentrated dose of potential learning experiences. The gorge is only 8 miles long—as the raven flies—from Hickory Nut Gap on the Eastern Continental Divide to Lake Lure. In this short distance, the elevation drops from 2,878 feet on the gap to about 1,000 feet at the lake, illustrating the transition from mountain vegetation to Piedmont vegetation. For the interested observer, the exposed rocks can reveal traces of the geologic history of the Southern Appalachians. The varied topography and the presence of a hornblende gneiss on top of the mountain peaks here create niches for a number of rare and unusual plant species and communities. Other important factors influencing plant distribution may be observed here: availability of water, exposure to the sun, and

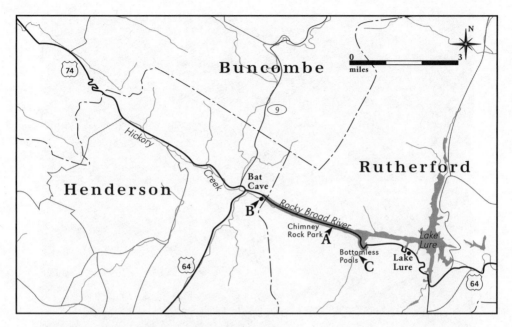

FIGURE 102. Hickory Nut Gorge tour route

position in the landscape. The influence of human activity is obvious, from the initial enhancement afforded by the lake—now marred by countless houses along its shores—to erosion problems, congestion, and noise in the valley, and the necessity of boardwalks on trails to protect the environment.

A. Chimney Rock Park

Most of what you can learn is best demonstrated in Chimney Rock Park. The park, a privately owned Registered Natural Heritage Area located on the face of a 500-foot cliff sitting 900 feet above the Broad River, is the major tourist attraction in Hickory Nut Gorge. You will find the entrance to the park in the small village of Chimney Rock. From Asheville, take US 74A East for about 25 miles. The best way to come from Rutherfordton is via US 74 West, then NC 9 North (New Prospect Exit), and US 74A West. From Hendersonville (and Interstate 26) it is about 12 miles on US 64 East, and NC 9 South comes in from Black Mountain and Interstate 40. For more information contact the park at 828-625-9611 or 800-277-9611, or e-mail visitximneyrockpark.com. You may also visit its Web site at http://www.chimneyrockpark.com.

From the park entrance, drive 3 miles to the parking lot at the base of the Chimney (Figure 103). The ticket office, where each driver receives a trail map, is

FIGURE 103. Chimney Rock. (Photo courtesy of Chimney Rock Park)

about halfway along this road. An elevator inside the mountain takes you up 258 feet to the Sky Lounge, a gift shop and snack bar. Outside of the Sky Lounge you will find steps leading to the top of the Chimney and to the official starting point of the Skyline-Cliff Trail Loop. A different access to the trail system is described in the next paragraph.

Three trails, all of which lead to the 404-foot Hickory Nut Falls, start by Moonshiners Cave, behind the big rock at the head of the parking lot. Two tall Norway spruces next to the rock mark the way. Trail guides, a geology guide, and a bird list are available here. You may have to ask for the plant list in the Sky Lounge. The stairs up the mountain lead to the Chimney, the Sky Lounge, and the start of the 1.5-mile-long Skyline-Cliff Trail Loop. The Skyline Trail, which may also be accessed by taking the elevator to the Sky Lounge, runs along the upper edge of the rock wall to the waterfall, where it connects to the Cliff Trail. This trail brings you back to the parking lot, crossing the cliff face on a natural ledge. You reach the Forest Stroll by taking the stairs down from Moonshiners Cave. It follows the base of the cliff for about 1.2 miles to the bottom of the waterfall and back.

Skyline-Cliff Trail Loop

As you walk from the parking lot through the tunnel to the elevator, you will find the first interpretive signs about the geology and rocks of the park. There will be others along the trails. Outside the Sky Lounge select the guides and lists that interest you from the display box. On the bridge you can observe an impressive example of the importance of water in shaping our landscapes. The nearby Chimney formed as a result of the removal of material by the action of water and ice along a network of cracks in the rock. This process continues today; in the future the Chimney will be ever farther removed from the mountainside, and its shape will change in the process. On the Chimney itself (Stop 4 in the Skyline-Cliff Trail Loop guide), take a look at the small holes on the surface. Ice pries tiny particles off the rock, and wind and water move them around to grind out the holes. Erosion is happening before your eyes.

The massive rock that forms the valley walls and the Chimney is called Henderson gneiss (a gneiss is a metamorphic rock that cooled slowly underground), and it is very resistant to erosion. Where the vegetation begins on top of the gneiss, the slopes are much less severe, an indication of a rock that erodes more easily. This rock is a mica schist that was placed above the gneiss sometime during the forming of the Appalachian Mountains. The vegetation line approximates the contact zone between the two rock types. The gneiss has been dated to be 509 million years old, but age and origin of the mica schist are unknown. (You will find a close-up view of a contact zone between these two rock types at Stop 16 on the Skyline Trail.)

The first part (Stops 5–10) of the Skyline Trail leads steeply up the east side of

Chimney Rock Mountain, which receives lots of sunshine on the thirty-five-degree slopes. An open forest of chestnut oak and hickory dominates here, though it is interspersed, in pockets of rich, moist soil, with white ash and eastern red cedar. Fringe tree is common on the very edges of the vegetation. Shrubs in this area are wafer ash (its leaves look very much like poison ivy leaves, but it does not cause dermatitis) and two species of mock-orange. Once considered endangered, Biltmore sedge is nearly ubiquitous throughout, even crowding out other rare plants. Seepage cracks are ideal locations for the rare Carey's saxifrage. White irisette, federally endangered, and yellow honeysuckle are also found here. Most of the plants here can withstand the sometimes severe droughts on the steep, exposed slopes; others disappear until growing conditions are favorable again.

Exclamation Point (Stop 11) is a special place with good views into the valley and toward the western horizon. The round-topped mountain in the distance is Bearwallow Mountain, at over 4,000 feet the highest point on the Eastern Continental Divide in our area. Hickory Nut Gap, where US 74A crosses the divide, is hidden near the lowest point on the horizon. The forests on the slopes are home to many nesting birds, among them several rare warblers: cerulean at the edge of the parking lot, Swainson's in dense rhododendron thickets, worm-eating along the Forest Stroll, and chestnut-sided at the edges of clearings on top of the mountain. More common birds that are normally found at much higher elevations, such as dark-eyed junco, black-throated green warbler, and black-throated blue warbler, regularly breed in the cool forests below the rocks. If you are very lucky, you may even hear ravens calling or glimpse a pair of peregrine falcons streaking by. The big birds soaring elegantly at eye level are not eagles but turkey vultures. Several interesting plant species grow around the edges of the woods. There are yellow honeysuckle, roundleaf serviceberry (one shoot has double flowers and is now in cultivation), ninebark, and streambank mock-orange. If the spring weather was favorable, there may be a small patch of pale corydalis at the edge of the rock. Here and there on the rock face, eastern columbine and purple phacelia add color to the thick mats of drab-looking twisted-hair spikemoss. At first glance these mats look like perfect footholds for other plants, but they are not rooted in the rock and are frequently washed away in heavy downpours. Up until the late 1980s, there were Table Mountain pines on Exclamation Point—most of them were about 70 years old. All of them died during one summer after several years of severe drought.

Here the trail swings to the north side of the mountain and follows the upper edge of the cliffs, affording great views of the valley and manmade Lake Lure. The vegetation changes drastically due to the much harsher living conditions, reflected in the smaller size of the trees. Chestnut oak with a thick shrub layer of Carolina rhododendron dominates on the drier, very acidic sites. In depressions, the presence of red oaks and deciduous shrubs indicates moister conditions and "sweeter" (less acid) soils. On black, dripping ledges you can see a thriving ninebark-over-

Biltmore-sedge plant community; and chokecherry, rare in the Southern Appalachians, is found directly below. (The black rock is an amphibolite-hornblende gneiss, the source of the calcium that makes the thin soils here on the upper slopes exceptionally rich.) Above the boardwalk just before the rain shelter is a special community type with hop hornbeam (look for slender trunks with thin-scaly bark and birchlike leaves) over streambank mock-orange; eastern shooting star is one of the outstanding flowering herbs here. From Peregrine's Rest (near Stop 15) you will have your first good look at Hickory Nut Falls to your left. To your right and across the small creek (it may not run during dry times) is a patch of a grasslike plant known as deerhair bulrush. It has a circumpolar distribution and is very much at home on the arctic tundra. In North Carolina it had been known to occur only above 5,000 feet elevation until it was found here in the cool conditions of the wet rock faces at 2,000 to 2,500 feet—a low elevation record. At Stop 16 there is a close-up of a contact zone between the Henderson gneiss, below, and the mica schist, above. The slaty appearance of the rock is an indication of the heat that was created by the friction between the moving rock masses. At Stop 17 a few stately Carolina hemlocks, Southern Appalachians endemics, are firmly anchored in cracks in the rock underneath the trail. A little farther along the trail a tunnel of rosebay, also called bigleaf rhododendron, leads you toward the waterfall.

From Hickory Nut Falls (Stop 18), the Cliff Trail leads back toward the Chimney. Its main attractions are the imposing cliffs and the various rock formations. At Stop 19-A an erosional process, called exfoliation or sheeting, is clearly demonstrated. The hanging slabs are created over time by ever-enlarging cracks in the rock. Eventually the sheets fall off, forming the typical rounded shapes of granitic and gneissic mountains (think of Stone Mountain in Atlanta, Georgia, and Looking Glass Rock in Pisgah National Forest). Some of the water of Nature's Showerbath at Stop 20 comes from the intermittent creek next to Peregrine's Rest on the Skyline Trail. Inspiration Point (Stop 23) is the only place in the park from which you can see both Hickory Nut Falls (Figure 104) and Lake Lure. Here you may inspect Carolina hemlock (notice the wind-sheared shape) and sourwood, another Southern Appalachian endemic, at eye level. At Stop 26, you are at the base of the Rock Pile, an unusual rock formation known to geologists as a hoo doo. Take either the Subway or the Needles Eye down to the parking lot. Both offer examples of interesting rock formations. However, if you are fond of the art of Bonsai, climb the spiral staircase to the top of the Rock Pile to see Carolina hemlock, naturally sculpted by the wind.

Forest Stroll

To reach the bottom of Hickory Nut Falls, take the Forest Stroll, which follows the base of the cliffs. Its outstanding feature is the big trees, some of which are over three hundred years old. Do we have remnants of a virgin forest here? Old pictures

FIGURE 104. Hickory Nut Falls. (Photo courtesy of Chimney Rock Park)

show that Chimney Rock Park as a whole was logged, just like any other place in the mountains. But it seems that the upper reaches of these slopes may have been too difficult to harvest without a road, which wasn't built until 1915, after logging had been discontinued. Along the way notice how erosion is creeping up the slope by undercutting the vegetation. Several natural rock chutes cross the trail, an indication that the mountain is constantly changing. Different forest types are more obvious here than they are on the upper trails. When you cross a ridge, which is always drier than a gully, step to the edge of the trail and observe the big chestnut oaks that often have Carolina rhododendron thickets underneath. This unusual plant community is found only on the steepest, driest ridges on a very acidic soil. In the adjoining depressions you will see a canopy of tulip poplar, basswood, red oak, and eastern buckeye (near the waterfall) with wild hydrangea and other deciduous shrubs underneath. These are examples of cove hardwood forests, which need moister conditions and "sweeter" soils. As you arrive at the base of the waterfall, rest a bit and enjoy the cool draft—you deserve it. From here Falls Creek continues in rushing cascades until it joins the Broad River, 900 feet below.

On the way out of the park, stop on the Meadows to visit the Nature Center, which is entirely focused on Chimney Rock Park. An interesting exhibit shows scenes from earlier years and introduces you to the family that has owned the park since 1902.

B. Bat Cave Preserve

The Bat Cave Preserve, managed by the North Carolina Nature Conservancy, is located between Bat Cave and Chimney Rock, about 2 miles up the river from the latter. Typically, the preserve would be accessible in the summer on scheduled hikes or by special arrangement with the Durham, North Carolina, office. As of this writing, however, the preserve is closed due to the fact that on September 4, 1996, the bridge across the river was washed away in a devastating flood. To inquire about the possible reopening of the preserve contact The Nature Conservancy (919-403-8558).

Due to the lack of limestone in the state, North Carolina does not have as many caves as some other southern states. Linville Caverns is our only sizable limestone cavern. The Bat Caves, however, are fissure caves and are the largest in the state. Big Bat Cave is also the largest known fissure cave in the world, with more than 1 mile of passageways. Several species of bats hibernate in the protected recesses of the caves, among them the endangered Indiana bat. Two rare spiders and two rare salamanders are found in and near the caves.

This is another area that has a wide variety of habitats for plants and animals.

The rich cove forest here is a prime example of its type with a seemingly endless variety of spring wildflowers. A chestnut oak forest is found higher up on the slopes, and a Carolina hemlock community occupies the bouldery areas above the caves. Among the unusual plants are dissected toothwort, nodding trillium, green violet, bleeding heart, bladdernut, roundleaf serviceberry, and walking fern.

c. Bottomless Pools

About 1.5 miles east of Chimney Rock Park on the main road (US 64/74A), the Bottomless Pools are a small tourist attraction. In the town of Lake Lure, take a right at the bridge across Pool Creek. There is a big sign pointing the way.

The short trail under bigleaf rhododendron along Pool Creek reveals three large potholes filled with clear water and connected by waterfalls. Upstream, a smaller pothole is visible. These holes illustrate the process of erosion. They started out, thousands of years ago, as small depressions in the creek bed where several joints had fractured the rock, giving flowing water a chance to attack. Sand at first, and then ever larger pebbles and stones, washed down the creek in high floods, are swirled around by running water, grinding the rock away. The stones themselves are ground to sand and flushed out, ending up as sediment in Lake Lure.

Thanks to determined conservation efforts of the owners, many old trees have been preserved on the property. The tall white pines, eastern hemlocks, and red and white oaks around the small parking lot are what the "Blizzard of '93" left standing. These trees alone would make the Bottomless Pools worth a visit. White oak has become uncommon in this area, probably due to the fact that it was harvested for making whiskey barrel staves. Only farther back in the Pool Creek valley is white oak still found in any appreciable amount.

To close out a worthwhile visit to this interesting area, drive to the marina just up the valley at the upper end of the lake and try to catch a boat ride on Lake Lure, toward the end of the day if possible. Seeing the mountains backlit by the setting sun is the indisputable highlight of a visit to the area.

Blue Ridge Parkway Tour
Asheville to Cherokee

J. DAN PITTILLO

This 76-mile trip takes you across one of the most scenic ranges on the Blue Ridge Parkway, the Richland and Plott Balsams of the Southern Appalachian Mountains. It begins in the French Broad River valley within the Asheville-Hendersonville Basin, crosses the crest of the Balsam Mountains, and terminates in the Great Smoky Mountains at Cherokee. Along the way you will pass through fourteen tunnels, scale the cliffs near the Devils Courthouse, and experience a vegetational change equivalent to traveling from the Piedmont of North Carolina to the coast of Maine. The Blue Ridge Parkway is gently graded with ample, sweeping curves and is posted with a 45-mile-per-hour speed limit, so it will take you out of the hustle of interstate highways. The driving time for this distance is about two hours, but you should allow ample time for stops, brief hikes, and picture taking. Picking vegetation on the parkway is prohibited, so enjoy the plants with your camera in hand. Drive slowly so you can see the plants, pull off frequently to allow traffic to pass, and enjoy the trip!

There are few restrooms along this section of the Blue Ridge Parkway; the only ones available are about 1 mile north of Balsam Gap (on US 23), on US 276 at the Cradle of Forestry, at the Mount Pisgah area, and at Waterrock Knob. Only the Mount Pisgah area has fuel and a camp store, but stores and filling stations can be located off the parkway at Balsam Gap and east of Soco Gap. Most travelers will wish to spend half a day on this magnificent section of parkway across the core of the Southern Appalachians. Opened in the 1960s, it now provides numerous overlooks, a small visitors center at Waterrock Knob, and a restaurant, lodge, and campground at Mount Pisgah for an overnight stay, if desired.

Perhaps the most important lesson to be learned during this tour is the fact that nature is constantly changing. Information obtained from the peat in the bog near Mount Pisgah has given researchers insight into the changes that have taken place in the mountains over the past twelve thousand years. And you can observe changes in the forests that have been taking place within your lifetime. You will probably notice differences in forest composition between the lowlands and the highlands and will feel the weather change with elevation—temperatures cool as

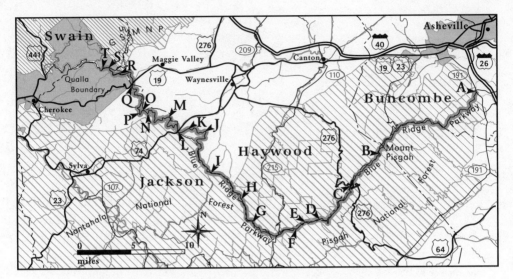

FIGURE 105. Blue Ridge Parkway tour route—Asheville to Cherokee

much as fifty degrees as you climb from about 2,100 feet in elevation to over 6,000 feet at the crest of Richland Balsam. You may also encounter patches of fog at different intervals in damp weather and see fog rising from the valleys after a rain, the basis for the term "smoky" in the Great Smoky Mountains range just west of Cherokee.

Follow Interstate 40 west of Asheville and turn south on Interstate 26 to the NC 191 exit (Exit 2); follow signs to the Blue Ridge Parkway. The parkway has numbered mileposts that will help in locating the parking areas described below. If you are coming from the west, go to Cherokee and continue north on US 441 to the Blue Ridge Parkway exit just inside the Great Smoky Mountains National Park. You would then follow the tour description in reverse.

A. North Carolina Arboretum and Sandy Bottoms

At the junction of the parkway, NC 191, and Bent Creek, at mile 393.6, an area apparently enriched by hornblende gneiss rocks has provided habitat for a rich diversity of plants. These can be seen from the mouth of the Blue Ridge Parkway's Shut-in Trail and along the floodplain of the French Broad River (Figure 106). This trail is reached by leaving the parkway and turning left on FR 479, then left again after 0.3 miles on FR 80, on which you will reach the trailhead parking area after about 500 feet. Among some interesting species here are southern nodding trillium, spring beauty, green dragon, and yellow oak, to name a few. Sandy

FIGURE 106. Floodplain of the French Broad River. (Photo by D. Pittillo)

Bottom Recreation Area is on NC 191 just south of the parkway junction. This is also important as a unique wildlife habitat and is a registered North Carolina Natural Heritage Area. A large portion of it was recently donated to The Nature Conservancy.

Along the French Broad River is a good location to observe water birds. Great blue herons, green-backed herons, wood ducks, spotted sandpipers, and belted kingfishers are often present. In addition, many warblers are often present during the breeding season—yellow-throated, northern parula, yellow, pine, and black-and-white warblers. Also there may be the common birds such as woodpeckers, flycatchers, blue jay, chickadees, and many others.

The entrance to the North Carolina Arboretum of the University of North Carolina is at the intersection of the Blue Ridge Parkway and NC 191. The arboretum, at a little over 2,000 feet elevation, extends from the mouth of Bent Creek westward and includes about 430 acres bisected by the creek. The site provides habitat for a significant number of native species, including a few rare ones. A modern visitors center and a plant propagating facility have been built on the western side of the arboretum. Extensive gardens accompany the area east of the visitors center, including the heritage quilt garden. A water garden is under development along Bent Creek, and an azalea garden occurs there along the floodplain. You could spend several hours walking and observing these gardens.

B. Mount Pisgah and Flat Laurel Gap

Return to the Blue Ridge Parkway and proceed to mile 407.4. A parking area located here near the Little Pisgah tunnel provides access to the 5,721-foot-elevation peak of Mount Pisgah. The 1.5-mile hike 700 feet up to the peak will take a couple of hours round-trip. The trail is moderate below but becomes steeper and more strenuous near the top. The local Asheville television tower occupies the summit, but a nearby viewing area gives an excellent 360-degree view of the Asheville-Hendersonville Basin and the Richland Balsam, Plott Balsam, Newfound, Walnut, Craggy, Black, and Blue Ridge Mountain ranges. If it is a clear day, you will be able to see Mount Mitchell atop the Blacks, and perhaps a portion of the Great Smokies beyond the Plott Balsams. In the gap below to the southeast is the Pisgah Inn and Flat Laurel Gap. The vegetation on the peak is pruned by the severe winds and ice storms that are prevalent at higher elevations. The damaging winds are mainly from the northwest, and you can note that tree tops trend toward the southeast as a result. Most of the trees on the slopes are oaks, but you will encounter a stunted beech forest near the peak. This beech forest, including its understory of the round-leaved galax, is rather unique. The peak itself is dominated by a mixture of heath shrubs with scattered trees, including serviceberry. During early June you may enjoy the deep pink of the purple rhododendron and perhaps the last of the spring's delicate pink mountain laurel blossoms (Figure 107). Brilliant flame azalea will also be blooming in June here. A dozen rare and endangered plants are found on this rugged peak.

High-elevation birds may be encountered along the trail, and the peak is a great place from which to observe spring and fall migration. The winter wren's gurgling song is often heard in the rhododendron thickets, though the bird itself is seldom seen. You may catch glimpses of the tiny golden-crowned kinglet, black-throated blue warbler, and Canada warbler. The ruffed grouse can be seen and is often heard, its low drumming lasting several seconds. Even the raspy voices of common ravens are commonplace here, and their aerobatic antics are a joy to behold.

One more mile farther south on the Blue Ridge Parkway, and about 740 feet lower in elevation, takes you to a site that has provided information on the past twelve thousand years of paleoecological history. A flat area of sediment dammed by a resistant rock mass to the west has evolved into a basin in which sediments and plant debris have accumulated over thousands of years. Bog vegetation and the associated layers of peat now sit here, at Flat Laurel Gap, next to a National Park Service campground. You can actually view the bog by taking a relaxing stroll through the campground, starting at the Pisgah store. Park in front of the lodge near the store or in the parking area at mile 407.8, where a trailhead is located opposite the parkway. The trail extends across from the store, and you may follow

FIGURE 107. Rhododendrons blooming on Mount Pisgah. (Photo by D. Pittillo)

the loops of the campground to the north and south of the Flat Laurel Gap bog. Researchers at the University of Tennessee and Western Carolina University have reconstructed the following scenario from studying pollen, other plant material, and sediments excavated from this bog site.

Around 12,000 years ago the permafrost associated with the last Ice Age melted. This area probably was covered by tundra vegetation—that is, mainly very low shrubs and no tall trees in a sparsely grassy area. Between 9,000 and 6,000 years ago, major deluges caused subsequent mass wasting of the slopes. This resulted in debris avalanches slumping into the flats and boulder fields sliding into the basin. (Note the large boulders left here from this event scattered at the junction of campground loops C and D.) In the muck at the center of the bog, pollen and prefossils indicate a continuous occupation of the site by heath species for the past 3,000 years, the longest heath record known for the Southern Appalachian region. Some of these species, such as leatherleaf and bog rosemary, have been extirpated from the site. The record also shows that Fraser fir disappeared in the late 1800s and American chestnut disappeared in the late 1930s.

Many bird species typical of high elevations are often seen or heard here. Winter wrens are commonly heard in the rhododendron thickets, and the haunting song of the veery often accompanies the arrival of evening and early morning in the campground. If you decide to camp here, you may hear, early in the morning or in the middle of the night, either the northern barred owl with its "who cooks for you" or the southern variety with its "who cooks for you-allll." In the parking lot of the Pisgah Inn, the American woodcock may be seen at twilight in March and April performing its aerial displays.

c. The Pink Beds and the East Fork Old Growth

A few more miles farther along in the southward direction on the parkway will bring you to another wet boggy site with an odd name. "The Pink Beds," named for the midsummer pink phlox that blooms here, is an unusually flat mountain valley that extends from Looking Glass Rock eastward to the gorge of the Mills River. This area is reached from the parkway, at mile 411.9, by driving south on US 276 toward Brevard for about 4 miles. Stop at the Pink Beds picnic area, where trails lead downstream. In this 2-mile-long flat valley, seepages have produced what is locally called Southern Appalachian "bogs." These are flat wetlands with scattered trees, shrubs, and ferns, and open gladelike areas dominated by grasses and sedges. Trails that radiate from the picnic area meander through the surrounding flat heathy woods. To the north is a loop trail through the area; to the south trails connect with the Cradle of Forestry, where an entrance fee is charged. A separate tour of the Cradle of Forestry and Pisgah National Forest is included in the next chapter of this book.

At mile 418.3 you will have an opportunity to pull off at an overlook from which you may observe a remnant old-growth forest. Most of the old-growth forests were cut from the mountains by the 1930s, but from the overlook here one can easily look down on a remnant of the former primeval forest that occupied the East Fork area. Note the snags of old trees and large specimens of eastern hemlock. The steep, rocky slopes opposite the overlook contrast sharply with the younger growth forest that can be seen further downstream.

d. Graveyard Fields Overlook

Graveyard Fields is the name given to this site because the large number of dead tree trunks on the ground looked like gravestones to early visitors. Today the site provides access to Yellowstone Creek and falls by following the trails downslope from the overlook parking area at mile 418.8 and turning right to Lower Yellowstone Falls or left (upstream) to Upper Yellowstone Falls. (The latter is reached by a hike of over 2 miles.) Successional scrub consisting of heath shrubs and small trees is found throughout the area. Pinkshell azalea and purple rhododendron give the entire area a pink cast in early May. Serviceberry is so abundant at this time that one might think the area is an old, overgrown apple orchard. Near the Upper

Yellowstone Falls several northern red oaks have begun to attain larger sizes. This is a very popular area and the parking may be limited.

Marcus Simpson has noted that the birds in this "hanging valley" (a tributary valley that enters another valley at some height above the floor) are a curious mixture of high-elevation and low-elevation species. A trail leads down to the flats where you may observe ruffed grouse, ruby-throated hummingbirds, downy and hairy woodpeckers, northern flickers, blue jays, common ravens, veerys, American robins, gray catbirds, cedar waxwings, solitary vireos, chestnut-sided warblers, black-throated blue warblers, Canada warblers, rose-breasted grosbeaks, rufous-sided towhees, and dark-eyed juncos.

E. Black Balsam Knob

The next stop is less than 2 more miles farther south on the parkway. The crest of Black Balsam Knob, reached from the paved U.S. Forest Service road (FR 816) at mile 420.2 and hiking up the Art Loeb Trail about 0.5 miles, is a good site from which to observe the Graveyard Fields area. Pisgah Ridge stretches to the northeast from here, and the crest to the north is Cold Mountain, which Charles Frazier made famous with his recent novel of the same name. Near the top of the knob (elevation 5,500 feet) you will notice charred stumps of the former spruce-fir forest that at one time covered this area. Following logging and subsequent fires in 1925 and again in the 1940s, this area was transformed into grass bald and scrub lands. Note that the swards of dominant grasses (hair grass) and sedges are occasionally punctuated with herbs such as wild celery or blackberry. If you are visiting the area when the wild celery is blooming, you might notice "drunken" bees wobbling over the flowers. Farther downslope shrubs become prominent, especially the heaths (rhododendrons, mountain laurel, blueberries, and others). In addition, trees are beginning to make a comeback, especially serviceberry, yellow birch, and mountain ash.

Many of the same birds noted at the Graveyard Fields stop are potentially visible here. In addition, alder flycatchers have taken up residence in the past couple of decades. From the peak, be on the lookout for common raven, northern harrier, and golden eagles. Even the northern goshawk and peregrine falcons have been reported from this vantage point.

F. Devils Courthouse and Mount Hardy

Rock outcrops represent one of the most important habitats for Southern Appalachian endemic plants and relict plant communities. At the Devils Courthouse (mile 422.4) you can view relict plants of the glacial period, such as deerhair bulrush (which turns the color of deerhair in fall) growing side by side with such endemics as fetterbush and mountain pieris. These exposures provide the open, full sunshine but cool habitats needed for species whose primary range is in the north. You may park at the Devils Courthouse Overlook (mile 422.1) and wander this area. Here in fall you can observe brilliant displays of mountain ash (fruits often hang on the trees after leaves have turned yellow and dropped), and you may hike up the steep trail to the cliffs. At any season, rock climbers frequent the area. The casual visitor, however, should not venture past the rock wall built by the National Park Service here: this is a dangerous place to "fool around."

The Devils Courthouse is probably the best location for observing saw-whet owls in the Southern Appalachians, according to Marcus Simpson. Here between dawn and dusk, from late March to June, often two or more can be heard and seen. A bright flashlight will be needed, and the best location to see them is at the sharp turn up the steep paved trail.

By stopping at Wolf Mountain Overlook (mile 424–25) you will be able to gain a view of the southern slopes of Mount Hardy, interesting for the outcrops that also provide habitat for a number of endemic species. In May there is a profusion of pinkshell azalea (in fall its leaves turn deep red in sun but yellow in shade), while in April fetterbush (the earliest flowering shrub) puts on a white show. In June this area is splashed in purple rhododendron. July is a good time to see yellow Blue Ridge dwarf dandelion and the cushionlike Blue Ridge St. John's wort. A stop at Wolf Mountain Overlook will provide close-up views of seepage cliff species, such as sundew, and in September one may see grass-of-parnassus rosettes, whose flowers have creamy white petals with green veins. At this same time, the deep blue hues of the closed gentians and monkshood give a gemlike quality to the flora. Be careful of the traffic at the overlook and along this part of the parkway.

In the gap below Mount Hardy is a good example of beech gap forest. This stand of nearly pure beech is undercarpeted, from April to July, with the light-green Pennsylvania sedge, which is replaced, by September, by the white snakeroot, the cause of "milksick" in early pioneers. If you have time, a footpath leads to the ridge and continues into the grass and heath balds of Fork Ridge, part of the Shining Rock Wilderness to the north.

G. Richland Balsam

At the parkway's Haywood-Jackson Overlook (mile 431) you will find a self-guided trail to the top of Richland Balsam. From this vantage point to the east, on a clear day you can see Pisgah Ridge and Mount Pisgah, from whence you came. On exceptionally clear days, the Black Mountains and Mount Mitchell are visible beyond Mount Pisgah. To the southwest the most prominent range is the Plott Balsams, and on the clearest days you might see the tips of the Great Smokies beyond. Up until the late 1970s, Richland Balsam Peak appeared nearly black from the valley below due to the "she balsams," or Fraser fir trees, dominating the forest. In the past, local herbalists referred to the Fraser fir as she balsam because they could "milk" the rosin from its bark blisters, whereas the "he balsam," red spruce, did not have these pustules. The Fraser fir forest here and in many other places in the North Carolina mountains was severely devastated in the late 1970s by an insect similar to an aphid—the balsam woolly adelgid. Only a few old trees survived for the past few decades, though numerous seedlings and saplings are now evident. The spruce trees have also been curtailed in vigor due to the pollution-laden clouds that bathe these peaks. The vegetation is undergoing a successional change, and there is a preponderance of blackberry, fire cherry, yellow birch, and mountain ash, making it appear quite scrubby.

At mile 431.4 you will be at the highest point of the Blue Ridge Parkway (6,050 feet). Here, at the Richland Balsam Parking Area, the extent of the death of the Fraser fir trees is most apparent. There is some indication that weakening of these trees resulted from air pollution effects on the soils, increasing the rate of the adelgid invasion. Some of the young trees are recovering, but most of the older, larger trees are dead.

H. Old Bald and Licklog Gap

Pull onto the right shoulder (off the pavement) at mile 434 and explore the meadows on the north side of the parkway. Many wildflowers (especially asters and goldenrods) can be observed among the extensive blueberry colonies (often producing brilliant red foliage in autumn). Cattle have been excluded from this area for over thirty years, but forests are much slower to reestablish in these challenging high-elevation environments.

Continue to mile 435.7, where a picnic area beckons you to pull off the parkway for another brief stop, this time at the Licklog Gap Overlook. To the north of the picnic area is an overgrown meadow. At the southwest end (opposite the picnic table) the Mountains-to-Sea trail parallels the parkway. To the south this trail crosses a periglacial boulder field with extensive colonies of false Solomon's seal and fancy wood-fern. To the west you will see extensive cove forest herbs (a word of caution: avoid the stinging nettle), and to the north the rock type changes and vegetation becomes sparse. There are buckeyes and yellow birches that exceed 2.5 feet in diameter on this fertile slope. Elevation here is about 5,365 feet; you have come down a little since the Richland Balsam Area.

I. Deep Gap and Steestachee Bald Boulder Fields

At mile 437 you will come to the Deep Gap Overlook (elevation 5,260 feet). As for many of the slopes of the high elevations, the site you will see here was apparently dominated by meadows in the past, perhaps within the last two hundred years. Note that some very large northern red oaks are flanked by generally shorter ones on both slopes near the gap. To get a close-up view of them, park at the Grassy Ridge Mine Overlook. If you would like to walk along the forested slope, the Mountains-to-Sea Trail can be entered just beyond the picnic table. July here is the most colorful, with many spring flowers, such as fire pink, blooming side by side with later summer ones, such as Carolina phlox.

Between mileposts 437.4 and 438.1 are five drainages filled with boulder fields created during past glacial periods. The Steestachee Bald boulder fields were actively moving during the glacial periods, when freeze-thaw action was breaking and moving large chunks of rock down from their source on the north-facing upper mountain slopes. The boulders vary in diameter from 1 foot to well over 6 feet. They are now covered with moss and vegetation, and the dominant tree growing among them is yellow birch. Consider why this might be so (hint: the germination and growth habits of yellow birch are different from other hardwood trees). There are several more typically northern species surviving in relict populations here, including the skunk currant and red raspberry.

J. Waynesville Overlook

One of the best places along the parkway from which to view fall foliage is the Waynesville Overlook, at mile 440.9. In middle to late April, across the roadway, you can see a colony of dwarf larkspur displaying a deep, royal purple. In October there are brilliant red and sugar maples near the overlook and scattered on the slopes below, creating brilliant red splashes among the yellows of the birches, striped maples, and mountain oaks (which turn later). This area is underlain by a fertile, basic soil, and sugar maples, white ash, black walnuts, buckeyes (along streams), beeches, northern red oaks, and bitternut hickories seem to grow well on this slope. These colorful slopes continue up Pinnacle Ridge of Wesser Bald as you pass from the Richland Valley around to the Allen Creek valley past the tunnel.

K. Redbank Cove, Standing Rock Overlook

Park at Standing Rock Overlook at mile 441.4 and walk across the parkway and down by the underpass to an old logging road. Continue up into the cove hardwoods. Dominant trees here include buckeye, American beech, sugar maple, basswood, northern red oak, and others. Especially large black cherry trees (flaky-looking bark) are also seen here. The understory herb layer is very diverse, with many especially showy spring flowers. The Mountains-to-Sea Trail crosses the stream at the point this logging road does. The trail traverses rich cove forests downhill and quickly enters drier, rocky heath uphill.

L. Balsam Gap

Balsam Gap, at mile 443.1 of the parkway, may be part of an ancient trench. The basic (greater than neutral pH) soils and the type of vegetation growing here suggest that it is underlain by limestone. Many locally rare plants occur here, such as glade spurge and Goldie's wood-fern. The site also harbors one of the ten populations of tall larkspur known to exist in North Carolina. This blue-flowered larkspur exceeds 6 feet in height and can be seen in full bloom in mid-July at the intersection of the connector to US 23/74. You have come down to 3,370 feet now, but will begin climbing again as you continue south on the parkway.

M. Mount Lynn Lowry Overlook

By mile 445 you have entered the Plott Balsams. From the Mount Lynn Lowry Overlook you are able to see the nearest peak, which is marked by a white cross, commemorating Lynn Lowry who was killed in an auto accident earlier this century. These forested slopes are particularly blessed with many rare species, including gnome lichen, saw-whet owl, brown creeper, golden-crown kinglet, and a ground beetle (*Trechus subtilus*), to name a few.

N. Woodfin Cascades Overlook

Stop at this overlook, at mile 446.7, and take a look across the valley to the north at the Woodfin Creek cascades. This site is on private land, and several homes can be seen from this area of the parkway. It also harbors several of the rare species mentioned for the last stop, in addition to an aquatic lichen.

O. Yellowface Overlook

Stop at the Yellowface Overlook (mile 450) and note that you have climbed to above 5,000 feet again. At this elevation (5,610, to be exact) you may notice that the trees are of smaller stature and the vegetation is more scrubby than you have been seeing below. This is due to devastating fires that followed timber clearing here around the turn of the century and in subsequent years. Yellowface and the eastern crest of the Plott Balsams from this point south to Sylva have recently been acquired by The Nature Conservancy; the property is to be transferred to the National Park Service, Blue Ridge Parkway, in coming years. You might notice that the rocks across the road now contain more mica—glittery flakes—than those you noted in the Richland Balsams to the east. As you cross over this crest, you move into a new group of rocks—part of the Great Smoky Group, a series of younger, metamorphosed sandstones and shales.

p. Waterrock Knob

Make a stop at mile 451.2, where you can visit a small visitors center on Waterrock Knob. This 5,718-foot peak is one of the gems for rare plants and animals in this region. Rare species, in addition to those earlier listed for Mount Lynn Lowry, include pinkshell azalea, Clingman's hedge-nettle, northern flying squirrel, and the avenger helix snail. You might enjoy the vigorous hike up the trail from the visitors center to the peak of Waterrock Knob, where you will have a 360-degree view of the Balsams, Blue Ridge, and Cowee ranges to the south and east, the Blacks (with Mount Mitchell) to the northeast on the clearest days (this is over 50 miles away), and the Smokies to the west and southwest.

q. Woollyback Overlook

Heath thickets or "balds" often cover the thin-soiled ridges at higher elevations. You will have a good view of such a bald at the overlook at mile 452.3. The site consists of a few trees and a thick cover of heath shrubs, mainly rhododendrons, mountain laurel, and blueberries. Local names for such places are "woollybacks" or "laurel/rhododendron hells/slicks." For anyone trying to traverse these thickets, "woolly" and "hell" seem appropriate adjectives. Black bears often frequent such sites, where they find it easy to dig into the thick duff mat to obtain bumblebee honey and larvae or yellow jacket larvae. Their thick fur protects them from the stings of these bees. Heath balds can be quite colorful when the bushes are in flower in early June.

r. Soco Gap

Soco Gap, at mile 455.7, is nearly 1,000 feet higher than Balsam Gap and provides the alternate route between Asheville and Cherokee: US 19 crosses the Blue Ridge here. Maggie Valley, known for years as the gateway to the Smokies for North Carolinians, occurs just to the east of this gap.

s. Plott Balsam Overlook

The overlook at mile 457.9 is a good vantage point for views of the north side of the Plott Balsams. Waterrock Knob is just to the immediate left, and the parkway crosses between Waterrock Knob and Yellowface, the peak to the right (south). Blackrock is the next highest peak to the south, followed by the long Pinnacle Bald and, finally, Perry Top before the ridges taper down to the Tuckasegee River valley at Sylva. us 19 can be seen below as it descends from Soco Gap toward Cherokee.

t. Heintooga Spur and Balsam Mountain Road

The Heintooga Ridge spur road at mile 458.2 connects the Blue Ridge Parkway with the Great Smoky Mountains National Park at Spruce Mountain. If you drive 1.3 miles down the spur you will come to a mile-high overlook, from which good views of Cherokee can be obtained. It is also an access point for a trail to Cataloochee Valley, but this would require a daylong hike of over 8 miles. The overlook is reached by just a short walk. Continue about 8 more miles to a picnic area at Balsam Mountain, where the forest is dominated by red spruce. A 27-mile one-way graveled road from here connects with Cherokee through the Big Cove Community, or you can return to the parkway and drive the remaining 10 miles to the southern terminus of the road, which intersects with us 441 in the Great Smoky Mountains National Park. Information on the park is provided in another chapter of this book.

Our Forest Heritage and Forestry Today

CINDY CARPENTER

This 27.5-mile tour takes you through the mountain valleys and coves of Transylvania County southeast of the Blue Ridge Parkway. You will see mixed hardwood forests with many species of trees, shrubs, wildflowers, and ferns. Roadside pull-outs invite you to stop to hear, and often see, a variety of birds and other animals along the route. You will also see areas managed for multiple uses and the implementation of several forest regeneration techniques. The tour circles Looking Glass Rock, a dramatic granite dome, and passes peaceful forest and streamside scenes, including Looking Glass Falls, a 60-foot vertical drop with a massive granite shelf towering above it. All along the route are trails to explore, and walks are suggested on many of them. For example, along the Pink Beds Trail on the route back to the parkway, you will see unique forest and bog communities and evidence of beaver activity on the banks of a scenic mountain river.

You will find two conservation education centers along this forest heritage tour, and both are worthwhile stops. Exploring the Cradle of Forestry in America Historic Site in the Pink Beds valley can significantly enhance your trip; the site is open from April through October. Here you will find easy wooded trails to historic cabins and a 1915-vintage steam locomotive. The Forest Discovery Center at the Cradle of Forestry presents interactive exhibits on forestry history, ecosystems, and forest management today. The Pisgah Center for Wildlife Education, another stop on the tour, offers indoor exhibits that focus on aquatic habitats across North Carolina. An outdoor exhibit area consists of eight learning stations focusing on wildlife management and protection, fish culture, and conservation education; these consist of interactive displays, audio exhibits, and hands-on activities. The center is open year-round except for Christmas, Thanksgiving, and New Year's Day.

The major learning experience of this tour is the opportunity to discover the relationship of forest resources to traditions of mountain living, the evolution of this relationship during the early days of the conservation movement, and the modern management practices carefully tailored to produce the forests of tomorrow. Let the scenery of today provoke your imagination to picture landscapes of

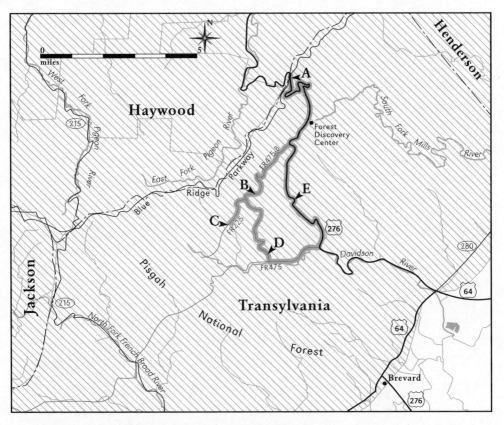

FIGURE 108. Forest heritage tour route—Transylvania County

the past—a past revealed by evidence of human occupation in the Davidson River valley and the Pink Beds for over four thousand years. More recently this land was kept open for livestock grazing and small-scale farming. Sunny fields of wild phlox gave the Pink Beds valley its romantic name, though these are now succeeded by a variety of trees, mountain laurel, and buckberry bushes. If you stop at the Cradle of Forestry you can learn the background history of the land, now public but once owned by George Vanderbilt. The area included in this tour was part of the 100,000-acre estate he purchased in the 1890s. Vanderbilt was the first landowner in America to hire a forester to manage his land and its resources. He hired Gifford Pinchot to serve as the forester at his Biltmore Estate from 1891 to 1895. Later, in 1905, Pinchot became the first chief of the U.S. Department of Agriculture's Forest Service. Carl Alwin Schenck, who started the first forestry school in America in 1898, succeeded Pinchot at Biltmore. The buildings, fields, and forests of the Pink Beds became the Biltmore Forest School's summer campus. Now renamed the Cradle of Forestry, the site exists today to further understanding of forest resources and their management, and to further enjoyment of the forest itself. For information on interpretive activities at the time of your visit call 828-877-3130.

After being exposed to the history and principles of forestry today, let the scenery along Forest Service roads (FR) 475-B and 225 provoke your imagination to picture future landscapes. To consider the condition of future forests—this is the major contribution of the forestry profession. During the late nineteenth century, when the nation's population was growing and demands on natural resources were expanding, the concept of nurturing the land so the forest can replace the trees removed was a new idea. Modern forestry is based on concepts of natural dynamics such as competition, mineral cycling, and succession, as well as an understanding of the need to extract some natural resources (wood) and to have places for outdoor recreation. The information given here only scratches the surface of all that is involved in planning harvests and managing ecosystems over time. If you view the sites along this tour with an analytical eye, you will receive a good introduction to the silvicultural techniques currently in use.

Pisgah National Forest's resources are managed in a variety of ways. Small tracts of timber are cut to provide hardwood lumber and to create openings for wildlife and young trees. Values considered are wood resources, clean water, protected soil, recreation experiences, game and nongame wildlife species, wilderness, cultural resources, old growth, threatened, endangered, and sensitive plants and animals and their habitats, and aesthetics. Along the route of this tour you will get a sense for the complexities of forest management today. You will see examples of group selection cuts, clear-cuts, and two-age shelterwood areas. You will also be exposed to a variety of recreational opportunities.

The North Carolina Wildlife Resources Commission establishes hunting and fishing regulations in the national forest. Some streams in the forest are stocked with trout raised at the Pisgah Fish Hatchery. At the Pisgah Center for Wildlife Education you can learn about aquatic habitats and fisheries across the state of North Carolina, wildlife management, conservation education, and fish culture. For more information on wildlife education programs at the time of your visit call 828-877-4423.

In keeping with nearby routes in this book, this forest heritage tour starts from the Blue Ridge Parkway on US 276 South toward Brevard. This tour can be easily accessed from the towns of Waynesville and Pisgah Forest near Brevard via US 276, from Asheville via Interstate 26 and NC 280 to US 276, and from Hendersonville via US 64 West.

A. Blue Ridge Parkway to the Cradle of Forestry

Exit the Blue Ridge Parkway at milepost 412 onto US 276 near the Cold Mountain Overlook. The road winds 4 miles down the mountain to the Pink Beds valley. Just past the Pink Beds Picnic Area on the left you may notice a lovely cabin and another building on the right. A bit farther on the left is the entrance gate to the Cradle of Forestry and the Forestry Discovery Center. Here you can get more information about where you will be traveling and find a detailed map (in the gift shop) of the area's features and recreation opportunities. When the Cradle of Forestry site is closed, you may park outside this gate and walk in to access the trails. This is a fee area during the open season, and the proceeds go directly to visitor services and maintenance of the site and its cultural resources.

B. FR 475-B to FR 225

The entrance to FR 475-B is not quite a mile from the Cradle of Forestry entrance gate. FR 475-B was historically called Headwaters Road. This was the main travel route from the heavily inhabited Davidson River valley and the towns of Brevard and Pisgah Forest to the Pink Beds valley and beyond. Part of the original draw road (so named because they followed creeks or "draws") can still be seen along the Biltmore Campus Trail at the Cradle of Forestry. Settlers drove livestock along this road from highland pastures to markets in South Carolina before the railroad came to Asheville in the 1880s. Today this gravel road provides access to Looking Glass Rock Scenic Area, timber management areas, and hiking, biking, primitive camping, and rock-climbing opportunities. It has only one lane, but frequent turnouts facilitate passing cars coming from the opposite direction. The road is not suitable for large vehicles, and it is sometimes closed during periods of heavy rain. Other than that it is a pleasant, though slow, 6.5-mile drive and gives you a sense of adventure and discovery away from the main highway. Once you are on the road, set your mileage counter to zero.

This part of the Pisgah Ranger District is managed for timber production, though the specific approaches are modified to emphasize visual quality and wildlife benefits. As set by the Forest Management Plan, the planned number of years between the start of timber regeneration and its final cutting (called the rotation) is 120 years. Habitat focus is for bear and other tree-denning animals such as owls, raccoons, squirrels, and bats. Recreation opportunities outside of developed areas abound.

When a timber sale is planned the Forest Service decides which trees are to be cut and which are to remain. Most of the timber is purchased by local sawmills, which sell lumber to the North Carolina furniture and building industries.

At mile 0.5 look to your left at an area that was clear-cut in 1992. (There is a small turnout on the right by a large red oak.) This stand was "born" in 1913 when the previous cut was made. There was serious oak decline here in 1992, and the Forest Service decided to harvest the trees while they were still merchantable. At mile 1.1 is a lovely stand of mixed hardwoods, which was commercially thinned in 1978. The goal of this thinning activity is not to regenerate new trees, but to add volume to the existing trees (reducing competition) until they reach rotation age. These "residuals" have been growing since 1883 and will be ready for harvest in 2003.

Red oak, chestnut oak, tulip poplar, and hickory are dominant species here. Typical associates are red maple, white ash, basswood, and mountain and cucumber magnolias. Dominant trees are those that affect the environment around them (for instance, by allowing a certain amount of sunlight to reach smaller plants) enough to determine what will grow nearby. Some species can tolerate full sunlight; others need the shady shelter of taller trees to become established. When planning harvests, the forester plans for regeneration and for specific desired dominant species, considering wildlife benefits as well.

After a hairpin turn at about mile 1.8, on the left you will see a clear-cut from 1982, now with young trees. This was a "firewood cut" during a time of high demand for fuelwood, when there was an oil shortage. Individuals selected by lottery could purchase up to two cords for $20. The Forest Service sold over 1,000 permits during a two-month period. The program lasted about five years. Firewood permits are still sold for dead and downed wood and some standing dead trees, but the demand has greatly decreased.

Good winter views of Looking Glass Rock are at mile 2.4. On the left at mile 2.9 is a mountain laurel "slick." This is an old farm field where no vegetation management is going on; what you see has grown back naturally. Years of plowing in the past with no erosion control has created a situation unsuitable for tree regeneration. Most regeneration in the national forest is natural from stump sprouts and seedlings. Trees are sometimes planted where regeneration of desired species needs a boost, and to introduce new quality genes to the ecosystem's diversity. On average, the Forest Service plants about two thousand hardwood trees annually (red and white oaks, black cherry, persimmon) and some white pines, with various rates of survival.

At mile 3.1 and the intersection of FR 225 (Upper Cove Creek Road) reset your mileage to zero. This side trip is a bit more adventurous than 475-B, the road being narrower and less traveled but usually in good shape. Several trailheads provide turnaround space if you don't want to drive the whole road. It is about 2.3 miles to a gate at the end, where there is room to turn around and backtrack.

C. FR 225

At 0.2 miles is a regenerating 18-acre clear-cut on the right from 1982. You are driving across the top of the cut. In 1983 the site was prepared for new trees by removing everything that would interfere with regeneration. In 1991 the Forest Service did a "precommercial thinning." In this treatment the tree sprouts and seedlings that should reach rotation age are selected and others are weeded out to give room to the crop trees.

At mile 0.3 is an older clear-cut from 1968 on the left. This immature stand is to be commercially thinned around the year 2008 to add volume to the tulip poplars and white pines. Tulip poplars typically dominate a clear-cut in cove sites with deep moist soils. They are fast growers when given plenty of sun. In this way they have filled a niche the American chestnut left behind when its dominance ended with the chestnut blight. In the days of Pinchot and Schenck, one out of every four trees was a chestnut. Valued for its wood and its tannin-rich bark, this tree was important to the economy and way of life wherever it thrived. It was also extremely valuable to black bear, turkey, deer, and other wildlife that depended on its protein-rich nuts. Flowering in June, well after danger of frost, the chestnut provided a more reliable source of hard mast food than oaks. The chestnut is not extinct, as stump sprouts still grow in the forest understory, but it is unusual for a tree to attain good size and produce viable nuts before succumbing to the persistent blight. Much research is being conducted to produce a chestnut hybrid with both American chestnut genes and blight resistance.

To produce hard mast for wildlife and valuable saw timber, the regeneration of oaks is quite important to forest planners. A regeneration technique widely used is the "two-age shelterwood." An example of this, created in 1993, is on both sides of the road at mile 0.4. Mature trees are cut, but a percentage of older trees are left to soften visual disturbance and provide hard mast until young trees produce nuts. To control the regeneration of maples, silverbells, and dogwoods—understory trees that would outcompete young oaks—the stump sprouts of these species are treated with herbicide injected directly into specific stems. This chemically girdles them and they die the next year.

Also at this milepost you may notice blue bands painted on three trees. These are witness trees identifying a songbird monitoring plot. From 1997 till 2002, this U.S. Forest Service Regional Land Bird Survey will gather baseline data on population trends in the South. There are forty plots of various forest types and ages on the Pisgah Ranger District of the national forest.

On the left at mile 0.7 is a "group selection cut," done in 1994. The last time trees were harvested here was in 1920, which therefore is considered the birth year of this stand. This is one of twenty-one group selection cuts of 0.25 to 1 acre in size being selectively managed over 120 years. Using this uneven age technique, eight cutting cycles are planned over that time. Every fifteen years the Forest Service will cut several groups of trees in this 95-acre area. The maximum size of the opening in a group selection cut is one to two times the average height of the dominant mature trees. Group cuts are spaced about 100 feet apart. Here hickories are among trees that will supply hard mast to wildlife. Grapevines provide year-round food for black bear, turkey, grouse, deer, and songbirds. Just before mile 1.0 on the right is a smaller group cut. A gated road on the left, the Caney Bottom Extension, offers a pleasant hike or bike ride.

A little farther down the road on the right at about mile 1.2 is a regenerating clear-cut from 1979. This is being managed so that tulip poplar, white oak, and red oak will be dominant. Herbicide treatment of undesired sprouts (precommercial thinning) was done in 1993. At that time foresters found a number of butternut trees resistant to and tolerant of a canker disease that is seriously threatening this native species. These trees are a genetic bank managed as a seed source to repopulate butternut in the South.

On the left at about mile 1.4 is another group selection cut. You may notice a large oak with a blue band painted on it. This sets the tree aside as a wildlife den tree. Oaks, magnolias, and sourwood are among species you will see here. All along the road and running perpendicular to it, "stringers" of uncut trees, including beautiful eastern hemlocks, mark riparian areas and protect water quality.

On both sides of the road at about mile 1.7 you may notice a sparse midstory with a dappled appearance on sunny days. This stand originated in 1890. In 1993 foresters wanted to start encouraging northern red oak regeneration on this high-quality site. They removed red maple, dogwood, sourwood, and silverbell from the lower canopy, creating partial shade that limits competition. This "shelterwood" method of giving young red oaks a chance was developed at the U.S. Forest Service's Bent Creek Forest Experiment Station near Asheville. For fifty years research has been conducted there to determine the consequences of various regeneration techniques in different forest situations.

It takes fifteen years for a northern red oak to grow 4 to 5 feet tall. Once the roots are well established and the tree is in this stage of advanced regeneration it grows fast and can compete with other understory plants. When 30 percent of the stand consists of oaks in this stage, the overstory must be removed using the most suitable harvest method for the site. The timing of this release is critical, because the oaks will die if they are suppressed at an age when trees need more sunlight. If they get the sunlight, they can compete with young, sun-loving, soft mast trees like red maple and tulip poplar. The average genetic lifespan of a northern red oak is about 120 years; a white oak can reach 400 years.

At the end of the gated road (mile 2.3) is another stand from 1890, thinned in 1977 to allow crop trees to grow larger. You may notice a thick understory here. In the increased light resulting from the thinning, soft mast species are regenerating better than the hard mast trees. The midstory treatment used in the previous stand was not used here. A closer look at regeneration in this stand is necessary before further cutting to be sure there is a good hard mast component. As at the previous site, the desired future condition here is for a sustained source of hard mast for wildlife.

FIGURE 109. Looking Glass Rock looms above a forest regeneration area. (Photo courtesy of U.S. Forest Service)

All along this road you have seen a mosaic of group selection cuts, clear-cuts, two-age shelterwoods, oak shelterwoods, and uncut areas. Every opening invites a new age class, desirable for sustainability. Scheduled harvests produce a variety of habitats over space and time. The timber management program paid for this road and others like it that provide access to backcountry for recreation opportunities, wildlife programs, and fire, search, and rescue emergencies. Enjoy the forest on the way back to Headwaters Road. Watch for glimpses of Looking Glass Rock along the way (Figure 109). Once you are back on Headwaters Road, reset your mileage counter before turning right.

D. Headwaters Road Lower Section to US 276

At mile 0.3 from the intersection of FR 225 watch on the left for a parking space and a view of Looking Glass Rock. This rock is very popular with climbers of all ability levels. Some climbing routes on this side of the mountain are closed when peregrine falcons nest. From this vantage point you may see the falcons on the hunt. At mile 0.5 is the Sunwall Trail to the bottom of the rock, a heavily used access point for climbers. Enjoy the drive through this area of woodland scenery. At mile 2.3 on the left are a small waterfall (sometimes almost dry), Slickrock Falls, and another popular trail to the base of the rock. Remember that waterfalls are slippery and therefore dangerous, even without a large volume of water. This one is well named to help you remember that risk. At mile 3.4 the road intersects with FR 475. Near here is the original location of a Black Forest Lodge. Two local craftsmen built at least a dozen of these unique cabins at the turn of the twentieth century to house Dr. Schenck's rangers. Turn left, and the road quickly becomes paved at the Pisgah Center for Wildlife Education.

The Center for Wildlife Education is located at the base of John Rock. A Civilian Conservation Corps camp was located on this site in the 1930s, as were farms and Native American settlements before that. Several hiking trails through this scenic area are accessible from the center's parking lot.

Continuing on the paved road, a spur of the Forest Heritage National Scenic Byway, you are paralleling the Davidson River, a famous trout stream. At mile 4.5 on the left is the trailhead for the Looking Glass Rock Trail, a 3.1-mile climb to a sweeping view of the area you have just traveled through.

At the stop sign turn left to continue north on US 276 and climb back up to the Pink Beds and the Blue Ridge Parkway. There are several picnic tables and turnouts along the road. Reset your mileage counter one more time.

E. US 276 North to the Blue Ridge Parkway

Most of this 10-mile section runs beside beautiful Looking Glass Creek (Figure 110). From the early 1900s to the 1930s, a logging railroad to the Pink Beds occupied the current road bed. Just ahead is Looking Glass Falls on the right. Steps take you to the bottom of the falls where you can feel the mist. At 1.3 miles is a trail to the bottom of Moore Cove Falls. This easy 1.5-mile round-trip walk goes through a lovely cove that is full of wildflowers in the spring. A mile farther on US 276 is the famous Sliding Rock Recreation Area, a natural rock slide where you can cool off or watch others slide. This can be a congested area in the summer.

Above Sliding Rock the forest understory is less dense and allows views farther into the forest. In the winter you can catch glimpses of nearby mountain ridges. Birches, hemlocks, mountain magnolias, and tulip poplars are common here. Near mile 3.3 look for a V-shaped wooden structure in the creek that creates a pool, where high levels of dissolved oxygen and substrate for macroinvertebrates provide trout with what they need. Hurricane Opal naturally created this habitat in October 1995 when it caused many trees and branches to fall into the creek farther up the road. Woody debris at least 9 inches in diameter is valuable to a healthy stream ecosystem and is part of riparian area management.

At mile 5.0 you have circled Looking Glass Rock and are once again at the beginning of Headwaters Road and the Pink Beds valley. The Forest Discovery Center is about 1 mile on the right, and the Pink Beds Picnic Area and trailhead are 0.25 miles farther. If you have a few hours, grab your map for a pleasant walk on

FIGURE 110. Looking Glass Creek—a peaceful scene along the Forest Heritage Scenic Byway. (Photo courtesy of U.S. Forest Service)

this loop trail. Depending on the activity level of beavers and rainfall, you may or may not be able to make the full 5-mile loop, but a shorter loop is available. Beavers arrived in the valley in 1993 and dammed the South Mills River. Over the years the increased sunlight from tree mortality has changed the vegetation. The wetland thus created provides habitat for a diversity of species and an open scenic area reminiscent of the West.

At mile 9.9 you are back on the ridge and can get on the Blue Ridge Parkway again or continue on the Forest Heritage National Scenic Byway toward Waynesville. Now in Haywood County, the byway exits the Pisgah National Forest, travels through rural communities, turns onto NC 215 South, and enters the national forest again between the Middle Prong and Shining Rock Wilderness Areas, where you will find many stream and mountain views. NC 215 intersects the Blue Ridge Parkway and continues south along the byway into Transylvania County to join US 64 west of Brevard. More woodland and rural scenery can be enjoyed along the way.

Cherohala Skyway to Joyce Kilmer Forest

J. DAN PITTILLO

This 18-mile tour provides some of the best views of the Southern Appalachians across the Unicoi Mountains just south of the Great Smoky Mountains. In many respects this tour matches the stunning views characteristic of the Blue Ridge Parkway as it crosses the Balsam Mountains between Asheville and Cherokee—a route described earlier in this book. Views of "mountains piled upon mountains" provide the dynamic relief that approaches 5,000 feet elevation, with the lowest valleys visible around 1,900 feet and the highest peak in the Smokies over 6,600 feet. The forests here range from cove hardwood and hemlock forests on the valley floors to mixed oak and pine forest of the lower slopes and weather-pruned northern hardwoods at the higher elevations, mainly those above 4,500 feet elevation. One may encounter animals—bear, deer, raccoons, foxes, turkeys, grouse—or perhaps brilliant fall leaf colors or pastel spring accents on the surrounding ridges. There are occasional exposed rocks composed of metamorphosed sandstones, slates, and schists.

The recently completed Cherohala Skyway has mile markers that start on the Tennessee line and end at Big Santeetlah Gap (the mileages are listed for each location, with the reverse mileage given in parentheses). Just north of Santeetlah Gap is Joyce Kilmer Memorial Forest, established in 1936 as a 3,800-acre primeval forest from which timber has never been removed; the forest is a part of the Joyce Kilmer–Slickrock and Citico Wilderness. To fully appreciate this driving tour, you should really stop at Joyce Kilmer and take a short hike through the grove of big trees at Poplar Cove. You should allow about two or three hours to visit Joyce Kilmer and another couple of hours to drive the Cherohala Skyway. The driving distance is a little under 40 miles round-trip, but the elevation gain from the base of Joyce Kilmer to the top of Hooper Bald is 5,429 feet.

This tour allows you to look backward at the mountains' glacial past: as you cross some of the most elevated landscapes of North Carolina you will see plants adapted to cooler climates that existed throughout the South 18,000 years ago. Botanists usually call the forests in this region "northern hardwoods" because they have many of the same species that are found in forests in the northern states and

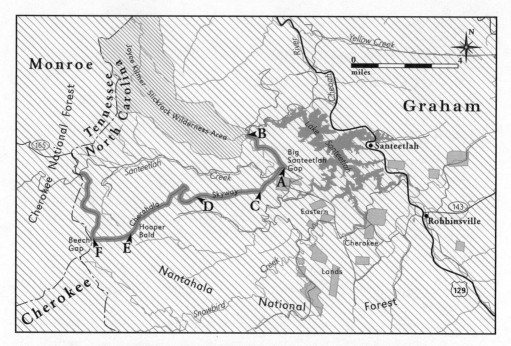

FIGURE 111. Cherohala Skyway to Joyce Kilmer Memorial Forest tour route

southern Canada. Our southern highlands, however, contain many species that have become locally adapted, and so we call them "endemics." So the total flora composition here differs from that of true northern hardwoods. At this latitude and elevation the vegetation does not include the more northern spruce-fir forest. However, paleoecologists have found evidence that both spruce and jack pine did extend to this location, and a little farther south into northern Georgia, during full glacial times. You will also learn about the effects that the weather at these higher elevations have on the vegetation, where the trees become deformed into krum-holtz or flag-formed shapes, often indicating the direction of the prevailing winds.

Most of the region was covered in primeval forests until the turn of the century. Babcock Lumber Company was logging the area to the north between 1915 and 1922, when it was forced to cease operations because Calderwood Reservoir was built along the railroad route. This area is the original site of introduction of the renowned "Russian boar." Five species of big game animals were initially introduced into the Hooper Bald game preserve in 1912. Only the boar remains.

The best way to reach this region is to follow Interstate 40 west of Asheville to the Waynesville and Sylva exit (Exit 27). Then follow the four-laned US 74 west to Alarka, where it meets NC 28. From here follow the two-laned NC 28 to NC 143, and follow the signs north via Robbinsville to Santeetlah Gap, where the Cherohala Skyway begins. If you are driving from Murphy, follow US 19 to Topton and continue to Robbinsville on US 129. In Robbinsville, intercept NC 143 and continue as above. This road (NC 143) connects with the Tellico Plains Road (TN 165) into Tennessee at Beech Gap on the Tennessee border.

A. Big Santeetlah Gap

Pull off at the overlook and information station at Big Santeetlah Gap, mile 17.8 (0) of the Cherohala Skyway. View to the north the valley of Joyce Kilmer Memorial Forest. In the foreground is Horse Cove Ridge. Strawberry Knob is to the far left (west), and Stratton Bald, at 5,341 feet, is on the horizon to the north, with Haoe Bald (5,249 feet) and Haoe Lead forming the margin of the basin. At this gap you are at 2,680 feet elevation. Consider turning back and driving down to the left (north), following signs 2.3 miles to the Joyce Kilmer picnic area, and hiking up to Poplar Cove.

B. Joyce Kilmer Memorial Forest

At the parking area for Joyce Kilmer Memorial Forest you will find restrooms with flush toilets during summer and chemical toilets during freezing weather. Picnic tables are also provided for those wishing to have lunch here.

Elevation is 2,200 feet at the entrance and 2,600 at the top of the loop. Two loop trails begin at the parking area and offer views of the lush, mature cove forest here (Figure 112). It will take about one or two hours to hike this moderate-to-easy loop trail and enjoy the scenery. The Poplar Cove contains some of the largest yellow poplars (also called tulip trees or tulip poplars) in the forest. There are some trees that have trunks over 6 feet in diameter and that are well over 100 feet tall. At the juncture of the figure-8 loop is a Canadian hemlock that is approximately 4 feet in diameter. It stands tall above the bronze plaque commemorating the poet Joyce Kilmer, who was killed during World War I. There are large American beeches, magnolias, sugar maples, mountain silverbells, basswoods, oaks, and hickories that add to one of the greatest plant diversities of any deciduous forest found in the world. The forest floor is carpeted early in spring with many flowers—spring beauty, trout lily, trilliums, violets, blue cohosh, hepatica, windflower, dwarf ginseng, buttercups—and later with overtopping summer herbs—ferns, sedges, cohosh, and little dolls' eyes.

You are likely to encounter birds here, especially in late spring when the Neotropical migrants return and begin to nest. You may hear the melodious gurgling of winter wrens in the rhododendron thickets, repetitive melodies of the vireos in the trees, and the many kinds of twittering that signal the presence of the warblers that inhabit these old-growth forests. The presence of Neotropical bird migrants is one of the important features of Joyce Kilmer Forest. Warblers—including black

FIGURE 112. Large trees in Joyce Kilmer Memorial Forest. Note downed chestnut log. (Photo by D. Pittillo)

and white, black-throated blue, chestnut-sided, hooded, and Canada—are especially notable here beginning in April as they return from the tropics and begin to nest. One of my favorite songs is uttered by the wood thrush, which is sometimes called the nightingale because it occasionally bursts into song late at night.

Evidence of black bears, bobcats, mink, raccoons, and gray squirrels has been observed in the forest here. You might see tracks of any of these in the mud along the trails. Black bears sometimes forage in the area, though you are more likely to see clawed-up logs or yellow jacket nests where they enjoyed a feast on the young grubs. (If you do come upon a nest of yellow jackets, try to avoid it; they are the cause of the greatest number of injuries sustained in the forests of the region.) Wild boars are frequent here because this is where boars trapped in the Great Smoky Mountains, just to the north, are released. Bobcats, skunks, and deer are also rather common in the area but are not usually seen during daylight hours.

If you drive a little farther, to mile 15.8 (2.0), you will come to a picnic area high on the ridge overlooking the region.

c. Camera Photo Point

After a hike and a picnic, you can return to the Cherohala Skyway, but for less than a mile. Stop at the overlook at mile 14.7 (3.2). Starting from the left (west) is

Stratton Bald, with Haoe Bald and Haoe Lead making up the middle ridges. Down in the foreground is Horse Cove Ridge, where even-age timber management is being carried out. The U.S. Forest Service manages the forest here by several methods, but in the most recent one they have cut small blocks (1–3 acres), leaving the larger trees between to be cut at a later date. In these cleared blocks, most trees, for instance oaks, resprout and regrow valuable trees in about eighty years. Other trees, such as tulip poplar (notice there is more of this species in these forested areas than in uncut ones), grow from seeds. At higher elevations black cherry is one of the most valuable timber species. Farther back on the horizon are the Great Smoky Mountains, beginning with Gregory Bald at 13 miles and, on the clearest days, Mount LeConte in Tennessee at 35 miles distance at the far right.

D. Wright Creek Old-Growth Hemlock and Hooper Bald Overlook

Stop at mile 12.3 (5.5) for a fine view of old trees. Grand old-growth Canadian hemlock forest occupies the valley along Wright Creek below to the right (Figure 113). Canadian hemlocks, the eastern counterpart of the better known western hemlocks, live to be nearly 1,000 years old (the record is 988 years, and 600 years is often attained). They often exceed 150 feet in height and 6 feet in trunk diameter in this region. Here, in the less protected higher elevations, these trees probably are closer to 100 feet tall and perhaps 200 to 300 years old. Nonetheless, their festoons of old-man's beard lichens (*Usnea* species) give them an ancient appearance among the younger beeches, birches, and other deciduous trees. There is some concern that these metaphors of the ancient Appalachians may be in jeopardy, just as our Fraser fir forests have been during the past couple of decades. The hemlock woolly adelgid is progressing down the Appalachian chain and now has reached the North Carolina border at Virginia. This may be a scene you will wish to photograph for posterity.

The Cherohala Skyway continues its ascent another 1,200 feet to the mile-high Hooper Bald. This is one of the most scenic sections of the tour. Much of the roadway through this region cuts through a highly acidic sulfurous rock known as Anakeesta schist. Excavations through this formation and exposure of the rock allows release of significant amounts of acidic water into the streams. This was discovered when a section of US 441 was constructed across the Great Smoky Mountains National Park in the 1960s. To correct for this, the rock must be carefully covered with soil to prevent the rapid release of acids into the stream, which causes a lot of fish and other aquatic life forms to perish.

As you follow the ascending highway you will swing around the headwaters of Wright Creek and enter briefly into the headwaters of Big Santeetlah Creek before

FIGURE 113. Wright Creek old-growth hemlocks laden with snow. (Photo by D. Pittillo)

continuing across the crest to Hooper Bald. You will be able to look back at the skyway as you progress up a major switchback. The forests at this elevation (about 5,200 feet) are usually called northern hardwoods forests. The dominant species here are northern red oak, yellow birch, and American beech. There are also red maple and serviceberry, along with heath bushes in the understory consisting primarily of blueberries, mountain laurel, and rhododendron. The earliest tree to bloom here is serviceberry, or "sarvis," opening in March at the lower elevations but as late as May in the upper elevations, here. The rhododendrons occur in the deciduous forms, mainly flame azalea, as well as the evergreen purple rhododendron and rosebay. In June the flame azaleas are still blooming as the purple rhododendrons begin their show. Mountain laurel, or calico bush as it is sometimes called, blooms just before the flame azaleas begin and continue into June and early July as well. July is a month for meadow flowers at these higher elevations, and the pink phlox, for which the Pink Beds in Transylvania County were named, will be increasing its appearance during the next couple of decades as the disturbed roadside vegetation undergoes the process of succession. You may spot fire pink (called a "pink" because of the notches cut in the petal tips, not because of its color)—a five-petaled crimson spring flower that lasts until July at these elevations. There are turk's-cap lilies bordering the woods, and various mints, especially bee balm, bergamot, and lemon mint, grow in patches along the borders of the highway. In the fall, the reds of the red maples and northern red oaks are framed by the yellows of the birches and by rusty brown beeches.

In the months of April and September the Hooper Bald area is a good vantage point from which to observe the spring and fall migrations of birds and butterflies. Spring migrations often are more colorful, as the birds flying north are in their spring breeding plumage. One of the most colorful is the goldfinch, the male decked out in his brilliant yellow plumage with black wings, or the scarlet tanager in equally brilliant scarlet plumage with black wings. Hawks, especially broadwing hawks, are particularly graceful and abundant as they fly north in the spring and south in the fall.

Winter at the high elevations can deal out some surprises. Supercooled clouds often pass over the crests of these mountains and the droplets freeze to the vegetation in a form called rime ice. The rime builds up in the direction of oncoming clouds, and sometimes rime coats two sides of a twig, indicating there has been a shift in the cloud movements during the past several hours. This rime ice may build up to several inches thick and may create hazardous conditions on the roadway. But the scenic rime-encrusted trees, often bending with the load, create some beautiful scenery.

While the bird diversity is lower in winter at these high elevations, there are nonetheless several species present. Grouse are often seen or heard, especially the low drumming sounds of the male as he beats his wings against his puffed-up breast to signal his territory. They can be seen in snow much more easily in winter, and their tracks are often evident. It is not uncommon to see a combined trail of grouse followed by a fox or bobcat. Thus, it will be instructive if you can find a calm sunny day after a snowfall to explore the area around Hooper Bald.

A game preserve established by George Gordon Moore here in 1912 once included five species of big game animals from Europe and the United States: buffalo (or bison), elk, mule deer, Russian brown bear, and wild boar. All the animals except the boar were extirpated. At some point in the early 1920s, during a grand hog hunt led by Cotton McGuire, a dozen or so dogs were killed or maimed and the hunters had to take refuge in the trees while the boars simply tore through the split-rail fences and escaped. These animals have successfully spread north across the Little Tennessee River and Fontana Lake and now are a problem in the Great Smoky Mountains National Park, where they are seriously impacting the native vegetation and other animals in their search for food, which generally involves extensive "rooting" in and tearing up of the forest floor.

E. Stratton Meadows and Gap

At mile 16.3 (1.5) on the skyway you will find the site of Absalom Stratton's grave, straddling the state line (the simple grave marker stands in the meadow at the gap). Anne Rogers, an archaeologist at Western Carolina University, relates the story that the federal highway administration asked her what would be needed to move the grave. She advised the agency that it would be easier to move the road, considering the necessary arrangements with two states and two national forests. Two weeks later a highway administrator called and said they would move the road. The Stratton family—Robert, John, and Absalom—were early settlers in this area. They built a house on Stratton Bald, where John lived for nineteen years. John was known as "Bacon John" due to his reputation for making "panther bacon" of the shoulders and hams.

F. Beech Gap

Stop at the overlook at Beech Gap, mile 0 (17.8): you are on the North Carolina–Tennessee line. To the west are the drier forested hills and mountains of the Cherokee National Forest of eastern Tennessee. To the east is Big Santeetlah Creek valley. The Cherohala Skyway continues down to Tellico Plains in Tennessee. If you look around at the beech trees here, you will note that many mosses and lichens inhabit their trunks and branches—an indication of the frequent rains and clouds that shroud this region. Though you could not call this a true "cloud forest," this feature gives you an idea of what a cloud forest would be like. From this vantage point you can also look into Tennessee and its portion of Great Smoky Mountains National Park, where further examples of high-elevation Southern Appalachian Mountain forests can be seen.

Blue Ridge Escarpment

Gorges of Lake Jocassee

GARY KAUFFMAN

This nearly 50-mile tour takes you past some of the most spectacular scenery in the Southern Appalachians. The tour route begins in the mountains of Transylvania County near Lake Toxaway, descends through Nantahala National Forest and state gamelands, past Whitewater Falls, and dips into South Carolina before reascending the Blue Ridge escarpment past Ellicott Rock Wilderness, the Chattooga River (made famous by the film *Deliverance*), and rich cove forests to the town of Highlands. You will then return to the starting point on US 64 past Whiteside Mountain and the craggy peak called Devils Court House. The trip down and up the steep south-facing escarpment gives you the chance to see the dramatic effects of erosion in an area of high (80 to 100 inches per year) rainfall. The streams that flow southeast and over the escarpment have cut steep, waterfall-filled courses through the hardest of rocks, while a more open, broader valley has been formed by the south-flowing Chattooga.

The major learning experience on this tour will come from exposure to the rare plant communities, spray cliffs, and granitic domes that are the keystone features of this region. Spray cliffs occur adjacent to waterfalls, where the constant humidity and moderate temperatures support the dominant fern, moss, and liverwort flora. The vertical to gently sloping rock faces that are kept constantly wet from the spray of waterfalls are inherently rare. Mosses, liverworts, and algae dominate this community, and vascular herbs have substantially less cover. Salamander diversity is high within these communities also, because most species require constantly moist substrate and high relative humidity. These sheltered sites rarely experience true freezing, also advantageous to salamanders. Rare bryophytes, disjunct from tropical or subtropical regions, are able to persist here given the relatively constant temperature and high humidity. Deeply sheltered grottoes, more commonly known as caves or rockhouses, are typically associated with spray cliff communities. These dark environs provide a habitat suitable for other rare plants that tend to persist only in deeply shaded environments. Given the appeal of the wild rushing water of waterfalls, there is a high risk for trampling damage from heavy recreational use of many of these sites.

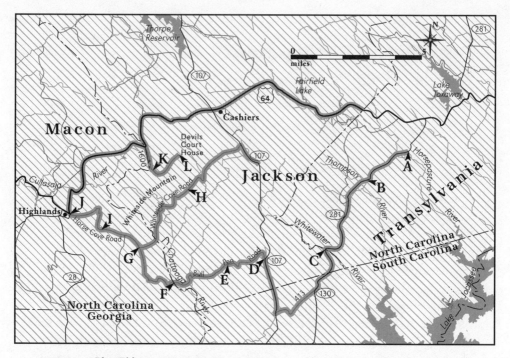

FIGURE 114. Blue Ridge escarpment tour route

The exposed rock outcrops within the Blue Ridge escarpment area are known as high-elevation granitic dome communities. Smooth, nonfractured bare rock dominates much of the surface. Soil development is minimal given the lack of crevices. These sites can vary greatly in steepness and in moisture availability. Zoned mats of various lichens, mosses, and the characteristic twisted-hair spikemoss adhere to the rock surface. This ancient evergreen spikemoss, more closely related to ferns than to mosses, provides an ecological barometer of available moisture content. It turns brownish-green and appears dead during dry periods, but rapidly transforms into a green carpet once the rains return. The true moss species tend to be abundant only in seepy examples of this natural community type. Larger herbaceous species survive only in some of the more highly developed older vegetation mats with the greatest soil depths. Two colorful herbs seen in such areas are the rock harlequin and the mountain dwarf-dandelion. It is not uncommon to see some yellowish-pink blossoms of the rock harlequin from April through November, although it is most vibrant during the springtime. Yellowish-orange blossoms of the mountain dwarf-dandelion are more plentiful in midsummer, although they are not uncommon from May through September. Many of the species typical of the high-elevation granitic dome community are primarily restricted to this type and are rare either within North Carolina or throughout their limited ranges. The edges of the rock may support woody species, typically rhododendrons, mountain laurel, and other members of the heath family that like acidic conditions.

Along much of the escarpment area you may actually notice a lack of herbaceous plant diversity. Shrubs tend to dominate on these highly acidic soils, which are usually sandy, have a high mica content, and are well drained, even though it is not uncommon for this area to receive 100 inches of rainfall annually. Most of the prominent shrubs are members of the heath family, the common deciduous species of which are huckleberry and various blueberries. The common evergreen members of the heath family are white rosebay (*Rhododendron maximus*), gorge rhododendron (*R. minus*), and mountain laurel. Few herbaceous species get enough light to survive within the dense shrub cover. While these areas can provide a spectacular rhododendron blooming display from year to year, the overall plant diversity tends to be sparse. Herbaceous flowering displays tend to be most visible in the summer and fall and are limited to roadside edges and sparsely forested areas. Many of the most frequently seen species are in the daisy, or aster, family. These include a diversity of asters, goldenrods, sunflowers, coreopsis, grass-leaved goldenaster, beggars ticks, Robin's plantain, ragwort, Joe-pye-weed, boneset, thoroughwort, black-eyed Susan, and white snakeroot. Other showy common species includes Carolina phlox, southern mountain-mint, flowering spurge, hairy angelica, tall milkweed, wild sage, basil bergamot, and bird's-foot violet.

This driving tour traverses a portion of three counties—Transylvania, Jackson, and Macon—and will cross four major river drainages—the Horsepasture, the Thompson, the Whitewater, and the Chattooga. It will skirt the Blue Ridge Divide in the very headwaters of the Cullasaja River. The main loop route covers about 48.5 miles in its descent from the US 64/NC 281 intersection south to Whitewater Falls, on to South Carolina, back to North Carolina, and across Bull Pen Road and Horse Cove Road, up to Highlands and Whiteside Mountain, and finally back down east of Cashiers returning to the starting point.

The first three rivers crossed on this tour flow through a new North Carolina state park. At the time of this writing, the new Jocassee Gorges State Park had not yet been established; therefore, trailheads and public access routes east of NC 281 may ultimately differ from those described here. Check with the Division of Parks and Recreation in Raleigh (telephone 919-733-4181) to get up-to-date information.

A. Horsepasture River

A temporary parking area on the east side of NC 281 South, about 1 mile south of the highway's intersection with US 64, is currently available on U.S. Forest Service lands for access to the Horsepasture River Trail. As this access point will undoubtedly change in the future, please respect private property in this area and follow the current roadside directions. Following the trail downslope will bring you to three prominent water features. The two cascading portions of the river that you will encounter first are known locally as Turtleback Falls and Drift Falls. Both of these areas are quite popular as sliding rocks and swimming holes in the appropriate season. Just a little farther down the trail, less than 0.75 miles from the parking area, is the truly spectacular Rainbow Falls.

B. Thompson River

You will cross the Thompson River next on NC 281, approximately 4 miles from the intersection with US 64. Here along the headwaters of the Thompson, the river seems quite small and tame—a mere dwarf of the mighty Horsepasture River. This area has just as much of a dramatic descent to the Piedmont with spectacular waterfalls as the Horsepasture River has. However, it is less accessible and has no designated trails. A significant portion of this watershed was just purchased in 1999 and will become a part of the Nantahala National Forest. The prominent peak visible to the east of the highway is Rocky Knobs, which separates the Thompson and Horsepasture River watersheds.

c. Whitewater River

You will cross the Whitewater River approximately 7.7 miles from the US 64 intersection. As you proceed to the Whitewater Falls recreation facility, less than 1 mile to the south, a small tree will become more noticeable on the forest edge—Hercules'-club or devil's-walking-stick. This plant is truly a four-season species of interest. In the dormant season you can get a good look at its impressive, finger-sized thorns at all the nodes (thus its common name). The "sticks" give way to lush tropical-appearing foliage in the spring, white flat-topped blossoms in the early summer, and colorful purple fruit in the fall. Hercules'-club is common across most of North Carolina, growing in openings and along roadsides. Here in the mountains it seldom is seen any larger than the size of a large shrub, 10 to 15 feet tall. Within the lower escarpment gorges it is more common than at other locations in the mountains and at times achieves tree height. A healthy tree-sized specimen, 30 to 40 feet tall, can be seen on the left near the bulletin board on the trail to the Whitewater Falls overlook.

The view of the upper Whitewater Falls at the end of the paved trail consists of a 411-foot drop in two steps (Figure 115). This is the most impressive waterfall in terms of sheer size in the entire Blue Ridge escarpment region. On the downhill side of the split-rail fence by the view is a nice clump of our only native bamboo in the mountains. This species has a curious bimodal distribution pattern in the

FIGURE 115. Upper falls of the Whitewater River. (Photo courtesy of U.S. Forest Service)

mountains, occurring in both wet floodplain forests and dry mountain slopes, as seen here at the Whitewater River. It was formerly much more abundant in the lowlands of the mountains and was a part of the historical "canebrakes"—large areas dominated by cane that Native Americans periodically burned to improve grazing for wildlife. Particularly prominent along the paved entrance trail and throughout roadsides along this tour is the snowy hydrangea, a Southern Appalachian endemic shrub. This species derives its common name from its densely white-hairy leaf undersides. It blooms with attractive white flat-topped clusters in May and June.

Follow the Foothills Trail down the steps to the view of the upper falls. On a rock outcrop here you can see the two native hemlock species side by side. The more common Canadian hemlock can be distinguished by the arrangement of the needle leaves in one plane on the twigs, resulting in a two-ranked or flat-leaf arrangement. In comparison, the endemic Carolina hemlock has a denser arrangement with the leaves radiating in all directions around the twigs, giving almost a bottlebrush effect. Carolina hemlock reaches the southern edge of its narrow range here in the Blue Ridge escarpment. Rarely do these two hemlocks co-occur, because Canadian hemlock prefers moist habitats while Carolina hemlock prefers dry upland bluffs.

Also sharing this rock outcrop is an inconspicuous shrub or small tree. Sweet leaf, or horse sugar, is most visible in the early spring, when it displays a show of fluffy yellowish-orange flowers. The common names refer to the sweetness of the leaves when chewed, although this can be quite variable from individual to individual and from one year to the next. Sweetleaf is common in the escarpment area, but only occurs sporadically in the rest of the mountains.

Given the inaccessibility of much of the forest here, the trail offers views of many large old-growth trees and numerous downed moss-covered logs. The Foothills Trail from the top overlook to the Whitewater River crossing is a 0.6-mile section of trail that drops from an elevation of 2,600 feet at the top to 2,100 feet near the river crossing. Forest communities here range from mixed white pine–oak forest, oak-hickory forest, acidic cove forest, and rich cove forest to Canadian hemlock forest. Much of the forest has a thick shrub layer composed of members of the heath family, which results in low overall herbaceous diversity. However, perhaps the most diverse cove forest in the escarpment area occurs on the lower half of the trail. A rare rock for this area, amphibolite, is suspected of having influenced the soil here, yielding a slightly higher pH and higher nutrient content. A spectacular springtime profusion of flowers highlight this area, including five different trillium species. Care should be taken to stay on the trail at all times since several rare plant habitats are crossed in the descent to the river.

From Whitewater Falls, proceed into South Carolina for 1 mile on SC 130, then turn right onto Wigginton Road (SC 413). A creek crossing 0.5 miles up this road provides a view of a mountain wetland to the right. This particular wetland has undergone a relatively recent hydrological change, as evidenced by the numerous dead white pines in the open area. A spectacular view of Lake Jocassee and the rolling topography in the South Carolina Piedmont is available from the roadside overlook 1.4 miles to the west. Wigginton Road connects to SC 107, where you will proceed to the right, back into North Carolina.

D. Bull Pen Road

You will cross the North Carolina state line about 1 mile from the Wigginton Road turnoff. Bull Pen Road (SR 1100) is the first gravel road on the left, another 1.3 miles to the north. For a 0.2-mile stretch on the west side of NC 107, just prior to reaching Bull Pen Road, a Southern Appalachian bog community is visible. Few intact marshy or bog areas remain in the mountains because these would have represented some of the scarce flat land available for cultivation by early settlers. Southern Appalachian bogs can vary among shrub-, sedge-, or grass-dominated communities, but all have an underlying mat of sphagnum moss. This particular bog is heavily dominated by swamp alder and swamp rose. The thick shrub layer hinders the herbaceous layer, which includes many of those rarer species that can occur in this community type. It may be that the hydrology has been modified here recently, or that some natural disturbance pattern, such as flooding or fire, has been disrupted, resulting in the denser shrub layer. Active management, such as shrub clearing or a prescribed fire, may be necessary here to maintain the present herbaceous diversity. Another wetland community is evident along Bull Pen Road about 1.3 miles west of the NC 107 intersection. Almost vertical seepy rock outcrops occur with sphagnum mats and various other herbs and mosses. Some bryologists refer to this community as a hanging bog.

A highly visible rare plant species transforms portions of this road into 4- to 6-foot-tall yellow flowering displays in midsummer. Fraser's loosestrife is a Southern Appalachian endemic primarily restricted to the escarpment area of North Carolina, South Carolina, and Georgia. The population located along Bull Pen Road is within the heart of this species' range and is one of the largest populations presently known. Typically, the limiting environmental factor for this species is light intensity. It has been noted to bloom more prolifically under higher light intensities, such as along roadside edges, which can mimic the species' native habitat in open woodland and on rock outcrops. While this plant is a disturbance-dependent species, it is the frequency of disturbance that most threatens this species. Low disturbance rates favor succession and competition from overtopping plants, which could result in localized elimination of a population, while high rates of disturbance could exceed the level of population maintenance and also result in localized elimination. The frequent maintenance requirements on roadside edges can and have resulted in rapid declines in populations of Fraser's loosestrife, unless efforts are undertaken to avoid the population centers. Recent efforts have improved the population along this road. Given its rarity and vulnerability, please only view this flower and do not disturb it here along the roadside.

E. Ellicott Rock Wilderness

The driving tour along Bull Pen Road traverses Ellicott Rock Wilderness to the south from 2.5 to almost 7 miles west of NC 107. Two separate trailheads occur along the road. The Bad Creek Trail begins 2.7 miles west of NC 107, while the Ellicott Rock Trail begins 6.7 miles from NC 107. Both of these trails are relatively gentle, primarily following old logging roads before they make a rapid descent into the Chattooga River Gorge near the North Carolina, Georgia, and South Carolina borders. The most common natural community encountered along these trails is a white pine–oak forest, usually with a huckleberry understory. This natural community type, here and in many other portions of the escarpment, has been significantly shaped by the former use of fire by Native Americans and the early European settlers. Accounts from the early 1900s suggest that white pine was not as abundant as it is today and may have replaced some of the dying American chestnuts and other species following the extensive logging completed in the Chattooga River valley in the early and mid-1900s. The recurrent use of prescribed burns practiced by the local folks up to the early 1900s undoubtedly killed white pines, a fire-intolerant species. With fire suppression being promoted and practiced at the time of the Chestnut decline, and the extensive logging, white pine, a fast-growing aggressive tree species, became codominant in many of the lowland to upland sites.

F. Chattooga River

The Chattooga River Gorge is characterized as a highly circuitous river gorge confined by both high and low mountains. This watershed drains across North and South Carolina and Georgia and is centered near the boundary of the three states. It is interesting to compare it to the three previous rivers, all of which have a predominantly southeasterly flow and a rapid descent into the Piedmont. In comparison, the Chattooga River flows predominantly southward and has a much broader river valley. As a result it has fewer waterfalls and tends to be less diverse than the other escarpment watersheds.

Visible downstream of the Chattooga River Bridge on Bull Pen Road is a small rocky island that formed in the bend of the river where the drag of the water forces the heavier sands and gravel to drop. A unique assemblage of plants tends to grow on frequently flooded sites such as this island: only those species with tenacious root systems can persist here. Particularly prominent is a sedge, *Carex torta*, that looks like a grass and tends to form extensive patches. An interesting common shrub that often establishes within these flooded communities and on streambank edges is yellowroot, so named for its distinctive yellow inner bark. It has unusual star-shaped, brownish-purple, pendulous flowers early in the spring before its lustrous green foliage even emerges. This extremely bitter plant was formerly (and is still) used by some local folks as a spring tonic; it yields a yellow dye as well.

G. Slick Rock

Toward the end of Bull Pen Road, about 7.5 miles west of NC 107, a trailhead leads to the left. An easy 0.1-mile hike leads to a high-elevation granitic dome natural community on Slick Rock. You will gain an appreciation for the varying size of this community after you compare this small example to others you will see later in the tour atop Whiteside Mountain. Note the weathered and pitted depressions in the rock that, during periods of high rainfall, provide microhabitats for various amphibian species. Fragile and small vegetation mats and amphibian habitats here are vulnerable to trampling damage, as evidenced by some of the abused spikemoss mats. Extreme care should be taken while viewing this site.

H. Whiteside Cove

If you wish to witness an awe-inspiring view of Whiteside Mountain, head to the right on Whiteside Cove road (SR 1107). From about 2.5 to 4.0 miles east of this intersection, the upper Chattooga River valley opens up with the white vertical face of Whiteside Mountain providing the backdrop. One can certainly see why the first white settlers to the Highlands and Cashiers area, the Barak Norton family, settled here in 1827—and why people continue to move here. The majority of this upper valley is privately owned. You will eventually cross the upper headwater slopes of the Chattooga River at 4.9 miles from the intersection with Bull Pen Road. The flat terrain here provides a dramatic contrast to the dissected landscape at the Chattooga River crossing downstream on Bull Pen Road.

Whiteside Cove Road eventually meets up with NC 107, south of the town of Cashiers. A side trip south on NC 107 for 1.5 miles will be worth the effort. You will have a chance to see, along a 0.2- to 0.3-mile length of this road within a wet lowland forest and under a powerline cut, a mass of pinkshell azalea. This deciduous shrub typically flowers in mid-May to mid-June prior to the emergence of its leaves. Many people consider this to be the prettiest native azalea; its reddish-pink buds change to pink flowers that gradually fade to a delicate white. This rare azalea is only known from North Carolina, extending from here, at its southernmost location, to Watauga and Caldwell Counties, its northernmost outpost. This species is readily available in the nursery trade if you want to add it to your landscape, as many folks have in this escarpment area. One other possible stop 0.6 miles to the south on the left side of NC 107 provides a close view of some of the smaller waterfalls that are scattered across this landscape. Silver Run Creek is a tributary to the Whitewater River.

I. Horse Cove

Horse Cove Road is to the right as you turn off of Bull Pen Road. It leads to a relatively flat broad valley, Horse Cove, with a majestic backdrop of Blackrock Mountain. While not quite as massive as Whiteside Mountain, it is impressive nonetheless, extending into the eastern edge of the town of Highlands. This mountain derives its name from the abundant seepage areas on the rock face, which can be seen from the cove; these seeps harbor dark moss mats. As you ascend the steep switchbacks in the climb to Highlands, you will get a closer view of Blackrock Mountain.

As you enter the cove about 0.5 to 0.7 miles west of Bull Pen Road, a mass of maidenhair grass can be seen both on the roadside edge and throughout a partially open forest community. This introduced grass from Asia is becoming aggressively weedy in portions of North Carolina and has recently been seen more frequently in rocky areas of Ellicott Rock Wilderness. If left unchecked the grass may eventually displace native species within open or partially open communities. Many cultivars of this species are quite popular in the nursery trade and are currently widely planted across the landscape. While the cultivars of this species do not seem as aggressive as the unimproved species documented here, at other locations some spread has been noted. A word of caution is advised to closely watch this species and its spread if you introduce it to your garden.

Although most of this cove has been logged at least twice, you will see evidence of the fertility of this valley by taking a 0.1-mile side trip onto Rich Mountain Road to the left. Park by the U.S. Forest Service bulletin board on the left side of this road. An old tulip poplar, greater than 4 feet in diameter and at least 127 feet tall, stands at the end of the short hiking trail on the right side of the road. The small area surrounding Rich Mountain is unique for the upper Chattooga River basin. Its soils have higher pH and are more productive than anywhere else in the watershed. Visual evidence of these unusual rich dark loamy soils can be found on road cuts in this area.

J. Highlands Plateau

The Highlands Plateau is characterized as a landscape with a relatively gentle terrain dominated by exposed rocks on the higher peaks and hemlock forest in the valleys. It represents the divide between the Tennessee River drainage and the Savannah River drainage. All the escarpment rivers drain to the south-southeast eventually reaching the Atlantic Ocean. In contrast, the Cullasaja River headwaters here in Highlands flow west to the Little Tennessee River, which heads on a northern course to the Tennessee River, the Mississippi River, and the Gulf Coast.

After climbing up to the plateau on Horse Cove Road, take a right turn in the middle of Highlands on US 64 and proceed east toward Whiteside Mountain. The gentle terrain over much of the Highlands plateau was conducive to the formation of small wetlands. Few intact examples of these scattered wetlands remain today. Most have either been filled in or have been subjected to other major hydrological changes, all related to the steady development of vacation homes and the vibrant tourist industry of the past century. Most of the remaining sites are shrub-dominated marshes. One example can be seen on the right side of US 64 about 3.7 miles east of the Highlands town square. A colorful shrub, meadowsweet, with white spirelike blossoms is clearly visible here in June and July.

K. Whiteside Mountain

The turnoff to Whiteside Mountain on SR 1600 is 5.5 miles east of the Highlands town square. Follow the paved secondary road for 1 mile to a graveled parking lot on the left at the foot of Whiteside Mountain (Figure 116). Notice the dense clump of a midsized shrub, mountain sweet pepperbush, to the left upon entering the parking area. Those of you fortunate to visit in July will be rewarded with a fragrant mass of white pendulous blossoms on these pepperbushes. This attractive flowering shrub also has striking peeling bark and has recently been promoted by the nursery industry.

The loop trail to the summit and back is a moderate hike of about 2 miles. The least strenuous hike is achieved by following the left portion of the loop, gradually climbing the mountain on an old roadbed. Numerous plant species are known to occur on this diverse mountain, but as in other parts of the escarpment region the heath family dominates. At least twenty-three different species from this plant family can be encountered along the trail from the foot to the summit. These range from the previously mentioned rhododendrons, mountain laurel, huckleberries, blueberries, and azaleas to the more unusual minniebush and sand myrtle.

Minniebush looks very similar to many deciduous azaleas and blueberries, but it has distinctly hairy leaves with a small extremely pointed tip (called a mucro) at

FIGURE 116. Whiteside Mountain—a high-elevation granitic dome. (Photo courtesy of U.S. Forest Service)

the end of each leaf. It is particularly common along both sides of the trail close to the parking lot. Sand myrtle is a creeping shrub with glossy evergreen leaves that tend to turn a bronzy color during the winter. It is a tightly compact shrub that seldom grows taller than 0.5 feet. A dense mass of flowers that are rosy in bud and open to a pinkish-white is present in May and June. Sand myrtle generally occurs only at the higher peaks of the escarpment region on the edges of both granitic domes and heath balds. Heath balds are dense treeless shrub thickets that primarily consist of members of the heath family. A few heath balds can be viewed on the south slopes of Whiteside Mountain. Curiously, sand myrtle is common in portions of wet pineland communities in the Coastal Plain, where it can become quite leggy and grow to a height of 4 to 5 feet.

You may observe various other communities along the trail on Whiteside Mountain. The lower slopes are blanketed with oak-hickory forest. A patch of northern hardwoods forest is present on the north-facing slope along the old roadbed. Northern hardwoods forest is relatively common at higher elevations in other portion of the Nantahala National Forest, but it is an exceedingly rare community type in the escarpment region. Yellow birch, a tree species that is more typically seen in the North, occurs here near the southern edge of its range. This tree can be distinguished by its yellowish or yellowish-gray peeling bark.

An old-growth red oak forest occupies the mountaintop. Recurrent ice storms and high winds have shaped the gnarled, relatively short red oaks that occur here at the highest point within this escarpment region. This forest gives way to extensive patches of high-elevation granitic dome communities—scattered patches of bare rock faces on the south side of the mountain. These vertical patches of white granite (commonly called Cashiers gneiss) lacking adhering plant cover justify the mountain's name.

A pair of peregrine falcons, a federally listed bird species, have nested and successfully raised young on Whiteside Mountain for the past ten years. They nest on the exposed rock face and can be occasionally seen hunting, cruising up to incredible speeds of 200 miles per hour, in the spring and summer.

L. Devils Court House

This craggy peak is clearly visible from Cowee Gap, back at us 64. Its jagged edges suggest that this peak has experienced more extensive weathering than any other mountaintop in the escarpment region. These are also some of the most inaccessible upper slopes of the escarpment. While preliminary surveys indicate that these slopes harbor similar high-elevation natural communities to those of other escarpment slopes, this northeastern extension of Whiteside Mountain has probably received less biological survey work than any other peak within the escarpment region.

From Whiteside Mountain Road, the return trip to the intersection of NC 281 and us 64 is 14.7 miles and passes through the town of Cashiers on the northeast edge of the Chattooga River basin. The two prominent peaks southeast of cashiers are Rocky Mountain and Chimney Top. Chimney Top has the sharper peak of the two. Both represent the Chattooga Ridge, here dividing the upper waters of the Chattooga River from the upper waters of the Horsepasture River. This is the closest point that waters from these two rivers ever come. Farther southeast the waters of both the Thompson River and the Whitewater River separate these two watersheds. Many of the same high-elevation natural community types seen earlier on the tour occur also on this final leg of the driving loop. Small granitic domes are particularly prominent along the north side of us 64 from Whiteside Mountain to Cashiers. The resinous sunflower (the name alluding to its sticky stems and flowers) is a distinctive 6-foot-tall bright yellow sunflower that is highly visible on this stretch of highway in August and early September. This distinctive sunflower, while common in the southeastern United States, is uncommon in the mountains and is primarily restricted to the escarpment region from Highlands to Brevard.

East of Cashiers you will pass by various smooth-alder-dominated wetlands. One wetland adjacent to a moist forest that follows a meandering stream has a particularly striking mass of one of North Carolina's native *Clematis* vines, virgin's bower. This large vine with dark green foliage grows up to 20 feet in length and carries white showy male flowers from July to September. Even more striking are the long, feathery fruits that persist through half the winter and tend to glisten at low sun angles. Watch for this colorful mass of virgin's bower about 5 miles east of Cashiers. One final mountaintop, Toxaway Mountain, is visible across the treetops to the north as you near the tour's starting point. A fire tower on this summit is still staffed with a lookout from the North Carolina Forest Service at times of high fire danger in the early spring.

Suggestions for Further Reading

DIRK FRANKENBERG

Biota

North Carolina's unusually high level of biological diversity makes recommending guide-books difficult. We have so many species that national or regional guidebooks usually include only the most common ones. State-specific guidebooks for particular groups (reptiles for example) tend to be scientific monographs written in a style that is difficult for the nonprofessional. As a result I recommend a two-step approach to finding guidebooks that meet your needs. First, check out the array of guidebooks in the nature, natural science, and North Carolina sections of a big bookstore. Many publishers put out guidebook series ranging in complexity from the simple Golden Books to near monograph sophistication. A short list of guidebook publishers includes the National Audubon Society, National Geographic, Reader's Digest, Little Brown (Stokes Nature Guides), DK Publishing (Eyewitness Handbooks), the Dover Handbook series, the Simon and Schuster Guide series, and IDG Books (Foster City, Calif.) with its "for dummies" series that now includes *Birdwatching for Dummies*. Somewhere in this spectrum you will find guides to biota written at a level you find appropriate and useful. The second step you might take would be to look over books written or published locally that cover subjects of particular interest to you. Several of these are listed below, but new ones come out all the time so expect this list to be outdated when you read it. The books listed are those that I have found particularly useful.

Animals

Birds

Bull, John, and John Farrand Jr. *National Audubon Society Guide to North American Birds*. New York: Knopf, 1994. 797 pp.

Fussell, J. O., III. *A Birder's Guide to Coastal North Carolina*. Chapel Hill: University of North Carolina Press, 1994. 540 pp. A compendium of where to go and what you'll see in some of the best bird-watching country anywhere along the Atlantic Coast and flyway.

Peterson, Roger Tory. *A Field Guide to the Birds East of the Rockies*. Boston: Houghton Mifflin, 1980. 384 pp.

Fish

Rohde, F. C., R. G. Arndt, D. G. Lindquist, and J. F. Parnell. *Freshwater Fishes of the Carolinas, Virginia, Maryland, and Delaware*. Chapel Hill: University of North Carolina Press, 1994. 222 pp. A useful treatment of the complex fish biota of southeastern and mid-Atlantic freshwater systems.

Mammals

Webster, W. D., J. F. Parnell, and W. C. Biggs Jr. *Mammals of the Carolinas, Virginia, and Maryland*. Chapel Hill: University of North Carolina Press, 1985. 255 pp. A useful guide to what I find to be a group rarely seen by casual observers.

Reptiles

Palmer, W. M., and A. L. Braswell. *Reptiles of North Carolina*. Chapel Hill: University of North Carolina Press, 1995. 412 pp. This book will flat out tell you all you want to know about the reptiles of our state.

Seashore Life (Including Common Marine Fish)

Ruppert, E. E., and R. Fox. *Seashore Animals of the Southeast*. Columbia: University of South Carolina Press, 1988. 429 pp. A thorough, accurate, and easy-to-use guide to all of the common and many of the less common animals found along our coast.

Spitsbergen, J. M. *Seacoast Life: An Ecological Guide to Natural Seashore Communities in North Carolina*. Chapel Hill: University of North Carolina Press, 1980. 112 pp. A shorter treatment focused on North Carolina.

Plants

Harrar, E. S., and J. G. Harrar. *Guide to Southern Trees*. New York: Dover Publications, 1962. 72 pp. An oldie but goodie—still useful more than thirty years after its second printing. (Who says botanists aren't immortal?)

Kraus, J. W. *A Guide to Ocean Dune Plants Common to North Carolina*. Chapel Hill: University of North Carolina Press, 1988. 71 pp. A short but very helpful guide to seaside plants.

Tiner, Ralph W. *Field Guide to Coastal Wetland Plants of the Southeastern United States*. Amherst: University of Massachusetts Press, 1993. 328 pp. An excellent guide to coastal settings—well illustrated with photographs, diagrams, and drawings.

Climate

There is bad news and good news about further reading on climate and weather. The bad news is that there is no treatment of North Carolina climate available. The good news is that Peter Robinson, Greg Fishel, and others have agreed to write such a treatment for the University of North Carolina Press in the near future. That book won't be out by the time you read this, but it should be coming along soon. Knowing the people involved in writing it, I am convinced that it will be a very useful reference. In the meantime, general treatments of weather and climate are the best we can do, though there are some academic papers that provide a North Carolina focus.

Two general books are worth having:

Ahrens, C. Donald. *Meteorology Today: An Introduction to Weather, Climate and the Environment*. St. Paul, Minn.: West Publishing, 1994. 950 pp. A widely adopted introductory text in meteorology; complete and well illustrated. This book is traditionally academic with many definitions and terms and, thus, may contain more information than lay readers may need.

Barnes, J. *North Carolina's Hurricane History*. Chapel Hill: University of North Carolina Press, 1998. 256 pp. A general description and specific history of the state's most powerful extreme weather events.

Robinson, P. "Weather and Climate." Subsection of "The Natural Environment," in *The North Carolina Atlas*, edited by Douglas M. Orr Jr. and Albert W. Stuart. Chapel Hill: University of North Carolina Press, 2000. An excellent summary of general climate features of the state. The best single source we have until the author's book on the subject is available.

Williams, Jack. *The Weather Book: An Easy-to-Understand Guide to the USA's Weather*. New York: Vintage Books, 1992. 212 pp. A readable treatment of weather phenomena copiously and skillfully illustrated by graphic artists from *USA Today*. Describes the climate system of the United States and the origins and characteristics of extreme events like thunderstorms, tornadoes, and hurricanes.

Ecology

Enger, Eldon D., and Bradley F. Smith. *Environmental Science: A Study of Interrelationships*. Dubuque, Iowa: W. C. Brown, 1992. 514 pp. An introductory text with excellent sections on ecological principles, energy, and human effects on ecosystems. Examples based on the Great Lakes and analysis of environmental risk analysis will be of less interest to North Carolina readers.

Godfrey, Michael A. *Field Guide to the Piedmont: The Natural Habitats of America's Most Lived-in Region, from New York City to Montgomery, Alabama*. Chapel Hill: University of North Carolina Press, 1997. 524 pp. A classic ecological description of a major region of North Carolina and its neighboring states. Absolutely first-rate exposition of the stages and process of plant succession with detailed descriptions of plants and animals characteristic of herbaceous, initial coniferous, secondary deciduous, and mature forest stages of the successional sequence in North Carolina and elsewhere.

Martin, William H., Stephen G. Boyce, and Arthur C. Echternacht. *Biodiversity of the Southeastern United States*. New York: John Wiley and Sons, 1992. A monumental work carried out over more than a decade by more than seventy volunteer authors. This compendium covers climate, geology, biota community descriptions, and analyses of human impacts on all of these. This three-volume work summarizes over fifty years of ecological science in the Southeast and is written at the scientific-review level of depth— that is, at a level accessible to interested lay persons but more easily by senior students and/or natural resource managers.

Savage, Henry. *Mysterious Carolina Bays*. Columbia: University of South Carolina Press, 1982.

Schafale, Michael P., and Alan S. Weakley. *The Natural Communities of North Carolina: Third Approximation*. Raleigh: North Carolina Natural Heritage Program, 1990. 325 pp. The best available summary of the diverse natural heritage of North Carolina. Uses scientific names of plants in the text but provides an appendix with common names of most species. There is no way to know what the plants look like without a separate identification guide. Such guides are recommended in the Biota section above. (May be purchased by writing to N.C. Natural Heritage Program, NCDENR, P.O. Box 27687, Raleigh, NC 27699-1615.)

Geology

Beyer, Fred. *North Carolina: The Years Before Man—a Geologic History*. Durham: Carolina Academic Press, 1991. 224 pp. An excellent, easy-to-read summary of North Carolina's geologic history and the characteristics of the state at various times in the past.

Carpenter, P. Albert, ed. *A Geologic Guide to North Carolina's State Parks*. North Carolina Geological Survey Bulletin 91. Raleigh: N.C. Geological Survey, 1989. 69 pp. A useful guide to its topic—especially as a supplement to the biologically oriented description of state parks by Biggs and Parnell cited below. Good glossary, maps, and color photographs.

Carter, J. G., P. E. Gallagher, R. Enos, and T. J. Rossback. *Fossil Collecting in North Carolina*. North Carolina Geological Survey Bulletin 89. Raleigh: N.C. Geological Survey, 1988. 89 pp. A useful guide to publicly accessible sites where fossils can be seen *in situ*, with a good description of the geologic formations in which they are found.

Fry, Keith. *Roadside Geology of Virginia*. Missoula, Mont.: Mountain Press, 1986. 278 pp. A good description of geologic processes and characteristics of the state that most resembles North Carolina. The geology, topography, and observable features of the two states are similar enough to make this a useful reference for North Carolina observers.

Kaczorowski, R. T. *The Carolina Bays: A Comparison with Modern Oriented Lakes*. Tech. Rep. no. 13-CRD. Columbia: University of South Carolina, Geology Department, 1977.

Rogers, John J. W. *A History of the Earth*. Cambridge: Cambridge University Press, 1993. 312 pp. An introductory, professional summary of geological periods and processes that have formed the Earth. Important processes are described in a style that is accessible to interested nongeologists, although careful reading and easy access to a good dictionary may be necessary in some places.

Natural Areas

Natural areas of North Carolina are described in books written for many purposes. As is the case with biota guidebooks, a good first step in finding a treatment that meets your particular needs is to visit your local bookstore. I list here several works that I found educational while working on this book, and one new title that provides historical and cultural information about many of the areas whose natural history is described here.

Cultural and Historical Information

Parent, L. *Scenic Driving in North Carolina*. Helena, Mont.: Falcon Press, 1998. Parent has excellent taste in scenic drives. He has independently selected drives through many of the natural areas described in this book. Parent provides excellent maps, driving directions, historical details, and scenic vantage points but not the natural history included here. As a result, the two books supplement each other in a way that was not planned, but that should be very useful to readers.

Natural Area Guides and Hiking Trails

Adams, K. *North Carolina Waterfalls*. Winston-Salem, N.C.: Blair, 1997. 208 pp. Remarkable coverage of these scenic but potentially dangerous remnants of the erosional flanks of our western mountains.

Adkins, L. M. *Walking the Blue Ridge: A Guide to the Trails of the Blue Ridge Parkway*. Chapel Hill: University of North Carolina Press, 1996. 255 pp. The latest, revised version of a long-popular summary of trails through natural areas that border "the world's cleanest highway."

Bannon, J., and M. Giffen. *Sea Kayaking the Carolinas*. Asheville, N.C.: Out There Press, 1997. 212 pp. Twenty-three recommended tours of the coastal region.

Benner, B., and D. Benner. *Carolina Whitewater: A Canoeist's Guide to the Western Carolinas*. 7th ed. Birmingham, Ala.: Menasha Ridge Press, 1996. 231 pp. A companion volume to the following, but focused on the more adventurous streams of our mountains.

Benner, B., and T. McCloud. *A Paddler's Guide to Eastern North Carolina*. Birmingham, Ala.: Menasha Ridge Press, 1987. 257 pp. Forty recommended tours of Piedmont and Coastal Plain rivers. Rates degree of difficulty, seasonality, water quality, and scenery.

Biggs, W. C., Jr., and J. F. Parnell. *State Parks of North Carolina*. Winston-Salem, N.C.: Blair, 1993. 339 pp. A compendium of information about the state parks, their location, attractions, facilities, biota, and available activities. Note also the companion volume on the geology of the parks, cited above.

Catlin, David T. *A Naturalist's Blue Ridge Parkway*. Knoxville: University of Tennessee Press, 1984.

De Hart, A. *North Carolina Hiking Trails*. Boston: Appalachian Mountain Club, 1996. 488 pp. The latest edition of the classic work on North Carolina's network of hiking trails through natural areas. De Hart provides more natural history per mile than almost anyone else.

——. *Trails of the Triad*. Winston-Salem, N.C.: Blair, 1997. 130 pp. This book and the following companion volume describe trails near two of the state's major population centers. Convenient for day-tripping naturalists.

——. *Trails of the Triangle*. Winston-Salem, N.C.: Blair, 1997. 163 pp.

Drake, D., and P. T. Bromley. *Natural Resources Inventory of North Carolina*. Raleigh: North Carolina Cooperative Extensive Service, North Carolina State University, 1997. 28 pp. A summary of natural resources, natural areas, and parks of the state. Includes many references to otherwise hard-to-find state documents.

Frankenberg, D. *The Nature of North Carolina's Southern Coast: Barrier Islands, Coastal Waters, and Wetlands from Portsmouth Island to Calabash*. Chapel Hill: University of North Carolina Press, 1997. 250 pp. This and the following volume describe environmental processes, natural field sites, and development issues that shape our dynamic coastline. The two differ in their specific focus, as the North Carolina coast is quite different north and south of Ocracoke.

——. *The Nature of the Outer Banks: Environmental Processes, Field Sites, and Development Issues, Corolla to Ocracoke*. Chapel Hill: University of North Carolina Press, 1995. 151 pp.

Johnson, Randy. *Winter Guide to Dixie*. Boston: Appalachian Mountain Club, 1987.

McDaniels, L. *Highroad Guide to the North Carolina Mountains*. Marietta, Ga.: Longstreet Press, 1998. Good general coverage and an excellent thirty-page section on Great Smoky Mountains National Park.

Manning, Phillip. *Afoot in the South: Walks in the Natural Areas of North Carolina*. Winston-Salem, N.C.: Blair, 1993. 256 pp. A well-written personal diary of a field naturalist simultaneously at work and at play. A pleasure to read.

Morris, G. *North Carolina Beaches*. Revised and updated ed. Chapel Hill: University of North Carolina Press, 1993. 294 pp. Beaches are natural systems, although what is found inland of them is increasingly developed. Finding nature among development is what this book is about.

North Carolina Department of Transportation. *N.C. Scenic Byways*. Raleigh: N.C. Department of Transportation, 1997. 143 pp. Although not a nature or trail guide, this inexpensive book is a useful supplement to the nature tours because many of the byways intersect or parallel routes described here. Good maps and comments on history and culture make it well worth the $5 contribution. Available from the Department of Transportation in Raleigh.

Roe, C. E. *North Carolina Wildlife Viewing Guide*. Helena, Mont.: Falcon Press, 1992. 96 pp. Ninety places from which wildlife can be viewed are described. All of these are in natural areas, most of which are also described in this book. Roe's book gives you the key to the brown signs carrying the image of binoculars seen along North Carolina's rural roadsides. The book and the signs resulted from a private/public partnership linking electric utility companies with state and federal agencies and two nonprofit organizations.

Schumann, Marguerite. *The Living Land: An Outdoor Guide to North Carolina*. Chapel Hill, N.C.: Dale Press, 1977. 178 pp. A privately published but excellent little book well ahead of its time as what would now be called "an ecotourist's" guide to the state. Provides both natural and human history of eighty-two sites, many of which are described in their current state in this book.

Simpson, Marcus B. *Birds of the Blue Ridge Mountains*. Chapel Hill: University of North Carolina Press, 1992.

Contributor Affiliations

Yates M. Barber—Elizabeth City, North Carolina

Vince Bellis—Department of Biology, East Carolina University

Carleton Burke—Western North Carolina Nature Center

Cindy Carpenter—Pisgah National Forest

B. J. Copeland—Zoology Department, North Carolina State University

Alex Cousins—Yadkin–Pee Dee Lakes Project

Allen de Hart—Friends of the Mountains-to-Sea Trail

Marshall Ellis—North Carolina Division of Parks and Recreation

Elisabeth Feil—Asheville, North Carolina

Dirk Frankenberg—Marine Sciences Program, University of North Carolina at Chapel Hill

Henry C. Hammond—Raleigh, North Carolina

Scott Hartley—Weymouth Woods Sandhills Nature Preserve

Elizabeth Hunter—Southern Appalachian Highlands Conservancy

Kim Hyre—Weymouth Woods Sandhills Nature Preserve

Mark Johns—North Carolina Wildlife Resources Commission

Gary Kauffman—U.S. Forest Service

Jean W. Kraus—North Carolina Maritime Museum

Ron Lance—North Carolina Arboretum

Diane Lauritsen—Mount Pleasant, South Carolina

Penny Leary-Smith—Raleigh, North Carolina

Harry LeGrand—North Carolina Natural Heritage Program

Ida Phillips Lynch—The Nature Conservancy

J. Merrill Lynch—The Nature Conservancy

Anne L. Maker—South Mountains State Park

Phillip Manning—Chapel Hill, North Carolina

Jeff Michael—The Land Trust of North Carolina

J. Dan Pittillo—Department of Biology, Western Carolina University

Stanley R. Riggs—Department of Geology, East Carolina University

Deidri Sarver—Crowders Mountain State Park

Michael P. Schafale—North Carolina Natural Heritage Program

Curtis Smalling—Ecos of the Blue Ridge

Lundie Spence—North Carolina Sea Grant, North Carolina State University

Alan Weakley—The Nature Conservancy

Laura White—Stevens Nature Center

Index